MW01124034

Everyone wants to know Go
to travel. Men and women he
to be a disciple. Their heart responds, but the way to do it remains unclear and vague. Beyond being taught and even being in Bible studies, there is a desperate need for clear, simple, and achievable steps to take. *The Path* does exactly that. It skillfully lays out a road to help people grow in Christ as disciples. As a Navigator, I love the "how to" coupled with a solid, biblical basis for growth. It is tested. It is grounded in years of experimentation. Don Willett has put this vital material in a form that churches, small group leaders, and individual disciples and disciplers can readily put into practice. I do not want to imply that discipleship is easy. It still requires work and commitment, but in a context of a proven *Path*. Walk down this path into biblical stages of growth. It will transform people and their churches.

—**Jerry E. White**, Ph.D.
Major General, USAF, Ret
International President Emeritus
Chairman Emeritus
The Navigators

Dr. Don Willet has done the church and the academy a valuable service with his research and practical instruction concerning the dynamics of spiritual growth. Many of us have grown weary of models of discipleship that identify external behaviors—like Bible reading and sharing our faith—as the benchmarks of spiritual maturity. Don offers instead a relational model of spiritual formation that takes into consideration what we know about human development and which stands on the bedrock of solid biblical exegesis. Few books spend as much time (a) in the biblical text and (b) in current literature on spiritual formation as *The Path*. I heartily recommend Don's book—and the accompanying workbook, *Stages of Faith*—to all who are interested in how we mature as followers of Jesus. Pastors will gain a theology of discipleship that will help us to craft meaningful and productive ministries for our people. Small group leaders will better understand their strategic roles in the lives of their group members. All of us will be better equipped to assess our own spiritual progress, as well as the progress of those whom we shepherd. Finally, my fellow-academics, particularly those involved in the field of spiritual formation, would do well to integrate Don's findings into their courses. *The Path* offers a promising corrective to the valuable—but incomplete—preoccupation with personal spiritual disciplines that currently characterizes the discipline in many circles.

—**Joe Hellerman**, Ph.D.
Professor of NT Language and Literature
Talbot School of Theology
Pastor-Elder
Oceanside Christian Fellowship
El Segundo, CA

The Path is a biblically informed and educationally relevant resource for any church's disciple-making emphasis. Dr. Don Willett formulates a practical and insightful pathway of fruitful growth toward Christian maturity for all believers, based on an intriguing spectrum of childhood, young adulthood, and parenthood spiritual benchmarks identified in 1 John 2:12–14. This pathway involves eight essential milestones emphasized in Scripture (Ch. 2–7) and commended by human developmental theory (Ch. 8–9, 11–13). The final chapter offers a variety of short-term and longer-term plans to teach the material that Willett has worked through in his own church ministry and seminars. A distinctive feature is a discussion of Willett's "Spiritual Growth Profile" as a means to assess one's journey along the eight milestones (Ch. 10). Each chapter ends with reflection questions to help readers review the material. Willett's heart and passion offer both encouragement and motivation for believers to press onward in Christlikeness.

—**Klaus Issler**, Ph.D.
Professor of Christian Education and Theology
Talbot School of Theology
Author of *Living Into the Life of Jesus*

Ever since spiritual formation has become the next new fad, writers have looked to a variety of sources for guidance. In *The Path,* Don Willet leads us into Scripture to understand guideposts that clarify stages of spiritual growth and provide practical help for anyone eager to help believers grow to maturity. I highly recommend this book.

—**Larry Richards**, Ph.D.
Author and Christian Educator

In *The Path,* Dr. Don Willett provides strong, biblical, and well-researched "stages of faith" and "milestones" of Christian growth and maturity. He gives seminary professors and Bible teachers an integrated framework for the development of faith, guidelines for pastors to follow, and a well-thought-out and useful "roadmap" for every Christian on his or her own faith journey. A must-read for anyone serious about helping people in spiritual growth and development.

—**Charlie Bradshaw**, Ph.D.
Executive Pastor, North Coast Church, CA
Adjunct Professor: Biola University and
Azusa Pacific University

Don Willett provides an extraordinary guide for the journey of faith for those longing to be and to grow deep followers of Christ. Not only does he describe what authentic spiritual maturity looks like, but also he intentionally addresses *how* stages of faith, stages of development, and one's life context and personality all contribute to becoming more like Christ for the building up of the body Christ and impact on the world around us. *The Path* avoids being formulaic. Don reminds us that "no believer becomes holy in a hurry" while challenging us through provocative and probing questions to understand and engage the opportunities, challenges, and obstacles of taking the next steps in pursuing Christ—the greatest journey of all!

—**Dr. Randy MacFarland**
Provost/Dean Denver Seminary

Seldom have I encountered a man with such a passion for practical godliness as when I met Dr. Don Willett. His passion is infectious. He has a heart for and has dedicated his life to discipling men to fulfill their call of being men of God. The principles in *The Path* are more than spiritual platitudes and nebulous theological jargon. They are divine truths that have been tried and proven as a "path" to spiritual maturity and a godly hunger for righteousness. Lives have been changed. Minds have been renewed, and man after man has committed himself to the journey of Christlikeness, which is routed on *The Path*. Dr. Willett is a spiritual traffic cop—used by the Holy Spirit to keep you on the path of righteousness! Practical. Portable. Powerful. Life-changing. Follow *The Path*—it leads to a blessing!

—Dr. Kenneth C. Ulmer
Senior Pastor/Teacher
Faithful Central Bible Church
Los Angeles

The Path represents Don's life work in helping others discover an intimate relationship with our Lord. It demonstrates careful research and maturity of thought. You will find a wealth of insights and practical steps to put these truths into practice. If you want greater insight as to how individuals grow in Christlikeness, you'll want to read this book.

—Dr. Norm Wakefield
Professor Emeritus, Phoenix Seminary

Thank you, Don Willet, for perceptively pointing out that just as there are ages and stages in one's physical life, so there are ages and stages spiritually, as well. And thank you for getting practical about that! You've re-positioned spiritual growth from a halo of good intentions to a realistic path that anyone can walk if they genuinely desire to follow Christ.

—Bill Hendricks
President of The Giftedness Center and
Author of *Exit Interviews: Revealing Stories of Why People Are Leaving the Church*

The Path is a tremendous resource for the Christian mental health professional in helping clients to integrate faith and psychology. Dr. Willet's stages of faith model is an invaluable tool, allowing the clinician to be sensitive to the client's spiritual needs. I highly recommend *The Path* for your library!

—Wayne Limm, Psy.D
Clinical Psychologist
Journey of Faith Counseling Center

Don is not a man sitting by a serene lake at sunset thinking about spirituality. He combines his experience-laden wisdom with serious research to develop a do-able spiritual maturation process. At a time when missiologists shout the need for depth in practical theological training, this book can serve as a handbook.

The Path is a guide for anyone, of any age or personality type, who is eager to grow in intimacy with the Father and ready to more deeply join in the joy/battle of helping another to grow. The best part for me, this week, is that *The Path* can help the four men I am discipling on Wednesday mornings and then can guide our church leadership in our task of equipping the saints to impact our community and world.

—Steve Draper
Navigator staff for thirty years

In my own walk as a Christian and as a small group leader for several years, I have noted differing levels of spiritual maturity among fellow believers. Reading *The Path* helped me identify their different levels of spiritual maturity and provided me with powerful insights into their current levels of maturity and the tools to understand the different levels of maturity of those in my group.

—Mike Wilson
Small Group Leader of Men, Manhattan Beach, CA

As a pastor involved for many years in the discipleship of new and newly growing believers, I have discover that the "deep people in the faith" who are available to spiritually guide others from God's perspective are greatly outnumbered by those seeking guidance. *The Path* couples a wonderful exposition of 1 John 2:12–14 with a grid of human development observations that wisely complement biblical truth in the shaping of these deep persons. Not only does *The Path* supply a comprehensive map for Christian direction, but also it guides the spiritual director to the diagnostic tools available in order to make most profitable the times we invest in people. *The Path* helped me understand the transitions I have gone through to become a deep follower of Christ and created a thirst to represent Christ more effectively to the many men with whom I am involved.

—Pastor Dave Cornell
First Baptist Church, East Stroudsburg, PA

THE PATH

Tobin –

THE PATH

HOW TO UNDERSTAND AND EXPERIENCE AUTHENTIC SPIRITUAL GROWTH

Go the distance!
1 John 2:12-14
Love ya,
Don Willett

DON WILLETT, PH.D.

AUTHOR OF STAGES OF FAITH

WinePress Publishing
Great Books, Defined.

© 2012 by Don Willett. All rights reserved.

WinePress Publishing (PO Box 428, Enumclaw, WA 98022) functions only as book publisher. As such, the ultimate design, content, editorial accuracy, and views expressed or implied in this work are those of the author.

No part of this book may be reproduced or transmitted in any form or by any means, electronic or mechanical, including photocopying and recording, or by any information storage and retrieval system, without permission in writing from the publisher.

Unless otherwise noted, all Scriptures are taken from the *New American Standard Bible*, © 1960, 1963, 1968, 1971, 1972, 1973, 1975, 1977 by The Lockman Foundation. Used by permission.

Scripture references marked KJV are taken from the *King James Version* of the Bible.

Scripture references marked MSG are taken from *The Message*. Copyright © 1993, 1994, 1995, 1996, 2000, 2001, 2002. Used by permission of NavPress Publishing Group.

Scripture references marked NET are from the *NET Bible*® copyright ©1996-2006 by Biblical Studies Press, L.L.C. http://bible.org All rights reserved.

ISBN 13: 978-1-4141-2192-5
ISBN 10: 1-4141-2192-X
Library of Congress Catalog Card Number: 2011914886

CONTENTS

ACKNOWLEDGMENTS

I SHEEPISHLY BUT purposely enrolled in the Educational Studies doctoral program at Talbot School of Theology, La Mirada, CA, in the Fall of 1986. Even then, my unswerving focus was on discipleship and influencing the spiritual growth of other followers of Christ. I felt "assigned" and entrusted with the creation of a biblical model that might be a clearer, less-obstructed path of spiritual growth to follow than what I had known.

I still remember the day I first encountered John Stott's observation on 1 John 2:12–14 in his commentary, *The Epistles of John:* John, the apostle, was "indicating not their physical ages, but stages in their spiritual development, for God's family has members of different maturity… They represent three different stages of spiritual pilgrimage." These words set my head swirling with questions to explore and possibilities to envision! The idea of biblical stages of faith was first conceived in a class I had with professor and Dean Dr. Dennis Dirks. And I have tirelessly and tediously developed this model over the last twenty-five years. This book, *The Path*, is the by-product of my doctoral research and dissertation combined with years of teaching in the classroom and small groups in churches.

I owe my determination and persistence to many people whose words of encouragement fueled me to continue when I could have given up. The men in Men Made New from Faithful Central Bible Church, Inglewood, CA, and from Journey of Faith in Manhattan Beach, CA, have been catalysts for me to keep pressing on.

But without a doubt, my biggest fan and cheerleader has been my wife, Barbara. I often tell her, "I'm a lucky guy!" This one-of-a-kind woman is dedicated to doing our life "assignment" together.

Too, I would like to thank and hug each of the following team members: John Hamilton, for all of the conceptual influence and design of graphics over the years; Erik Svendsen (Reddoor), for his fresh design of the *Stages of Faith* logo; Mel Andrews, for his original work; and Lisa Guest, for her editorial craftsmanship. These four gifted friends have contributed so much to this project. *The Path* is a result of us! I am happy with the outcome and hope you are too.

PREFACE

WHAT A PRIVILEGE to be called into God's family—to have our eyes and hearts open to God's gracious provision of His Son as the perfect sacrifice for your sins and mine! What a life of hope we can lead as we look forward to eternity with Him, where Jesus will reign and there will be no more sorrow, pain, or tears! But what are we to do in the meantime, between naming Jesus our Savior and Lord and going to be with Him?

Thankfully, we aren't left on our own to figure that out. Instead, we work in cooperation with the Holy Spirit's guidance and empowerment. One way He guides us is with the truth of God's Word, and 1 John 2:12–14 is an example. Those three verses, penned by John the apostle, offer a path toward Christlikeness, the ultimate goal of our salvation, and that path is the focus of this book.

Why This Book?

Over the years, I have observed some serious shortcomings in how we, the church, disciple and educate people for spiritual growth. I have been a youth pastor and a pastor of adult ministries and discipleship; I served seven years on staff with a disciple-making and church renewal organization. I have enjoyed the world of higher education at Biola University, where I was the director of the Adult Degree Completion Program. Eager to learn, I earned a Ph.D. in Educational Studies at Biola (1997) with an emphasis on spiritual development, during which time the idea for *The Path* was conceived. Additionally, I am hard-wired to focus on those believers who, like the world-class athlete, want to excel and go farther than the ordinary. Finally, my twenty years of teaching both the workbook *Stages of Faith* and the ideas in *The Path*—in small groups, churches, and a Christian university—have shaped this work and compel me to tirelessly advance it.

This book needs to be in the hands of men and women who will help change the way we think about spiritual growth and the way we guide others in the faith. The curious, the small-group leaders, the professors at evangelical undergraduate and graduate schools, the pastors of churches large and small—why not accept the challenge to lead the way? It will take God-loving, passionate leaders to get this work into the mainstream of discipleship tools.

Starting with You

- Every church needs a disciple-making strategy. *The Path*, with its companion workbook, *Stages of Faith*, provides a clear path and describes the key milestones by which a believer's progress can be measured. In churches today, however, spiritual growth is too often talked about in terms of *more*—more study, more commitment, more memorization, more service, more attendance, etc. This focus on external behavior and performance leads to discouragement and disillusionment. *The Path* provides an alternative approach that is simple, comprehensive, and transformative.
- *The Path* provides skilled guidance to pastors who are committed to investing deeply in the lives of a few people, and the *Stages of Faith* workbook enhances any disciple-making efforts.
- The teaching pastor in the pulpit as well as Sunday school teachers and leaders of numerous other ministries speak to a range of people: some are in their Childhood stage of faith, others are in the Young Adulthood stage, and still others are

in the Parenthood stage. Every individual in the congregation is unique in his or her level of spiritual maturity, and pastors will be surprised to learn what stage of spiritual development their people are at and what is slowing or even preventing their growth. These pastors and other church leaders will then be better able to help people move forward to the next stage of spiritual development.

- Individuals assigned to oversee and train small-group leaders as well as the directors of mens' and womens' ministries should be armed with this text and the *Stages of Faith* workbook. Both books also belong in every small-group leader's toolbox.
- Spiritual formation courses at colleges and seminaries are increasingly popular. The current trend in spiritual formation looks to the Desert Fathers, ancient wisdom, and spiritual paradigms provided by medieval mystics like Bernard of Clairvaux, John of the Cross, and Theresa of Avila. *The Path* and *Stages of Faith* step in to provide a clear, biblical path and the promise of sure footing for every believer.
- Countless disciple-making ministries are doing God's kingdom work across the United States and around the world. Each staff member will benefit from *The Path* text, the *Stages of Faith* workbook, and the Spiritual Growth Profile as they disciple and mobilize believers. Furthermore, the staff of these ministries will come to care for one another more effectively as they better understand how the story of their spiritual growth has been shaped.

I Commission You!

Accepting this invitation to walk the path John outlines in his first epistle means setting out on an adventure that may surprise you with unexpected discoveries and impact you with some unforgettable experiences. In fact, you may never be the same after this journey!

—Don Willett
July, 2012

CHAPTER 1

UNCOVERING A NEGLECTED PATH

MAYBE YOU'VE NOTICED it too. And you may have noticed it years ago or only recently. You may have seen it in your church as well as others, or maybe the issue has come up when you've done some reading on church history or Christian growth. I'm talking about the serious shortcomings in the way we—the church, God's people—disciple, educate, and prepare believers for spiritual growth.

Many Christ-followers are like world-class athletes: they want to excel and go farther in their faith walk. For them, mere proof of membership and an official gym bag won't do. And that's where *The Path* can help. While other books claim to bring a fresh insight or new challenge to today's followers of Christ, *The Path* is truly one-of-a-kind. It's not another initiative in spiritual formation or a novel spin on how to grow spiritually. It's not another disappointing ten-step, how-to program for becoming more like Christ. Instead, taking an entirely different approach, this book is designed to change the way you think about the Christian journey and to offer ideas about how believers can grow, as well as how they can guide others in spiritual growth.

Surprisingly fresh and different, *The Path* provides clear direction to guide you on your journey. Based on 1 John 2:12–14,

The Path identifies three dynamic stages of spiritual development and the eight milestones that comprise those stages. Believers will discover how far they have come as they explore how the process of sanctification—of becoming more like Christ—happens in predictable stages over a lifetime. The unique Spiritual Growth Profile provides a map to help believers determine what stage of faith they are in, what may be slowing their spiritual growth, and how they can tailor a plan to get in better shape.

And the church desperately needs believers who are in good spiritual shape, believers who are mature Christ-followers. According to Richard Foster, however, that goal is quite countercultural. Commenting on the value our society places on immediate gratification, a value that opposes long-term, deep spiritual progress for the Christian, Foster has insightfully observed that "superficiality is the curse of our age. The doctrine of instant satisfaction is a primary spiritual problem. The desperate need today is not for more intelligent people nor gifted people, but for *deep* people."[1]

Addressing this need, *The Path* is an invitation to think about your journey of faith in a distinctively different way, a way probably unfamiliar to you and not much like your experience. This path to deepening spiritual maturity, rooted in the New Testament writing of the apostle John, has been left largely unexamined, neglected, and for many believers, quite hidden. May this study inspire further exploration of this model and benefit readers like you who are looking for a path that gives proven direction for their own journeys of faith.

One more reassurance: *The Path* doesn't urge you to jump through prescribed hoops, practice certain disciplines, or outline specific formulas, all of which can emphasize *more*—more commitment, more Bible study, more surrender, more memorization, more service, more prayer, and more attendance. Through the years, we Christians have likely prescribed these for ourselves, with the expectation that we would grow spiritually. Despite our good intentions, however, what eventually resulted was undoubtedly a weary admission of disillusionment and disappointment. Any call to *more* is sure to leave you guilty, discouraged, and exhausted.

And *more* doesn't heal or transform a believer. There is a better way—and that is the biblically grounded but largely unexamined path to spiritual maturity we find in the New Testament. Again, as stated above, John the apostle offers a perspective by which you can chart your course for the lifelong journey of spiritual growth.

Like the cords of a rope, three intertwined factors reveal why reading and applying the principles of *The Path* is a worthwhile and significant assignment. Each one of these three components will help you to find sure footing on a path that will be rich and rewarding. These three aspects of *The Path* will also make your personal journey more direct and your ministry to others more focused.

1. A Biblically Grounded Path

Too many of us have not discovered this biblically based path that can guide our lifelong journeys of faith, and that is exactly what the apostle John offers. He describes three stages of spiritual growth—the Childhood stage of faith, the Young Adulthood stage of faith, and the Parenthood stage of faith—and notes the distinguishing characteristics of each stage. First John 2:12–14 sets forth an entirely different way of looking at one's spiritual progress. How will you benefit?

- Christian travelers can determine the distance they have already traveled as well as plan for the distance yet to be covered. Specific, biblical milestones will be identified to help believers ascertain their strengths, note their progress, identify their weaknesses, and attend to those and any other factors that slow spiritual growth.
- *The Path* offers insights as to why many adults need to enrich the three vital aspects of the Childhood stage of faith; suggests why too many adults plateau or stall in the borrowed, secondhand faith of the Young Adulthood stage; and describes the deep and seasoned Parent in the faith.
- Younger believers will get a look at what is ahead and save themselves lots of time, uncertainty, and discouragement.

- Older believers may realize they need to revise their assumptions about how spiritual growth occurs.

As pastors, small-group leaders, Christian educators, and disciple makers, we hope to see Christians grow and mature throughout their lives. We want to facilitate their transformation into Christlikeness. That, in fact, is God's job description for us as leaders in His church, and we know that conversion marks the beginning of one's progress toward spiritual maturity and Christlikeness. Needless to say, some believers are more mature and farther along in their progress than others, and all these people will hear and respond to any message according to their stages of spiritual growth.

That is one reason why *The Path* is a valuable addition to your ministry toolbox. As you become familiar with both *The Path* and its companion, *Stages of Faith*, you will become more skilled at discerning where others might be in their spiritual growth, helping them identify what is holding them back, and pointing them forward on their own journeys. Whether you are a pastor or a lay leader, the biblical principles set forth in these resources will, ideally, become part of the fabric of your church's discipleship process. Sermons and teachings on the 1 John stages and on how spiritual growth occurs can also help that happen.

Various denominations, however, offer distinctly different paths for believers to follow and different milestones by which to measure one's progress to spiritual maturity. As a result, rather than a consensus, much confusion about spiritual growth exists. In *Christian Spirituality: Five Views of Sanctification*, author Don Alexander observed that the ongoing debate about these divergent paths and distinctive emphases leads to confusion. He concluded that these paths are a "riddle of sanctification" and a "dilemma of the call to personal holiness."[2] The apostle John's model of stages described in *The Path* enables us believers to see beyond what appears to be a riddle and a dilemma so that we can more confidently navigate our way to personal spiritual growth. Furthermore, *The Path* and *Stages of Faith* work well with the various denominational traditions represented in a church.

In addition to the various denominational perspectives, also clouding a believer's understanding of the Christian's journey is James Fowler's model of faith development, in which he sets forth a different destination in his universalizing stage of faith, which very few ever arrive at—other than Mahatma Gandhi, Mother Teresa, Martin Luther King, Jr., and Dietrich Bonhoeffer. Fowler's view of faith is different from a biblical understanding of faith. Also, slowing down the spiritual growth of many believers is the conventional model of discipleship, with its focus on the content of the Christian's belief system and its neglect of the process that results in a deepening, maturing faith. Yet the renewed and widespread curiosity about the Desert Fathers and Catholic spirituality (Theresa of Avila and John of the Cross, among others) leaves us insisting on a biblical vision of a transformative relationship with Christ. Setting forth yet another scenario, *The Path* describes the apostle John's path of sanctification and a destination that is holistic and restorative. This paradigm will be easy to understand, biblically faithful, and sophisticated; yet it will remain user-friendly.

The Path identifies and describes stages of faith in a Christian's journey so that each of us can better understand where we are in the process of spiritual growth and better cooperate with God as He works in our lives.

We will develop the model of stages of faith from the Word of God in the following chapters:

2. The Case for Stages of Faith
3. Evidence Beyond a Reasonable Doubt
4. An Aged Apostle's Ideas About Spiritual Progress
5. The Childhood Stage of Faith: The Birth of Faith
6. The Young Adulthood Stage of Faith: The Ownership of Faith
7. The Parenthood Stage of Faith: Empowering Faith

2. A Developmentally Informed Path

A second noteworthy aspect of *The Path* is its integration of developmental theory with the biblical model of stages of faith. What might John's model of stages of spiritual development look like when informed by three developmental perspectives? The answer is a compelling description of the *how* of spiritual growth that enables us to better understand the process, sequence, rhythms, tempos, and patterns of spiritual development over the whole of the adult's life span. This section also describes the range of possibilities, the boundaries of the process, and the mechanics of development and change. The distinctive structure and content of John's model begins to come alive. As *The Path* outlines the various dimensions of the stages of faith model, what emerges is an unique, heuristic, and holistic model of a journey toward Christian maturity, a model that is firmly derived from Scripture, grounded in God's truth, and then enriched by human development theories.

Believers today are more accustomed to thinking about faith in terms of *what* people should believe, but healthy spiritual growth needs to look farther than the content of faith. Perry Downs explains:

> Historically evangelicals have attended to content but have ignored structure. We have been so concerned with guarding what people believe that we have failed to listen to how people believe. We have ignored the possibility of stages of faith, striving only to make faith stronger without being concerned with making faith more mature. We have tended to police its content and tried to strengthen its power, but we have neglected its maturity.[3]

Downs then describes the advantages enjoyed by the Christian educator and caregiver who employs a model of stages of faith that attends to the *process* of faith, not just the *content* of faith:

> As Christian educators become sensitive to the stages of faith they will be able to hear the structure as well as content, and maturity as well as strength. They will understand people more deeply and have a more realistic perspective on the health of their congregations. Moreover, they will have better possibilities for designing educational approaches fit to the level of maturity of their people.[4]

If you've been a Christian for any length of time, maybe you've noticed that discipleship materials often fail to address how the journey of faith progresses over a lifetime, especially through adulthood. The longest period of life, adulthood, offers us an unique opportunity to experience in ever-deepening ways the profound truths of our Christian faith as well as a spirituality that is genuinely transformative. After all, we shouldn't expect our experience of faith in our younger years to suffice in our later years—and that's not God's plan either.

But back to the *how*: Exactly how does faith grow through these three stages of spiritual development? As mentioned above, this focus on the process is noticeably absent in literature addressing Christian growth. Instead, discipleship books are largely content and information driven, and they emphasize disciplines to master. So *The Path* and *Stages of Faith* offer readers a refreshing and challenging alternative.

As we examine twelve specific characteristics of spiritual growth, we'll find vital clues about how to provide, care for, give direction to, and disciple fellow believers. Ideally, we will then be better able to listen to *how* people come to believe, and believe more deeply, even as we pay attention to *what* they believe. We can be concerned about making faith more mature, not just stronger. Two chapters explore these twelve conclusions of how spiritual growth occurs:

8. The How of Spiritual Growth, Part 1
9. The How of Spiritual Growth, Part 2

Then, in Chapters 10–12, each of the three stages of faith—Childhood, Young Adulthood, and Parenthood—and their particular milestones are integrated with human development theories. Building on ideas from Chapters 8–9, John's model now invites the believer to follow a journey of spiritual growth that is both clear in its direction and compelling in its process.

10. The Journey of the Childhood Stage of Faith
11. The Journey of the Young Adulthood Stage of Faith
12. The Journey of the Parenthood Stage of Faith

3. Skilled Guides for the Journey

Third, *The Path* offers important insights about spiritual growth to spiritual caregivers and leaders, pastors, educators, missionaries, Sunday school teachers, parents, Christian counselors, and disciple-making organizations. This biblical model for spiritual growth enables church leaders to appraise the health and growth of those they are shepherding. *The Path* can also help leaders determine what to do to shape spiritually mature Christians—whether their programs are effectively fostering spiritual growth or what are delaying growth in their people—and what they can do to enrich their ministry and encourage movement toward spiritual maturity. Based on what they learn here, spiritual caregivers can then tailor a plan for a specific individual's growth.

The identification and training of such skilled guides is essential if the Christian church is to be a center of spiritual formation. Said another way, the success and longevity of any discipleship plan will depend on the quality of the shepherds and guides—and, sadly, there is a dire shortage of such skilled guides. In *Soulguide*, Dr. Bruce Demarest notes this crisis:

> Where can a disciple who is eager to grow spiritually find a person who will listen, discern, keep his feet on the fire, and point the way home? Where can one find a supportive spiritual companion endued with wisdom, compassion, humility, and grace? Advice givers and problem solvers are as common as coal in Newcastle.
>
> But where are the godly and competent spiritual guides—those who to a significant degree reflect the pastoral qualities exhibited by the Lord Jesus? There may be a shred of truth in the opinion that "Good spiritual directors are as rare as hen's teeth."[5]

Richard Foster's plea that believers become "deep" is a timely one, and the existence of divergent paths of sanctification that lead to confusion must be remedied. Believers in Christ need to become familiar with a way forward and upward that is biblical, sensible, and compelling. And there must be a cadre of spiritual guides to help lead the way.

It is indeed a lofty statement to suggest that *The Path* can help believers—seminary trained and lay alike—understand more clearly how to develop increasingly deep, mature Christian adults. It is indeed a lofty statement to claim that *The Path* will be of vital, practical, and broad importance to the Christian community, Christian educators, counselors, disciple-makers, and mentors. But, by God's grace, neither one is an impossible goal. May He use these tools for His glory as well as for the good of His people ... starting with you.

Questions for Reflection and Action

1. Consider the ideas set forth in this chapter. What point about spiritual growth did you find especially intriguing? Why?
2. Where did you see yourself or your faith journey described in this chapter? What statements accurately describe your church?
3. When have you attempted to do *more* of something—more Bible study, more commitment, more Scripture memorization, more service, more church attendance, etc.—in hopes of becoming more spiritually mature, more like Christ? Describe your efforts, the outcome, and your reaction to that outcome.
4. Richard Foster has made this observation: "The desperate need [in the church] today is not for more intelligent people nor gifted people, but for *deep* people." Do you agree or disagree? Why?
5. What nudge to action, if any, did you sense as you read this chapter? Going on to read the next chapter counts!

Chapter 2

THE CASE FOR STAGES OF FAITH

RICHARD FOSTER'S INSIGHTFUL observations bear repeating: "Superficiality is the curse of our age. The doctrine of instant satisfaction is a primary spiritual problem. The desperate need today is not for more intelligent people nor gifted people, but for *deep* people."[1] The church definitely needs deep, mature followers of Christ. Offered in hopes of helping to meet that need, this chapter invites you to think about the believer's journey of faith in a distinctively different way, specifically, as a path—largely unexamined—to deepening spiritual maturity. May this study inspire further exploration of John's model and benefit those readers looking for direction for their own journeys.

Before looking at the direction John offers, consider that our spiritual journeys can be derailed, a fact that prompted William Hendricks, author of *Exit Interviews*, to try to determine why so many Christians withdraw from church. He interviewed people who had been Christians for more than ten years, some for two or three times that long, yet who were dissatisfied with their spiritual progress. The attrition rate is not all that surprising in light of the fact that evangelicals have developed a clear theology about salvation (the beginning of the journey) and eschatology (the ultimate end of the journey) but have been less helpful in describing the lengthy process of the journey itself. Hendricks therefore suggested that a root cause of believers' dissatisfaction with their spiritual growth is their deficient understanding of the process of sanctification:

> Over the course of the church's history, some brilliant thinking has been put forward on the nature and process of salvation, or justification. Likewise, good work has been done on the question of our future hope in Christ, or glorification. But, there's a gap in our theology when it comes to sanctification. What happens between coming to faith and meeting Christ?
>
> Along these lines, we tell people that the goal is "spiritual maturity." What is that? What are its characteristics? Is spirituality a destination or a direction? How long should it reasonably take to arrive at "maturity," whatever it is? Or do we ever get there? If not, how do we stay motivated? How do we mark our milestones? How do we even know if we're making progress?[3]

Hendricks raises these specific and poignant questions about the process of spiritual growth, and the progression outlined in 1 John 2:12–14 offers answers. Contemporary Christians want a biblical description and explanation of spiritual growth; they want to travel farther toward spiritual maturity and be able to mark their progress along the way.

Hendricks' questions continue:

> What is that process? Can its steps or stages be discerned? In 1 John, the writer says that he is writing to "little children," "young men," and "fathers." Are these phases of spiritual development? If so, what are their characteristics?
>
> I know of no single body of work that has thoroughly explored these issues and others like them. Yet spirituality is probably the foremost theological category in people's minds today. As long as the church lacks a cogent doctrine in this area, it will keep losing credibility—which is to say it will keep losing people.[4]

Habermas and Issler, who also discuss a biblical path to spiritual maturity, note that children, young men, and fathers are mentioned in the 1 John 2:12–14 passage:

> The identification of such biblical phases seems to offer a promising way to delineate the maturation process within believers. But more study is needed of these and related passages, if we desire to recognize critical milestones of growth in our Christian pilgrimage.[5]

Yet Tom Ashbrook, the director of spiritual formation for Church Resource Ministries, identifies another key problem, specifically, the fuzziness and confusion about what "spiritual formation" is.

> Careful not to get labeled or boxed in to a narrow understanding or regimen, writers advocate a little of this and a little of that. For example, Richard Peace concludes, "So in place of a single model, I suspect that in the new millennium we will see a blending of approaches. I can imagine an evangelical bookshelf containing ... a list of books from varied traditions." The trouble is that in the effort to be inclusive and holistic, there is little clarity about either the goal or the process of spiritual formation. Will an eclectic library and a dabbling in the spiritual disciplines accomplish true spiritual formation?[6]

Good question, Dr. Ashbrook!

The Case for Stages of Faith

Images and analogies for a Christian's spiritual growth are many and varied, and one of the most instructive comes from 1 John 2:12–14, the passage that serves as the foundation for this Stages of Faith path of spiritual growth. These three verses outline the Christian journey toward maturity and Christlikeness—and this is not merely a twenty-first-century view of the passage. As the following discussion will show, the conclusion that John's words are a description of stages of faith proves true to the apostle's teaching, his meaning, and his intent.

Four Questions Regarding the Interpretation of 1 John 2:12–14

Through the years, though, 1 John 2:12–14 has prompted questions about stages of faith. These are questions that must be dealt with in order to ensure an accurate interpretation of the passage. The four issues most commonly raised in discussions of this passage are:

1. Is John talking about stages of faith or literal ages of believers?
2. How many groups is John addressing in this epistle?
3. Why does John use two words for "child"?
4. Why does John change the verb tenses?

We invite you to carefully consider the answers to these questions, which have been offered by knowledgeable biblical scholars and commentators. May their expertise encourage you to embrace the path toward spiritual growth that John the apostle outlines in his first epistle.

Question #1: Is John referring to stages or ages?

Commentators as well as laypeople ask, "Does 1 John 2:12–14 refer to chronological ages or metaphorical stages? Is John noting physical ages or levels of spiritual maturity? What does the author mean when he describes his readers as children, young men, and fathers?"

Option 1: Chronological Age

Some commentators believe that the references to children, young men, and older men may have a literal meaning. John Calvin notes that John "mentions three ages, the most common divisions of human life."[7] But there are at least five difficulties with this literal interpretation.

1. Most significantly, John uses *little children* (*teknia*) elsewhere to include all of his readers (1 John 2:1, 28; 3:18; 5:21).
2. The order in which the three groups are mentioned is not consecutive. If John is addressing the chronological ages of

the people in his congregation, there seems no reasonable explanation for the groups to be listed out of chronological order.

3. References to the ages of his congregation appear to contribute nothing to the meaning and development of John's argument. That there would be Christians of differing ages among John's readers is self-evident.
4. Smalley suggests that the naming of "fathers" and "young men" indicates a male-dominated community.[8] Yet no support exists for any sectarian character or male-dominated quality in the Johannine community.[9]
5. Finally, it is patently clear that advancing age is no guarantee of spiritual progress. Advancing chronologically does not automatically mean greater spiritual maturity. Rather, spiritual growth comes from the intensity, not just the extensity, of the years of following Christ. A believer may be a Christian for many years yet remain stuck in prolonged spiritual immaturity (1 Corinthians 3:1–2; Hebrews 5:11–14).

According to these five arguments, a literal interpretation of the ages John mentions seems inadequate in advancing his pastoral thought, intent, and concerns.

Option #2: A Metaphorical Understanding of Stages

Some commentators maintain that John is addressing Christians who are at different stages of spiritual growth and that he is describing these believers metaphorically as children (recently converted), young men (farther along in Christ), and fathers (those still more developed and seasoned in the faith). The following eight scholars strongly support this view, and they also offer particular insights about the distinctive characteristics of the three metaphorical stages of spiritual development mentioned in 1 John 2:12–14. Together, these commentators provide a basis for understanding how believers develop a mature faith.

- John Stott clearly differentiates three "stages of spiritual development," each one representing a more mature and stable believer. At each stage, the believer is qualitatively, constitutionally different from the stage before:

> [The apostle John] is indicating not their physical ages, as some have thought, but stages in their spiritual development, for God's family, like every human family, has members of different maturity ... They represent three different stages of spiritual pilgrimage. The dear children are those newborn in Christ. The young men are more developed Christians, strong and developed in spiritual warfare; while the fathers possess the depth and stability of ripe Christian experience.[10]

- Guy King challenges the reader with his comments, based on 1 John 2:12–14, that the new birth is only the beginning of one's faith journey and that the growth process is not automatic and can therefore stall.

> The entrance to the Fellowship is not a stopping-place, but a starting-place—as in all life, there is to be growth, progress. Some people miss so much for lack of this onward spirit ... There is even danger, as well as loss, in failing to get on.
>
> The New Testament is full of this idea of progress. John, by means of yet another illustration, pointing the same salutary lesson—some have grown in spiritual stature to be as "fathers"; some are spiritually vigorous "young men"; some, for all their physical age, are yet "little children" in grace.[12]

- Robert Law notes "stages of growth" in 1 John 2:12–14, where each stage is characterized by a more advanced attainment; a riper, calmer, and deeper faith experience; and a greater capacity to see life differently. At the end of this process, a constitutionally different person emerges.

> The apostle next addresses his readers according to their stages of growth; and, first, the "fathers," among whom would be included ... all who, in contrast with the "young men," were most advanced and, presumably, of riper Christian attainment ... We look to mature experience for a largeness of view, a calm untroubled depth of conviction, a clear-eyed judgment upon life, which youth cannot have.[13]

Law also notes in 1 John 2:12–14 a curriculum or map of movement toward Christian maturity.

> To take as the starting point the gift of God in Christ, the forgiveness of sins and the knowledge of the Father; then to advance, with this as our strength and the Word of God as our weapon, to faithful and victorious warfare; finally through this, to arrive at the sure perception of the everlasting, in union with whom our human life and its results become an eternal and blessed reality—such is the curriculum which St. John maps out for human experience.[14]

- Calling 1 John 2:12–28 "Degrees of Growth in the Family of God," August Van Ryn describes specific features of individual spiritual growth and the experience of three groups of believers:

> All have life in Christ alike, all alike are the recipients of every spiritual blessing in virtue of the grace of Christ, but there is a difference in spiritual apprehension and experience. Thus a special message is given to each of these three groups. Fathers in spiritual growth have reached the stage where the Lord Jesus Christ fills their vision, and so no warning is needed or given them. Young men are in danger of moral seduction; hence they are warned against the world, the flesh and the devil. Children are in danger of spiritual seduction; hence they are warned against false doctrine, against anti-Christian lies.[15]

- Arthur Pink argues for three "grades," "stages of spiritual development," or "degrees of the stature of Christ" in 1 John

2:12–14 and declares that progress is measured not merely with the passing of years. One's chronological age is descriptive of the years one has lived, but the number of years one has lived does not define one's spiritual maturity.

> In 1 John 2:12–14 believers are not graded according to their natural ages, nor even according to the length of time they have been Christians, but according to the spiritual growth and progress they have made in the Christian life... But during this present life are different stages of spiritual development reached by Christians, different forms in the school of Christ to which they belong, different measures of progress made by them. Broadly speaking there are three degrees of the "stature of Christ" reached by believers in this life, though the highest of them falls very short of that which shall pertain to them in the life to come.[16]

- Similarly, F. F. Bruce comments on the factors of experience, time, and chronological age in the process of moving experientially from stage to stage toward spiritual maturity.

> The threefold grouping relates to spiritual maturity, not years reckoned by the calendar. Even if, in the Christian third generation, there was a growing tendency for spiritual maturity and natural age to coincide, nevertheless, it is spiritual experience that is emphasized.[17]

- Vine observes that spiritual growth comes as a result of advancing years and greater life experience. The "father" is the most experienced among the family of faith. These seasoned, older believers can draw on their faith experience as they guide and give care to others in the faith. They are highly regarded and worthy of both respect and imitation.

> Children are the youngest believers, newborn spiritual babes. Young men are those who have had some experience of spiritual conflict. *Fathers* refers to those who have been Christians the longest and have the deepest, ripest, and most

> mature development. They are the older men in the heavenly family; those who by reason of experience are looked up to for sympathy, guidance and assistance.[18]

- James Montgomery Boice also distinguishes three metaphorical stages of faith, calling attention to the increasing wisdom, strength, and depth of character that believers gain with time and experience.

> The children are those who have recently come to the knowledge of God and of sins forgiven. The fathers have acquired the gift of spiritual wisdom, having lived longer in the faith and thus have come to know Him who is from the beginning in a deeper way. The young men are those who are bearing the brunt of the church's spiritual warfare.[19]

These respected commentators offer strong evidence and persuasive arguments for understanding 1 John 2:12–14 as referring to three metaphorical stages of faith. Some believers, regardless of their age, are children in the faith; some have advanced to the Young Adulthood stage; and others have progressed to the last stage of being fathers or Parents in the faith. Clearly, the apostle John is employing a metaphor of development as he uses images of three ordinary family members to represent different levels of spiritual growth. Implicit in this metaphor is the concept of a goal, an endpoint, and a fulfillment of purpose. Basically, the journey of faith is the progressive movement of the believer toward the goal of full-grown, genuine Christlikeness.

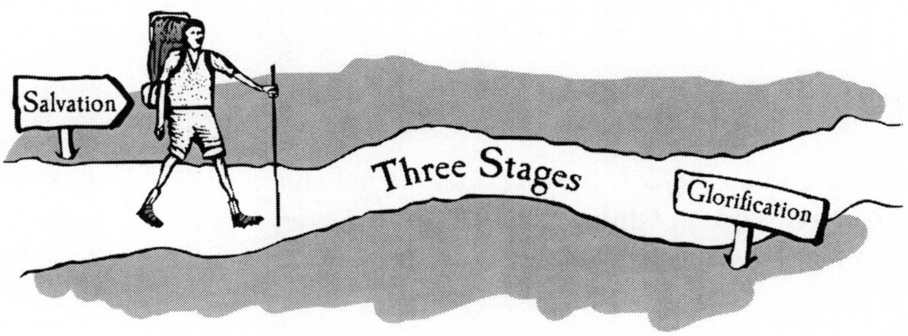

But 1 John 2:12–14 does not stand alone or in opposition to other key passages of Scripture. What follows are three key additional passages, each similar to 1 John 2:12–14 in its identification of a path of three successive stages of spiritual maturity. Note that the journey has a beginning stage, a destination stage, and a stage of a lengthy distance in between. The prominent theme of each passage is summarized, offering insight into the process or "how" of spiritual growth and pointing to possible causes of its delay.

Hebrews 5:12–6:3	Infancy to Maturity
Theme: Getting in Shape for the Journey. *Believers were stalled in the stage of infancy, needing to practice and train in order to become skilled in moral reasoning.*	

1 Corinthians 2:14–3:4	Infancy to Maturity
Theme: Developing a Firsthand, Owned Faith. *Believers are stuck in the stage of infancy due to performing* for *and conforming* to *the approval and conventions of significant others.*	

Ephesians 4:12–16	Children to Maturity
Theme: Relationships That Transform. *Paul emphasized community; spiritual growth has an interpersonal dimension to cultivate that cannot be neglected.*	

The evidence supporting stages of spiritual maturity—evidence from 1 John 2:12–14; Hebrews 5:12–6:3; 1 Corinthians 2:14–3:4; and Ephesians 4:12–16—is compelling and soundly defensible. The journey toward spiritual maturity and Christlikeness is neither a puzzling dilemma nor a disconcerting riddle.

Three Challenges to the Metaphorical View

Some commentators, however, have challenged the metaphorical interpretation of 1 John 2:12–14 on three main points, and these challenges are addressed below.

1. Commentators have argued that the order does not follow a chronological sequence. John first addresses the children, then the fathers, and last, the young men. Zane Hodges suggests that "the sequence—which makes the 'fathers' the middle term—is somewhat strange."[20]

But by placing young men last, John may be emphasizing that particular stage. As we will discover in Chapters 6 and 12, this is the stage where many believers plateau and stall, and that fact might explain why John describes the stage of Young Adulthood more fully than he does the other two stages.

Also, the non-chronological order may be explained stylistically. John may first give the two extremes of the stages (the beginning and the ending) and then refer to the intermediate stage, "young men." After all, John's epistle is full of sharp contrasts (light and darkness, truth and error, love and hate, etc.). Here, possibly, the contrast is between child and parent, with the young men mentioned afterward.

Last, the question as to why the order should be sequential needs to be raised. This may purely be the expectation of a western interpreter, a linear thinker, when the non-chronological order may be very typical of Jewish writers like John. As mentioned above, the non-chronological order of child, father, and young men does not at all support the case for the literal interpretation of the ages. Actually, this issue of the sequence appears quite irrelevant to both views.

2. Another argument against the metaphorical interpretation of 1 John 2:12–14 contends that the "children-fathers-young men" triad lists spiritual qualities that should characterize all Christians at any time (Dodd, Brown, Barclay, Marshall, Boice, Hodges). The reasoning is that, whatever the ages of his readers, John can properly say to them all, "Your sins have been forgiven; you have known Him who has been from the beginning; and you have conquered the evil one." Similarly Dodd says, "All Christians are (by grace, not nature), children in innocence and dependence on the heavenly Father, young men in strength, and fathers in experience."[21] This

approach argues that there is no obvious reason why each quality mentioned should not be typical of all Christians, not just one group at a particular stage of spiritual growth.

Marshall, however, offers a compelling counterpoint when he observes that the characteristics to which John refers are, in each instance, particularly relevant to the group being addressed: The young convert would be especially conscious of God's forgiveness. The mature Christian would know God in a deep way. And growing believers would have the spiritual motivation and strength to conquer the evil one.[22]

Furthermore—and still in response to Dodd's viewpoint—how is it possible to describe a new Christian as being strong in the faith or as a father in the faith? The qualities mentioned are simply not true of all Christians, and they cannot rightly be expected of all Christians. Dodd's view does not recognize the marked differences among believers in the depth and maturity of their Christian faith and life. Another compelling argument against Dodd's view is that nowhere else in 1 John or even in the rest of Scripture are the terms *fathers* and *young men* ever used to describe all Christians.

3. Finally, the metaphorical interpretation is challenged by the fact that the qualities of faith mentioned cannot be sharply distinguished from one another and sometimes overlap.[23] You know the Father (2:13), for example, is directed to the "children" in the faith, and "you know Him who has been from the beginning" (2:14) is directed to the "fathers" in the faith. This argument can, however, be soundly refuted.

The fathers in the faith are those believers whose knowledge of God as Father has developed and become mature. As a result of the seasoning of time and experience, these fathers have come to know the Eternal One, and they fully trust Him. The depth of their knowledge and intimacy with Him is lacking in the child. "All Christians, mature and immature, have come to know God. But their knowledge of Him ripens with the years … [More mature believers] are already consciously living in eternity."[24]

Furthermore, "Him who is from the beginning" may refer to Christ rather than to the Father. If so, John is not saying the same thing to the children that he is to the fathers. Even if verse 14 refers to the Father and not to Christ, that is not a weighty reason for dismissing the view that distinct stages of faith are outlined in this 1 John 2:12–14 passage.

In conclusion, the evidence supporting a metaphorical understanding of stages of spiritual maturity is far more compelling and defensible than evidence suggesting that John is referring to chronological ages.

Question #2: How many groups is John addressing?

A second question commentators ask about 1 John 2:12–14 is: "How many groups is John addressing—and who are those groups?" Some commentators propose three groups, and others suggest only two.

The Three-Groups View

The least confusing and most plausible interpretation of the biblical text is that the author divides his readers into three groups, and then he addresses each of these trios twice. The following table illustrates this viewpoint:

Trio	Group One	Group Two	Group Three
First	Little children (*teknia*)	Young men	Fathers
Second	Children (*paidia*)	Young men	Fathers

John undoubtedly repeats these designations for the three groups as well as his messages to them in order to emphasize his points. This repetition appears to advance, not merely repeat, John's argument; the repetition also prepares the reader for the teaching that is to follow in verses 15–17. In form, verses 12–14 consist of two sets of three parallel affirmations that appear in a highly structured, almost poetic form. They are even set as lines of poetry in the Greek as well as in most English translations.

The Two-Groups View

It has been suggested that, by *children*, John means all the members of his congregation. After all, Jesus uses *teknia* and *paidia* in the gospel of John to address all of His followers. Elsewhere in 1 John, *little children*, *teknia*, refers to the whole community of faith (cf. 2:1,28; 3:1,2,7,10,18; 4:4; 5:2,21). Within this community of faith, John then goes on to address two groups—young men and fathers (Westcott, Candlish, Ross, Plummer, Vincent, Brooke).[25] In this case, John may be referring to titles of church leaders. Others have proposed that the two groups represent two levels of Christian maturity. We will now explore these two views.

- **Two Titles for Church Leadership**

The argument goes that, within this community of *teknia*, the apostle addresses the fathers and the young men as two specific groups. If so, John may have two specific sets of church officers in mind, and he is using the formal titles "fathers" (*pateros)* and "young men" (*neaniskoi)* as the equivalent of the terms *presbuteroi* (elders or presbyters) and *diakanoi* (deacons or servants), terms that were coming into use as designations for the leaders of the church and their assistants in the New Testament period.[26] However, no such equivalency is found elsewhere in the New Testament. Also, if the fathers and young men in this passage are understood exclusively in terms of office, why isn't what is said to be true of one group true of both? Deacons and young men, for example, are not the only Christians who should know the conquest of evil. Also, why wouldn't John have used *presbuteroi* (elders) instead of *fathers* if that is what he meant?

- **Two Levels of Maturity**

Another suggestion is to understand *fathers* and *young men* in a general sense: as the older and the younger Christians in John's community of believers. According to this argument, John first addresses all of his readers and then subdivides them into fathers and young men, seniority being addressed before young men.[27] *Fathers*, then, would refer to believers who are older, chronologically or spiritually or both. In contrast, the term for young men was commonly used to designate people between twenty-four and forty years of age (Lenski, Westcott, Plummer).[28] So these young men would be younger in both physical and spiritual maturity.

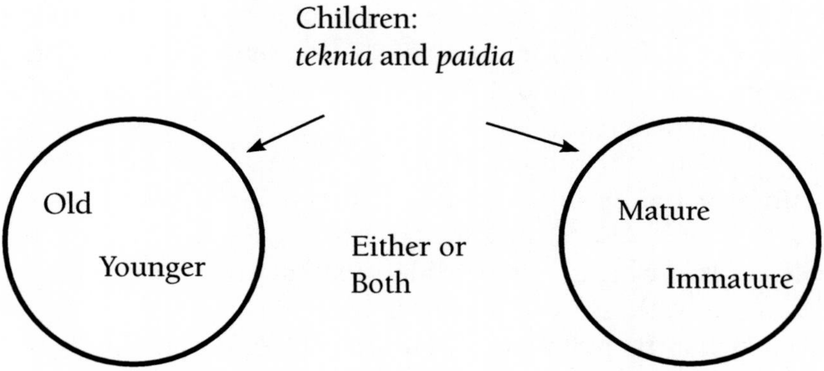

Supporting this argument, other New Testament writers refer to these two categories of believers in similar terms (see 1 Timothy 5:1; Titus 2:1–8; 1 Peter 5:1–5). Paul, for instance, advises Timothy to approach various age groups as he would corresponding members of his own family. As a young man, Timothy is to treat other young men as brothers, older men as fathers, older women as mothers, and young women as sisters. In Titus, Paul addresses the older men (2:1–2) and women (v. 3) and the younger women (vv. 4–5) and men (vv. 6–8). In both of these letters, the focus is on age rather than a stage of spiritual growth.

Westcott, however, divides the readers "by the length of their Christian experience,"[29] a view also held by Greek fathers as well as by Law, Brooke, Ross, and Hiebert. The two groups are the mature and the immature, corresponding to the familiar Pauline "babes in Christ" and the "mature in Christ" (1 Corinthians 3:1; Colossians 1:28). This position admits to two stages of faith, the fathers and the young men, an argument for the metaphorical rather than the chronological interpretation of 1 John 2:12–14. Westcott remarks, "The characteristic of 'fathers' is knowledge, the fruit of experience; that of the 'young men,' victory, the prize of strength."[30]

Two Challenges to the Two-Group View

The first shortcoming of this two-group position is that two stages alone do not comprise the whole of Christian experience. The stage of childhood is conspicuously absent if John is addressing only the young men and fathers in the Christian community. In contrast, the division of believers into three groups covers the full range of the Christian experience.

A second shortcoming of the two-group position is that the distinctive intent and content of the epistle's message is best understood as addressing three groups. In 1 John 2:12–14, John wants to assure his Christian readers that they have passed the tests of genuine faith. However, John notes that some Christians have progressed farther along in this journey of faith than others have. Some believers are more like Christ than others. Some believers resemble Christ in their obedience (Test #1) more than others do; some believers resemble Christ in their ability to love (Test #2) more than others do; and some are more discerning, seeing as He sees (Test #3). So John writes that some Christians are in the Childhood stage of faith, some have advanced to the Young Adulthood stage of faith, and some have progressed to the seasoned Parenthood stage of faith.

In 1 John 3:2, the apostle speaks of the day that will come when the believer will be fully and ultimately "like" Christ: "Beloved, now we are children of God, and it has not appeared what we will be. We know that when He appears, we will be like Him, because we will see Him just as He is." While we are here on this earth, it is God's purpose that believers become progressively like Him. That likeness happens in stages. The process is a journey from salvation to glorification.

But, again, a paradigm of two groups—young and old or immature and mature—does not adequately describe this growth and progress as well as a model of three groups does. In John's model of three stages of faith, the new converts are associated with a fresh knowledge of the forgiveness of their sins, the mature Christians with a deep knowledge of God, and the young men with vigorous strength to overcome.[31] Again, the "little children" are those newborn in Christ; the young men are more developed Christians, strong and victorious in spiritual warfare; and the fathers possess the depth and stability that come with long-term, Christian experience.[32] In conclusion, the clearest and least confusing interpretation of 1 John 2:12–14 is that the author divides his readers into three groups and then addresses each group twice.

Question #3: Why does John use two words for "child"?

A third question commentators ask of this passage is why John uses two different Greek words to refer to children. Twice in 1 John 2:12–14, the apostle uses the same Greek word to refer to both the young men and the fathers, but he selects two different words for child. How is *teknia* ("little children" in verse 12) different from *paidia* ("children" at the end of verse 13)? And what, if anything, are we to conclude about this use of two different Greek words?

As the table (page 23) clearly shows, the author has three groups in mind. "Little children" and "children" are not separate stages. John seems to use both words in order to round out the description of one group—the Childhood stage of faith. Another perspective is that the usage of two different terms is merely a stylistic variation.

The term *teknia*, translated "little children" or "my little born ones," is used in 1 John seven times (2:1,12,28; 3:7,18; 4:4; 5:21). The cognate verb—*tiktō*, "to bear, to give birth to"—suggests kinship or the closeness of the birth relationship. *Teknia* is therefore an expression of affection and endearment used in the context of child and family. Because it is neuter, the noun refers to both men and women. This term also emphasizes the community in which all Christians will grow. Throughout his epistle, John emphasizes this interdependent life of believers, a context that provides relationships similar to that of parents and children. Also, consider that John is approximately ninety years old as he addresses these Christians. They must indeed have seemed very much like little ones to this aged apostle.

The term *paidia*, translated "children," refers to an infant through age seven, to the baby and very young child who is dependent and in need of training, guidance, protection, and nurturance.[33] *Paidia* is found in 1 John twice—in 2:13 and in 2:18, where he introduces a passage (2:18–27) on living in the "last hour." John therefore seems to be addressing Christians in the Childhood stage of faith, who are particularly vulnerable to the deception and lies of antichrists. Remember that John has described the young men as having overcome the evil one (2:13, 14) and the fathers as seasoned in the faith.

Of course, however, no Christian is ever too mature to be seduced (2:15–17; 3:7). After all, a believer's three archrivals—the world, the flesh, and the devil—conspire to conform and condition every Christian, but the *paidia* is uniquely susceptible in the last hour. As children mature in the faith, they move away from this stage of susceptibility to deceit and counterfeits and toward genuine, discerning faith.

Question #4: Why does John change the verb tenses?

A fourth question commentators raise is: "Why does John change verb tenses from *I am writing* to *I have written*?" John begins his first three statements with "I am writing you …" (present tense) and the second three with "I have written you" (aorist tense). This change in tense has given rise to much discussion.

Some commentators suggest that *I have written you* refers either to a former letter[34] or to the earlier part of the epistle,[35] while the present-tense verbs refer to the whole letter. "More likely John is simply thinking of the words he is writing when he uses the present tense and of what he has already written when he uses the aorist."[36]

It is also possible that the aorist is an epistolary aorist (a verb tense suitable for letters); in which case, there is really no difference in meaning between the aorist verbs and the present-tense verbs.[37] The present and epistolary aorist both consider the entire letter with no real difference in meaning. In fact, the New International Version translates all six occurrences as the present tense *I write to you*. This last view seems the most reasonable explanation for the change of tenses. Ultimately, the difference in tense really adds nothing to our understanding of the process of spiritual growth.

Four Questions of Interpretation: Final Conclusions

Commentators offer a range of views and explanations in response to each of the four questions about 1 John 2:12–14 considered here. These questions and problems—and the answers and solutions—are important to an accurate interpretation and biblical understanding of 1 John 2:12–14.

- This passage is best understood to mean that the apostle John saw the believer's journey of faith progressing through three distinct, metaphorical stages of spiritual development toward Christlikeness, with that destination finally being reached at glorification, either by our death or Christ's return.
- The passage is best understood when we see the apostle John as implicitly teaching that the believer's journey of faith progresses through three discrete, metaphorical stages of spiritual development, in which some believers are more "like" Christ than others are; some Christians are more mature, more obedient, more loving, and more discerning than their brothers and sisters in the faith are.
- Finally, John's passage can also be understood and appreciated as an encouragement and challenge to modern readers to keep growing and maturing in a faith that will point people to Christ and glorify Him.

Questions for Reflection and Action

1. Why do you think people withdraw from the church? If you have done so at one point or another, what brought you back? If people you know have withdrawn from the church, what were their reasons?
2. What conclusions have you come to regarding each of these four issues? As you explain your stance, refer to some of the scholarly arguments above.

    a. Is John talking about stages of faith or literal ages of believers?
    b. How many groups is John addressing in this epistle?
    c. Why does John use two words for "child"?
    d. Why does John change the verb tenses?

3. What encouragement and challenge to keep growing in your Christian faith do you find in 1 John 2:12–14?

"I'm a Christian. Now what?"

As a pastor and teacher, I find that question very refreshing and encouraging, because naming Jesus as Savior and Lord is not at all like crossing a finish line. Making that declaration of faith is instead the first step in a lifelong spiritual journey.

As a pastor and teacher, I have an answer for the "Now what?" question: We who are followers of Christ are to be continually transformed by God's Spirit in deep and substantial ways so that we will be more like Jesus. As demonstrated in the Chapter 2 discussion of "The Case for Stages," this dynamic growth process will take Christ's apprentices on a journey through three stages of spiritual development—Childhood, Young Adulthood, and Parenthood.

Before we look more closely at this pattern of spiritual growth, note the apostle Paul's fundamental conviction that transformation is an ongoing process:

> Those whom he foreknew he also predestined to be *conformed* to the image of his Son, that his Son would be the firstborn among many brothers and sisters.
>
> —Romans 8:29 NET (emphasis mine)

> And we all, with unveiled faces reflecting the glory of the Lord, and being *transformed* into the same image from one degree of glory to another, which is from the Lord, who is the Spirit.
>
> —2 Corinthians 3:1 NET (emphasis mine)

> Do not be *conformed* to this present world, but be *transformed* by the renewing of your mind, so that you may test and approve what is the will of God—what is good and well-pleasing and perfect.
>
> —Romans 12:2 NET (emphasis mine)

> My dear children, for whom I am again in the pains of childbirth until Christ is *formed* in you.
>
> —Galatians 4:19 NET (emphasis mine)

And a theological word for that process of transformation into Christlikeness is *sanctification*.

Sanctification

Wayne Grudem's *Systematic Theology* defines *sanctification* as "a progressive work of God and man that makes us more and more free from sin and like Christ in our actual lives."[1] The sanctification of us Christians in our totality—our becoming more like Christ in our intellect, emotions, will, motivations, and purposes—will take place progressively, and this process of gaining freedom from the power of sin will continue throughout our earthly lives. Much of Scripture instructs and motivates believers to walk with God. During this earthly journey, we Christians are designed and equipped to make ongoing progress as we cooperate with the Spirit in our transformation into the image of God. Professor and theologian Gregg Allison states, "This original image, defaced because of the fall into sin, was so ravaged that it became a hideous parody of its pristine reality. Because of redemption, however, this marred and tainted image is being progressively restored through the ongoing process of sanctification."[2]

Why is this transformation into Christlikeness a key point for the apostle Paul? Consider that each of us has, since birth, been shaped, misshaped, and twisted, not only by such factors as our sin nature, family of origin, personal temperament, choices, habits, and patterns of thinking but also by the influence of outside sources, including the world and the Adversary. No wonder we can expect it to take a lifetime to bring about the radical changes that need to occur in our lives! The apostle John's transformational journey from the Son of Thunder to the Apostle of Love took more than sixty-five years.

In *Foundations of Spiritual Formation*, Paul Pettit, director of the spiritual formation program at Dallas Theological Seminary, emphasizes that such authentic growth is indeed an ongoing and *lifelong* process:

> Make no mistake: maturing as a Christian is a process. It is not a second step, a higher plane, a sacred blessing, or a lightning bolt moment when God invades and brings the Christian to a perfected place. A lifelong transformation is set into motion when one places his or her faith in Jesus Christ and seeks to follow Him.[3]

And this lifelong transformation will occur in predictable stages, a fact that is patently and convincingly clear in passages other than just 1 John 2.

CHAPTER 3

EVIDENCE BEYOND A REASONABLE DOUBT

NO MODEL FOR spiritual growth and development—in fact, no argument for any aspect of the Christian faith—should be based on a single passage. Therefore, it is crucial to demonstrate that the apostle John's portrayal of spiritual growth as a three-stage process is not unique in Scripture; nor is it in conflict with other passages of Scripture. In fact, an important step in sound, biblical interpretation and an important step toward building a compelling case for stages of faith is made when the 1 John 2:12–14 passage is aligned with other scriptures. Three vital New Testament passages will be examined in detail: Hebrews 5:11–6:1; 1 Corinthians 2:14–3:4; and Ephesians 4:12–16. Then, we will learn more about the process of spiritual growth from 2 Peter 1:5–9. We will see that these biblical passages do not contradict or refute the 1 John 2:12–14 case for three stages of faith. Rather, these passages complement and even complete John's model. *The Path* will help you to see your own way more clearly as we explore this distinctively different path of spiritual progress.

Also, remember that in the preceding chapter, "The Case for Stages," we saw that some commentators (Westcott, Candlish, Ross, Plummer, Vincent, Brooke) argue for only two groups, the young men and the fathers. These advocates of two groups, however, might be persuaded otherwise if they came to terms with the following discussion of faith development in Hebrews 5; 1 Corinthians 2–3; and Ephesians 4:12–16. These three passages soundly refute the two-group arguments. In addition, several New Testament verses argue for a process, a progressive movement, from immaturity toward full-grown spiritual maturity. Many biblical passages definitely help us better understand the journey of faith.

1. Hebrews 5:12–6:1

> For though by this time you ought to be teachers, you have need again for someone to teach you the elementary principles of the oracles of God, and you have come to need milk and not solid food. For everyone who partakes only of milk is not accustomed to the word of righteousness, for he is an infant. But solid food is for the mature, who because of practice have their senses trained to discern good and evil. Therefore leaving the elementary teaching about the Christ, let us press on to maturity, not laying again a foundation of repentance from dead works and of faith toward God.

Hebrews 5:12–6:1	The Path from Infancy to Maturity
Theme: Spiritual Fitness and Getting in Shape on the Journey. *Stalled in the stage of infancy, these believers need to practice, train, and become skilled in moral reasoning.*	

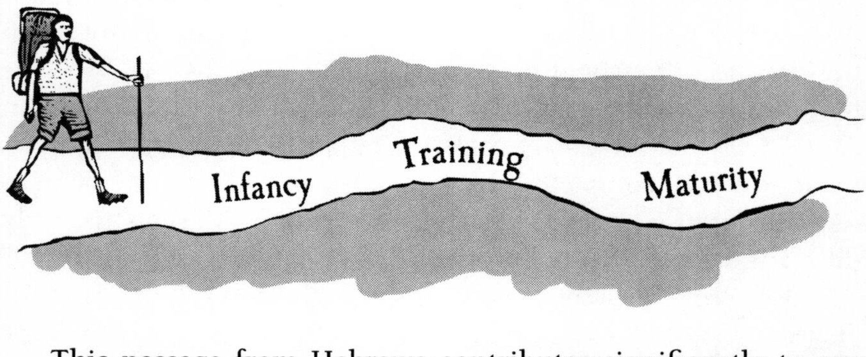

This passage from Hebrews contributes significantly to our understanding of the process of spiritual growth, and it clearly supports the three stages of faith found in 1 John 2:12–14.

First, consider the illustration above. There is a stage at the beginning of the journey, then the destination of maturity, and in between, a lengthy stage for training. Commentator H. P. Owen asserts, "Amid much that is obscure one thing is clear. The author here divides the Christian life into successive stages."[4] Owen describes a three-stage process that begins with the infant in Christ, who receives only the milk of the Word (5:13). These Hebrew Christians were stuck in this infant stage, not "accustomed to the word of righteousness" (5:13). They had a genuine, saving faith in Christ, but their growth stalled because they hadn't shed their reliance on works and performance; they continued to try to earn God's acceptance. They never grew deep in the assurance that His love is absolute, unconditional, undeserved, and non-repayable (addressed in Milestone #1 of the Childhood stage of faith). The faith of these believers was not growing: it remained largely secondhand and borrowed, rather than firsthand and owned (these qualities are emphasized in the apostle John's Milestone #4 of the Young Adulthood stage of faith).

Between the two endpoints of "Infant" and "Mature" is a definite intermediate stage. In that stage, Owens contends, Christians gain skill in the personal application of biblical truth to beliefs and values, and they practice distinguishing between good and evil. This moral reasoning is based on God's Word, not on what significant others think or what beliefs the new believer grew up with. This stage 2 is an ethical and practical stage of growth, of assimilating one's beliefs and behaviors, and of getting accustomed to a faith that is firsthand and owned. The believer's choices are now affecting his or her character. Interestingly, the Greek word for *train* is the athletic term *gymnazō* (from which we get our word *gymnasium*), meaning "to get in shape, work out, exercise." These followers of Christ are in the gym, exercising their faith muscles and applying what they are learning. And this stage clearly parallels the apostle John's Young Adulthood stage of faith.

Once the Christian "has acquired a reasoned pattern of behavior based on experience he can proceed to stage 3 and receive the solid food,"[5] the stage of the mature believer (5:14). The lifestyle of these Christians has resulted from training and practice in the application of biblical truth to real-life situations. These are *deep*, seasoned, in-shape believers; they are, to use John's analogy, parents in the faith.

To summarize, this passage in Hebrews describes spiritual progress as taking place in three discrete stages of faith, stages that clearly parallel the three-stage progression described in 1 John 2:12–14.

2. 1 Corinthians 2:14–3:4

> But a natural man does not accept the things of the Spirit of God, for they are foolishness to him; and he cannot understand them, because they are spiritually appraised. But he who is spiritual appraises all things, yet he himself is appraised by no one. For WHO HAS KNOWN THE MIND OF THE LORD, THAT HE WILL INSTRUCT HIM? But we have the mind of Christ. And I, brethren, could not speak to you as to spiritual men, but as to men of flesh, as to infants in Christ. I gave you milk to drink, not solid food; for you were not yet able to receive it. Indeed, even now you are not yet able, for you are still fleshly. For since there is jealousy and strife among you, are you not fleshly, and are you not walking like mere men? For when one says, "I am of Paul," and another, "I am of Apollos," are you not mere men?

1 Corinthians 2:14–3:4	The Path from Infancy to Maturity
Theme: Developing a Firsthand, Owned Faith. *Believers were stuck in the stage of infancy due to performing for and conforming to the approval and conventions of significant others.*	

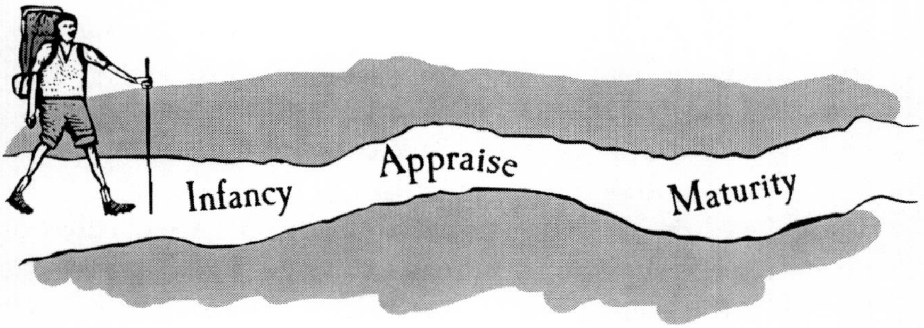

This key passage not only clarifies some of the obstacles that commonly slow spiritual progress, but also it highlights key characteristics of this growth process. Paul's message also contains some instruction for gaining spiritual maturity. The passage shows that spiritual growth is not automatic and that we believers can get stuck and can stay stuck, frozen in time, largely due to excessively relying on, performing for, and conforming to the approval and conventions of significant others (in this case, Paul, Cephas, and Apollos). In other words, this Corinthian passage describes the movement—in John's terms—from the Childhood stage of faith into the Young Adulthood stage of faith. Spiritual maturity involves moving away from a secondhand, borrowed faith and coming to a firsthand and owned faith.

Three Characteristics of "He Who Is Spiritual"

First Corinthians 2:14–3:4 addresses the nature and process of spiritual development by considering the "spiritual" believer and the "fleshly" believer. First, in 1 Corinthians 2:15, Paul referred to "he who is spiritual," but that is not an elite group of advanced Christians. "He who is spiritual" simply means a person who is filled with or controlled by the Spirit, and this passage says three things about such a person.

First, a spiritual person "appraises all things," and the word *appraise* is a legal term that means "to bring to trial before the presiding judge who examines all the evidence." The appraisal is the questioning process—the cross-examination, interrogation, investigation, inquiry, and reflection—that precedes the verdict. This analogy teaches that a spiritual person's faith is meaningful because he/she constantly examines and applies God's truth to personal and pressing real-life situations. Spiritual people appraise "all things"; they exercise discernment on a broad range of issues that affect their own spiritual development as well as other people's. They find functional answers to crucial questions. How unlike the carnal Corinthian Christians whose lives, values, attitudes, and beliefs remained unexamined!

Second, a spiritual person "is appraised by no one" (verse 15). Spiritual people are able to stand alone, directed by God and living a lifestyle shaped by principles from God's Word—regardless of what others think. Spiritual people are not motivated by external approval or the need to rely on people who matter. Motivated only by the truth of God's Word, spiritual people own their faith. In sharp contrast are the baby Corinthian Christians who let Apollos, Cephas, and Paul do their thinking for them (1:12; 2:4). These babies gathered around their heroes of the faith and conformed to their ideas in order to win their approval. Consequently, these babies experienced no personal growth.

Third, spiritual people have "the mind of Christ" (2:16), and having the mind of Christ enables them to both exercise discernment as they appraise all things and then stand alone when their understanding of the truth leads them to nonconformity. The carnal Corinthians do not have the mind of Christ. They have only the wisdom of man (2:5, 8, 9; 3:4).

Five Characteristics of an Infant Believer

The portrait of a spiritual person becomes clearer when it is contrasted with a sketch of a so-called carnal believer, a person controlled by the flesh. These baby Christians experience an unduly prolonged spiritual infancy, and their growth is stunted. The first four verses of 1 Corinthians 3 identify five symptoms of spiritual immaturity and thereby teach much about healthy growth.

First, sufficient time has passed for these believers to have progressed much farther than they have. Five to seven years after their salvation, these Corinthian adults are still infants in their faith. Childish characteristics have continued into adulthood, as Paul's words suggest ("not yet," "even now," "still"). Normal spiritual development has not occurred (3:2–3), and these believers must take personal responsibility for that failure. Spiritual growth is not automatic, nor does the mere passing of time guarantee progress.

Second, these Corinthian Christians have had an inadequate diet: "I gave you milk to drink, not solid food" (3:2). Mother's milk is essential to normal growth, but relatively soon, solid foods

(Hebrews 5:11–15) must be included in a baby's diet in order to sustain healthy growth and development. Milk alone would be insufficient. Likewise, spiritual infancy, with a diet of only milk, is an expected stage of development, but it is only the beginning of growth. Because these Corinthians were stuck at the infant stage and failed to move on to solid food, "God's wisdom" (1 Corinthians 2:7), the "deep things of God" (verse 10), and "the mind of Christ" (verse 16) have eluded them.

Third, the Corinthians suffer from an eating disorder as well as a poor diet. Despite their age, they are "not yet able to receive" solid food. It is not a matter of these Corinthians being ignorant and in need of more information. Paul asked ten times, "Do you not know?" (3:16; 5:6; 6:2, 3, 9, 15, 16, 19; 9:13, 24). They do not lack the biblical knowledge necessary to grow. The issue is that their beliefs have not affected their behavior. The Corinthians have failed to apply what they already know. They have not examined the issues they faced, exercised discernment where appropriate, or tried to live out what they already know. In other words, they have not ingested their food. The nutrients have not been absorbed. The food simply passed through their bodies without contributing to their growth. As a result, they are spiritually emaciated. Since the Corinthians have failed to appraise all things, their values and behaviors remain unchanged.

Another basic reason for the Corinthian Christians' immaturity is their reliance on the approval of their religious heroes and significant others. They are conformists, choosing to follow a specific faith hero like Paul, Apollos, Cephas, or even Christ (1:12; 3:4). The Corinthians focus on personalities and, rather than relying on self-chosen principles, let these celebrities and authorities do their thinking for them. These Corinthian believers do not own their faith. Theirs is an inherited or borrowed faith, shaped by the experiences they had with those people who have influenced their faith. Sparked by the believers' prolonged immaturity, interpersonal conflicts—"jealousy and strife" (3:3)—were rampant.

Last of all, the lifestyle of the Corinthian brethren shows no evidence of spiritual growth. Their behavior is indistinguishable from the "natural man" (2:13) who never claimed to be a Christ-follower. Paul asked, "Are you not walking like mere men?" (3:3).

To summarize, distinctive qualities of genuine spiritual growth were largely absent from the community of Corinthian believers. While revealing that truth, this passage from 1 Corinthians supports the vital aspects of the spiritual growth process found in the 1 John 2:12–14 stages of faith.

3. Ephesians 4:12–16

> ... for the equipping of the saints for the work of service, to the building up of the body of Christ; until we all attain to the unity of the faith, and of the knowledge of the Son of God, to a mature man, to the measure of the stature which belongs to the fullness of Christ. As a result, we are no longer to be children, tossed here and there by waves and carried about by every wind of doctrine, by the trickery of men, by craftiness in deceitful scheming; but speaking the truth in love, we are to grow up in all aspects into Him who is the head, even Christ, from whom the whole body, being fitted and held together by what every joint supplies, according to the proper working of each individual part, causes the growth of the body for the building up of itself in love.

Ephesians 4:12–16	The Path from Children to Maturity
Theme: Relationships That Transform. *Paul emphasized community; Spiritual growth has an interpersonal dimension to cultivate that cannot be neglected.*	

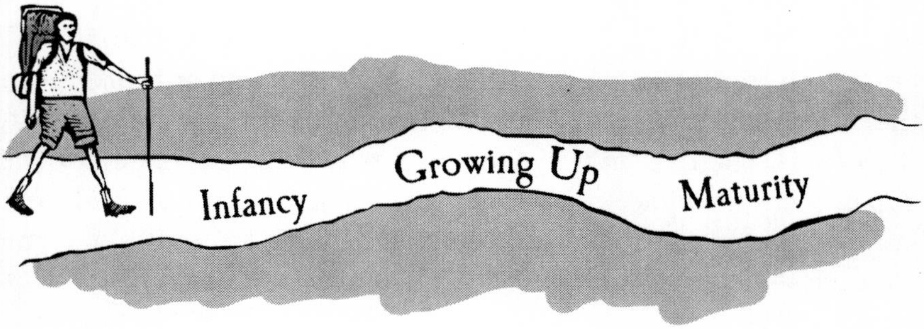

Note that, once again, this time in his epistle to the believers at Ephesus, Paul describes spiritual growth as having a beginning stage and final stage connected by a path leading from infancy to maturity. The destination of the spiritual life is defined in verse 14: "until we all attain to the unity of the faith, and of the knowledge of the Son of God, to a mature man, to the measure of the stature which belongs to the fullness of Christ." Between the moment of conversion and the attainment of some degree of spiritual maturity lies a lengthy, winding path of growing up. By emphasizing both the individual and the community—the interpersonal aspects of spiritual growth—this Ephesians 4 passage offers significant insight into the movement from the infant stage to a point of maturity. Such growth requires believers to understand how much they need one another. After all, God calls us out of the world and into relationship with one another. Paul emphasized this intentional development of mutual, reciprocal friendships with those who help one another become more like Christ. By God's grace and design, there is transforming power in the community of believers.

Ephesians 4 underscores the kind of interpersonal relationships that need to exist among believers if personal spiritual transformation is to occur. This passage highlights the role of gifted believers we walk with on the journey. God's children, Paul taught, can expect to become increasingly connected with other believers and therefore less isolated and self-reliant, to become less independent and more interdependent—and what a fundamental, even miraculous shift in focus that is! We move from being self-oriented to others-oriented, and that new orientation involves both *giving to* and *receiving from* others. In community, believers learn to let go of their isolated, self-seeking lives and to establish relationships with people who are dedicated to loving God and one another. The collective transformation that results in such a community supersedes all polarizing differences, including race and ethnicity. And Paul knew that these communities serve as a winsome alternative, an appealing counterculture that attracts the attention and then the hearts of unbelievers.

But merely attending a small-group Bible study is not necessarily being involved in life-changing community. Unfortunately, too many believers are not exposed to—or are resistant to—the types of relationships and influences that stimulate transformation. It seems that too many believers seldom, if ever, are connected to the support and challenge of healthy and redemptive relationships. Christian community can and must be intentional about creating an atmosphere conducive to transformation and spiritual growth in the Christian faith. Paul underscored a few of the critical dynamics that need to be operative in such groups. If those traits are absent, we cannot expect spiritual growth to occur.

Consider again the picture of community found in Ephesians 4:

> Speaking the truth in love, we are to grow up in all aspects into Him who is the head, even Christ, from whom the whole body, being fitted and held together by what every joint supplies, according to the proper working of each individual part, causes the growth of the body for the building up of itself in love.

First, growing up in the faith requires believers to courageously speak the truth in love to one another (verse 15). Making it a priority to be boldly honest in our interpersonal relationships means learning to discard pretense, hiding, and masquerading so that we can minister to one another with the gifts of the Spirit. We need to belong to a community in which each of us can know people, be known, and grow spiritually at our own pace. This kind of integrity and vulnerability can transform relationships between believers, whatever the context. Healthy growth toward spiritual adulthood and the fullness of Christ is triggered as relationships in the body of believers mature and deepen.

Next, the Ephesians 4 passage makes it clear that pastors and teachers are to shape the vision of the community and guide its corporate spiritual growth. This emphasis on transformational community cannot be expected to happen without the intentional direction of informed and committed leadership. Besides enabling believers to skillfully minister to one another—a key element of Christian community—leaders are to model what living in community looks like. Especially when they're feeling broken and vulnerable, believers need to be shown how to live in relationship with others. But, of course, leadership can easily get distracted by the many peripheral issues that come with ministry today. Additionally, today's leaders may not even know that they are responsible for fostering community, or they may not know how to or have time create and sustain this relational emphasis.

When you read the biblical job description in Ephesians 4, notice the pastor's primary role (shown in the chart below). First and foremost, a pastor is to be an equipper and trainer of believers so that they can fulfill their roles in the building up of the body of Christ (strengthening community) or ministering to one another and serving the world. Even the leader's preaching and teaching are to draw attention to and insist on the vision of the interpersonal nature of transformation. What a difference it would make in the body of Christ and the world at large if all believers saw themselves as ministers called and enabled to serve and be used as agents of spiritual growth and transformation in one another's lives.

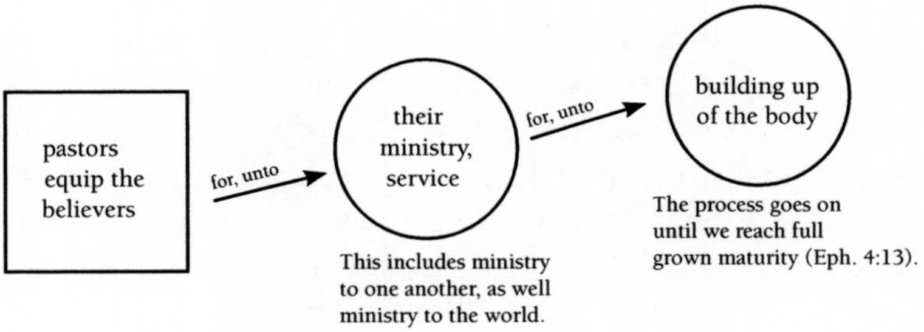

What has caused the loss of this focus? What has contributed to a pastor's multifaceted job today? The case could be made that the King James Version and the Revised Standard Version translations of Ephesians 4:11–12 contributed to the misunderstanding, and the problem continues to this day.

> And He gave some, prophets; and some evangelists; and some, pastors and teachers; for the perfecting of the saints, for the work of ministry, for the edifying of the body of Christ. (KJV)

The fateful structure of this passage gives the impression that pastoral leadership involves three jobs.[6] If that were true, the call to prepare believers for their own ministry would be quite unnecessary because—according to this translation—all "the work of ministry" would be done by the "professional" ministers. And that is not a biblical model.

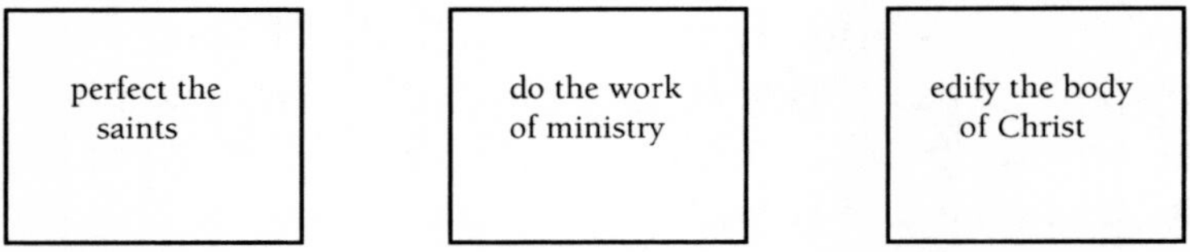

Back to the subject at hand: As we pastors and leaders shepherd and guide believers, we can't miss the role of truth and doctrine in believers' coming to maturity. In Ephesians 4:15, Paul pointed out that believers can remain stuck as immature children: "As a result, we are no longer to be children, tossed here and there by waves and carried about by every wind of doctrine, by the trickery of men, by craftiness in deceitful scheming." When internalized, the Word of God gives believers poise and stability, and even more so as they become increasingly skilled at discerning and standing strong against deceptive, damaging messages from the world, the flesh, and the devil. It is simply not possible to be ignorant of the Bible and spiritually mature at the same time—but it is possible to know the Bible and *not* be spiritually mature.

The Bible must be taught and studied as truth to be lived, not as information that one will be tested on and required to prove proficient in. The educational process must include examining one's own inadequate assumptions as well as narrowing the gap between one's professed beliefs and personal behaviors. Those who lead believers toward transformation will be careful to guide believers beyond information. God's truths will be taught and understood but also—and crucially—applied in a person's life, impacting behavior, mind, emotions, and will.

As we have seen, the essential context for spiritual learning and growth is the Christian community, and, of course, within that community, believers will be at various stages of progress—Childhood, Young Adulthood, and Parenthood. That truth adds to the richness of the fellowship as well as to its importance in the life of a believer.

Consider now the winsome description of such a Christian community by Quaker writer and scholar Elton Trueblood. As you read his words, remember that we leaders face this challenge, which is at the same time a great privilege, of shaping this kind of community in church, small groups, and classes.

> What we need is not intellectual theorizing or even preaching, but a demonstration. One of the most powerful ways of turning people's loyalty to Christ is by loving others with the great love of God. We cannot revive faith by argument, but we might catch the imagination of puzzled men and women by an exhibition of a fellowship so intensely alive that every thoughtful person would be forced to respect it. If there should emerge in our day such a fellowship, wholly without artificiality and free from the dead hand of the past, it would be an exciting event of momentous importance. A society of genuine loving friends, set free from the self-seeking struggle for personal prestige and from all unreality, would be something unutterably priceless and powerful. A wise person would travel any distance to join it.[7]

One More Passage

Having looked at what Hebrews 5:11–6:1; 1 Corinthians 2:14–3:4; and Ephesians 4:12–16 teach about the process of spiritual growth, consider now what the apostle Peter adds to our understanding:

> Now for this very reason also, applying all diligence, in your faith supply moral excellence, and in your moral excellence, knowledge, and in your knowledge, self-control, and in your self-control, perseverance, and in your perseverance, godliness, and in your godliness, brotherly kindness, and in your brotherly kindness, love. For if these qualities are yours and are increasing, they render you neither useless nor unfruitful in

> the true knowledge of our Lord Jesus Christ. For he who lacks these qualities is blind or short-sighted, having forgotten his purification from his former sins.
>
> —2 Peter 1:5–9

In this passage, Peter emphasized the need for virtuous living. Peter's readers were "in danger of moral apostasy, under the influence of teachers who evidently held that immorality incurred no danger of judgment."[8] In response to the false teachers' indifference to morality, Peter taught that moral effort is required because Christ has given the believer everything necessary for godly living (verse 3) as well as the promise of eternal life (verse 4). The promise of escape from mortality imposes a strong ethical condition (verses 5–9) as well as the exhortation to Christians to be committed to a life of moral progress in order to become "partakers of the divine nature" (verse 4).

To what did Peter attribute this moral progress? Commentators debate about whether Peter was defining a progression of spiritual growth or simply using a literary device. In other words, does each virtue contribute to the existence of the next, or is the list of seven virtues merely intended to give a general impression of the kind of virtuous life that the Christian faith should foster?

In explaining verse 8—"if these qualities are yours and are increasing"—Paine observes that the matter of increasing "implies Christian growth and the Spirit's fullness or full control as experienced by believers."[9] The word *increasing* suggests that some believers have experienced these virtues more fully than others have. If the believer progressively exercises the virtues, the knowledge of Christ will be neither "useless nor unfruitful" (verse 8). Bauckham explains that believers who do not "carry through the moral implications of this knowledge have effectively become blind to it again,"[10] as seen in verse 9, and their growth will stall.

The Christian is therefore to make every effort, or "apply all diligence" (verse 5), to the development of these seven virtues. It is not clear, however, how each virtue listed in verses 5–7 is supposed to give birth to the next. How are the qualities interconnected so that one develops out of another? Stephen Paine suggests that the progression moves believers from the elemental to the more advanced:

> Peter urges these young believers to move on from step to step in divine grace ... It would be amiss to picture these beautiful graces as compartmentalized and attainable only in this order. No, their presentation here seems to observe an order from the more elemental to the more advanced.[11]

Readers and commentators alike have asked other questions about this 2 Peter passage. Concerning the order of the seven virtues, how are we to understand the position of faith at the head of the list and love at the end? Are faith and love like bookends to the list, giving meaning to the selected virtues listed in between? Does love comprise or encompass all the other virtues? Is the list of seven meant to be comprehensive of the ethical life?

It is noteworthy that the virtues grow from the rich soil of saving faith: "For he who lacks these qualities is blind or short sighted, having forgotten his purification from his former sins" (verse 9). This statement echoes the grace-based Milestone #1 of the Childhood stage of faith mentioned in 1 John 2:12–14. Restorative grace is the basis for the believer's growth toward spiritual maturity. The last virtue in Peter's list—love—may parallel John's Parenthood stage of faith, the point at which the believer has become a seasoned caregiver.

Images of Growth and Transformation

Biblical writers used various images to describe the complexities and nuances of spiritual growth. Perry Downs talks about the images of human development and botanical growth:

> Thinking about growth in faith in predictable ways is not a new idea. Scriptures use numerous metaphors of growth to describe how our faith should come to maturity. Metaphors of milk and solid food imply that spiritual development is like physical development. The Hebrews were rebuked because they still needed

> milk rather than solid food (Heb. 5:11–14). Also, metaphors of seeds and plants indicate that spiritual growth is like botanical growth, moving from a preliminary stage to a later mature stage. The calls of Scripture to maturity are calls for growth, and the pattern of growth is to some extent predictable.[12]

What follows are seven scriptural truths about spiritual growth and some illustrative verses for each. The sheer volume of biblical verses that speak to the process of spiritual growth is impressive.

1. **Spiritual growth is implied in discussions of the differing degrees of character traits or virtues.**
   - As we have seen in 2 Peter 1:5–9, the apostle listed seven Christian qualities and then exhorted the believer to "apply all diligence" (verse 5) to see to it that "these qualities are yours and increasing" (verse 8).
   - Aware of relational problems in the Philippian church, Paul prayed "that your love may abound still more and more in real knowledge and discernment" (Philippians 1:9). Implied is the idea that some believers demonstrate more love and greater relational skills than other believers.
   - Colossians 3:12–13 offers another list of Christian traits, and it comes after Paul taught that these traits take root because of "the new self who is being renewed" (verse 10), a present-tense, constant renewal.
   - In 1 Timothy 4:15, Paul encouraged a younger pastor to attend to his instructions "so that your [spiritual] progress may be evident to all." Arndt and Gingrich define *progress* as "advancement, furtherance, go[ing] forward."[13] The believer's progress is to be observable to others in the Christian community.

These passages affirm that believers are to move steadily away from spiritual infancy and consistently toward spiritual maturity, making gains in behavior as well as in character development.

Clearly, the lives of some Christians offer greater evidence of character transformation and progress than others do.

2. **God commands every Christian to continuously pursue spiritual growth.**

Christian growth is clearly commanded of all believers, regardless of their age or stage of spiritual development.

- "Do not be conformed to this world, but be transformed by the renewing of your mind" (Romans 12:2).
- The growing believer is in the process of displacing the "old man" with its controlling "lusts of deceit" and being progressively "renewed in the spirit of your mind" (Ephesians 4:22–23).
- "Let endurance have its perfect result, that you may be perfect and complete, lacking in nothing" (James 1:2–3).
- "Let us press on to maturity" (Hebrews 6:1).
- "You received from us instruction as to how you ought to walk and please the Lord, that you may excel still more" (1 Thessalonians 4:1).
- "Grow in the grace and knowledge of our Lord and Savior Jesus Christ" (2 Peter 3:18).
- "Like newborn babes ... grow in respect to salvation" (1 Peter 2:2).

In this spiritual growth process, some believers are farther along than others.

3. **The process of growth and change is predictable, sequential, and maturational, but not irreversible.**

- There is a path that leads from being "infants in Christ" (1 Corinthians 3:1) to "mature" (2:6) and "spiritual" (2:15) believers.
- Paul described his own spiritual growth as a process of moving away from a time "when I was a child" and a moving toward "when I became a man" (1 Corinthians 13:11).

- Paul prescribed a path for all Christians: "no longer to be children ... we are to grow up ... to a mature man" (Ephesians 4:11–16).
- A Christian grows from being "an infant" (Hebrews 5:13) to being among "the mature" (verse 14) who are "teachers" (verse 12).
- Metaphorically speaking, food or diet is a clue to the distance and depth of the believer's growth. For instance, in 1 Corinthians 3:12, the infant believer was still feeding only on "milk" and had not yet progressed to "solid food," even though sufficient time had passed. In the Hebrews 5 passage, believers "dull of hearing" could only be fed "milk"; they could not assimilate solid food (5:12).
- In Hebrews 5, the spiritual "infant" is identified by inexperience and a lack of practice in applying Scripture to daily life situations (5:13).
- Conversely, "solid food" is for the "mature," for those believers who have, like an athlete, practiced and trained and become skilled at applying "the word of righteousness" (5:12) to issues requiring personal "discernment of good and evil" (5:14).

By God's grace, maturing believers make progress in the personal, ethical, and practical realms of life.

4. The ultimate goal of the journey of faith is Christlikeness.

This goal is to be the centering hope and realization of the Christian pilgrimage.

- "When He appears we shall be *like Him*... And everyone who has this hope fixed on Him purifies himself, just as He is pure" (1 John 3:2–3, emphasis mine). This progress toward the likeness of Christ is a process that is to continue until the believer's death or the Lord's return.
- Until our ultimate arrival at our heavenly home, the process of sanctification is partial and unfinished. According to

the apostle John, in 1 John 2:12–14, some believers are Children, some have progressed to the Young Adulthood stage, and yet others have moved into the Parenthood stage of Christlikeness, but no one this side of heaven moves into a stage of purity and holiness.

- "Whom He foreknew He also predestined to become conformed to the image of His Son" (Romans 8:29).
- The final goal of spiritual growth is "until we all attain to … the fullness of Christ" (Ephesians 4:13).
- Becoming more like Christ is a movement in the direction of the repair and restoration of the image of God in us: "We all … are being transformed into the same image from glory to glory" (2 Corinthians 3:18). The original image of God in us was dimmed, not erased, and by the power of His Spirit, it is now being progressively renewed.

5. **The process of spiritual growth should continue throughout a believer's lifetime.**

Maturity is not the result of a singular event but of a long-term commitment of faithful, continual obedience to a process. Aging does not automatically bring maturing, but age and experience are essential ingredients.

- "Though our outer man is decaying, yet out inner man is being renewed day by day" (2 Corinthians 4:16).
- The apostle Paul passionately resisted stalling in his spiritual growth: "Not that I have already obtained it, or have already become perfect [mature, *teleios*], but I press on" (Philippians 3:12).

Several New Testament writers demonstrate that their ministry to other Christians was driven by the desire that other believers not stall or permanently plateau.

- These writers encouraged believers to "increase in the [experiential] knowledge of God" (Colossians 1:10).

- "You received from us instruction as to how you ought to walk and please the Lord, that you may excel still more" (1 Thessalonians 4:1).
- "Grow in the grace and knowledge of our Lord and Savior Jesus Christ" (2 Peter 3:18).

Again, believers are to sustain and continuously nourish their spiritual growth throughout their lives.

6. **Christians can find themselves stuck and not growing at all.**

- Some believers are "carnal," stuck in a prolonged stage of infancy (1 Corinthians 3:1–4).
- Some believers described in the book of Hebrews were "dull of hearing" (5:11). "By this time [they] ought to be teachers" (5:12), but they were stuck in a stage of spiritual infancy (5:13) and had "come to need milk not solid food" (5:11). These Christians are commanded to "press on to maturity" (6:1).
- Some believers regress in their spiritual life, leaving "their first love" (Revelation 2:4, 5).
- Spiritual progress can be impaired: "You were running well; who hindered you from obeying the truth?" (Galatians 5:7).
- Like the apostle Peter, Christians may experience a crisis of faith and need restoration (Galatians 6:1).
- Peter said that some believers are "blind or short sighted" (2 Peter 1:9) and not growing in the Christian virtues he listed (verse 8).

Spiritual growth may not stall or plateau permanently, but neither will spiritual growth just happen automatically with the passing of time.

7. **Differing results are evidence of varied degrees of growth.**

- The parable of the seeds teaches that seeds sown on good ground can bear fruit either one hundredfold, sixtyfold, or thirtyfold (Matthew 13:3–23).

- Jesus told the disciples to expect to "bear fruit … bear more fruit … bear much fruit …" (John 15:2, 5, 8). Productivity, not activity, is a mark of the health and growth of the believer.

Though some believers yield more fruit than others, it is not wise to conclude that the quantity of fruit is evidence of greater spiritual growth than others have experienced.

Conclusion: Numerous New Testament verses either reflect or clearly imply a process to Christian growth, a progressive movement away from spiritual immaturity toward fuller maturity, a personal transformation that involves qualitative changes in character and lifestyle throughout one's lifetime. The Bible offers much solid evidence that each believer will mature toward Christ's likeness in stages, growing from children to young men and then to fathers.

Questions for Reflection and Action

1. Why is it significant that many passages from Scripture support the idea that spiritual growth is a process?
2. What argument for stages of faith did you find most convincing in the discussion of the following key passages?

    Hebrews 5:11–6:1
    1 Corinthians 2:14–3:4
    Ephesians 4:12–16
    2 Peter 1:5–9

3. Review the description of "He Who Is Spiritual" (pages 37–38). Where do you see yourself? What encouragement about where you are or where you want to be do you find here?
4. According to God's design, relationships with fellow believers need to exist if personal spiritual transformation is to occur. Think about your own experience. Whom has God used as an agent of spiritual growth and spiritual transformation? And how has God used you to grow a person toward Christlikeness? Comment on the value of this design.

5. Look back at the seven scriptural truths about spiritual growth (pages 48–53). Which one(s), if any, offered a new perspective on transformation? Which one(s) most convicted you about making your journey toward Christlikeness a priority?

Among its countless treasures, the Word of God outlines a largely unexamined but all-important path for believers to travel. This path for spiritual growth is a model for spiritual development, a model that offers direction for disciples who desire to become more like Christ.

In this next chapter, we see the rich context of the 1 John 2:12–14 path, a context that enhances the panoramic and scenic route the apostle outlines. The results will both surprise readers and ground them in a biblical spirituality.

If you asked the apostle John to discuss spirituality, he would highlight five essential aspects:

- A friendship in two directions (1:1–4)
- Living without pretense (1:5–2:2)
- Evidence of genuine growth (2:3–11)
- Progress through three stages (2:12–14)
- The enemies of spiritual progress (2:15–17)

The next chapter will present the main concepts in John's epistle, demonstrate how the concept of stages of faith fits in the flow of John's epistle, and clarify the meaning and purpose of 1 John 2:12–14.

CHAPTER 4

AN AGED APOSTLE'S IDEAS ABOUT SPIRITUAL PROGRESS

TO BETTER APPRECIATE the apostle John's message, let us consider in greater detail the story of his own transformation, a lifelong journey of sanctification. When Jesus first invited the rugged John to leave his vocation as a fisherman and follow Him, this disciple was nicknamed the Son of Thunder (Mark 3:14). He was loud, self-centered, impetuous, and known for his fiery temperament. Over the next sixty-five years, though, God slowly transformed this high-voltage, impulsive, and ambitious man into the Apostle of Love.

We find evidence of John's transformation in his account of the Last Supper, the Passover meal Jesus shared with His disciples before dying on the cross as the holy and sacrificial Lamb of God. On the night before Jesus' death, when He was sequestered in the Upper Room with the Twelve, John was seated next to Jesus. This was the place of honor; John had become the Lord's closest confidant and friend. John, "the disciple that Jesus loved" (John 13:34), was now content to find his true identity in simply being loved by Jesus. John had learned to draw near to the heart of God, and it was enough for him to be close to Jesus and loved by Him.

Church history reports that John, who outlived all the other apostles, became a godly pastor and a faithful elder statesman of the church at the end of the first century. It is noteworthy that John, in the writing of his gospel, three epistles, and the book of Revelation, never referred to either himself as the author or his calling to be an apostle. He no longer needed to be noticed.

The Epistle of 1 John: The Context of 1 John 2:12–14

The broad context of 1 John provides important background information about the whole into which 1 John 2:12–14 fits. This passage is congruent with the direction, purpose, and intent of John's main message in the epistle. Attention to the whole will heighten awareness of the meaning and nuances of the 2:12–14 passage. Conversely, if this step of biblical interpretation is neglected, we may gain only a superficial understanding, a trivialization, or worse, a misrepresentation of 2:12–14.

A specific and urgent situation in the church prompted John to write this epistle. The issue was the insidious propaganda of certain false teachers (2:26; 3:7) who led people astray with their pernicious lies. The apostle Paul's prophecy to the Ephesian elders about "savage wolves" (Acts 20:29–30), later repeated to Timothy (2 Timothy 3:1–7; 4:3–4), had apparently been fulfilled. At one time, these wolves passed as loyal members of the church, but now they had withdrawn from the body (2:19; 4:1). As a result of their departure (2:19), some of the church members who remained must have been left wavering and insecure about their faith, so John wrote to reassure and strengthen them. His words are frank, realistic, and positive, "seeking to affirm and reinvigorate doctrinal direction, ethical urgency, relational integrity, and a forward-looking faith in God, generally in a geographical setting and temporal era in which relatively young churches were facing the challenges of longer term existence."[1]

The opponents and deceptive teachers whom John addressed are very possibly the direct forerunners of the adversaries denounced by Ignatius in the following generation. In fact, John's letter apparently reflects spiritual conditions in the region of Ephesus in the closing decades of the first century. Sources such as Irenaeus and Clement of Alexandria affirm that, in roughly 70–100 A.D., John was a resident in Ephesus and ministered there.[2] The short letters in Revelation 2 and 3 also offer insight about the church in this area and this era, for Ephesus was a leading city in the Roman province of Asia. Church historians describe an incipient philosophy, antecedent to the Gnosticism that would increasingly be a voice jockeying for prominence and recognition in the second century. Its heretical statement of faith could have had lethal consequences in the church, especially in the areas of Christology and ethics.

Though commentators do not agree on an outline for the epistle of 1 John, I suggest that the epistle can be seen as three cycles, each one of which expands, elaborates on, and reinforces John's message. The first cycle (1:1–2:27) introduces five elements of John's message, each one a key aspect of authentic spiritual growth. (The second cycle is found in 2:28–4:6, and the third cycle spans 4:7–5:5.) Together, these five elements offer dynamic clues about spiritual progress, a truth that will be developed in the pages that follow. Furthermore, these five elements serve as the broad context for 1 John 2:12–14, where the apostle revealed that the process of spiritual growth takes places in three stages.

1. **Friendship is Both Vertical and Horizontal** (1 John 1:1–4)

The prologue of 1 John addresses the heresy that denies that Jesus is the Son of God or the Christ in the flesh. "The believers in question were in danger of succumbing to heterodox tendencies; they were leaning in the direction of a Christology which was either too strong or too weak in character."[3] Thus, John's primary purpose in 1:1–4 was to answer these heretical extremes, set out a perfectly balanced Christology, and establish the historic identity of Jesus Christ. John emphasized two particular aspects of Jesus' identity: First, Jesus has existed from eternity past and will exist into eternity future. Second, Jesus was a flesh-and-blood person in history. The first-century false teachers denied that Jesus was fully man. The purpose of the Incarnation—of Jesus coming to earth in human form—was to fully disclose God to us. The apostles, whose words we read in the New Testament, saw, heard, and touched Jesus, so they offer conclusive and compelling evidence that He was fully and genuinely both God and man, rather than a phantom, ghost, apparition, illusion, or emanation as the false teachers claimed (1 John 1:1–2).

Historic Christian spirituality centers on Jesus Christ, who is God incarnate. Christian spirituality is not like some Eastern faiths in which followers seek to lose their identity through rigid asceticism. Nor is Christian spirituality linked with a monastic commitment to meditation and worship, highlighted by momentary, numinous experiences of unity with God. Instead, Jesus charged His apostles to tell others about Him. Obeying, these eyewitnesses invited people into fellowship with them as well as into fellowship with the Father and His Son. This *koinonia* meant sharing, to have in common, and each follower of Jesus shares with God and in the resulting relationships they share with one another. The verse 3 clause "you may have fellowship with us"—meaning the apostles and Christian community—highlights the horizontal dimension of fellowship, and the clause "our fellowship is with the Father, and His Son Jesus Christ" points to the vertical dimension. These two dimensions of spiritual growth are not mutually exclusive. Spirituality is an inseparable two-dimensional relationship. This combination of "Jesus and me" and "Jesus and we" is both/and, not either/or. "If I have God, I won't need other people" is an utterly false assumption. Certainly God is sufficient, but His sufficiency doesn't exclude the people through whom He will manifest His love in our lives. We are to love God with all our beings, we are to love others as ourselves, and we will experience His love from Him directly as well as through His people.

The apostle John understood that genuine, full, complete joy (1:4) results from both the vertical/internal relationship with God and the horizontal/external relationships with fellow believers. Believers are to know and love Jesus and to know and love one another. "Jesus and me" is a very personal relationship, but it is never an exclusive, private one. "Jesus and we" is interpersonal, communal, and essential because together, in community, believers experience God's presence. John addressed the need for believers to balance these two dimensions in their life experiences.

In regard to the horizontal and vertical dimensions of believers' faith, some believers are deeper, farther along, and more mature than others. Some are in the Childhood, others are in Young Adulthood, or still others are in the Parenthood stage of faith. There is always room for growth and progress in both dimensions of fellowship.

2. **Living Without Pretense** (1 John 1:5–2:2)

In the next section of John's epistle, the apostle exposed the impoverished and disturbing tenets of the opponents who viewed ethical conduct and love with indifference. John's emphasis here is on the moral implications of the apostolic message: personal integrity, truthfulness, and transparency are essential to cultivating *koinonia* (fellowship) with God and within the community of faith. Pretense or dishonesty is, after all, a powerful deterrent to spiritual maturity and Christlikeness.

Other opponents of Christian truth represented the renegade movement with its "supremacy of the intellect and the superiority of mental enlightenment to faith and conduct."[4] Also characteristic of these dissenters was belief in the radical and unbridgeable distinction between spirit and matter, coupled with the conviction that matter is inherently evil and that spirit alone is good. If matter is evil, the argument went, how could God Himself take on a human body? This view can also lead to either antinomianism (the philosophy that sin does not matter) or a rigid asceticism, (pleasure is sin and mastered by austere self discipline).

John made a bold summary statement that "takes his audience back to the fundamental basis of all Christian belief and experience."[5] He reminded readers of the essential character of God Himself. John frequently used the metaphor of light to describe God (John 1:4–5, 7–9; 3:19–21; 8:12; 9:5; 12:35–36, 46; Rev. 21:23) and referred to Him as the "Holy One" (1 John 2:20). In sharp contrast to dark and twisted human nature, God is pure, flawless, and undiminished light; "In Him there is no darkness at all" (1 John 1:5). The false teachers would hijack believers by compromising both God's absolute holiness and their own personal ethics.

However, the God who invites believers into intimate relationship is absolutely holy and morally perfect. Imagine the radical change in our lives if we understood that God's light exposes, penetrates, and diffuses the darkness and reveals the concealed. The Christian is fully known by Him: "There is no creature hidden from His sight, but all things are open and laid bare to the eyes of Him with whom we have to do" (Hebrews 4:13).

In 1 John 1:6–10, John exposed and refuted three unsettling claims of the troublemakers. The first was the denial that sin interrupts or interferes with our fellowship with God (1:6–7); the second claim was the denial that sin exists in our nature (1:8–9); and the third claim was the denial that sin shows itself in our conduct (1:10–2:2). John argued that our spontaneous first—and very human—reaction to God may be one of pretense, flight, alienation, and defense mechanisms as we face the sharp contrast between God's lofty, unattainable (at least in our own power) desires for us and our sinful nature and consequently low achievements.

What are the implications of the truth that God is light for those who profess to know Him? And how are we sinners to respond to the invitation to enter into a relationship with a holy God? The statement that "God is light" carries with it an inevitable moral challenge: His followers must walk in the light. "Living in the light" implies a "conscious and sustained endeavor to live a life in conformity with the revelation of God."[6] First of all, it is essential that one's conduct is consistent with one's desire to know God personally. The pseudo-spirituality of a mere profession of faith or a superficial familiarity with Christian doctrine does not equate to relationship or intimacy with God. In other words, personal holiness is not optional; there can be no moral indifference for the believer. The follower of Christ must learn to walk in the light. As believers do so, however, the enormity of our sinfulness, our radical fallenness, and our dismal failure to be like Jesus become increasingly apparent. Fellowship with God results in a far greater awareness of God's holiness and our own unholiness or sin.

John revealed two options for dealing with this predicament—one that leads the Christian in a downward spiral, away from the light of God, and the other that leads the Christian in an upward spiral, toward His light. The first option involves ignoring, denying, excusing, and/or defending one's sinfulness and the deep spiritual and personal needs that accompany it (1:6, 8, 10). John warned that this grim dishonesty will only lead us away from truth and reality … and toward deeper illusion, deceit, and darkness. As William Shakespeare said, "God hath given you one face, and you make yourselves another."

Recall Robert Louis Stevenson's words in *The Strange Case of Dr. Jekyll and Mr. Hyde:*

> There is a face that we hide
> Till the nighttime appears,
> And what's hiding inside,
> Behind all our fears,
> Is our true self
> Locked inside the facade!

As adults, we have likely learned the exhausting role of professional imposter—masquerading, posing, performing, posturing, acting for others. Sin turns all of us into pretenders who are working hard to keep up appearances. And this effort produces such inevitable effects as shame, blame, fear, denial, and anger—until we run back to God and His offer of healing. It is costly to fail to honestly admit to self, God, and others our sins, our inconsistencies, and our rationalizations of these failings. Wearing masks will only sabotage our authentic relationship with God and with others. For some of us, however, honesty about our journeys may be too painful or terrifying to face. Can we find the courage to look at the truth about ourselves and to live openly and honestly, without masks and pretense? Some believers are too insecure to admit they are powerless over their habits, hang-ups, and hurts. Slow to let go of their secrets, inhibitions, and pretenses, these believers tragically fail to walk in God's light.

The other and spiritually healthier option is for believers to candidly and courageously, plainly and honestly, admit ("confess") their personal failings to God (1:7, 9; 2:1). In the context of 1 John, when believers confess their unbelief, disobedience, and lack of love, they can be confident that God extends forgiveness and cleansing as He shapes them more into His likeness. Put differently, honesty releases God's restorative grace, and believers then progressively experience a reality-based Christian life. The God of light (1:5) breaks through the darkness of sin.

Clearly, the basis of relationship with God is not one's sinlessness but His unexpected and undeserved forgiveness. Growing Christians learn to make this unconditional love the basis of their day-to-day experience. They rely on the truths that "He is faithful" (1:9) and trustworthy. As they walk in the light, they can expect to see themselves as they really are; yet as they see their sin, believers need not be threatened or intimidated by God's holiness. They are simply to admit to themselves and to God their sins as well as their rationalizations of those failings. There is no use in trying to hide their sin or pretend it doesn't exist. Instead, Christians can let go of sin and secrets and know freedom from condemnation and pretense. Fully accepted and unconditionally loved, Christians can enjoy an intimate and transformative relationship with a holy God.

It is noteworthy that, in addition to revealing sin, light also warms and heals. Believers can better face the bad news about their sin and the reality of their woundedness when they focus on the good news of God's total acceptance of them through Christ. Believers must learn to live in honesty and openness in order to know Jesus and one another deeply. Over the span of their lives of faith, authentic spirituality moves Christians toward transparency, vulnerability, and bold integrity.

The word *truth* offers another clue about a believer's spiritual growth. While *truth* refers to the content of Christianity as the absolute truth on which to base one's life, Arndt and Gingrich define *truth* (as used in 1:6, 8; 2:4) as "reality as opposed to mere appearance," "real and genuine," "true in accordance with truth."[7] Truth needs to be seen as more than orthodox formulations and propositions. Truth exists in contrast to appearances and illusion. Biblical truth is a reliable portrait of reality.

In Chapter 8 of John's gospel, it is patently clear that information does not guarantee freedom for the believer (see verses 31–32). The appropriate response to biblical revelation is not mere intellectual assent, but action. Christian spirituality, then, involves a shift from the cognitive alone to the personal, experiential, and lived-out meaning of biblical truth. Being faithful to God's teachings will bring greater knowledge of the truth about God, self, and others, and that will mean walking to a greater degree in the freedom of God's light.

In response to the teaching of 1 John 1:5–2:2, some believers have become courageously honest with God and others, have discarded defenses and pretenses, and have grown more accustomed to walking in the light than other Christians have. Some believers have progressed from Childhood to the Young Adulthood or even to the Parenthood stage of faith in their ability to live according to God's revelation and to live out His truth. Clearly, John's hope is that Christians recognize in themselves the need for continued spiritual growth.

3. **Evidence of Genuine Faith** (1 John 2:3–11)

The epistle's general introduction to the essential relationship between the believer's life and God's truth is now particularized in three tests that serve two purposes.[8] We will consider the purposes before we look at the tests.

First, these tests distinguish between authentic Christians and their adversaries who claimed to know God. The false teachers did not know God. Their claim was spurious; their beliefs were aberrant. Second, the tests offer Christians specific evidence of what it is to know God and salvation in Him. Three times in this brief letter, John referred to these tests, and each subsequent time the test is more probing. The reader cannot afford to miss that the apostle's repetition underscores that these truths are to progressively shape the believer's life. These tests make us aware that there is always room for us to progress, learn, and improve—and, ideally, these tests will motivate us to keep pressing on. Who among believers can say that he or she walks as Jesus walks, loves as He loves, and sees as He sees? None of us has yet to arrive at Christlikeness; yet without this holy discontent, our faith will otherwise entropy and stagnate; we will lose our desire to become more like Jesus. But as we Christians learn to live in God's light and let go of pretense, we can honestly admit ways in which our obedience (Test #1), love (Test #2), and discernment (Test #3) fail to measure up to God's ideal.

Clearly, though, the lives of some believers indicate that they are deeper and farther along than others when it comes to passing these tests or reaching these benchmarks of spiritual progress. Again the point is made: Christians are in differing stages of spiritual growth. Some are in the Childhood stage, others are in Young Adulthood, and some are in the Parenthood stage of faith development.

Sixteen hundred years ago, Augustine prayed, "My soul is like a house, small for You to enter, but I pray You to enlarge it. It is in ruins, but I ask You to remake it. It contains much that You will not be pleased to see: this I know and do not hide."[9] This kind of awareness of our brokenness, accompanied by our openness to God's work in our hearts, leads us to candidly admit that we fail these tests. That's when we open ourselves to God's transforming work and become "deep."

Test #1: John's first test was the moral test of obedience (2:3–6). This test measures the believer's progress in the vertical dimension of faith, focusing on "Jesus and me," a key concept first introduced in 1:3. Believers are to increasingly walk as Jesus walked.

The following verse is stunning:

> The one who says he abides in Him *ought himself to walk in the same manner as He walked.* (2:6, emphasis mine)

Remarkably, believers are commanded to walk as Jesus walked, to resemble Him in His absence, and even to be mistaken for Him. Our behavior is to mirror His. What believer doesn't have room to grow! Those who claim to have fellowship with God increasingly prove it by their actions, not just with an orthodox, verbal profession (see also 2:28–3:10; 5:2–3). Believers are to become progressively skilled at identifying and resolving hindrances to full obedience. As believers let go of pretense, they can honestly admit where their ways do not resemble Jesus' ways. The actions of some Christians, however, will resemble Christ more than the actions of other Christians will.

So how can Christians be sure that they truly know Jesus? And how can genuine Christians be distinguished from the spurious (cf. 5:13)? John introduced this formula: "we know that ..." (verse 3), "this is how we know ..." (verse 5b), and "here is the test by which we can make sure that we know Him" (NEB). To know God is not a matter of biblical thought processes or doctrinal correctness but of a genuine spiritual relationship with the Lord. Knowledge of God is not intellectual and speculative but experimental and dynamic.[10] Authentic knowledge of God is both personal and practical.

Dodd writes that, in this passage, John "is not only rebutting dangerous tendencies in the church of his time, but discussing a problem of perennial importance, that of the validity of religious experience."[11] John insisted that no religious experience is valid if it does not have obvious moral consequences in the life of the proponent. It is not the person who claims both to be a Christian and to know God who is presumptuous but those people whose claim to know God is contradicted by their conduct. Those individuals are liars (1:4)—and that is a strong word that will haunt us as we honestly face the truth that too often we fail to follow Him fully. And that truth should bring us to the truths that God loves us in spite of our failures and that we need not hide from Him.

Furthermore, believers come to know God better only by obeying His commands. Only if we obey Him can we claim to know Him. Our verbal proclamation of faith will be tested—will be proved or disproved—by our obedience. If we disobey God's commandments, our claim to know God is a lie; our conduct contradicts our profession of faith and proves our faith to be false. If anyone obeys God's Word—and that means obeying His commands in particular as well as His teaching in general, regarding them as the two parts of a single and complete revelation of His will—these people are showing by their obedience that they are indeed true Christians (verse 5a).

Obedience to God's commands, however, does not establish relationship with Him; rather—as has been stated—one's relationship with the Lord is demonstrated by obedience to His commands. True love for God is defined not by sentimental language or mystical experience but by moral obedience. The proof of love for God is loyalty to His values and standards: "We cannot claim to abide in Him unless we behave like Him."[12] The Christian must increasingly walk as Jesus walked. Jesus is a model to be imitated, and this imitation of Christ is a dynamic, lifelong process. The basis of this obedience is a growing trust in the rightness of God's ways. In a believer's walk of obedience, pretense is unnecessary, and a grace-based relationship replaces the effort to perform in order to earn acceptance. Obedience is not an attempt to merit God's approval, to compensate, pay back, cover up, or impress. Obedience is a response of love and loyalty.

Clearly, believers fall far short of complete, 24/7 obedience; we fail to "keep His commands" (2:3). Even in the course of a single day—a single hour—we Christians quite often fail the test of obedience. All believers can grow in obedience; none of us fully resembles Jesus or walks exactly as He walks. Instead, our love for God, as demonstrated by our obedience, is increasingly "perfected" (2:5); it progressively reaches maturity or completeness in the obedient Christian. So John rightfully observed that some believers are farther along than others in this matter of walking as Jesus walked. Some believers resemble Christ in their actions more than others do. Some are in the Childhood stage, others are in the Young Adulthood stage, and some are in the Parenthood stage of faith.

Test #2: After discussing the moral test of obedience, John moved on to the test of love, or the relational test (2:7–11). Having already written about the Christian's obligation to keep God's commandments (verses 3–4), John next singled out one commandment: the challenge to love. Believers are to increasingly love as Jesus loved. This test focuses on the horizontal dimension of faith: the "Jesus and we." To walk in God's light is to walk in His love. Those who claim to know God will progressively give evidence of this reality through their love for others. Those who claim to know God will give evidence of this knowledge through their love for others (see also 3:11–18; 4:7–21; 5:1–3). Remarkably, we are to resemble Jesus in the way He loved. Note that this is an imperative, not a suggestion. *Ought* is a strong word, a command:

> We know love by this, that He laid down His life for us; and *we ought to lay down our lives for the brethren.* (4:16, emphasis mine)

Believers are to become progressively skilled at loving and receiving love. We are to increasingly resemble Jesus in the ways we care for others and allow others to care for us. Genuine spirituality is observable in the quality of our interpersonal relationships. In fact, John taught, the genuineness of our Christian faith is revealed in our relationships of love to God and to fellow human beings. If by God's transforming grace we are letting go of pretense, we can more easily and more honestly confess our self-absorption and self-centeredness. We can open ourselves to God's making us more loving individuals—and it is very apparent that some Christians are farther along the path of loving others just as Christ loves others.

Jesus Himself commanded: "As I have loved you, so you must love one another" (John 13:34; 15:12, 17). He then explained, "By this all men will know that you are my disciples, if you have love for one another" (John 13:35). Certain of salvation and secure in our status as God's children, believers can grow to love others more freely and to let others love us. As believers love, our words and actions serve as evidence that "the darkness is passing away" (or fading) and that the real or true light of God is shining in us and through us (2:8).

This kind of transformation is quite evident in John's life. Early on, this young and passionate Son of Thunder angrily wanted to call down fire from heaven upon the Samaritans who rejected Jesus (Luke 9:54). On another occasion, this self-centered John sought his own advantage at the expense of the other disciples (see Matthew 20:20–28). But later, John described himself as "the disciple whom Jesus loved." John knew firsthand that the persistent, undeserved, and unexpected love of God had changed him. No wonder he exclaimed, "See how great a love the Father has bestowed on us that we should be called children of God; and such we are" (1 John 3:1). Regardless of what stage of faith we believers are in, God's transforming love is a vital contributor to our growth in faith.

So, in the first test, the falsity of the claim to be living in God's light was revealed by a believer's disobedience; in this second test, the absence of authentic love revealed the falsity of one's claim to be following God. "Lack of love implies lack of God."[13] Hatred distorts the believer's perspective. By contrast, love sees straight; thinks clearly; and gives one a balanced outlook, godly judgment, and Christlike conduct. A believer's personal relationships are to be marked by unselfish and caring love. In fact, the essence of such love is self-sacrifice, which was perfectly manifested in Christ and which should characterize the lives of His followers as well. Just as Cain is the supreme example of hate (see Genesis 4:1–10), so Christ is the supreme example of love. But the self-sacrifice of Christ is not just a revelation of love to be admired; it is an example to follow. As the apostle said, "We ought to lay down our lives for our brothers" (3:16).

The test of love is further explained in 4:7–12. In that passage, the apostle's refrain was "let us love one another" (verse 7), "we ought to love one another" (verse 11), and "if we love each other ..." (verse 12). John wanted this divine imperative to be clearly understood: Christians are to love God and one another because God has revealed Himself to us in Christ's self-sacrificial love. God is love (verses 8, 16). God has loved us in Christ (verses 10–11). And God continues to love us and love others through us (verses 12–13). These are reasons for believers to learn to love one another.

As mentioned earlier, believers often fail to demonstrate the deep quality of God's love for others that characterized the life of Christ. Again, all believers can improve on this count; none of us fully resembles Jesus and His way of loving self-sacrificially and unconditionally. As believers learn to increasingly let go of our defenses and pretenses, we can more honestly and fully confess our self-absorption, self-centeredness, and failure to serve and minister to others as Christ did. And, again, some Christians are more like Jesus than others are in their ability to love God and love fellow believers. Some of us are in the Childhood stage, some are in the Young Adulthood stage, and others are in the Parenthood stage of faith.

Test #3: To the moral test of obedience and the relational test of love, John added the doctrinal test of discernment (2:18–27). Those who claim to follow God will increasingly demonstrate their loyalty—the genuineness of their commitment to the Lord—by accurately discerning counterfeits to faith, identifying lies and fabrications about God's truth, and noting false teachings about Christ's character and mission (see also 4:1–6; 5:1, 4, 5). Believers are to progressively come to see as He sees, becoming more and more skilled at recognizing God's truth and abiding in it. As believers let go of pretense, they can honestly admit where they do not fully see life and others as God does. Also, they will move away from reliance on teachers in order to gain a firsthand, personally examined, and personally owned faith (2:27). Some Christians see more clearly and more carefully than others do. Some Christians have advanced beyond others in thinking as Jesus does. Yet each of us is to increasingly see all of life as Jesus does.

John clearly distinguished between false teachers and genuine Christians (verses 18–21), defined the nature and effect of the heresy (verses 22–23), and finally, described two safeguards against heresy (verses 24–27). His readers' loyalty to God's truth is contrasted with those who had defected from the church. The false teachers were the antichrists who opposed and denied the truth about the person of Christ. Their theology was defective and diabolical. John taught that if believers are to guard against error, two things must "remain" in them, the message that "you have heard from the beginning" (verse 24) and "the anointing you received from Him" (verse 27).

The present tense of the command "do not believe every spirit" (4:1) suggests that John's readers were tending to accept uncritically all teachings that claimed to be inspired. So John urged them to investigate every allegedly inspired utterance. The searching test is applied in two ways: first, with reference to the teacher (4:1–3) and then with reference to the hearers (4:4–6). True faith examines its object before placing confidence in it. Before Christians trust any spirits, we must test those spirits. God's people are to listen to God's Word rather than the teachings of the world.

Again, every believer can grow in the ability to see as Jesus sees. Some Christians see more clearly, more carefully, and more as Christ sees than others do. Some believers have become more advanced and skilled at recognizing God's truth and abiding in it. Some believers are in the Childhood stage, others are the Young Adulthood stage, and still others are in the Parenthood stage of faith.

Progressing Through the Three Stages (1 John 2:12–14)

Walking in obedience as Jesus walked, loving as He loved, seeing as He sees—passing these tests is completely impossible. We all fail these tests again and again in the course of a day. No wonder John was quick to reassure his readers of their salvation, as well as to affirm them for their spiritual progress. He reiterated that they are in the family of God and that they can rest assured of that fact:

> [John] does not mean to give his readers the impression that he thinks they are in darkness or that he doubts the reality of their Christian faith. It is the false teachers that he regards as spurious, not the loyal members of the church ... His purpose in writing is as much to confirm the right assurance of the genuine Christian as to rob the counterfeit of his false assurance.[12]

But—as we've seen—genuine Christians are all at different stages of spiritual development:

> I am writing to you, little children, because your sins have been forgiven you for His name's sake. I am writing to you, fathers, because you know Him who has been from the beginning. I am writing to you, young men, because you have overcome the evil one. I have written to you, children, because you know the

> Father. I have written to you, fathers, because you know Him who has been from the beginning. I have written to you, young men, because you are strong, and the word of God abides in you, and you have overcome the evil one.

Notice John's writing style: he spoke in the sharp contrasts of light vs. darkness, love vs. hate, truth vs. error, keeping His commandments vs. lying. There are no in-betweens. You either know God (and that will be evidenced by how you live) or you don't know Him. But we don't live entirely in these extremes. Rather, John wanted his readers to see that believers will progress and grow in our ability to live out our knowledge of God. It makes sense—and it is reassuring—that as believers move from the Childhood stage to the Young Adulthood stage and then to Parenthood in the faith, we will grow more deeply in our experience of God's light, love, and truth.

So John pointed out in 2:12–14 that some members of the family are farther along in their faith development. In other words, some believers have progressed beyond others in their obedience to God's commands, loving Him and His people, and discerning God's truth. Some Christians are children, some are young men, and others are fathers in their spiritual progress. These three groups are best understood as representing metaphorical stages, not chronological ages.

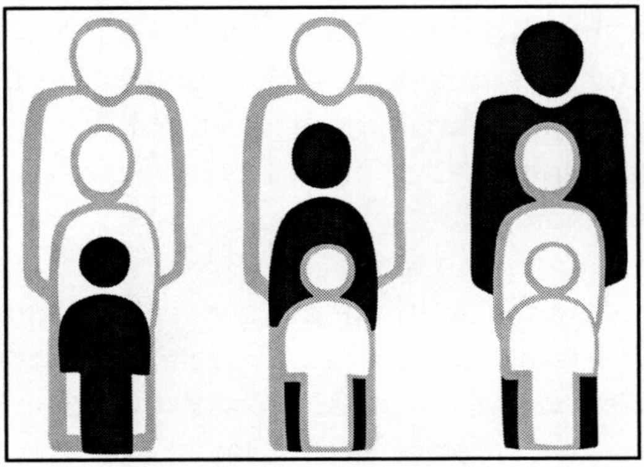

John also explained in this passage that specific milestones, or characteristics, inherent to each stage differentiate the three stages from one another. Each of the eight milestones contributes to a believer's ongoing growth in holiness and wholeness, and together the eight comprise God's agenda for a lifetime of spiritual growth. No other biblical writer identifies the marks or characteristics of spiritual progress as clearly and specifically as John did. (The exegetical basis for the three stages of faith has been developed in Chapter 2, "The Case for Stages," and is further supported in Chapter 3, "Evidence Beyond a Reasonable Doubt," where we explored the spiritual growth paths described in Hebrews 5:11–6:1; 1 Corinthians 2:14–3:1; and Ephesians 4:12–16.) These milestones are the catalysts or prime movers for a Christian's growth, and these eight milestones are examined carefully in Chapters 5–7 and 11–13 and are the focus of the *Stages of Faith* book.

The Enemies of Spiritual Progress (1 John 2:15–17)

The path of spirituality takes believers through a very real battleground. First John 2:15–17 warns that whether believers are in the stage of Childhood, Young Adulthood, or Parenthood, they can be sure to encounter three rivals to their spiritual growth: the world (outer conflict), the devil (outer conflict), and the flesh (inner conflict). This trinity of evil can indeed be hazardous to one's spiritual health as they take aim at authentic and lifelong spiritual growth. Then, in 2:18–27, John warned about the false teachers who deceive and about false believers who defect from the faith. John was pleading for Christians to develop discernment (2:18–27; 4:1–6; 5:1, 4–5). John also reminded believers of the role the Holy Spirit plays in helping them obey God, love Him and one another, and detect counterfeits to faith.

John's message was, bottom line, that spiritual growth is never automatic. Christians are never too mature to be seduced by these persistent and pervasive enemies. Growth toward deeper and more genuine faith can be impaired and delayed by the world, the flesh, and the devil, and it is quite possible to get stuck at any of the three stages. *The Path* and its companion *Stages of Faith*, however, will help you become more aware of how these enemies conspire to interfere with the development measured by the eight milestones of spiritual growth, and that awareness is the first step toward developing a healthy defense.

The first enemy, the world or *cosmos*, refers to the process by which believers unthinkingly absorb the warped and twisted values, perspectives, and attitudes unique to a culture and how these Christ-followers are powerfully shaped and misshaped by those false standards. The world system socializes, secularizes, and conditions each person in ways that do not foster Christlikeness.

John then described the second enemy, the Evil One, the mastermind behind the forces of the world and the flesh. Satan's lies and deceptions are designed to keep believers from moving toward wholeness and fully developed Parenthood in the faith.

The third enemy is the enemy within, the flesh, comprising the "lust of the flesh, the lust of the eyes, and the boastful pride of life" (2:16). Lust (*epithumia*) refers to the believer's instinct-driven desires, habits, and motives that compete for mastery and control of one's life. The lust of the flesh is the desire for sensual pleasure: "I want what I feel." The lust of the eyes is the desire for the pleasure that comes with acquisition: "I want what I see." Last, the boastful pride of life is the desire for the pleasure that comes with recognition: "I want to be first—and I better be anything but last!" Christian maturity means that believers face the reality that the fulfillment of all of one's appetites and impulses does not lead to genuine satisfaction in life.

And that's only one reason why believers are not to buy into the world's message. John provided two other reasons why Christ-followers are not to love the world. First, love for God and love for the world are incompatible and mutually exclusive (2:15–16). The ideals and aspirations of the world are utterly antithetical to faith. Second, everything that is in the world is transitory and will fade away. The transience of the world is contrasted with the eternal permanence of those who do God's will (2:17). In 1 John 2:15–27, John suggested that some Christians have not yet found Jesus to be enough for them. In other words, some Christians have found more victory over their inner and outer enemies than others have. Some are in the Childhood stage, others are in the Young Adulthood stage, and still others are in the Parenthood stage of faith.

Take-Aways from 1 John

An overview of 1 John offers a context for 1 John 2:12–14 that makes those verses more significant and compelling.

- The seasoned apostle John was well aware that his congregation consisted of believers in three stages of spiritual development. Some were deeper and farther along in both the vertical ("Jesus and me") and horizontal ("Jesus and we") dimensions of faith than others were (1:1–4).
- John also knew that a primary obstacle to spiritual growth is pretense, so he called Christians to be open, truthful, and honest with God and with one another (1:5–2:2).
- John outlined three benchmarks of authentic Christian growth: the moral test of obedience (2:3–6), the relational test of love (2:7–11), and the doctrinal test of discernment (2:15–17). John acknowledged that some believers are more experienced at walking as Jesus walked, loving as He loves, and seeing as He sees than other Christ-followers are.
- In 2:18–27, John warned that believers in any stage will encounter inner and outer enemies to their progress in the faith.

In this epistle, the apostle John prepared and guided readers to the truth of 1 John 2:12–14, where he identified three stages of faith and described the primary characteristics that distinguish each stage from the others. By God's grace, may John's words prompt in you and me the desire to grow in our obedience to God's commands, our ability to love Him and others, and our ability to recognize and live out His truth.

Questions for Reflection and Action

1. By God's transformational grace, the Son of Thunder came to be known as the Apostle of Love. What evidences of your transformation toward Christlikeness are you aware of? If you're not sure, ask someone who knows you well and has known you for a while. If your small group has been meeting for a significant length of time, what evidences of transformation can you affirm in one another?
2. *Friendship is Both Vertical and Horizontal*: Which aspect of your faith—"Jesus and me" or "Jesus and we"—do you struggle with more? Why do you think that is?
3. *Living Without Pretense*: In what ways can pretense be protective, habitual, and unhealthy? Why do we hide behind pretense? What can believers do—what can *you* do—to take a step toward living without pretense?
4. *Evidence of Genuine Faith*: Obedience, love, discernment—these are the three tests of genuine faith. Why is each important to your relationship with the Lord? Why is each important to your witness for Him in this world?
5. Of what value is a believer's "holy discontent"? What can you do to fuel that holy discontent and further motivate yourself to pursue Christlikeness?

CHAPTER 5

THE CHILDHOOD STAGE OF SPIRITUAL GROWTH

THE BIRTH OF FAITH

IN CHAPTERS 5 through 7, the distinguishing biblical marks of the three stages of faith—Childhood, Young Adulthood, and Parenthood—will be identified and explored, providing believers with a reliable pathway of spiritual growth. In order to optimize this transforming work of God in their lives, Christians are to nurture the characteristics described here. As we make a solid case for a biblical paradigm of spiritual growth, know that these characteristics are not exhaustive and comprehensive, as if John were intending to encapsulate in 1 John 2:12–14 all there is to say about spiritual growth.

Yet, in 1 John 2:12–14, the apostle twice addressed three distinct groups of believers: children, young men, and fathers. These three groups are best understood as metaphorical stages of faith. Throughout *The Path*, the group of children refers to those believers in the Childhood stage of faith, the young men to those in the Young Adulthood stage, and fathers to those in the Parenthood stage. The attributes addressed in each of these stages will be referred to as *milestones,* an allusion to those roadside markers or signs that tell the distance to a particular place. Each milestone shows travelers that they have made some progress and are heading in the right direction, toward their intended location.

This metaphor emphasizes the believers' role in their own spiritual growth and their responsibility to follow the eight markers that guide them to maturity. These eight milestones are rooted in the biblical text itself: Three are characteristics of the Childhood stage. Three characteristics are distinct to the Young Adulthood stage. And two are characteristics of the Parenthood stage.

Table 1 shows that each of the eight milestones is rooted in the 1 John 2:12–14 passage. Specifically, each milestone is based on the biblical phrase noted in the table below.

Table 1: John's Stages and Milestones

The Childhood Stage of Faith

- Milestone #1 "Your sins have been forgiven you for His name's sake" (2:12)
- Milestone #2 "You know the Father ..." (2:13c)
- Milestone #3 "Little children" (*teknia*, 2:12) and "children" (*paidia*, 13c)—the familial, relational, interpersonal context of spiritual growth

The Young Adulthood Stage of Faith

- Milestone #4 "You are strong" (2:14)
- Milestone #5 "The word of God abides in you" (2:14)
- Milestone #6 "You have overcome the evil one" (2:13, 14)

The Parenthood Stage of Faith

- Milestone #7 "Fathers" (2:13, 14)
- Milestone #8 "You know Him who has been from the beginning" (2:13, 14)

The 1 John 2:12–14 passage is something like a skeleton, providing the structure as well as the foundational content for three stages of faith. After we look at these three stages in Chapters 5–7, Chapters 8 and 9 will address "The *How* of Spiritual Growth," a discussion informed by developmental theory, and you will be surprised to see the skeleton come to life. Then, in Chapters 10 through

12, we will integrate the biblical with the developmental; we will add flesh, movement, expressions, personality, and individuality to the skeleton as we acknowledge the ways human developmental theory complements the process of faith development and fashions a compelling model of stages of faith.

The Childhood Stage of Spiritual Growth

The following three milestones provide the foundation for spiritual growth in the Childhood stage:

- Milestone #1: Experiencing God's Grace and Forgiveness
- Milestone #2: Embracing God as Father
- Milestone #3: Growing Up Together

Every believer who attends to these milestones will deeply personalize the three key truths noted below.

Table 2 (below) lists the three milestones that characterize the metaphorical Childhood stage of faith. In a structure that also appears in the following overviews of Young Adulthood and Parenthood, alongside each milestone is the "Biblical Source," noting the milestone's origin in 1 John 2:12–14, and the "Biblical Truths" that are to be nurtured by the believer during this stage of growth. In the last column is the desired "Outcome" that reflects the milestone's primary purpose.

Table 2: John's Childhood Stage of Faith

Milestone	Biblical Source	Biblical Truths	Outcome
#1	"I am writing to you, little children, because your sins have been forgiven you for His name's sake." (1 John 2:12)	Assurance of forgiveness, certainty of God's love and acceptance, status as son or daughter of God	*Experiencing God's Grace and Forgiveness*

Continued

Milestone	Biblical Source	Biblical Truths	Outcome
#2	"I have written to you, children, because you know the Father." (1 John 2:13)	God's trustworthiness and reliability, believer's call to trust and surrender	*Embracing God as Father*
#3	"I am writing to you [*teknia* and *paidia*]" (1 John 2:12, 13)	Relationships in God's family, the matrix of spiritual growth	*Growing Up Together*

The Childhood stage of faith embraces three formative milestones that help shape the believer's inner and outer world. These milestones address fundamental and far-reaching core issues that, once in place, guide believers toward spiritual maturity. These matters are also basic to the promised joy (1 John 1:4) that too often eludes Christians.

Milestone #1: Experiencing God's Grace and Forgiveness

> The biblical source for Milestone #1 is the promise of 1 John 2:12, "I am writing to you, little children, because your sins are forgiven you for His name's sake." The biblical truths invite the formation of a distinctive identity based on one's security, significance, and worth in Christ. The outcome of this milestone is for a believer to fully experience and rest in God's grace and forgiveness.

The perfect tense of the verb *forgiven* communicates the idea that grace and forgiveness begin to be experienced in Childhood and continue to be the believer's indispensable lifeblood throughout each successive stage of faith. Greek grammarians Dana and Mantey define the perfect tense as "a combination of two ideas: it looks in perspective at the action, and regards the results of the action as continuing to exist; that is, in progress, at a given point."[1] The use of the perfect tense in this context means, "I am saved when I place my faith in Christ, and my salvation is ongoing."

Little children (*teknia*) is a term of endearment and affection. The Christian can enjoy the privileged status as a son or daughter of God (John 1:12). As Paul wrote elsewhere, "He predestined us to adoption as sons ... to the praise of the glory of His grace, which He freely bestowed on us in the Beloved" (Ephesians 1:5–6).

Saving Grace

In the Bible, grace can be understood as both saving grace and sanctifying grace. First, saving grace focuses on the fact that a believer's salvation is assured. Each of the following verses, all penned by the apostle John, emphatically teaches the certainty of God's love and forgiveness.

- John 3:36; 5:24: "... *has* [not hope to have or might have] eternal life"
- 6:37, 39: "I will *certainly not* cast out ... I lose nothing"
- 10:27–29: "They will never perish, and *no one* will snatch them out of My hand ... and *no one* is able to snatch them out of the Father's hand."
- 1 John 5:12–13: "These things I have written to you ... so that you may *know* that you have eternal life."

Salvation is assured! We receive salvation and the forgiveness of our sins by virtue of our faith in Jesus' sacrificial death on our behalf. James Boice comments on 1 John 2:12 and 13: "John writes to the newborn in Christ to assure them that he is writing, not because they are not saved (which some of his remarks might lead them to question), but because they are and because he wants them to progress in their Christianity."[2]

How are we to respond to this amazing grace? The apostle John is clear that the journey of faith is rooted in grace. Although John, in

1 John 1:5, described God as "light, and in Him there is no darkness at all," there is no need to pretend or hide in fear or denial. Though we believers are fully known by God, we are also fully forgiven. The Bible clearly teaches that the intimate relationship with God and the divine restoration that He offers His children are the result of His non-repayable forgiveness and His unconditional love. Other verses reassure us of God's love and forgiveness (Romans 5:1–2; 8:1; 8:31–39; Colossians 2:13–15; Hebrews 10:14, 17, 23). We discover that salvation is the beginning of a friendship with God; a believer is totally accepted, and forgiveness is final and complete. Christ's death fully pays the penalty for human sin: "In Him we have redemption through His blood, the forgiveness of our trespasses, according to the riches of His grace, which He lavished upon us" (Ephesians 1:7–8). This grace is unearned, unending, unwavering, unmerited, undeserved, and not something we can ever repay. And our gracious God delights in us.

In 1 John 3:1–2, even though the apostle John was over ninety years old, he still marveled at the extent of God's mercy and at his status as God's son: "What marvelous love the Father has extended to us! Just look at it—we're called children of God! That's who we really are" (MSG). Like John, as we age and mature in our faith, we can continue to marvel at God's gracious acceptance and love, and as a result of resting in that love, we can more easily admit our tendency to condemn ourselves, justify ourselves, and hide behind protective masks of pretense. Rather than invest energy in those fruitless efforts, we can instead choose to trust in the strong and persistent love of God.

First and foremost, God loves His people unconditionally, even though He is very aware of our sins, faults, shortcomings, and free will. Second, God's love is causeless (people can do nothing to earn or deserve it), ceaseless (He loved every person before his or her birth, and He will never stop loving any of His children), and measureless (God's love is infinite, never changing, never ending). When individuals accept Jesus Christ as Savior and Lord, they are forgiven of their sins and eternally secure in God's love. God can heal any destructive sense of inferiority or superiority. His children can live free of past hurts and grounded in the love God has for them. Their sense of significance and self-worth is based entirely and unshakably on their identity as God's son or daughter. Imagine the practical differences this new way of thinking can make in a person's life!

Can Salvation Be Lost?

An errant but, sadly, not uncommon teaching is that people can lose their salvation. This is not true, but this toxic teaching threatens a believer's experience of God's grace and forgiveness. Passionately committed to obstructing a Christian's spiritual growth, Satan will readily deploy this lethal weapon of false belief.

If believers are to travel far spiritually, they must resolve the question, "Can my salvation be lost?" Read it here in black and white: forgiveness is irreversible. Also, rely on the truths of such verses as the already-cited Romans 5:1–2; 8:1; 8:31–39; Colossians 2:13–15; and Hebrews 10:14, 17, 23. We believers are to trust the biblical statements of God's full acceptance of us, not our fickle heart's condemnation. Scripture says, "We will know by this that we are of the truth, and will assure our heart before Him in whatever our heart condemns us; for God is greater than our heart and knows all things" (1 John 3:19–21).

Sanctifying Grace

Saving grace does exactly that: the grace of being able to acknowledge one's sin and then accept Jesus as Savior and Lord saves an individual from eternal separation from God. Sanctifying grace focuses on the lifelong process of sanctification that follows salvation, the process of becoming less bound to sin and more like Jesus Himself. At salvation, the believer is introduced to God's unconditional love and forgiveness. Whereas salvation is birth, sanctification or spiritual formation is growth. Regeneration is instantaneous and complete, but spiritual formation is progressive and incomplete. No believer becomes holy in a hurry. Sanctifying grace is the continuous grace-based process of renewal toward maturity, and this grace precludes shame, self-condemnation, self-justification, and reliance on performance to earn and maintain God's what-would-be conditional acceptance. Salvation is the starting point for what the theologian Francis Schaeffer called "the substantial healing of the total person."[3] Note, however, the word *substantial* as opposed to *complete*. Believers can and do experience real and significant healing, but healing is never entirely complete on this side of eternity. "Man is born broken. He lives by mending. The grace of God is the glue."[4] When God's children are glorified in heaven, then every emotional wound will be healed.

While God's children walk this earth, His grace repairs, rebuilds, and strengthens their inner lives (Acts 20:32). God's grace frees believers from the control and patterns of sin (Romans 6:14). This is the grace to which Paul attributes his own personal transformation (1 Corinthians 15:10), and his ministry flowed naturally from this grace-based renewal. Grace removed the fears that held Paul back and kept him from admitting weaknesses and neediness (2 Corinthians 12:9). Where Paul was vulnerable, God was very much accessible.

Like Paul the apostle, believers today are to progressively "grow in the grace" (2 Peter 3:18) and be increasingly "strengthened by grace" (Hebrews 13:9). Paul prayed, "May grace and peace be yours in fullest measure," suggesting that the Christian's experience of grace can grow (1 Peter 1:2). And Peter blessed his readers this way: "Grace and peace be multiplied to you in the knowledge of God and of Jesus our Lord" (2 Peter 1:2). In the Childhood stage of faith, believers will become increasingly familiar with such amazing grace.

Commenting on this amazing grace, Lewis Smedes observed that God's people can increasingly experience the grace of God on four different levels.[5] First, when believers initially experience grace as *pardon*, they are forgiven for wrongs done. Pardoning grace is the antidote to guilt. Second, when believers experience God's grace as *acceptance*, they are reunited with God as well as with their true self. This accepting grace—being cradled, held, affirmed, and loved by God—is the answer to shame. Third, when Christians experience God's grace as *power*, they find in His grace spiritual energy to shed the heaviness of shame and to move toward the true self God means each individual to be. Fourth, when God's children experience grace as *gratitude*, they marvel over and rejoice in the gift of life, enjoying a sense of wonder and sometimes even elation at the lavish generosity of God. Together, these four levels of grace mean that believers can anticipate a more comprehensive experience of personal renewal over a lifetime.

What Must I Do to Preserve My Salvation?

Another misleading and false teaching—one that is closely related to the unfounded notion that believers can lose their salvation—is that a person's relationship with God is based on his or her performance. Even if not explicitly taught, this message appeals to a part of twisted human nature that does better with earning than simply receiving because, after all, earning means people have at least some power in the transaction. But God's grace is to be received. Entertaining any thought that His acceptance is conditional, any burden of oughts and perfectionism, will undermine the lessons of Milestone #1 and a believer's freedom to experience God's grace and forgiveness. The journey of faith begins when a person chooses to rely on God's saving grace—and on that grace alone—for forgiveness and salvation. Spiritual progress continues and spiritual growth happens as the believer learns to develop a grace-based way of relating to God.

What is grace? "Grace is God acting in our lives to accomplish what we can't accomplish on our own."[6] The idea that one's personal performance can increase God's acceptance, love, or grace must be rejected. Each believer must thoroughly denounce this toxic message.

In fact, growing Christians need to fully attend to Milestone #1—to trusting and resting in God's grace and forgiveness—if they are to move toward spiritual maturity and wholeness. To grow spiritually, believers need to trust that they are loved by God absolutely and unconditionally. Then, certain of God's forgiveness and confident of their acceptance in Christ, God's children will be able to increasingly discard any masks, pretenses, phoniness, need for performance, bargaining, guilt, self-condemnation, sense of unworthiness, and feelings of inferiority. Sin will no longer prompt hiding, ignoring, denying, resisting, self-defense, projection, or rationalizations (1 John 1:9; 2:1). Grace allows believers to accept God's love and the truth that, in Christ, they are worthy of that love. God's grace frees Christians to come out from behind the people-pleasing efforts and performance by which some try to earn the Lord's acceptance. Believers—men and women, boys and girls—who have put their faith in Jesus are anything but inadequate and defective.

Lewis Smedes described the transforming impact of grace this way:

> Grace overcomes shame, not by uncovering an overlooked cache of excellence in ourselves but simply by accepting us, the whole of us, with no regard to our beauty or ugliness, our virtue or our vices. We are accepted wholesale. Accepted with no possibility of being rejected. Accepted once and accepted forever. Accepted at the ultimate depth of our being. We are given what we have longed for in every nook and nuance of every relationship.
>
> We are ready for grace when we are bone tired of our struggle to be worthy and accepted. After we have tried too long to earn the approval of everyone important to us, we are ready for grace. When we are tired of trying to be the person somebody sometime convinced us we had to be, we are ready for grace. When we have given up all hope of our being an acceptable human being, we may hear in our hearts the ultimate reassurance: we are accepted, accepted by grace.[7]

J. I. Packer described how thoroughly and irreversibly God knows and loves the believer; yet He is not disillusioned or surprised by what believers say, do, or think:

> What matters supremely, therefore, is not, in the last analysis, the fact that I know God, but the larger fact which underlies it—the fact that He knows me. I am graven on the palms of His hands; I am never out of His mind. All my knowledge of Him depends on His sustained initiative in knowing me. I know Him because He first knew me and continues to know me. He knows me as a

> friend ... There is tremendous relief in knowing that His love to me is utterly realistic based at every point on prior knowledge of the worst about me, so that no discovery can now disillusion Him about me.[8]

Amazing grace indeed—and believers are cautioned not to negate this grace of God (Galatians 2:21 says, "I do not nullify the grace of God ...") by trying, for instance, to earn His love. Paul was angry that the Galatian Christians were no longer relying on grace ("you have fallen from grace" [5:4]). The writer of Hebrews warned that believers who rely on performance and conformity to external standards "insulted the Spirit of grace" (10:29) and "come short of the grace of God" (12:15). Instead, in dark or uncertain circumstances, believers are to turn to God and "find grace to help in time of need" (4:16).

Furthermore, forces exist that have the express purpose of diminishing the Christian's experience of grace and thereby delaying or stalling the believer's spiritual growth. Along the journey of faith, believers will encounter the following five, all-too-common, and very strong opponents of grace. Christians therefore need to learn to overcome these anti-grace forces, for they will attack a believer's experience of God's grace and forgiveness throughout the lifelong journey of faith.

1. The first rival of grace resides *within the believer* (Hebrews 10:1–23): internal feelings of guilt, shame, self-condemnation, and self-justification are deadly to personal transformation. Also, believers may magnify their flaws and discount their strengths. Human nature seems resistant to grace and forgiveness and instead to be inclined to both earning God's approval and paying Him back in order to gain His continued acceptance. Neither God's approval nor His ongoing acceptance can be earned. The heart of the matter is grace.
2. A second opponent of grace is located *in the church* (Colossians 2:6–23). The church is too often home for

legalistic moralizers who emphasize external behaviors done out of a sense duty. Such legalism will sabotage a Christian's growth. Codified rules and mandated conformity to oughts and shoulds are powerful thieves of grace. One's faith can become secondhand and shallow, too reliant on the group and its controlling norms and expectations.

3. Another rival to grace is found *in the home* (Ephesians 6:4; Colossians 3:21). Children naturally expect parents and significant others to be trustworthy and to provide care, nurture, warmth, and affection. Instead, mothers, fathers, and other important people may bring disgrace and shame when they fail to acknowledge the infinite worth of each person. In the home specifically, a rules-based approach to the Christian life clouds grace. When that happens, Christians may grow up feeling unaccepted, unacceptable, and utterly unworthy of God's love.
4. Certain *aspects of culture* also oppose grace (Mark 4:19–20; Romans 12:2; 1 Corinthians 1:20). In part, people in the West are programmed to base their identity and self-concept on their performance and on the opinions of others. Some individuals have been rejected by and felt unaccepted by those they relied on to embrace and validate them. That burden is made heavier by a culture that says people must be the way others want them to be; individuals who do not measure up are simply not acceptable. This cultural message can crowd out God's grace.
5. The last of grace's opponents is *Satan* himself, who is seated in high places (Revelation 12:9–11). Satan often uses guilt and self-condemnation to powerfully shape and misshape a believer's inner world, and this strategy can effectively slow a Christian's spiritual growth.

In summary, Milestone #1: Experiencing God's Grace and Forgiveness is about personalizing God's grace in thorough, deep, and restorative ways. As Christians progressively awaken to God's wholehearted and unshakable acceptance of them, they will be more able to travel deeper and farther in their faith.

In Milestone #1, there is to be the formation of the believer's identity or self-concept. Change and growth toward spiritual maturity take place when believers know that they are fully accepted and forgiven. God's grace restores brokenness and replaces shame. If believers neglect this Milestone, self-condemnation, legalism, or perfectionism will misshape their faith as well as their identity. Believers will not likely be able to honestly face their sin and brokenness.

Milestone #2: Embracing God as Father

The biblical source of Milestone #2 is the apostle John's statement in 1 John 2:13, "I am writing to you, children, because you know the Father." In Milestone #1, the biblical truths to be attended to focus on the formation of a new identity in Christ and therefore one's self-concept. Next, Milestone #2 emphasizes a believer's concept of God. The primary purpose of this second milestone is to enable a believer to embrace God as Father.

The Greek word John used for "children"—*paidia*—refers to very young and dependent children, not yet seven years old, who need protection, training, guidance, and discipline.[9] Second, the Greek word for "know" speaks of knowing something firsthand through direct, personal experience. This knowledge goes beyond merely knowing about a certain something or someone. *The Dictionary of New Testament Theology* defines *know* (*ginōskō*) as "grasping the full reality and nature of an object under consideration. It is thus distinguished from mere opinion, which may grasp the object half-correctly, inadequately, or evenly falsely."[10] Finally, John specifically referred to God as "the Father." God is, first and foremost, above and beyond anything else, a Father to His children. Christians can trust their heavenly Father without resistance, reluctance, or reservation. Perhaps in sharp contrast to one's earthly parents, God the heavenly Father is absolutely trustworthy and utterly reliable.

John also taught that God is absolute holiness and light; yet naturally sinful believers are not to withdraw from Him in uncertainty or fear. Instead, the apostle John invites Christians—then and now—to experience perfect fellowship with the Father (1 John 1:3). Forgiven by God and accepted because of the substitutionary death of Jesus Christ, Christians can walk in the light of a holy God without hesitation, apprehension, or fear; they can walk with perfect openness and honesty (1 John 1:5–10). God in His mercy is absolutely trustworthy and utterly reliable. Furthermore, God is not austere or exacting, so there is no need to hide from Him. God is instead perfect love (1 John 4:8) and is therefore a flawless Father for His sons and daughters. Christians can trust God wholly and follow Him fully. Indeed, as J. B. Phillips wrote, "God is truly Perfection, but He is no Perfectionist."[11]

No wonder that, in the time of Jesus, the name of this holy and perfect God was so sacred that ordinary people were not even supposed to speak it. In fact, the Jews had used the letters *YHWH* to refer to God, and only the High Priest could pronounce that word—and then only when he entered the Holy of Holies on the Day of Atonement. Readers of Scripture who came to these letters would say, "Adonai" ("Lord") or "Master" instead of "Yahweh." When writing about God in Romans 8:14, 17 and Galatians 4:6, however, Paul used *Abba*, the Aramaic term for "father" and one of the first words a child spoke (similar to the English-speaking child's *Papa* or *Dada*). Likening the Christian's relationship with God to the relationship between a child and his/her daddy was abhorrent to an orthodox Jew. But Jesus Christ bridged that unbridgeable chasm between the holy Father God and sinful human beings, and now believers have the freedom and privilege of addressing God as "Father." In fact, *Father* is Christianity's distinctive title for God.[12]

Finally, it is impossible to have a healthy relationship with God without having an accurate and biblically sound concept of who He is. An incorrect concept of God will result in incorrect responses to Him. Likewise, a confused concept of God will mean a confused response to Him. And a distorted concept of God will prompt only distorted responses to Him. Believers are to respond to the God they know as He reveals Himself in His Word, His Son, and His Holy Spirit. As A. W. Tozer said, "What we believe about God is the most important thing about us."[13]

A Father's Forgiveness

You may be familiar with Luke 15 and Jesus' story of the prodigal son. As that parable so aptly illustrates, one of the greatest challenges to a believer's spiritual growth is learning to rest in the Father's unconditional acceptance and in the undeserved, yet unshakable, status as His child. Expecting the father's love to be conditional, the younger son, who had left home, doubted whether he would even be welcome when he returned. So, as he headed for home, the son practiced a speech (Luke 15:17–19), in which he offered to be treated as a hired servant rather than a forgiven child. As he was about to say, "I am no longer worthy to be called your son," the father interrupted (verse 21) and welcomed him home with a great celebration.

Likewise, a Christian's heavenly Father doesn't want to hear rehearsed scripts, and He does not want His children expecting, as the prodigal son did, to be benched, to be treated as a second-string player, when they return home. The holy, loving God wants His children to live joyfully as His forgiven and beloved sons and daughters. And that status is worth celebrating, just as the prodigal son's restored status was.

Luke 15:20–24 describes the homecoming. The father ran to his son and embraced him. Imagine the son's surprise as his father threw a party in honor of his son's return home. His father fully accepted him, without any reservations at all. Just as the father celebrated his love for his son upon the boy's return, so also God's children are to celebrate their heavenly Father's great love.

An important way to celebrate is to choose to let go of any guilt rooted in the past. Believers can fully trust their heavenly Father's gracious forgiveness and celebrate wholeheartedly, knowing that they have not disqualified themselves from receiving His undeserved love and absolute forgiveness. Believers need to have in their hearts and minds a new script that emphasizes God's grace and mercy—and they do well to rehearse that script often in celebration of their identity as God's son or daughter. Christians have reason to continually party in their souls as they journey through life. And

Christians are blessed with the ever-present opportunity to pause for a few minutes to enjoy simply being home with their Father. At such a soul-party, believers find freedom and laughter and maybe some tears as they surrender themselves to His care.

Rembrandt's painting of the prodigal son and his older brother depicts the son broken and kneeling before his father. The father has gently placed his hands on his son's back, and the boy—head shaved, dressed in dirty rags, with only one tattered sandal remaining—feels embraced by the father's love. Henri Nouwen confessed, "For years I had instructed students on the different aspects of the spiritual life… But had I, myself, really ever dared to step into the center, kneel down, and let myself be held by a forgiving father?"[14]

Growing Christians need to adequately attend to this second Milestone en route to spiritual maturity and wholeness. In fact, to ensure spiritual growth, believers need to know God the Father as the provider and caregiver who can be trusted and to whom they can surrender their lives. In order to develop a mature, adult faith, believers need to recognize and correct any distorted images, misconceptions, or caricatures of God that are wrongly influencing their thoughts about God. Believers also need to identify and discard any myths they are holding onto as truth.

In Milestone #2, there is to be the formation of one's God-concept and of a felt sense of God as Father. Believers learn to trust and surrender to God as He re-parents them. If Christians neglect this milestone, their distorted, damaging ideas about God will persist and cripple their full trust and total surrender to Him.

Milestone #3: Growing Up Together

This third milestone does not emerge exegetically from the text in the same way the other milestones do. Milestone #3 is not preceded by a *because* clause as other milestones are. This milestone that calls for togetherness is, however, strongly established in John's model for the following five reasons.

First of all, Milestone #3 stems from the apostle John's statement, "I am writing to you, little children" (*teknia*), in 1 John 2:12. *Teknia* refers to a child in relation to parents or family. The term also expresses affection and endearment. Clearly, with his use of *teknia*, the author has family relationships in mind. Believers in the Childhood stage of faith need to experience the mutually supportive and challenging relationships that can be found in the family of God. In Milestone #3, Christians begin to be reshaped within the grace-based relationships they form with fellow Christians. Believers can grow spiritually when God's people extend His grace and unconditional love to one another.

Next, this milestone's call to togetherness is supported by the larger context of John's epistle, where the apostle refers to his readers (*teknia*) as "brothers" (3:14), "one another" (2:11), and "beloved" (4:7). This relational need for affection, attachment, protection, and nurture begins to be met in the Childhood stage of faith as believers find a new home, a new place to belong, and a synergy of care. This relational dimension is crucial to every infant in the faith.

Third, John's model of faith development would be incomplete without this horizontal dimension of faith. In Milestones #1 and #2, believers attend to the vertical dimension of faith; now, in #3, they move to the horizontal dimension of faith. Recall that John wrote his epistle so "that you may also have fellowship [*koinonia*] with us," even as "our fellowship is with the Father, and with His Son Jesus Christ" (1:3). True joy (1:4) results when God's children experience a faith rich in the vertical as well as in the horizontal dimension.

Growing up in Christ together with fellow believers is not optional or negotiable. Impoverished faith may be at least partly attributed to inadequate relationships with brothers and sisters in Christ. After all, a believer's concepts of both self (Milestone #1) and God (Milestone #2) are experienced, relearned, and validated in community (Milestone #3). Certain of their salvation and secure in the status as God's children (Milestone #1) and trusting God as Father to re-parent them (Milestone #2), believers can love others and let others love them (Milestone #3). The formative milestones of Childhood are nurtured in community. Close, caring relationships are a prerequisite to healthy spiritual growth, and that growth process begins with the believer's new birth. Believers need to be living in relationship with one another and regularly interacting with fellow Christians because transformation takes place in the context of relationships.

A fourth reason why fellowship with believers—community—is key to spiritual growth is John's second test of genuine Christian faith, the test of love (2:7–11). God's children are to increasingly love as Jesus loved. This relational dimension is commanded, not just descriptive, of the believer. Those who claim to know God will increasingly give evidence of this reality in their love for others. In 3:11–18, John explained that the believer's personal relationships are to be marked by unselfish and caring love, that the essence of Christian love is self-sacrifice, that such sacrifice has been perfectly manifested in Jesus, and that sacrificial love should characterize the lives of His followers. Simply put, but not always easily done, "we ought to lay down our lives for our brothers" (3:16).

The test of love is further described in 4:7–21 and 5:1–3: "Let us love one another" (4:7); "we ought to love one another" (4:11); "if we love each other" (4:12). Christians are to love one another because God has revealed Himself in Christ as self-sacrificial love. God is, in His very essence, love (4:8, 16). God has loved the believer in Christ (4:10–11). And God continues to love people through believers (4:12–13). God's love is experienced in relationships. Clearly, as Milestone #3 sets forth, togetherness with fellow believers is vital to an individual's spiritual progress. To John, who viewed spiritual growth as mutual, collaborative, and cooperative, a Christian's relationships with other believers are imperative to the journey toward Christlikeness and maturity.

Fifth, evidence of the importance of Milestone #3-type togetherness is found throughout the New Testament. Consider the many verses in the New Testament that highlight the characteristics of community. Specifically, we are commanded to love one another; serve one another; bear with one another; be devoted to one another; encourage one another; build up one another; accept one another; not slander one another; instruct one another; admonish one another; carry one another's burdens; be kind and compassionate to one another; forgive each other; speak to one another with psalms, hymns, and spiritual songs; submit to one another; not lie to each other; spur one another on to love and good deeds; confess sins to each other; pray for each other; be clothed with humility toward one another; greet one another; be at peace with each other; and comfort one another (John 13:34; Galatians 5:13; Ephesians 4:2; Romans 12:10; Hebrews 10:25; 1 Thessalonians 5:11; Romans 15:7; James 4:11; Romans 15:14; Colossians 3:16; Galatians 6:2; Ephesians 4:32; 5:19; 5:21; Colossians 3:9; Hebrews 10:24; James 5:16; 1 Peter 5:5; 5:14; Philippians 2:3; Mark 9:50; 1 Thessalonians 4:18). Believers living in relationship with one another are partners in spiritual growth, empowering one another toward maturity and further Christlikeness. Grace is much more than the means of our salvation; grace is also the transforming community, the very place of our maturing and our life together.

For the five reasons noted above, Milestone #3, "Growing Up Together," is key to the apostle John's model of spiritual growth. The growing Christian will need to attend adequately to Milestone #3—to relationships with fellow believers—in order to move toward Christlike maturity and wholeness.

Furthermore, one's concept of self and one's concept of God are clarified and reinforced in community. Tragically, this "Jesus and we" aspect of the spiritual life is too often neglected: believers too often ignore the truth that relationships with one another are powerfully linked to personal spiritual progress. In fact, relationships can either prompt or impair spiritual growth. Milestone #3 encourages intentional focus on relationships with fellow believers, for in those relationships with members of the grace-based family of God, individuals can be healed, encouraged, and transformed. In fact, believers continue to grow spiritually by both extending God's grace and unconditional love to one another and receiving those life-giving elements in return.

The idea of fellowship is summarized in the Greek word *koinonia*, meaning "sharing your life in common with." For instance, Luke used the word *koinonia* to describe the business partnership between the two pairs of brothers, James and John and Andrew and Simon. As joint owners of a little fishing fleet, they were colleagues, engaged together in the fishing trade and committed to developing a successful business together. *Koinonia* is also used to describe the mutuality and intimacy of a marriage relationship. In authentic, biblical *koinonia*, the people in relationship to one another are partners in spiritual progress, committed to empowering one another toward maturity and Christlikeness.

Theologian John Stott has this to say about *koinonia*:

> There are two ideas of the religious life. There is the tramcar idea and the fireside idea. In the tramcar you sit beside your fellow-passenger. You are all going in the same direction, but you have no fellowship… Then there is the fireside, where the family meets together, where they are at home, where they converse one with another of common pursuits and common interests, and where a common relationship binds all together in a warm bond of love and fellowship… And when we concentrate on this, we are no longer facing in the same direction, we are gathered in a circle, facing each other.[15]

In *The Safest Place on Earth*, author Larry Crabb envisions a spiritual community where men and women find a commonality in their brokenness and recognition that they really do need each other.

> Why is spiritual community so rare? I suspect it has to do with the requirement of brokenness. We'd much rather be impressively intact than broken. But only broken people share spiritual community… It is our weakness, not our competence, that moves others; our sorrows, not our blessings, that break down the barriers of fear and shame that keep us apart; our admitted failures, not our paraded successes, that bind us together in hope. A spiritual community, a church, is full of broken people

> who turn their chairs toward each other because they know they cannot make it alone.[16]

A tramcar, by the way, is a British trolley car or a cable car, and Stott suggests that these passengers don't always know even the names of the people sitting near them. Clearly, such relationships would not transform anyone. But in fireside relationships, people know one another's names as well as their hearts and hurts, their dreams and desires. In fireside relationships, believers clearly need one another if they are to go higher and farther on the journey of obedience, love, and belief.

But people who have been Christians for a long time may never have experienced *koinonia* or mutual caregiving. Such relationships call for openness and vulnerability, and that involves risk. Yet believers must take risks in their relationships with one another if they are to enjoy an authentic and mature Christian faith. Milestone #3 invites God's people to experience "group grace," a sense of truly belonging, collaborative care, interdependence, and efforts to ensure each person's wholeness in Christ.

In Milestone #3, there is the formation of one's concept of others. Christians need one another. Within the matrix of interpersonal relationships, believers move toward wholeness and Christlikeness. If believers neglect this milestone, they will lack the kind of support and challenge necessary for spiritual growth.

The Childhood Stage of Faith: A Stage of Vulnerability

The original Greek of 1 John 2:18–27 makes it clear that the apostle was addressing those believers who have work yet to do in the Childhood stage of faith. Verse 18 begins, "Children [*paidia*], it is the last hour." John then closed that section with, "These things I have written to you [*paidia*] concerning those who are trying to deceive you" (verse 26). As noted above, *paidia* is the Greek word for the young child who needs guidance, protection, and instruction, a description that fits believers in the Childhood stage, who are particularly and uniquely vulnerable to the deceptions, lies, and counterfeits that the world, the flesh, and the devil (2:15–17) use in their attempts to stall spiritual progress. Further evidence that 1 John 2:18–27 targets those in the Childhood stage of faith is found in the fact that those in the Young Adulthood stage have already overcome the Evil One (Milestone #6).

The apostle also reminded vulnerable Children in the faith that they have the Holy Spirit as the Resident Tutor within them (2:20, 27). The Spirit's job is to help believers recognize false teachers (verse 27). In addition, John wanted the young believers in his audience to know that, living in the "last hour," they must rely on the authority of God's Word to guide their spiritual journeys rather than depending on teachers and peers. But this relocation of authority—this confident reliance on the Spirit-empowered ability to understand Scripture—is beyond the experience of these believers.

A Review of the Childhood Stage of Faith

Milestone #1: Experiencing God's Grace and Forgiveness
Milestone #2: Embracing God as Father
Milestone #3: Growing Up Together

The writings of John the apostle clearly justify placing the vertical dimension of faith (Milestones #1 and #2) ahead of the horizontal dimension (Milestone #3). "We love, because He first loved us" (1 John 4:19), and that love enables us to obey. As 1 John 4:11 says, "Beloved, if God so loved us, we also ought to love one another." The three Childhood milestones are, however, interrelated, interdependent, and synergistic. The three milestones work in concert, growing believers into Christlikeness.

In relationships characterized by grace, for instance, God's love and forgiveness come alive. The truths set forth in Milestones #1 and #2—the truths that believers are forgiven by God and can surrender their will and very life to Him—are more fully realized in the context of Christian relationships. Similarly, any unfinished work left over from Milestone #1 and Milestone #2 will manifest itself in these relationships, but being able to identify those weak places helps believers grow rather than stay stuck.

Milestones #1, #2, and #3—relationship with God, relationship with self, and relationships with others—can be seen as a unit. Being renewed by these milestone truths is a precondition to a successful transition into the Young Adulthood stage of faith.

Questions for Reflection and Action

Milestone #1: *Experiencing God's Grace and Forgiveness*

1. Your own story of your accepting God's amazing grace is a powerful tool of evangelism. Practice telling it to someone who is new to the Christian faith. In other words, avoid Christian jargon and fancy theological words. Be sure to include why believers can't lose their salvation ... and why we don't have to work to preserve it.
2. Review the five rivals of grace. Which is most powerful in your life? What can believers do to stand strong against these rivals? Choose a statement from Lewis Smedes or J. I. Packer (pages 86–87) to help you stand strong against those rivals.

Milestone #2: *Embracing God as Father*

1. Why did Jesus tell the story of the prodigal son? What aspect of the truth that God is your loving, forgiving Father does it help you more fully embrace?
2. Why is J. B. Phillips's comment that "God is truly Perfection, but He is no Perfectionist" good news? Give evidence from your own life that you are or are not living in that truth.
3. A. W. Tozer observed, "What we believe about God is the most important thing about us." Do you agree or disagree? Why?

Milestone #3: *Growing Up Together*

1. Review the five arguments for the importance of Christian community. Which do you find most compelling?
2. What Christian community are you involved in—or where could you get involved?
3. What degree of involvement will enable you to experience God's transforming power? (Remember Stott's tramcar?)

CHAPTER 6

THE YOUNG ADULTHOOD STAGE OF SPIRITUAL GROWTH

THE OWNERSHIP OF FAITH

WHO ARE THE "young men" in the faith? And what distinguishes them from children in the faith? The Greek word for young men, *neanisko*, refers to men of peak strength who are in the prime of life. Philo and Josephus used the word to describe the twenty-four-year-old to forty-year-old man, when he reaches full development and the height of his vigor and strength (Lenski, Westcott, Plummer).[1] Clearly, these young men of the New Testament are not to be confused with modern-day adolescents. (Since both time and experience move us toward maturity, the role of age as a factor in spiritual development will be addressed in Chapter 8, "Issue: The Importance of Age" and "Conclusion 5: Stages are loosely linked to chronological age.")

Table 4 (below) lists the three milestones of the Young Adulthood stage of faith. Alongside each milestone is the "Biblical Source" (noting the milestone's origin in 1 John 2:12–14) and the "Biblical Truths" that are to be nurtured by the believer during this stage of growth. In the last column is the desired "Outcome" that reflects the milestone's primary purpose.

Table 3: John's Young Adulthood Stage of Faith

Milestone	Biblical Source	Biblical Truths	Outcome
#4	"I am writing to you, young men, because you are strong." (1 John 2:14)	Personal, examined convictions	Owning a Firsthand Faith
#5	"I am writing to you, young men, because the word of God abides in you." (1 John 2:14)	Applying and internalizing God's Word, experiential knowing	Linking Truth and Life
#6	"I am writing to you, young men, because you have overcome the evil one," the world, and the flesh. (1 John 2:15–17)	Confronting three rivals to spiritual progress, transcendent realities	Defeating the Enemies of Spiritual Progress

John identifies three characteristics that are to distinguish the Christian in the Young Adulthood stage: "I am writing you because you are strong"; "I am writing you because the word of God abides in you"; and "I am writing you because you have overcome the evil one." Burdick and Westcott see three separate, distinct characteristics of these "young men,"[2] and these three characteristics appear to build naturally on one another. The apostle John challenged believers to continue to grow, even though the stage of Young Adulthood involves conflict and warfare.

Milestone #4: Owning a Firsthand Faith

> Based on 1 John 2:14 ("I have written to you, young men, because you are strong ..."), Milestone #4 addresses the core issue of becoming a Christian of distinction, of living one's life according to God-guided, personal choices rather than bowing unthinkingly to the pressure to conform to other believers. The truth to live out here is, "I am determining and owning the Christian values and biblical beliefs that, regardless of the cost, will guide my faith journey."

In Milestone #3, we focused on community, the horizontal dimension of our Christian faith. We acknowledged the basic human need to belong and the importance of supporting and challenging one another to grow in the walk of faith. Milestone #3 emphasized interdependence, a bonding attachment, and mutual support and challenge with fellow believers. Believers develop relationships with believers who wash one another's dirty feet.

Now, in Milestone #4, believers learn to confidently stand alone, not relying on the influence of the group to do their thinking and choosing for them. Here in Milestone #4, a key task is separation, and these two—separation and attachment—remain in dynamic tension throughout a believer's journey toward Christlikeness. After all, the purpose of community is neither conformity (we all believe and behave alike) nor obsessive reliance on others (we let others think for us). In healthy relationships, we are liberated to come into our own internalized, biblical faith. Clearly, the step from the Childhood stage of faith to Young Adulthood is a major transition.

From	To
"We"	"Me"
"I belong"	"I stand alone"
Peers	Principles
Membership	Ownership
Convention	Conviction
Secondhand faith	Firsthand faith
Borrowed faith	Owned faith
Bonding attachment	Separation
External authority	Inner authority

Paul wrote 1 and 2 Corinthians and Romans quite awhile before the apostle John wrote 1 John. So John would certainly have been familiar with Paul's use of the word *strong* and the fact that strong believers and weak believers are fundamentally different from one another. It will become apparent that "strong" Christians in the Young Adulthood stage have developed a faith that has become their own—a firsthand faith, rather than a secondhand, conventional faith. The core issue of this milestone centers on "Owning a Firsthand Faith." It appears that too many Christians get stuck rather than fully transitioning to the Young Adulthood stage of faith. Why do these believers plateau? The answer in part lies in the question "How do I get beyond conformity and the control of the group?" The challenge is to dare to be different. And daring to be different—in any era, in any aspect of life—calls for strength.

To better understand the meaning of the word *strong,* we will look at: 1) other New Testament passages; 2) the broad context of 1 John; 3) the context provided by the three milestones of Childhood; 4) the strong-weak paradox in 2 Corinthians 12:9–10; and 5) the usage of the word in Romans 14–15, a lengthy strong/weak passage. This five-part analysis will help us become strong in the Young Adulthood stage of faith.

People of Distinction

First, the word *strong* appears in many New Testament passages, as these verses illustrate: "binds the *strong* man (Matthew 12:29); "seeing the *strong* wind, he became afraid"(Matthew 14:30); "a *severe* famine occurred in that country" (Luke 15:14); "*loud* crying and tears" (Hebrews 5:7); "became *mighty* in war" (Hebrews 11:34); "the sound of *mighty* peals of thunder" (Revelation 19:6); "the *strong* city, Babylon" (Revelation 18:10). The word *strong*, also translated *mighty*, *loud*, and *severe*, sets apart whatever is being described. It is a demoniac whose inordinate, excessive strength needs the restraint of chains. It is a wind that is distinct among winds. It is not just crying but crying that stands out. It is not just an ordinary city but a special city that is notable or conspicuous.

So, for the apostle John, a strong Christian is one who is set apart from other believers, specifically from those still in the Childhood stage of faith. Strong Christians are determined not to be ordinary believers, satisfied with merely conforming to the status quo. Strong believers refuse to be mediocre and are instead committed to doing all they do with excellence for the Lord's glory and honor. Strong Christians are becoming distinct, prominent, extraordinary, brave, powerful, conspicuous, striking, and unique in their faith. They genuinely pursue being transformed into Christlikeness—and they won't settle for less.

Second, it seems reasonable to assume that the strong Christian has more thoroughly processed the five ingredients of authentic spirituality (see Chapter 4) than a Child in the faith has. Consider how those five aspects of spirituality, all mentioned in 1 John, flesh out the meaning of the word *strong*:

- A Friendship in Two Directions (1 John 1:1–4): Strong believers will have rich *koinonia* in both the vertical ("Jesus and me") and horizontal ("Jesus and we") dimensions of faith. Their experience of joy (1:4) is also likely to be fuller.
- Living Without Pretense (1:5–2:2): The strong have learned to relate to God and others without hiding behind facades, posing, or masquerading. Integrity and transparency

are essential to cultivating a rich friendship with a holy God and with others. Strong believers enjoy an intimate relationship with the Lord and with fellow believers based on His transforming grace and unconditional love, not on oughts and shoulds. Also, the strong are more apt to face their woundedness and sin rather than hide or ignore it.

- Evidence of Genuine Faith (2:3–11, 18–27): The strong have become practiced in the tests of obedience, in "walking as Jesus walked" (the vertical dimension of faith), in "loving as Jesus loved" (the horizontal dimension of faith), and in discernment—"seeing as Jesus sees" (recognizing the toxic influences of false teachings).
- Progress Through Three Stages of Spiritual Growth (2:12–14): The strong have progressed farther toward wholeness and Christlikeness than believers in the Childhood stage have. They are also gaining experience in following the map of the eight milestones of spiritual development.
- Enemies of Spiritual Growth (2:15–27): Strong believers are able to deal with counterfeits to deep and authentic faith, personal vulnerabilities, and lies that deter spiritual progress.

Third, strong Christians have attended to the three formative milestones of the Childhood stage of faith: they have addressed the core issues of self-concept, God-concept, and their relationships with others. The strong Christian has established a foundation on which to construct an increasingly holistic and personal faith. Having worked through Milestones #1, #2, and #3, strong Christians now have a healthy foundation on which to continue to build their faith. Commentator James Montgomery Boice expands that idea:

> Believers must learn that the forgiveness of sins and the knowledge of God which they have enjoyed from the initial moments of their conversion are not the sum total of Christianity. Rather

> they must seek to *grow strong* so that they may take their proper and needed place in the Christian warfare.[3]

Fourth, "young men" in the faith are God's "strong/weak" people because, in the Christian faith, strength has the paradoxical nature of recognizing its weaknesses.

> [The Lord] has said to me, "My grace is sufficient for you, for power is perfected in weakness." Most gladly, therefore, I will rather boast about my weaknesses, so that the power of Christ may dwell in me. Therefore I am well content with weaknesses, with insults, with distresses, with persecutions, with difficulties, for Christ's sake; for when I am weak, then I am *strong*."
>
> —2 Corinthians 12:9–10

Strong Christians acknowledge their need for God's restorative grace and empowerment, and they feel no need to wear masks in an effort to cover their weaknesses. They have learned not to masquerade or pretend that they have it all together and are doing just fine.

Fifth, the strong believers and the weak are fundamentally different from one another. The faith of the strong, for instance, is firsthand and owned rather than secondhand and borrowed. Strong believers have experienced an inner reorientation, and they have thought through their faith, perhaps rejecting longstanding beliefs and behaviors. They have learned to recognize and be free of petty differences in nonessential faith issues and personal matters of conscience.

In sharp contrast, weak believers expect everyone to regard nonessentials as essentials; they are weak, legalistic, and fearful. And they have left their beliefs and behaviors largely unexamined, allowing their beliefs and behaviors to be dictated by "What will other people think? Will I disappoint them?" Spiritual transformation that is genuine and lasting cannot be based on living up to other people's expectations in matters that are morally neutral. The strong extend grace to others, while the weak hurl criticism and cast blame.

Consider now the context of Paul's teaching in Romans 14 and 15. The early church in Rome consisted primarily of Gentile Christians; Jewish Christians were in the minority. But both groups had to deal with an important question about conformity: Would the Jewish Christians continue to conform to their deeply rooted, historical traditions and practices? According to Paul, the Gentile Christians did not need to conform to those Jewish ways, but what would that ruling mean for the fellowship? At stake in the church at Rome was much more than food taboos and which feast days to observe. Jewish Christians faced nothing less than a serious crisis of identity, and church unity was threatened.[4]

Born a Jew, Paul understood why Jewish Christians were alarmed by the idea of abandoning the very traditions that had given them their identity as God's chosen people. Laws governing their diet and the observance of the Sabbath were among the clearest boundary markers that set Jews apart from Gentiles. The Sabbath, with the accompanying profound devotion to this ancestral custom, had become a badge of ethnic identity. Paul, however, was also concerned about the harsh insensitivity of the Gentile Christians who did not understand either the Jewish customs or their value to the Jews.[5] These stronger, "liberal" believers regarded the scruples of the traditionalist Jews as tolerable but worthy of contempt. The weaker, "conservative" Jewish believers—fewer in number and lower in social and political standing—regarded the freer practice of the liberal Gentiles as completely intolerable. So, as Christianity, an essentially Jewish movement, began to develop its own distinctive character and identity, it had to confront these very sensitive issues. At issue was Christianity's earliest understanding of itself. Conformity for conformity's sake was not the solution for either the Jewish believers or the Gentile believers, all of whom who had a personal relationship with Jesus.

For this community, at this important crossroads, Paul addressed the question, "What should be the church's response to the minority opinion of the weaker Jewish believers?" Put differently and in timeless terms, "What should be the church's response to questions about conformity within the church?" That question is relevant not only for church bodies but also for individual believers. Will you choose to conform to the faith that you've grown up with, the faith that you've settled comfortably into, the faith that you've borrowed or adopted and that may be too dependent on the approval of other people—or will you examine your Christian values, identify essential and nonessential differences between yourself and fellow believers, and arrive at biblical convictions about your faith, convictions that you truly own? Choosing the latter can result in a personal crisis of introspection and profound wrestling with key issues, but the effort is worth it. As commentator F. F. Bruce said of Paul, who fully models the "strong" Christian for us, "Never was there a Christian more thoroughly emancipated from non-Christian inhibitions and taboos. So completely emancipated was he from spiritual bondage that he was not even in bondage to his emancipation."[6]

Faith at a Crossroads: Firsthand and Owned or Secondhand and Borrowed

In the Roman church, the weak in faith were being tripped up by their Jewish heritage and their cautious, scrupulous abstinence from the freedoms that Gentile believers enjoyed. As commentator James Stifler put it, they were "weak in their faith, but strong in scruples."[7] They put too much weight on the outward form they felt they needed to maintain as the covenant people (Romans 2:17–29) and on their status as the chosen people of Israel (13:14). An understanding of grace and the acceptance of God's unconditional love were not the basis of their lifestyle, worldview, or faith. Even today—and this has been true through the centuries—a weak Christian's faith is largely unexamined and secondhand. His or her beliefs and values are dependent upon the approval of other people. Christians can become dulled, cautious, stiff, and proper when the focus is on the question, "What will others think?" Author Charles Shelton described the danger like this:

> A reliance on significant others to such an extent that personally held beliefs and values are never consciously adopted or reflected upon. What arises is a truncated value system in which one

> simply "buys into" the values of others in his or her life who are admired.[8]

Consider what Paul wrote: "Accept the one who is weak in faith, but not for the purpose of passing judgment on his opinions" (Romans 14:1), and "let not him who eats regard with contempt him who does not eat" (verse 3). Paul's message is that the strong, although they are in the majority, should not seek to impose their views and practices on the weak; neither should the strong laugh at or despise the weak as narrow-minded and superstitious. Paul knew that the strong believers infuriated the weak who considered eating meat an immoral issue rather than an amoral one. He therefore told the strong, "Don't be angry at the weak over their convictions, ungrounded as they are, and don't be impatient with them. There is no room in the community of believers for contempt of the weak and their convictions. You who are strong cannot claim freedom for yourself without allowing freedom to the other."

Paul pointed out that the controversy is over mere "opinions" (verse 1) as opposed to key matters that Scripture clearly identifies as sin. Nonessentials had become flashpoints of division and controversy. The weak ascribed biblical authority to nonessentials, turning amoral issues (eating meat, days, diets) into moral issues. These nonessentials were ancillary aspects of the faith. The weak were defensive, inflexible, and exclusive.

Inevitably, believers will have different opinions on various issues. In his commentary on Romans, James Dunn reminds us that "boundary markers" define who is in the group and who is not.[8] Groups establish boundary markers to make such distinctions, but then the outward conformity to boundary markers too often substitutes for authentic transformation. Conformity masquerades as evidence of a changed life.

The Good News set forth in the Bible, however, is all about faith in Jesus, not faith *plus* special days and special practices and not faith *less* certain activities. Making a list of things to do in addition to believe or a list of things to refrain from if you believe results in a false definition of Christlikeness, a substitute for authentic change, and the façade of pseudo-transformation—and the same happens today. The Christian community should allow members the freedom, *within the limits of orthodox and biblical Christianity,* to embrace divergent views and different lifestyles. The Christian community should not find it necessary to achieve a common mind on every point of possible disagreement.

Paul, therefore, told the weak in the church at Rome and the weak among us today not to judge the strong. Neither are the weak to accuse—publicly or privately—the strong believers among them of compromise, spiritual indifference, or lack of discipline (verses 3–4). Likewise, the weak, given to acting as if they are superior to the strong, are not to criticize and condemn the strong as unscrupulous and irreverent. Nor are the weak to simply comply and imitate the strong. Instead, the weak are to accept the strong into the family of believers just as God Himself has. Rather than try to persuade the weak that their scruples are baseless in an attempt to avoid a schism, Paul encouraged the strong to let God continue to do His work in the hearts of weaker believers.

A Catalyst for Firsthand Faith: Strong Community

Paul knew that the weak in the church at Rome wanted to make their laws binding for all believers—to standardize and codify external conduct and certain behaviors into absolutes and so guarantee uniformity. That is not acceptable, but neither are the efforts of the strong to seek uniformity by forcing their insight on the weak. The Roman church was embroiled in conflict, and the believers were polarized. Commentator C. E. Cranfield summarizes this point: "If the strong should not try to force the weak into a frightening liberty where guidelines are far less clearly drawn, neither should the weak seek to restrict the strong within the limits of their own more tightly defined liberty."[9] The freedom that comes when people are accepted despite different opinions and behaviors is vital to healthy spiritual development, both corporate and personal.

Author Charles Swindoll captured the intent of this passage from Romans 14:

> If we genuinely desire to help fellow believers along in their transformation, we must set them free from demands—ours and anybody else's... We can allow them room to breathe, room to try new things (and fail!), room to discover for themselves what God would like to change. Without frowns and demands and the chatter of other believers to distract them, they will be freed to feel the tug of the Holy Spirit and then experience genuine, lasting growth.[10]

When Paul wrote to both the weak and the strong in the Roman church, he emphasized the important distinctives of a Christian community: "So we who are many, are one body in Christ, and individually members of one another... Let love be without hypocrisy... Be devoted to one another in brotherly love... Be of the same mind toward one another... Be at peace with all men" (Romans 12:5, 10, 16, 18). The Christian community is to function like a greenhouse and optimize the growth of the individual members. The strong and the weak are to accept and welcome one another. This acceptance cannot be conditional, even when substantial differences of opinion exist, and there can be no forced conformity in the Christian community.

Another Catalyst for Firsthand Faith: The Lordship of Christ

Paul knew the difference between doing something to conform to an external convention and doing something as a result of internal conviction. He therefore urged the strong and the weak alike to be "fully convinced in [their] own mind[s]" about their faith and their actions (14:5, 22). The faith of the weak is largely unexamined, so Paul emphasized the responsibility of each believer to arrive at his/her own values, beliefs, and convictions about amoral issues, but Paul was also clear about the parameters. Paul did not simply demand that the weak comply to his arguments or to the arguments of the strong (with whom he sided). Instead, Paul encouraged the believers to establish relationships characterized by love, edification, and mutual accountability. This kind of accepting and affirming environment can foster genuine spiritual growth. This kind of dynamic Christian community can empower individuals to explore issues for themselves and make their own decisions. A Christian community should definitely support the believer's conformity to Christ, but it should never coerce conformity to the group's expectations. In such a community, believers are able to work out the tension between independence and interdependence.

So what can believers do to move away from a borrowed, secondhand faith? An answer lies in Romans 14, where nine times, in verses 4–11, Paul referred to Jesus as "Lord." We Christians are to determine our personal convictions based on the ultimate approval of the Lord because, after all, "we are the Lord's" (verse 8). With this statement, Paul took both the strong and the weak believers back to the fundamental issue of their personal relationship with the Lord. Controversial issues are not to be settled by relying on other people's opinions or conforming to group pressure. God is the ultimate Judge and the only Audience that matters. All of our Christian beliefs and values are to be determined by the answer to the question, "What does the Lord think?" rather than, "What do others think?"

A Third Catalyst to Firsthand Faith: The Judgment Seat of God

Paul has noted two catalysts to faith that run counter to the forces of conformity and secondhand faith. In Romans 14:10–12, Paul introduces a third catalyst: the future "judgment seat of God" before which "each one of us [the strong as well as the weak] will give an account of himself to God" (2 Corinthians 5:10; 1 Corinthians 3:12–15). Our future judgment should shape our present convictions, and it is this shift of authority, this recognition of God's supreme authority over us, which is critical to our becoming a strong believer. Strong Christians realize that they are ultimately accountable to God rather than to the authority and approval of others. The strong live by a higher calling: to please God.

At that future judgment, we will not only be asked whether or not we received Jesus Christ as our Lord and Savior (the basis of our salvation) but also *how* we were a Christian—*how* we came to own our beliefs and behaviors. Do I merely comply with the conventional status quo of my denomination or a certain faith hero? Will I modify my today, knowing I will stand before Him in the future? Learning to personally practice this third catalyst will have a huge impact on weak and strong believers, and this transformation is the agenda of believers in Milestone #4.

The Whims of the Weak

That said, are strong believers to, in an effort to be at peace with fellow Christians, accommodate their behavior to the wishes of the weak and thereby be shackled by the lack of understanding and insight these less-mature believers have? Put differently, are the strong to avoid conflicts at all costs and ask about their every action, "What will others—what will weaker, younger believers—think?" Paul was aware that the weak can manipulate the strong and suffocate the liberty available to them in Christ. Commentator Anders Nygren explained it this way: "It often happens that in his very weakness he has an effective weapon for making the circumstances comply with his view. Not infrequently it is the weak who is the real tyrant. In his judgment of others he finds a compensation for his weakness."[11]

Paul's words aimed at the weak members of the church at Rome were blunt, direct, and overdue: "Grow up! Focus on the essentials of the Christian faith, not nonessentials. Stop being defensive and so easily offended. As you examine and revise your beliefs and behaviors, and as you transfer your allegiance to the Lord and His Word rather than to some group, know that you are loved and valued in the body of Christ."

Writing to strong believers as well as weak ones, Paul said this: "Let us not judge one another anymore, but rather determine this—not to put an obstacle or a stumbling block in a brother's way" (verse 13). All of us who claim Jesus as Lord need to be considerate of our brothers and sisters, and we are wise to try to see issues from their point of view. But Paul was not calling strong Christians to give in to the whims of the weak. Neither was he merely concerned about the strong disappointing or hurting the feelings of the weak. Instead, Paul called believers to resist the temptation to insist on one's rights and on the primacy of one's own convictions.

Responsible love in the Christian community means living with sensitivity to one another and helping fellow believers grow in their faith. Such love seeks to understand another person's perspective. Paul therefore urged strong and weak believers alike to consider the needs of others rather than insisting on their own personal rights. Believers are to be open to ideas different from their own. Paul called Christians in Rome—and God uses his words to call us today—to "pursue the things which make for peace and the building up of one another" (verse 19), but this peace is not to be achieved by merely avoiding friction or keeping quiet about important matters.

Paul opened Romans 15 with further instructions for the strong: "Now we who are strong ought to bear the weaknesses of those who are without strength and not just please ourselves. Let each of us please his neighbor for his good, to his edification" (verses 1–2). The strong are not to just wait for the immature to catch up to where they are. The strong are to intentionally reach out and build relationships with their weaker brothers and sisters in Christ. Again, Paul was addressing strong believers who "are full of goodness, filled with all knowledge, and able to admonish one another" (verse 14). This ability to admonish one another suggests that more than superficial relationships exist here. Paul called believers then and now to talk to one another in order to resolve differences. This process enables people to clarify issues, increase mutual understanding, and communicate unconditional love; thereby encouraging spiritual growth and authentic Christian community.

In summary, strong Young Adult Christians have developed a faith that has become their own. They are living out a firsthand faith rather than a secondhand, conventional faith. At Milestone #4, these believers have addressed the issues reflected in these basic questions: "Why do you believe and behave as you do?" and "To what degree are your beliefs and values largely determined by the approval of other people?" A Christian's beliefs cannot be dictated by parents, a pastor, a denominational statement of faith, a peer group, or a faith hero and truly be firsthand, owned, and yours! Strong Christians have clarified and owned the biblical values and beliefs that will guide their journeys of faith. They have learned to stand alone and confidently in their faith.

Milestone #5: Linking Truth and Life

Milestone #5 is based on the promise of 1 John 2:14, "I am writing to you, young men, because the Word of God abides in you." The core issue of this milestone is linking God's truth to everyday life. To grow spiritually, believers need to allow God's Word to transform them—their heart, their thinking, their lives, their daily experiences in the world. These Christians move beyond merely receiving head knowledge from the Bible to applying its truth to life. The Word of God resides in and has a centering influence on those believers who have begun the lifelong work of Milestones #1–4.

The Greek word for *abide* (*menō*) is used twenty-two times in 1 John and eight times in John 15. *Abide* means "to settle down, be at home, remain." The present tense of the word implies learning that lasts a lifetime, suggesting constancy and steadiness. In *The Dictionary of New Testament Theology*, *abide* is used of place, meaning "to remain, to stay in a place, lodge, dwell, sojourn (Luke 19:5); not to depart, not to leave, to continue to be present." Figuratively, *abide* also communicates the idea of holding fast, of "remaining steadfast, continually, permanently; or to stand firm, pass the test."[12] To abide is to "remain, last, persist, continue to live." In the present tense, *abide* denotes a continuous, enduring, personal communion. [13]

Young Adults in the faith have understood John's five elements of spiritual growth (recall Chapter 4), including obedience to God (moral test of obedience) and love for the brethren (relational test of love), and they are using the knowledge (doctrinal test of discernment). They are applying the teachings of God's Word to real-life situations: His truth is directing their experiences, shaping their values, and guiding their judgments. God's Word is informing the Young Adult's behaviors, not just his/her beliefs.

The text of 1 John 2:12–14 clearly reveals the sequential process preceding Milestone #5. First, the three Childhood milestones must be attended to and nurtured. In Milestone #1, the Christian obeys God's Word, certain of His love and forgiveness, experiencing a renewed identity, and free of legalism and oughts. In Milestone #2, the believer obeys, not to earn acceptance or because a perfectionistic God will punish disobedience. The believer has discarded such myths and caricatures of God. Believers obey because they love God. In Milestone #3, a believer counts on the support and challenges of others who long to be shaped by the Word. Then, in Milestone #4, believers are moving away from obeying and believing just because obedience and faith are expected; they are also moving away from copycat conforming to others. These four milestones are preparatory to God's Word abiding in the strong Christian.

J. I. Packer wrote about the purpose of this abiding and of God's revelation of Himself in the Scriptures being fundamental in the life of a strong believer. Packer's words clarify that abiding involves a relationship; it is far more than merely knowing. He states:

> Why has God spoken? The truly staggering answer which the Bible gives to this question is that God's purpose in revelation is to make friends with us. It was to this end that He created us rational beings, bearing His image, able to think and hear and speak and love; He wanted there to be genuine personal affection and friendship, two-sided, between Himself and us—a relation, not like between a man and a dog, but like that of a father and a son, or a husband and a wife. Loving friendship between two persons has no ulterior motive; it is an end in itself. And this is God's end in revelation. He speaks to us simply to fulfill the purpose for which we were made; that is to bring into being a relationship in which He is a friend to us, and we to Him, He finding His joy in giving us gifts and we finding ours in giving Him thanks.[14]

Abiding is not to be mistaken for accumulating abstract doctrine or gaining a merely cognitive understanding of the Christian faith. Such efforts do not lead to mature Parenthood in the faith, to wholeness, or to Christlikeness. Factual knowledge of God is incomplete without experiential knowledge of Him. Genuine Christian faith is grounded in the Bible and lived out in the day-to-day world.

Therefore, at Milestone #5, Christians will experience, not merely accept, the truth of God's Word. Christians will become competent at thinking in a distinctively Christian way and living according to a distinctively Christian worldview. The Scriptures will progressively define, modify, and order the believer's world. In the Young Adulthood stage of faith, believers move beyond simply knowing about Scripture to integrating God's Word into a Christian lifestyle and letting it gradually transform their whole person. In the first century, the heretical teachers intended to deceive and mislead the Christians (1 John 2:26). Today, Christians will also learn to better recognize and resist counterfeits that oppose or would diminish their faith (1 John 2:18–27; 4:1–4; 5:4, 5). Discerning believers notice anything inaccurate or artificial about the horizontal and vertical dimensions of their faith. For believers at this Young Adulthood stage, the Word of God gives the ultimate perspective and insight into reality; it presents life as He means it to be lived.

Obedience: Seeing Jesus Despite His Absence

The night before Jesus was crucified, He assured His eleven faithful disciples that their relationship with Him would continue even though He would physically die. He said, "In My Father's house are many dwelling places… I go to prepare a place for you" (John 14:2). He also said, "If anyone loves Me, he will keep My word; and My Father will love him, and We will come to him, and make Our abode with him" (John 14:23). The Greek word for *dwelling place* and *abode* is one and the same. The twofold truth expressed in these verses is, first, the fact that Jesus (interestingly, a carpenter by trade) was returning to heaven to prepare a residence for His disciples to inhabit with Him in the future. Jesus' absence from His people would be temporary—and what a reunion and homecoming await His disciples!

Jesus also wants to craft a residence within the earthly life of every believer. What does Jesus do to prepare such an abode in His followers? Jesus explained it this way:

> He who has My commandments and keeps them, he it is who loves Me; and he who loves Me will be loved by My Father, and I will love him, and will *disclose Myself to him.*
>
> —John 14:21

Though Jesus is physically gone, as we obey His Word, He settles down and makes Himself at home in us. Obedient believers therefore experience new insights into the love of the Father and His Son, as well as fresh revelations of Jesus. Milestone #5 is all about developing this intimate relationship so that, despite Jesus' physical absence from this earth, you are still in an exciting, dynamic relationship with Him. At Milestone #5, believers experience God's Word firsthand as it makes the fourteen-inch journey from the head to the heart.

Faith as a Noun and Faith as a Verb

We will now consider two dimensions of knowing: objective and subjective, the head and the heart. It is imperative for the Christ-follower to both recognize this distinction and understand the relationship between the two kinds of knowledge. A word of caution: We cannot neglect or overemphasize either dimension without experiencing toxic side effects. The two must be kept in balance as we live out a truly authentic Christian faith. When our head knowledge and our heart knowledge are in balance, knowing God is very real and very exciting.

First, one dimension—the objective dimension of knowing—focuses on the content of a biblically informed faith. This is faith viewed as a *noun*: the *what* of faith ("My commandments" [John 14:21], "My word" [John 14:23]). The Christian's faith is definitely based on God's revealed, propositional truth, on His commandments and His Word. God's truth as revealed in Scripture is to serve as the framework of a biblical spirituality, but the goal is not mere information. The goal of this kind of knowing is transformation.

Two additional passages describe this faith as a noun: "... constantly nourished on *the words of the faith* and of *the sound doctrine* which you have been following" (1 Timothy 4:6) and "I felt the necessity to write to you appealing that you contend earnestly for *the faith which was once for all handed down to the saints*" (Jude 3).

In addition to the objective dimension of knowing is the experiential or subjective and personal side of knowing; this kind of knowing focuses on owning one's faith and applying it to the particulars of life. This knowledge comes as a result of lived experience. This is faith viewed as a *verb*: the *why* and *how* of faith ("has My commandments and keeps them" [John 14:21]).

Here are three other verses that reflect the reality of faith as a verb: "[Abraham] did not waver in unbelief but *grew strong in faith*, giving glory to God" (Romans 4:20); "*fight the good fight of faith*" (1 Timothy 6:12); and "*your faith is greatly enlarged,* and the love of each one of you toward one another *grows even greater*" (2 Thessalonians 1:3).

Note carefully that verses 21 and 23 tie both dimensions of knowing together. Although He will be absent from the disciples, Jesus will reveal Himself, show Himself, make Himself known to them experientially—and to anyone else who shows a love for Jesus by obeying Him. Don't miss this! Although Jesus is physically absent right now, preparing a future home for us, He is also within each believer, preparing a place for Himself. He promises that, as we choose to follow His commandments and obey His Word, He will reveal Himself in a unique way to assure us that we are loved and that we will get a fresh, firsthand glimpse of Him.

Anointed: The Holy Spirit as Tutor

The Holy Spirit is actively involved in a believer's spiritual growth. John the apostle explained it this way: "You have an anointing from the Holy One… The anointing which you received from Him abides in you, and you have no need for anyone to teach you; but as His anointing teaches you about all things …" (1 John 2:20, 27). Just as Old Testament kings and priests were anointed to fulfill their roles in God's kingdom, every single New Testament believer—and that includes you and me—is anointed with the Holy Spirit at the moment of salvation, and He plays a crucial role in our spiritual growth. One of His responsibilities, for instance, is to be every believer's Resident Tutor. Note that John was *not* saying that Christians don't need teachers. After all, John himself was teaching with these very words! John was, however, emphasizing that believers don't need to rely only on others to learn God's truth, understand His Word, and apply it to life. Our Resident Tutor helps us to discover both the meaning and the application of the Scriptures.

Believers in the Young Adulthood stage of faith come to be governed by the Scriptures; they stop looking to the group or to a significant other as their primary authority. Most importantly, head knowledge and heart knowledge are coming into greater balance, and knowing God is very real and very exciting.

In Milestone #5, the core issue is that God's Word becomes internalized and is the centering, orienting influence for all that believers do. If believers neglect this milestone, their spiritual life will be that of secondhand orthodoxy, without personal ownership. One would merely accept God's truth rather than experience its power. The lordship of Jesus Christ would merely be a matter of cognition and creed, without passion and action. At Milestone #5, the Scriptures increasingly transform, not just inform believers; God's Word increasingly defines, modifies, and orders the Christian's world. Moving beyond merely receiving biblical information to experiencing personal transformation, beyond knowing about God's truth to truly applying it to real life, is what Milestone #5 is all about.

Milestone #6: Defeating the Enemies of Spiritual Progress

The biblical source of Milestone #6 is 1 John 2:13, 14: "I am writing to you, young men, because you have overcome the evil one." At this milestone, believers come to understand the lethal strategy of their three archenemies—the world, the flesh, and the devil—and how to successfully recognize and stand strong against each. Knowing that healthy spiritual growth is impaired by neglecting or inadequately completing the milestones of spiritual development, the believer will continue to work on the milestones they attack. The title of Milestone #6 is therefore "Defeating the Enemies of Spiritual Progress."

Milestone #4 challenges believers to move past merely conforming to the beliefs and behaviors of others who matter to a faith that is personally owned and that informs one's life. Milestone #5 focuses on the centering and transforming influence of God's Word. Key to linking God's Word to everyday life (Milestone #5) is having worked on Milestone #4 as well as having attended to Milestones #1–#3. Otherwise, the potential impact of Milestone #5 will be minimized.

And one reason for that—perhaps the metaphor is startling—is that spiritual growth truly is a battle. The conflict outlined here is inevitable, and it is not a result of a lack of faith. Three enemies are working to sabotage every believer's journey at every stage of faith. The world, the flesh, and the devil compete for the Christian's loyalties, energy, and trust. These three deadly enemies conspire to block the growth that can be sparked by working through the 1 John milestones. Threatening purity as well as progress, these perverse enemies strive to thwart spiritual growth in the Childhood and Young Adulthood stages, thus curtailing the formation of mature, seasoned, mentoring Parents in the faith.

None of a Christian's opponents, however, is omnipotent or unbeatable. With courage rooted in the Lord and trusting in His power, believers can boldly confront any challenge that comes their way and continue to grow toward wholeness and Christlikeness. The apostle John neither sensationalized nor minimized spiritual warfare in our Christian life, and he also made it clear that spiritual growth is never automatic.

The perfect tense *have overcome* does not mean that the battle is already over, but rather that the believers stand assured of victory. They have overcome in Christ, and that overcoming continues in the present. The word for *overcome* comes from the Greek word *nike*, which appears as the logo on our athletic gear and means "victory." As commentator Henry Alford remarks, "Whatever conflict remains for them afterwards, is with a baffled and conquered enemy."[15]

John Stott adds the following about the young men in conflict who are overcoming areas where sin's power has been present:

> The young men are busily involved in the battle of Christian living. The Christian life, then, is not just enjoying the forgiveness and

> the fellowship of God, but fighting the enemy. The forgiveness of past sins must be followed by deliverance from sin's present power, justification followed by sanctification. So in both messages to the young men it is asserted that they have overcome (NEB, "mastered") the evil one. Their conflict has become a conquest.[16]

Mentioned earlier, the three archenemies of spiritual growth and wholeness are identified in 1 John 2:15–17 as the world, the flesh, and the devil. These opponents conspire to detain the growth of the Child, Young Adult, and Parent at each step of the spiritual journey. The believer is never too mature to be seduced; there can be no vacation from the struggle of spiritual growth. This trinity of evil conspires to lure every pilgrim off the path toward wholeness and Christlikeness. The battle is waged within the believer's heart (the flesh) as well as by forces outside the individual (the world system and the devil). Together, these enemies—that may actually transcend one's awareness—powerfully shape ideas and guide actions. At every step of the journey, Christians must be alert to any forces that have been or would be injurious. Again, these enemies do not limit their activities to the Young Adulthood stage of faith; yet at this stage, believers become experienced in identifying and countering those opponents.

Enemy #1: The World—Programmed to Conform

Six times in two verses (2:15–16), the word *kosmos* (the world) appears. This word has been defined as "the life of human society as organized under the power of evil." *Kosmos* refers to the present culture and age, with its values, goals, attitudes, models, messages, and lifestyles apart from God. Held in the grip of the evil one (1 John 5:19), this world system does not know the Lord (1 John 3:1) and, consequently, hates His followers (John 15:18–21; 17:14). The essential mark of the world system is the distortion of the value of created goods and legitimate needs. The New English Bible says, "Do not set your hearts on the godless world or anything in it" (1 John 2:15). Robert Law wrote, "Do not court the intimacy and the favor of the unchristian world around you; do not take its customs for your laws, nor adopt its ideals, nor covet its prizes, nor seek fellowship with its life."[17] C. S. Lewis warned, "Enemy occupied territory—that is what the world is."[18]

Christians are not to love this world or things in this world system because love for the world and love for the Father are totally incompatible. Three succinct phrases describe the nature of the world system: "the lust of the flesh and the lust of the eyes, and the boastful pride of life." Furthermore, Christians are not to love the world because every aspect of it is transitory, passing away, and headed for destruction. Only the person who does the will of God remains forever (1 John 2:17).

No wonder God is uncompromising in His command to not love the world (1 John 2:15). We Christians are to love God (2:5) and our brothers and sisters in the Lord (2:10), but we are not to love the world. We Christians are to resist the powerful influences of its fleeting values and instead embrace the eternal values of God. Consider T. S. Eliot's epitaph for those people who, deeming spiritual matters irrelevant, choose to love the world:

> Here were a decent godless people:
> Their only monument the asphalt road
> And a thousand lost golf balls.

Through the process of socialization or enculturation, we thoughtlessly absorb the values and perspectives of our culture, and we are powerfully shaped—and misshaped—by them. Sin becomes entrenched in our lives. The secular world system conditions us and even programs us to conform to its ways; it desensitizes, entangles, entices, pollutes, and distracts us. The growing Christian must therefore rely on the truth revealed in Scriptures in order to recognize and stand strong against the culture's many counterfeits.

In the West, for instance, we battle the influences of an increasingly secular culture that values achievement (status), acquisition (affluence), appearance, and self-sufficiency. In our pluralistic culture, we face postmodern moral relativism (the stance that there are no truths that apply in every situation, in every place, and to every person), its virtue of tolerance, and its commitment to rationalism. These warped and twisted values—and the pressure to conform to them—compete with God's truth, numb our need for Him, muffle His voice, and often derail our progress toward maturity and Christlikeness. The Young Adult, however, is skilled at identifying these seductive and toxic influences.

Enemy #2: The Flesh—Chronic Dissatisfaction

The Bible offers countless illustrations of man's twisted, tangled, insidious human nature, and God's commands are intended to help the believer curb any instinct-driven habits. The biblical writers knew that each of us can be energized by evil desires and motives and guided by distorted ideas about God, His world, and ourselves—the "trinity of evil." Enemy #1 (the world) and enemy #2 (our radically sinful nature) capitalize on that fact and conspire with enemy #3 (the devil) to block spiritual growth and compete for the control of our lives. This enemy strategy is aimed at the chronic and sinful dissatisfaction within the believer's soul.

In the Young Adulthood stage of faith, believers become skilled at countering the urge to acquire ("the lust of the eyes"), the pursuit of sensual pleasure ("the lust of the flesh"), and the desire for recognition ("the boastful pride of life"). The Greek word for *lust* (*epithumia*) means "strong desire" and suggests compulsions, indulgent habits, urges, hungerings, and longings too strong to resist—without the Lord's help. All believers will encounter sensual temptations that could become an addiction and deprive them of inner freedom and joy. Puritan preacher Jonathan Edwards referred to these as "fondest lusts." The delusion is that we need and deserve more, that we will be happy when we have more or when our circumstances are better. Spiritual maturity means facing the reality that the fulfillment of all of one's appetites does not mean satisfaction in life. John analyzed the ideals that are accepted and even prized in the world but are antithetical to Christianity. To love God is to move away from such values. To love the world is to drift increasingly away from love for God and thereby also lose love for others.

- "The lust of the eyes"—or "I want what I see"—refers to the desire for *acquisitional* pleasure. It is easy to be captivated by outward appearances and the desirability of material things. But wants become needs, and possessions become deified. Lust of the eyes is "the tendency to be captivated by the outward show of things, without inquiring into their real values."[19] It includes "the love of beauty divorced from the love of goodness."[20]
- "The lust of the flesh"—or "I want what feels good"—refers to the desire for *sensual* pleasure. Fueled by hormones and compulsive instincts, the lust of the flesh leads to self-indulgence. The focus is on gratifying legitimate needs in illegitimate ways.
- "The boastful pride of life"—or "I want to be first, and I better be anything but last!"—reflects the desire for *recognitional* pleasure. The goal is not so much keeping up with the Joneses as getting ahead of them; this pride is evidence in one's boasting about all that one has and all that one does. A desire to be significant can easily lead to drivenness, the tyranny to excel, and narcissism. This attitude fosters self-promotion and self-exaltation by individuals striving for achievement, power, prestige, and status.

In *The Pursuit of God,* A. W. Tozer wrote this prayer:

> Father, I want to know Thee, but my coward heart fears to give up its toys. I cannot part with them without inward bleeding, and I do not try to hide from Thee the terror of the parting. I come trembling, but I do come. Please root from my heart all those things which I have cherished so long and which have become a very part of my living self, so that Thou mayest enter and dwell there without a rival. Then shalt Thou make the place of Thy feet glorious. Then shall my heart have no need of the sun to shine in it, for Thyself will be the light of it, and there shall be no night. In Jesus' name, Amen.[21]

Enemy #3: The Devil—The Architect of Deception

The "evil one" (2:13) is the vicious, injurious, and destructive devil, the pernicious mastermind behind the forces of the world (conformity) and the flesh (chronic dissatisfaction). Satan's lies and deceptions are designed to keep believers from ever becoming mature Parents in the faith.

During the Young Adulthood stage of faith, believers become more skilled at recognizing and overcoming rivals to Christlikeness. In 2:18–27, John warned of this dark presence of antichrists active in this "last hour," who are "trying to deceive you" (1 John 2:26). These heretical teachers are prompted by the evil one.

Clearly, spiritual growth is a long journey toward the goal of becoming "like Christ" (1 John 3:2), and these three enemies do all they can to jeopardize a believer's journey toward spiritual maturity and wholeness. That's why these enemies are the focus of the final milestone of Young Adulthood. Spiritual growth can be impaired and delayed by the world and the devil as well as by one's own flesh. These enemies never stop whispering to us that we will be happier if we could just have a little more, and this often-urgent drive and accompanying sense of dissatisfaction cause believers needless suffering and joylessness. And, tragically, in this war, there is no ceasefire, no truce, no time out, and there are no prisoners.

Furthermore, these enemies are with us wherever we are on the journey toward spiritual wholeness; no believer is ever too mature to be seduced by them. Christians can take no vacation from the struggle against these ever-present and very motivated adversaries! At every step of our journeys, and in every stage of our growth, these rivals conspire to block the Childhood milestones of the Birth of Faith, the Young Adulthood milestones of the Ownership of Faith, and the Parenthood milestones of Modeling Faith. Since spiritual growth is never automatic, it is essential that we identify our own particular vulnerabilities, hurts, habits, and hungerings. Then we can more easily and more fully yield to God's presence, power, and purposes.

The Young Adulthood Stage of Faith: Reviewing the Milestones

The following summary presents the core issues of each of the three important milestones of the Young Adulthood stage of faith as well as the consequences of neglecting or only partially completing any of these three milestones.

In Milestone #4, the believer is self-governing and determining his or her own values and beliefs apart from people who are deemed important but whose ideas may be different. The believer will continue to need the support and challenge of other believers, but he or she is no longer dependent on them to dictate what to believe or to approve of his or her beliefs or decisions. Having examined one's faith, the believer now owns it. Believers who neglect Milestone #4 remain weak Christians, motivated primarily by the need to conform and the desire to win the approval of people who are deemed significant. Critical thinking skills stay un- or at least underdeveloped, and obedience to God remains mechanical, obligatory, and burdensome.

In Milestone #5, God's Word has become internalized and is the centering, orienting influence for all that this person does. The believer's walk has become congruent with his/her talk. Christians who neglect this milestone live an orthodox life rather than a vibrant life that incarnates Christ's presence. These believers merely accept God's truth rather than experience its power. The lordship of Jesus Christ remains merely a matter of cognition and creed rather than the foundation for life.

In Milestone #6, the believer is well aware that spiritual growth occurs on a battleground. The powerful forces of the world, the flesh, and the devil seek to conform and condition each Christian, but at this Milestone #6, the believer learns to recognize and overcome each of these enemies. Christians who neglect this milestone will be unprepared, unprotected, and quite vulnerable to the enemies' strategies in the spiritual battle that is unavoidable in this world.

Questions for Reflection and Action

Milestone #4: *Owning a Firsthand Faith*

1. Look again at this statement: "Separation and attachment ... remain in dynamic tension throughout a believer's journey toward Christlikeness. After all, the purpose of community is neither conformity (we all believe and behave alike) nor obsessive reliance on others (we let others think for us). In healthy relationships, we are liberated to come into our own internalized, biblical faith." When have you experienced this tension between separation and attachment? What spiritual growth can this tension prompt?
2. Explain how—by God's grace—community, the lordship of Christ, and the judgment seat act as catalysts for firsthand faith. Comment too on when you have seen or, better yet, experienced each catalyst prompting your own spiritual growth.

Milestone #5: *Linking Truth and Life*

1. In what ways, if any, are faith as a noun and faith as a verb out of balance in your Christian life? What are the consequences of that imbalance? What specific step will you take this week to try to get the two more in balance?

Milestone #6: *Defeating the Enemies of Spiritual Progress*

1. Comment on the aptness of this metaphor of war. Why do believers not need to fear the battle? What encouragement did you find in the discussion of this battle (pages 121–122)?
2. The world, the flesh, and the devil—which of these enemies of your spiritual growth is/are currently most pressing? What can you do to stand strong against it/them? Be specific, and be sure to take action.

CHAPTER 7

THE PARENTHOOD STAGE OF SPIRITUAL GROWTH

WHAT DOES SPIRITUAL maturity look like? Where is this lifelong journey of faith taking the Christian? What is the ultimate goal of growing in one's faith? What fruit will these stages of faith and their respective milestones bear? John's model of faith development offers solid answers to such probing questions.

The Goal of Spiritual Growth: Full-Grown Faith

In the New Testament, the Greek term *teleios* refers to a mature or perfect faith (see Ephesians 4:13; Philippians 3:12, 15; Hebrews 5:14; 6:1). *Teleios* means completed growth, full development, and the fulfilling of one's potential or purpose to the point of lacking nothing. As faith matures and spiritual development progresses, holiness and wholeness merge. At this point, faith is reaching its fullness. Believers are living according to their purpose in the Lord and attaining to some degree the God-given goal of their existence: they have become more like Christ. Again, Parenthood in the faith is the stage where wholeness and holiness merge.

The journey of faith, the process of maturing in one's Christian walk, begins at salvation and ends on the other side of the grave, with the believer's glorification. It is important to understand, however, that there are two dimensions to spiritual maturity—the relative dimension and the absolute dimension. *Relative or progressive maturity* is the maturity that comes as we increasingly become "like Him" in the here and now. During our days on earth, God molds us more and more into Jesus' likeness; and, anticipating His return, we who are His children cooperate with that process. The apostle John spoke to this truth: "Everyone who has this hope fixed on Him purifies himself just as He is pure" (1 John 3:3). This growth is a process: "We are being transformed" (2 Corinthians 3:18) in stages from Childhood, to Young Adulthood, to Parenthood in the faith (1 John 2:12–14).

Absolute or ultimate maturity is complete likeness to Jesus, and that is the ultimate destiny of every believer. Through the apostle John, God promises us this glorification: "Beloved, now we are children of God, and it has not appeared as yet what we will be. We know that, when He appears, *we will be like Him*, because we shall see Him just as He is" (1 John 3:2). Believers are predestined to this likeness (Romans 8:29). Our friendship with God and our likeness to His Son will be consummated at either our death or the Second Coming of Christ (2 Corinthians 5:18).

Based on 1 John 2:12–14, Table 4 shows the two milestones of the Parenthood stage of faith. Given at each milestone is its "Biblical Source" (ensuring its origin in John's writing), "Biblical

Truths" (to be embraced by the Christian), and an "Outcome" that describes the milestone's primary purpose.

Table 4: John's Parenthood Stage of Faith

Milestone	Biblical Source	Biblical Truths	Outcome
#7	"I am writing to you, fathers ..." (1 John 2:13–14)	Mature model, procreating and guiding other believers	Empowering Others
#8	"I am writing to you, fathers, because you know Him who has been from the beginning." (1 John 2:13–14)	Full-grown faith, longstanding obedience	Seasoned by Time and Experience

Around 95 A.D., the aged apostle John wrote to a first-century church in which some people had known Christ for as long as sixty years. These aged, experienced, seasoned veterans in the faith had become the fathers or Parents in the faith and, in some ways, had become like the heavenly Father. Such experiential knowledge of the faith comes only with much experience of walking with the Lord—with the intensity, not just extensity of years. Salvation has progressed since Childhood, through the rigorous Young Adulthood stage, and now into a deep fellowship with God. A believer is now mature and wise. John wrote that the fathers "know Him who has been from the beginning," wording that gives the impression that these believers have been Christians a long time and, in that sense, are both older than and more spiritually mature than other believers.[1]

Pateres ("father") is a word always used with respect for the age of the person being addressed. John was writing people who were physically aged and spiritually mature, older believers who had a longstanding experience with God.[2] (The biblical term *fathers* will be changed to *parents* throughout this book in order to include both male and female readers.)

If the young men are between twenty-four and forty years of age, these fathers or Parents in the faith would likely be older than forty. The age distinctions are not exact, but neither are they arbitrary or fanciful. The point to be noted is that spiritual depth, seasoned maturity, greater likeness to Christ, and wisdom come with time and experience in walking with the Lord. This long-term process cannot be avoided or recklessly accelerated.

Although he addressed these fathers twice, John did not change his statement. As E. H. Hiebert observed, John's "assurance concerning their mature knowledge only needed reemphasis. As mature believers, they could not afford to relax their spiritual growth."[3] Similarly, John Stott recognized that the fathers are "the spiritually adult in the congregation. Their first flush of ecstasy in receiving forgiveness and fellowship with the Father was an experience of long ago. Even the battles of the young men are past. The fathers have progressed into a deep communion with God."[4] These fathers in the faith have come to recognize that no accomplishment in this life transcends knowing Christ intimately and empowering others to do so as well. These two eternal values govern the life of Parents in the faith.

The following authors have discerned vital clues about believers who are in the Parenthood stage of faith. (Each of these references also was presented in Chapter 2.)

Table 5: Parents in the Faith

John Stott	"Fathers possess the depth and stability of ripe Christian experience."
Guy King	"Some [believers] have grown in spiritual stature to be as fathers."
W.E. Vine	"Fathers refers to those who have been Christians the longest and have the deepest, ripest, and most mature development. They are the older men in the heavenly family; those who by reason of experience are looked up to for sympathy, guidance, and assistance."

Robert Law	"Finally ... to arrive at the sure perception of the everlasting, in union with whom our human life and its results become an eternal and blessed reality—such is the curriculum which St. John maps out for human experience."
August Van Ryn	"Fathers in spiritual growth have reached the stage where the Lord Jesus Christ fills their vision, and so no warning is needed or given them."
Arthur Pink	"There are three degrees of the 'stature of Christ' reached by believers in this life, though the highest of them falls very short of that which shall pertain to them in the life to come."
F. F. Bruce	"The threefold grouping relates to spiritual maturity, not years reckoned by the calendar. Even if, in the Christian third generation, there was a growing tendency for spiritual maturity and natural age to coincide, nevertheless, it is spiritual experience that is emphasized."
James Boice	"The fathers have acquired the gift of spiritual wisdom, having lived longer in the faith and thus having come to know Him who is from the beginning in a deeper way."

Milestone #7: Empowering Others

The biblical source for Milestone #7 is 1 John 2:13–14 ("I am writing to you, fathers ..."). Living out the biblical truths of this milestone, Parents will assume the God-given responsibility to care for and guide in spiritual matters other members of His family, offering experience from their own spiritual journeys and directed by the core issues of the other milestones. The Parents will work to acquire the skills needed to effectively impact others toward Christlikeness and wholeness. The outcome is a title that encapsulates the meaning and purpose of this milestone—"Empowering Others."

As with Milestone #3, Milestone #7 is not supported exegetically to the same degree as other milestones are, nor is it preceded by a "because" clause in the biblical text. Consider, then, the basis for this seventh milestone.

To start, *fathers* is not simply a term for the older male members of a church, since chronological age alone does not guarantee spiritual progress or indicate how much one has grown spiritually. Van Gorden suggests that the term *fathers* implies that these men were "believers in Christ who themselves had grown in grace and had begotten children in the gospel."[5] Larry Richards notes that "in biblical times, the father guarded and provided for his family. But his primary responsibility was to communicate a living faith in God to the next generation."[6] A believer becomes a spiritual father after attending to the milestones of Childhood and Young Adulthood. E. H. Heibert points out that the term *father* "naturally implies some authority and leadership as characteristic of those mature in the faith."[7] John's stages of faith paradigm suggests a rich form of caregiving, supporting, and challenging offered by the Parent and received by the Child and Young Adult.

A father is, first of all, procreative, involved in bringing to life the next generation, and that makes a father different from a husband or a man who does not have children. While not every Christian may be directly procreative—may not be personally leading others to Christ—every Parent in the faith will be generative, intentionally extending care and nurture to fellow believers who are not as far along in their journeys toward wholeness and Christlikeness. The metaphor of procreating is straightforward in 1 Corinthians 4:14–15: "I do not write these things to shame you, but to admonish you as my beloved children. For if you were to have countless tutors in Christ, yet you would not have many fathers; for in Christ Jesus I became your father through the gospel." A Parent seasoned in the faith can uniquely present the gospel to the lost. Such personal witness flows naturally out of a transformed life. And the experienced Parent can mentor the younger believers with sensitivity. His generative concern is to pass on the lessons and life he has experienced in his own faith journey.

Milestone #3 highlighted the interactive nature of community—the Christian faith is best communicated person-to-person—and the mutual support and challenge that a Christian community offers. In Milestone #7, the focus is on the special contribution of the Parent in a community of believers, a contribution one can better appreciate after having looked at the demands of each preceding milestone. We believers need more than a map: each of us needs a personal, skilled, experienced, and sure-footed guide. W. E. Vine put it this way:

> *Fathers* refers to those who have been Christians the longest and have the deepest, ripest, and most mature development. They are the older men in the heavenly family; those who by reason of experience are looked up to for sympathy, guidance and assistance.[8]

Children and Young Adults in the faith need mature Parents in the faith who have worked on the six milestones of spiritual growth. These more mature believers are uniquely qualified to empower Children and Young Adults in their growth. It can't be emphasized enough that less mature Christians need the personal guidance and the godly, real-life wisdom of the Parent.

Again and again, Scripture affirms the value of someone who models a mature Christian faith (Luke 6:40; Philippians 2:19–21; 3:17; 4:9; 1 Thessalonians 1:6–7; 1 Timothy 4:12; and Hebrews 13:7). The Bible attests to the fact that observational and imitative learning is key to spiritual growth. Children and Young Adults in the faith need to see Christian values and behaviors lived out by people who are not distant heroes of the faith. Some models need to be nearby, people with whom the Child and Young Adult can closely identify. Everyday interactions and a strong emotional connection make a Parent in the faith an invaluable resource for the journey toward spiritual maturity. Faith is then caught as well as taught.

In their book *Nurture That Is Christian: Developmental Perspectives on Christian Education*, John Dettoni and James Wilhoit underscore the importance of Parents in the faith who provide skilled care and guidance to other believers:

> Christians do not emerge from the spiritual experience of being born again as full and complete Christians, but as childlike Christians, who, like human children, have all the potential for growing into complete and mature adults but need to be nurtured and guided. The implications of this are staggering, and we oftentimes do not honor this commitment to the lifelong growth of Christians enough.[9]

Marching Orders from Jesus

The apostle John wrote much about "bearing fruit" (John 14:5–14; 15:2, 5, 8, 16, 27; 17:20), clearly communicating that a believer's witness is to be increasingly effective as he or she travels toward a more mature faith. In John 14:12–14, for instance, Jesus taught that His disciples have work to do until He returns. Then John identified four degrees of impacting others as we obey these marching orders: we bear no fruit (15:4), some fruit (verse 2), more fruit (verse 2), or much fruit (verses 5, 8). The branch bearing the most fruit has been pruned the most; that branch—that kind of believer—is aged and seasoned in abiding in Christ.

The Lord's disciples are to impact their world for Jesus, who said, "You did not choose Me but I chose you, and appointed you that you would go and bear fruit, and that your fruit would remain, so that whatever you ask of the Father in My name He may give to you" (15:16).

Let's develop Jesus' metaphor more fully. Think for a moment about fruit and its purpose. Fruit exists for hungry people to eat and enjoy. Fruit does not exist for itself, simply so it can look attractive on the vine or branch.

Now consider this truth personally. Are you fulfilling your purpose and bearing fruit for God's kingdom? More specifically, are you living to reach out to spiritually hungry people and to influence the lives of spiritually thirsty people? In other words, are you committed to obeying Jesus' marching orders—to impacting people with His truth—regardless of the cost to you?

Jesus commands us to die to self and to live for Him and others, but many Christians don't make this shift. We are to affirm our identity as God's chosen and appointed followers. If we have surrendered our lives to Jesus (that means a change in ownership) we will be keenly aware of whom we belong to. Each believer is to learn to live under new management—under the Lord's management—and no longer be defined by self-rule.

Jesus' mandate is clear: His followers are to "go and bear fruit." Fruit includes both one's character development and one's love for others, but Jesus' disciples—in His day and now—are also commissioned to impact others for Christ through efforts in evangelism as well as discipleship, in winning the lost as well as providing spiritual guidance for fellow believers.

John has provided a map of faith development from the stage of Childhood through Young Adulthood to Parenthood. A Parent who serves as a guide, who is skilled in using John's map, is essential to the growth of other believers. But where are those Parents in the faith who will guide Children or Young Adults in the faith? Tragically, it seems that too few men and women have assumed responsibility to skillfully and sacrificially care for the growth of other believers. When believers do not experience the empowering presence and life-giving care of a mature guide, their spiritual development will be deficient, spiritual progress will be delayed, and the journey will be far more treacherous and much less enjoyable.

Brother Lawrence, a seventeenth-century Carmelite monk in France, lamented that he could have enjoyed a richer relationship with God much sooner had someone shown him how. In the closing paragraph of his book *Practicing the Presence of God*, he shared his regrets:

> If I had only known Him sooner, if I had only had someone tell me then what I am telling you, I should not have so long delayed in loving Him.[10]

In *Soulguide*, author Dr. Bruce Demarest calls attention to the shortage of those who can skillfully guide others:

> Where can a disciple who is eager to grow spiritually find a person who will listen, discern, keep his feet on the fire, and point the way home? Where can one find a supportive spiritual companion endued with wisdom, compassion, humility, and grace? Advice givers and problem solvers are as common as coal in Newcastle. But where are the godly and competent spiritual guides—those who to a significant degree reflect the pastoral qualities exhibited by the Lord Jesus? There may be a shred of truth in the opinion that "Good spiritual directors are as rare as hen's teeth."[11]

At Milestone #7, Parents in the faith increasingly gain skills in walking with, attending to, and empowering brothers and sisters as they travel farther and higher on their journeys. Meanwhile, the Parents also continue to attend to their own milestones of Childhood and Young Adulthood.

Milestone #8: Seasoned by Time and Experience

> The biblical source for Milestone #8 is 1 John 2:13–14 ("I am writing to you, fathers, because you know Him who has been from the beginning"). The biblical focus for the believer is the experiential knowledge of God that comes from longstanding, consistent obedience to Him. In this second milestone of Parenthood, the Christian moves into a deep, refined, and stable communion with God. By this point in the spiritual journey, the Parent in the faith knows God and His ways intimately and experientially. Parents in the faith have become more like the heavenly Father, and holiness and wholeness are merging.

Growing Christians need to conscientiously attend to the work of Milestone #8 if they are to move toward spiritual maturity and wholeness. To grow spiritually, believers need to press on, continuing to work on all of the milestones of spiritual development so that they may know God better. Growing believers will not be content to let themselves plateau or relax as the years go by. Instead, these believers will continue to nurture a deep and life-giving relationship with their heavenly Father.

Note that the apostle John explained that he wrote to the Children because they have "known Him." John Stott points out that "the verb is the same as that used of the little children (*paidia*). All Christians have come to know (*egnōkate*) God. But knowledge of Him is to ripen with the years. The children know Him as 'Father' (13c); the fathers have come to know Him as Him who is from the beginning."[12] It is the fathers in the faith whose personal experiences with and knowledge of God as Father have become more fully developed. It is the fathers who, as a result of being seasoned by time and experience, have come to better know and more fully trust the Eternal One. This depth is lacking in the *paidia*. "All Christians, mature and immature, have come to know God. But their knowledge of Him ripens with the years... [The fathers] are already consciously living in eternity."[13] The perfect tense of the Greek verb suggests a past knowledge that remains and yet grows, a knowledge centering on a Person characterized by His permanency.

Next, the apostle John explained that he was writing to the fathers because they have "known Him who is from the beginning." In 1 John 2:13–14, the emphasis is not on knowing *about* God, as if knowing Him is to remain merely cognitive or theoretical. This is not knowledge by investigation, observation, or speculation. Rather, it is experiential knowledge, gained as a result of maturity.[14] In this context, "to know" is personal, experiential, and intimate: "It is no mere speculative knowledge that is here in view, but knowledge which has become part of a man's own being."[15]

The verb is in the same tense John used when he wrote of the "little children" (2:13) knowing the Father (Milestone #2). By now, however, the believer's personal experience with God and knowledge of Him have become richer and deeper. It is the fathers who, as a result of a lifetime of spiritual experience, know the Eternal One and have come to more fully trust Him. Interestingly, the path to maturity is through the conflicts inherent to the Young Adulthood stage of faith. As commentator Robert Law noted, "There is a 'knowing,' that of the 'children,' which must precede the fight; and there is a 'knowing,' that of the 'fathers,' which comes after it."[16] The fathers know a maturity that is no stranger to suffering and pain. Romans 5:3–4 points out that experiencing "suffering produces character, and character hope." The word translated *character* is *dokia,* meaning "testedness; a quality of provedness which is possessed by faith when it is stood up to testing," according to Cranfield.[17]

Bruce Demarest, in *Seasons of the Soul*, stresses the importance of allowing our unique experiences on life's journey to transform us:

> The unsettling seasons we encounter on the journey are necessary both for our transformation in Christ and for gaining the wisdom to guide others on their homeward journeys. Our greatest need, therefore, is not to avoid distress and suffering, but to live into the process and patiently permit our hardships to do their transforming work. [18]

Parents in the faith have come to know what it is to be centered in Jesus Christ, and they are guided by a single-minded passion for God. Only people whose faith has been seasoned by time and by years of experience in walking with the Lord will have matured to a point of wholeness and holiness from which they can disciple and guide fellow believers. For Parents in the faith, the process of divine repair has brought them to a degree of strong spiritual health, and they have known God and His ways intimately and experientially. A Parent's love for God is no longer grounded in the blessings God gives, the rewards He promises, or even the warmth of His love. A Parent in the faith loves God simply because He is God. These Parents enjoy a deep, stable, and intimate communion with God.

For some of John's readers, the first flush of ecstasy that came when they, as Children, received forgiveness and entered into fellowship with the Father was an experience of long ago. Even the struggles to learn to think critically, the stretch of evaluating their faith, and the battles of Young Adulthood happened long before John wrote to them. Yet Parents cultivated their friendship with God through the formative milestones of Childhood and the rigorous milestones of Young Adulthood. Now they assume a God-ordained responsibility to care for fellow believers, even as they enjoy a rich fellowship with God.

Only longstanding obedience to the commands of the Lord and sustained attention to the milestones of spiritual development can sculpt a mature, Christlike Parent in the faith. So the Parent presses on, attending to each of the eight milestones of spiritual development and unwaveringly passionate about knowing God better and finishing the journey well.

Parents Know Him Deeply

Clearly, the purpose of the milestones of spiritual development is to liberate and guide the growing Christian to know God more deeply. Each milestone frees the believer to experience God in more transforming ways and to become progressively more like Christ, well, and whole. The milestones are not ends in themselves. Instead, each is a means to the goal of lifelong, life-giving fellowship with God. In Childhood, the *paidia* come to know God as Father. Years later, as Parents in the faith, they have come to know Him in a deeper way, as "Him who has been from the beginning."

Note that John described the Child in the faith as knowing the Father and the Parent in the faith as knowing "Him who has been from the beginning." The new element is the reference to time—"from the beginning." Boice comments:

> This suggests the idea of God's unchanging faithfulness together with the spiritual trust and wisdom which such knowledge brings. It is the fathers who, as a result of a lifetime of spiritual experience, have known the Eternal One and have come to fully trust Him. John writes to them because, having known God in this way, they will be able to rejoice in the truths that the aged apostle enunciates and support him in what he says.[19]

So, in 1 John 2:13–14, the apostle wrote to people who have known "Him" long and well and described that "Him" as the One "who has been from the beginning." Who does *Him* refer to—God the Father or Jesus the Son? The New Testament offers support for both interpretations, and significantly, there is no essential difference between the two interpretations.

Some interpret "Him who has been from the beginning as the Son." The first verse of 1 John ("What was from the beginning, what we have heard, what we have seen with our eyes, what we beheld and our hands handled, concerning the Word of Life") and the opening of John's gospel ("In the beginning was the Word, and the Word was with God, and the Word was God… And the Word became flesh, and dwelt among us, and we beheld His glory, glory as of the only begotten from the Father, full of grace and truth" [1:1, 14]) support the idea that *Him* refers to Jesus. John clearly taught Jesus' pre-existence and eternal deity in his gospel as well as in his epistles. In John 14:7, 9, for instance, Jesus stated, "If you had known Me, you would have known My Father also … He who has seen Me has seen the Father; how do you say, 'show us the Father'?" Earlier in the epistle, John wrote, "Indeed our fellowship is with the Father, and His Son Jesus Christ" (1:3). Fellowship with God (*koinonia*) is with both God the Father and God the Son.

The phrase "from the beginning" may refer to the beginning of all things, i.e., the creation.[20] After all, John 1:1–14 presents the Word as the One in whom the whole course of history is wrapped up, emphasizing Christ in His pre-incarnate and eternal existence. Another line of thinking is that "from the beginning" may be understood to refer to the beginning of Jesus' self-revelation among His disciples in ministry.[21] The latter view seems in line with the thrust of the epistle.

Again, referring to the phrase "Him who has been from the beginning," White notes that using this designation "would have no particular significance here as a title for God, whereas the incarnation of the Logos, who was from the beginning, is the crux of the faith John writes to defend."[22] When the heretical teachers taught that Jesus was the son of Joseph and that the Spirit of the "Christ" came upon Him at His baptism and left Him before His crucifixion, the mature Parents in the faith knew better. These Parents would have known the truth about Jesus' identity for many years. They had encountered, recognized, and dismissed counterfeits and deception before now. John "drew assurance from his realization that their years of pondering the gospel message and their experiences with the incarnate Christ had stabilized them so that they would not be misled by the novel Christologies of the Gnostics."[23] Again, time plus experience are essential to attaining the Parent's level of spiritual maturity.

Some Bible scholars, however, understand "Him who has been from the beginning" as being the Father, the Ancient of Days.[24] One reason is that, in 1 John, the pronoun *Him* seems to refer more often to God the Father, and the word *Father* appears explicitly twice in the immediate context of 2:15–17. If "Him who has been from the beginning" refers to God the Father, the sentence suggests God's unchanging, immutable faithfulness and reliability. The eternal God does not change with advancing years as human beings do. God is forever the same. Longstanding experience with this faithful, unchanging God brings wisdom and deep trust.

As already mentioned, beginning their spiritual growth by knowing God as "Father," as their "heavenly Parent" (Milestone #2), believers then work to discard any unfounded and distorted ideas they have about God's true character, ideas that would delay their growth toward wholeness. God the Father then re-parents the Child. As the years go by and their journeys of faith continue, believers become Parents in the faith, confident that God never changes and is always trustworthy. Time plus experience are essential to reaching this degree of spiritual maturity.

A Review of the Parenthood Stage of Faith

The questions "What does spiritual maturity look like?" and "Where is this lifelong journey of faith taking the believer?" have been asked. Some answers to those questions are found in the discussions of Milestones #7 and #8. Milestone #7 states that mature believers, Parents in the faith, enter into caregiving relationships with other believers in order to empower them on their spiritual journeys.

Milestone #8 addresses how time and experience forge a seasoned and profound faith. A Parent in the faith, who by now knows Christ and His ways intimately and experientially, continues to have a passion for the Lord and a desire to finish the journey of faith well.

God's desire is to so transform Christians that they more and more exhibit the character of God and live according to His purposes, just as Jesus Himself did. At any moment, some believers are in the Childhood stage, others in the Young Adulthood stage, and still others in the Parenthood stage of this transformational process. The Parent now has a seasoned and mature Christian faith and therefore offers a compelling witness of a deep spiritual reality. Parents in the faith have become more like Christ, and for them, holiness and wholeness are merging.

A Parent in the faith enjoys a rich, two-dimensional faith. The Parent is intimate with Christ (the vertical dimension of the faith) as well as with fellow believers (the horizontal dimension of the faith). The Parent in the faith is living out what John describes in 1 John 1:3: "What we have seen and heard we proclaim to you also, that you also may have fellowship [*koinonia*] with us; and indeed our fellowship [*koinonia*] is with the Father, and His Son Jesus Christ."

In 1 John 2:3–6; 2:28–3:10; and 5:2–3, John described the vertical dimension of faith. The Parent now *walks* much as Jesus walked. Mature faith and love for God have been deeply seasoned over the years. The Parent now richly abides in Jesus, knows God deeply, and keeps His Word. Mature believers examine their progress and work through obstacles that hinder their obedience.

In 1 John 2:7–11; 3:11–18; 4:7–21; and 5:1–3, John addressed the horizontal dimension of faith. The believer now *loves* others much the way Jesus loves. The resemblance is striking. In the Parenthood stage, the believer's love for fellow believers has matured. Now skilled in caregiving and in guiding others toward maturity, the Parent extends love and healing grace to those in the community of faith, and that love empowers people toward transformation and Christlikeness. A Parent is able to love deeply, reflecting God's love, and that ability enriches his or her relationships with other believers. Mature believers examine their progress and confront obstacles that hinder their loving and being loved.

In 2:18–27; 4:1–6; and 5:1, 4–5, John highlighted the test of discernment. The believer now *sees* much the way Jesus Himself sees. The mature Parent is able to identify counterfeits to authentic faith, examine spiritual progress, and confront obstacles that interfere with deeply knowing and experiencing God's truth.

Besides incarnating God's character and growing deeper in their faith, Parents live in the awareness that only a life centered on the eternal is satisfying and meaningful (2:15–17). Parents in the faith clearly understand that they are on a pilgrimage to another country (Hebrews 11:14), and this understanding gives purpose and meaning to life. C. S. Lewis said this about the pilgrimage through this world:

> Creatures are not born with desires unless satisfaction for those desires exists. A baby feels hunger: well, there is such a thing as food. A duckling wants to swim: well, there is such a thing as water. Men feel sexual desire: well, there is such a thing as sex. If I find in myself a desire which no experience in this world can satisfy, the most probable explanation is that I was made for another world. If none of my earthly pleasures satisfy it, that does not prove that the universe is a fraud. Probably earthly pleasures were never meant to satisfy it, but only to arouse it, to suggest the real thing. If that is so, I must take care, on the one hand, never to despise, or be unthankful for these earthly blessings, and on the other hand, never to mistake them for the something else of which they are only a copy, or echo, or mirage. I must keep alive in myself the desire for my true country, which I shall not find till after death; I must never let it get snowed under or turned aside; I must make it the main object of life to press on to that other country and to help others to do the same.[25]

Questions for Reflection and Action

Milestone #7: *Empowering Others*

1. When have you been guided or mentored by a Parent in the faith? Briefly describe the benefits of that relationship—or, if you weren't so blessed, how having such a mentor might have helped you grow in your faith and come to be more like Christ.
2. Even before we are Parents in the faith, we are to obey Jesus' marching orders. In what way(s) are you fulfilling your purpose and bearing fruit for God's kingdom? More specifically, what are you doing—or what could you be doing—to reach out to spiritually hungry people and/or to influence the lives of spiritually thirsty people?

Milestone #8: *Seasoned by Time and Experience*

1. Knowing *about* God is very different from *knowing* God. Explain that difference and describe when you first made that discovery and what contributed to that awareness.
2. Describe a "rich, two-dimensional faith": What characterizes the believer's relationship with God? The believer's relationship with fellow believers? Comment too on your own growth. In what specific ways are you walking more as Jesus walked? Loving more as He loves? Seeing more as He sees? What can help you further develop such Christlike traits?
3. What do you most appreciate about the C. S. Lewis quote that closes this chapter? Why?

CHAPTER 8

THE *HOW* OF SPIRITUAL GROWTH, PART 1

- Describe when and how your journey of following Christ began. In other words, what unique circumstances led up to your decision to follow Christ?
- How far have you come in your spiritual growth since your journey of faith began?
- What do you need to understand and do in order to go farther in your spiritual progress and enjoy a deeper relationship with your heavenly Father?

YOUR ANSWERS TO those first two questions will offer some clues about the story of the birth and growth of your faith. Your answer to the third will, ideally, get you thinking about where you go from here.

In addition to helping you appreciate the story of your faith journey, this chapter and the next will help you to acknowledge certain aspects of that story that you may not have thought about before. Also, as you consider your story, keep in mind that you might benefit from having a close friend help you see your story for what it is. And don't forget to think about how the Twelve Conclusions you read about here might help you to better understand and more skillfully guide the growth of believers for whom you are a Parent in the faith.

Before we get to those Twelve Conclusions, though, we need to remember that two factors are key in everyone's journeys. Growth in our Christian faith must, first, be biblically grounded (which we've covered in Chapters 2–7). And, second, our growth must be developmentally informed (which we'll address in this chapter and the next). Both this biblical grounding and our sensitivity to human developmental issues will help us wisely navigate our own paths of spiritual growth and effectively impact others' paths.

One more word: The outcome of the spiritual growth process described in this chapter and the next may not be exact, but the description is comprehensive. Spiritual growth is an orderly process of stages, but because every human being is unique, any description of spiritual growth is imprecise and multifaceted, never a rigid or static formula. What emerges in these next two chapters is a unique, heuristic, and holistic model of the journey toward Christian maturity, a model that is—as stated earlier—firmly derived from Scripture, grounded in God's truth, and enriched by human development theories. We are to grow up and mature, and these two chapters show us what that growth might look like.

How *Not* to Measure Growth

As you have already seen, the apostle John offers an entirely different way of looking at one's spiritual progress. In 1 John 2:12–14, John describes three stages of spiritual growth: the Childhood, the Young Adulthood, and the Parenthood stages of faith. He then notes distinct milestones for each of these stages. Relatively few Christians are aware of this biblically based path for Christian growth, but a quick field trip to a prestigious hospital, a classroom at an eminent university, a top-notch athletic gym, and finally, some experienced pastors in their church offices will help us understand why that may be the case. As we visit these different venues, keep in mind that we expect—and are willing to pay for—these well-trained and experienced medical professionals, educators, and coaches to, respectively, restore us to physical health, prepare us to be academically competent, and enable us to excel on the sports field.

Professionals in these areas of expertise are always searching for new and better solutions.

First, on our visit to the hospital, we find medical doctors and nurses measuring physical growth with high-tech equipment, diagnosing a patient's health with sophisticated instruments, and then prescribing treatments and medications to remedy pains and illnesses. Next, at the university campus, we meet educators who have excelled in their specific fields, guiding their students' learning and then evaluating their students' competence by examinations, papers, and oral presentations. Then, as we drop by the gym, experienced coaches are vigilantly evaluating the athletes' performances using a stopwatch, relying on statistics, and analyzing footage of games. The coaches then develop a plan for losing weight, increasing muscle mass and strength, rehabilitating after an injury, or developing a specific skill. All three of these trained and experienced professionals analyze, diagnose, and prescribe to help their clients reach goals of healing, learning, or excelling. The results are often very apparent and easily measured.

Now come our visits with several pastors of churches both large and small; specifically, we will talk with pastors who specialize in the care and development of a believer's spiritual life. We often bring into our discussions church leadership teams, elders, deacons, and a few parachurch staff to see how they might answer our questions. We want to know three things:

- What do you regard as marks of a spiritually healthy church?
- How do you measure an individual's spiritual growth and transformation?
- What can and does your church do to help broken people regain their spiritual health and progress toward full-grown maturity?

What answers do we receive? Here is what we both heard and observed in response to the question, "What do you regard as marks of a spiritually healthy church?":

- The number of members
- The frequency of salvations and baptisms
- Attendance at worship services
- The percentage of the congregation involved in a small group
- The state of the church's budget (is the church functioning in the red or the black?) and the number of members giving generously and tithing faithfully
- The percentage of members serving in the church in some capacity
- Demonstration of certain spiritual gifts
- The size and condition of the church campus
- The number of church programs currently in effect
- Political muscle

As you read through this list, did you notice that church leaders referred to observable, measurable, and quantifiable behaviors? But do any of those activities really reveal how genuine or deep a believer's faith is or how much spiritual growth he/she has experienced? Church leaders have no tool or instrument (like medical doctors do) that will reliably scope out the innermost, private conditions of the believer or measure their spiritual health and growth. Despite that lack of information, these church leaders often prescribe certain disciplines—more commitment, more Bible study, more surrender to God's will, more memorization of Scripture, more service in the church and community, more prayer, and more attendance—to help believers get in shape.

We wondered, *Do any of these factors really help us understand how deep and far a believer has come? So am I healthy, whole, and mature in the faith if I do any or all these things? Does* more *mean* deeper? In a word, no.

Finding a Biblical Path

We then ask the church leaders we're visiting another important question: "At your church, is there a prescribed path of Christian growth or discipleship that leads believers toward greater spiritual maturity? Have you set forth specific, biblical criteria that indicate how far a believer has progressed toward spiritual maturity?"

Implied in these questions is the idea—the fact—that spiritual growth is an ongoing process. Church leaders had not really stopped to consider either this perspective or the reality that some believers are at different stages of spiritual maturity and have grown to different degrees of Christlikeness. Instead, some leaders seemed to regard salvation as the whole package.

We then explored how a given church's programs, groups, and classes might be helping believers grow in their faith and become increasingly transformed and more like Jesus. We reminded the leaders that their flock's busyness at church and their involvement in worship and fellowship do not mean that transformation into Christlikeness is occurring. So we, using the words of Donald Alexander, asked the leaders, "What are you doing to help solve the 'riddle of sanctification' and the 'dilemma of the call to personal holiness'?"

Clearly, church leaders do not have access to the same kinds of diagnostic and prescriptive tools that doctors at the hospital, professors in the classroom, and trainers and coaches at the gym have, and that does make their job harder—as author and theologian John Stott addressed in an October 13, 2006, *Christianity Today* article. When asked to evaluate the "immense growth of the church worldwide, largely along evangelical lines," Dr. Stott said this:

> The answer is "growth without depth." None of us wants to dispute the extraordinary growth of the church. But it has been largely numerical and statistical growth. And there has not been sufficient growth in discipleship that is comparable to the growth in numbers.[1]

Dr. Stott's concern for the Christian church was, more simply put, its growth in size without a corresponding growth in substance.

Once again, the word *depth* has surfaced, and Stott looks to discipleship to reverse the trend of shallow and stagnant Christians.

In *Invitation to a Journey*, Robert Mulholland also addresses the issue of spiritual growth, proposing that it is best understood as a journey of deepening personal growth from brokenness and bondage to wholeness and Christlikeness:

> I do not know what your perception of Christian discipleship might be, but much contemporary spirituality tends to view the spiritual life as a static possession rather than a dynamic and ever-deepening growth toward wholeness in the image of Christ. When spirituality is viewed as a static possession, the way to wholeness is seen as the acquisition of information and techniques that enables us to gain possession of the desired state of spirituality ...
>
> When spirituality is viewed as a journey, however, the way to spiritual wholeness is seen to lie in an increasingly faithful response to the One whose purpose shapes our path, whose grace redeems our detours, whose power liberates us from our crippling bondages of the prior journey and whose transforming presence meets us at each turn in the road. In other words, spirituality is a pilgrimage of deepening responsiveness to God's control of our life and being.[2]

Read again that rich phrase: "a pilgrimage of deepening responsiveness to God's control of our life and being." John's words in 1 John 2:12–14—the stages model we have been looking at—is a biblically grounded description of exactly that kind of pilgrimage. As John's insights reveal, this journey takes us through three stages of growth en route to greater spiritual maturity. Church leaders who heed the wisdom of this biblical passage will be better able to provide skilled guidance to the believers in their care.

Gaining Insight from Developmental Theory

In addition to being biblically grounded, spiritual growth will also be developmentally informed. We will, therefore, consider the question, "What might John's model of stages of spiritual development look like when informed by developmental perspectives?"

The answer we offer is a compelling description of the *how* of spiritual growth. Christian educator Perry Downs boldly states that all developmental approaches "can be understood as descriptions of how God has designed people to develop."[3] So, with insights provided by widely accepted psychology and developmental theory, we will better understand the process, sequence, rhythms, tempos, and patterns of spiritual development over the whole of an adult's life span. This chapter and the next present the range of possibilities, the boundaries of the process, and the mechanics of development and change. Developmental theory will be integrated into the stages of the 1 John model, thereby clarifying the spiritual growth process and showing how becoming more like Christ (sanctification) is an ongoing process throughout a believer's lifetime.

The distinctive structure and content of John's stages model becomes animated and is galvanized as it takes on potential, shape, and vitality. The outcome may not be exact, but it is comprehensive. Though spiritual growth is an orderly progression of stages, it is still messy, imprecise, and multifaceted; spiritual growth does not walk in lockstep according to a set course. These two chapters of *The Path* describe and explain the various dimensions of the stages of faith model, resulting in a rich model of the believer's journey toward Christian maturity. We are to be transformed, and these two chapters show us what that transformation might look like.

In *A Theology for Christian Education*, Greg Allison acknowledges the impact of human development on spiritual growth:

> God created us as developmental beings. While we are wholly human from conception, we are not wholly formed adults for many years. We grow up! We grow and mature through a process of human development. However, the Scriptures are not a developmental psychology text. They simply reflect the observable growth of individuals and report on them phenomenologically.[4]

For example, we read in Scripture these statements: "Now the boy Samuel was growing in stature and in favor both with the Lord and with men" (1 Samuel 2:26), and "the Child continued to grow and become strong, increasing in wisdom; and the grace of God was upon Him... And Jesus kept increasing in wisdom and stature, and in favor with God and men" (Luke 2:40, 52). The apostle Paul himself noted the changes that occur naturally between childhood and adulthood: "When I was a child, I used to speak like a child, think like a child, reason like a child; when I became a man, I did away with childish things" (1 Corinthians 13:11). These biblical observations about the growth process in human beings include the physical, cognitive, social, moral, and spiritual dimensions.

Author and Christian educator John Dettoni refers to developmental theorists as "sculptors" in the sense that "the Sovereign Lord enabled them to make their valuable discoveries, shape their findings from their own words and backgrounds, and exhibit their work to others."[5] Dettoni then refines his statement: "Actually, our Creator is the *sole Sculptor*, so technically, these theorists discovered prominent ideas within specific areas of human life that correlate with the Creator's earlier portfolio."[6] As we will continue to see below, God's special revelation shines through His general revelation. To echo Dettoni's point, some of the observations of modern social scientists are compatible and consistent with the essential foundations of Christian theology.

Of course it goes beyond the scope of this book to review every theory of developmental psychology. Social scientists such as Jean Piaget (cognitive development), Erik Erikson (psychosocial development), Lawrence Kohlberg (moral development), James Fowler (faith development), and Lev Vygotsky (socio-contextual theory) have empirically researched and described their particular theories about how we move through predictable stages of development from childhood through adolescence and into adulthood. Each of these aspects of human personality can be discussed and considered separately, but human beings are integrated wholes, and each aspect interacts with and influences the others. (To learn about these theories of human characteristics from a distinctively Christian perspective and consider their applications for Christian education, see the three resources suggested in the endnotes.) As shapers of faith, Christian educators and pastors can learn from these developmental theories without allowing them to supplant or trump the final authority and contributions of the Bible.

Christian educator John Yeatts signals a cautionary note and regards a developmental paradigm of Christian formation to be "helpful, but inadequate." While it is *helpful* to include human development theories in our understanding of spiritual development, we cannot simply equate Christian formation with one of the prevailing theories of human development.[7]

Twelve Conclusions: The Process of Spiritual Growth

The Path first made a case for three stages of spiritual development (Chapter 3), and this model was supported by other key passages (Chapter 4). Next, Chapters 5–7 presented the distinctive structure and content of John's model of spiritual growth. Now we'll consider the *how* of spiritual growth. What happens? How does faith grow through these three stages of spiritual development? What kinds of changes occur through the years? Why do believers sometimes stall or get stuck? The dynamic process and the possibilities of change and growth at each of the three stages and eight milestones will become clearer. We will find a paradigm of spiritual growth that is broad in its scope and compelling in its explanatory power—a credible pathway for others to travel. All the while, we are careful not to present the findings as exhaustive, but rather as descriptive of areas that a Christian can choose to nurture. Other researchers could amplify the nuances and facets of the individual stages and their milestones.

Notably, this focus on the process, on the *how,* is commonly absent in church pulpits, discipleship materials, and resources addressing Christian growth. This focus is a significant contribution of *The Path* as we clear the way for a biblical and unique route leading believers to deepen their faith and be transformed—without confusion, riddle, or dilemma. This focus, too, will not only encourage our personal growth, but also learning about these Twelve Conclusions will provide vital clues for those of us who offer care, direction, and discipleship to fellow believers. Prepare to find yourself better able to, as Perry Downs encourages us to do in

Chapter 1, listen to how people believe, pay attention to what they believe, and be concerned about making their faith more mature.

Now to the promised discussion of the Twelve Conclusions that together offer a description of the dynamic process of spiritual growth and will thereby help you better appreciate and understand your own pilgrimage in the faith. What might John's model of stages of spiritual development look like when informed by the developmental perspectives? The biblical evidence is that the believer's growth toward Christlikeness (1 John 3:2) takes place through three predictable stages—from the child, to young men, to fathers. Looking through the lenses of developmental theory, what can we know about these stages and the process of spiritual maturity?

I encourage you to think about your own personal and one-of-a-kind faith story as you study these Twelve Conclusions. Get past thinking about these truths as mere theory or rigid assignments that must be completed. Instead, let God use these conclusions to free you from past events that have misshaped you spiritually, to restore you from any hurts that have delayed your spiritual growth, and to prepare you to know Him more deeply and serve Him more naturally and wholeheartedly. You have a unique and special faith story to share with others, and only you can tell it. So invite God to open your heart and mind to His presence and to enable you to discover all that He has for you on your journey of faith. He has traveled with you this far, and He wants to walk with you even more closely from this point on.

A quick note about our approach. I will rely on professor N. J. Salkind's insights about certain recurring issues of development to guide us through the maze of diverse and multifaceted developmental theories.[8] Using Salkind's outline from her book *Theories of Human Development*, as well as ideas presented by other experts in human development and growth, I have formulated the following conclusions about the *how* of spiritual growth. Clearly, developmental clues about the process of growth integrate well into the John's model. Salkind's questions (on the left) and my Twelve Conclusions (on the right) are outlined here:

N. J. Salkind	Twelve Conclusions
The Nature of Development What is the major force that influences the course of development?	1. Nature and nurture interact, as do various rivals of spiritual progress and certain counter-forces.
The Process That Guides Development What is the process primarily responsible for changes in development?	2. Spiritual growth is holistic. 3. Stages of faith are normative. 4. Stages of faith are descriptive.
The Importance of Age What role does age play as a general marker of changes in development?	5. Stages of faith are loosely age-linked.
The Rate of Development and Critical Periods Are there certain sensitive or critical periods of development, and if so, how are they related to the rate of development?	6. Change is triggered by scheduled as well as unscheduled events.
The Shape of Development Is development smooth and continuous, or do changes occur in abrupt stages?	7. In general, change is discontinuous, but some continuity is evident. 8. Stages of faith are sequential. 9. Stages of faith are cumulative. 10. Stages move the believer toward spiritual maturity and, ultimately, Christlikeness.
Individual Differences How does the theory explain differences in development between individuals of the same chronological age?	11. Spiritual growth is idiosyncratic. 12. Spiritual growth is not inevitable.

In light of Richard Foster's timely plea that believers become deep, we need to remedy the confusion caused by the divergent paths of sanctification that exist. Believers in Christ need to become familiar with a way forward and upward that is biblical, sensible, and compelling. Recall that Christian educators Ronald Habermas and Klaus Issler consider further study of biblical stages a promising way of describing the spiritual maturation process. *The Path* has sought to lift some of the fog by providing such a path of biblical stages by which believers can locate where they are on a challenging path to becoming increasingly transformed followers of Christ.

> As you read this chapter and the next, you will find a whole new vocabulary because developmental literature has its own language. So don't let yourself be overwhelmed, and don't ignore the new words or new usages. The words are rich with meaning.

Believers in Christ need to be familiar with a way of spiritual growth and maturation that is biblical, sensible, and compelling, and what you'll read in the rest of this chapter and the next will flesh that out. John's stages of faith model will become more alive and personal as you start to see how God shapes us, His beloved children, into Christlike people.

Issue: The Nature of Development

Conclusion 1: Nature and nurture interact.

Dr. Salkind first asks, "What is the major force that influences the course of [human] development?" In response, theorists share their view of human nature, discuss how the environment affects development, and offer their thoughts as to what degree the two forces interact.

Briefly, human development—including spiritual development—is shaped by both nature and nurture: who we are when we are born and the environments in which we live as we grow up are interactive influences. The impact of nature and the impact of nurture, of heredity and environment, are inextricably intertwined. The influence of the one is impossible to understand without considering the influence of the other. Neither heredity nor environment alone causes development. Our personal growth is linked to both inner and outer causes, as well as to the genuine choices we have even in the face of these strong forces. Our freedom is not absolute, but neither is the power of the very real influences in our lives. The external environment either enables or hinders our development, but it does not fully control it. Also significant but not all-powerful is one's inner experience of these forces, an experience that is dependent on one's innate personality.

Now let's look to the apostle John to help us shape a Christian view of these dimensions of nature and nurture. First John 2:15–27 shows that all believers, whether they are in the Child, Young Adulthood, or Parenthood stage of faith, must contend with the world, the flesh, and the devil. These inner and outer deterrents to spiritual progress parallel the nature/nurture issues raised by the developmental theorists. The conflict believers face consists of the inner enemy (the flesh) and two outward enemies (the world and the devil). We are bent, deformed, misshaped, and twisted by these enemies of the Christian faith; we are crooked people living crooked lives in a crooked world. Our spiritual growth can be impaired and delayed by any of these three forces as they interfere with our work on the eight milestones of faith. The secular theorist, however, does not acknowledge either the very real existence of sin or the harmful impact our sin nature can have on our development.

The Inner Conflict: In John's model of spiritual growth, our sin nature, or heredity, is the enemy within. The Bible clearly teaches that mankind is not morally neutral; rather, every human being is a sinner by nature (Romans 3:23). To use a biblical term, the flesh—that chronic dissatisfaction we battle—is fueled by the lust of the flesh (sensual pleasure), the lust of the eyes (acquisitional pleasure), and the boastful pride of life (recognitional pleasure). *Lust* describes believers' congenital corruption and those instinctual desires, impulses, compulsions, and motives that compete for mastery in our lives.

The Outer Conflict: In John's model, nurture—or the environment—wars against the soul in the form of the world and the devil himself. Believers, for instance, have unconsciously absorbed and been misshaped by the world's warped and ungodly values, perspectives, and attitudes. The world system socializes, secularizes, and conditions each of us in ways that do not lead to Christlikeness and spiritual maturity. In addition to these cultural forces, the evil one battles to keep us from walking on the narrow path of sanctification. Satan uses his lies and deceptions to prevent believers from moving toward wholeness and full-grown Parenthood in the faith.

Also, Bates identifies normative as well as non-normative triggers of developmental change that can impair all aspects of human development.[9] These triggers prompt change during the events, interpersonal encounters, and decisive happenings of one's life, as well as through the inner and subjective impressions one has along the way. To be more specific, the non-normative triggers of change are those idiosyncratic events that do not occur at any predictable time but do come to mark a turning point in the believer's life. These influences are unique, unexpected, and unscheduled moments in life that decisively shape the individual. As a result of our different life journeys, we each need to face, and resolve as best we can, the significant hurts that block our spiritual, emotional, and psychological growth.

Note that it is not the events of life themselves or age alone or timing that can explain our individual responses to the challenges that come our way. Rather, it is our perception of those events, based on the personal context in which we experience them, that is central to the impact of those events on our hearts and souls. Our perceptions of these triggers of change determine the effect of the outer enemies—the world and the evil one—and the ways that those external influences may shape, misshape, or deeply hurt and wound us. These non-normative influences often indicate areas where we believers need to go to God for healing and deep transformation. Not turning to God so He can meet those needs will stall our journeys to spiritual health and wholeness.

Yet, even according to developmental theorists, we believers are not powerless against the anti-change, anti-growth forces of the world, the flesh, and the devil. Neither are we at the mercy of non-normative triggers of change. As the apostle John makes clear, Christians have four sources of strength to help them stand strong against their spiritual enemies.

As John emphasizes in 1 John 2:18–27, the Holy Spirit is one source of strength we can rely on when we are battling these persistent and pervasive spiritual enemies. As we believers grow through the predictable stages of Childhood, Young Adulthood, and Parenthood, identifying the world's particular appeals and our flesh's vulnerabilities and appetites along the way, we will need to learn to progressively yield to God's presence, power, and purposes in our lives. When we believers go deeper and farther in our faith through the years, we can expect an increase in our reliance on the Holy Spirit and a consequent decrease in our enemies' power over us.

In 1 John 3:16–18, the apostle identifies the body of Christ as another source of strength for us in our battle against the world, the flesh, and the devil. Relationships with fellow believers—the horizontal dimension of "Jesus and we" (Chapter 4)—are essential to our walking in the light and growing toward Christlikeness. Unfortunately, we too often approach spiritual formation as a very personal and individualistic endeavor. Perhaps we are simply not convinced that we need one another. Spiritual growth, however, happens most profoundly in the context of a group of believers. A Parent in the faith, for instance, can significantly contribute to the spiritual growth of a Child or Young Adult in the faith by helping those brothers and sisters identify, attend to, and make new meaning of these rival forces.

In addition to the Holy Spirit and the body of Christ, John teaches about the strength we can find in our new nature as a believer. This new nature begins as a seed (the Greek word *sperma*) that progressively matures and increasingly stands strong against the control and power of one's sin nature, the influences of the world to which one is vulnerable, and the deceptions and lies of the Evil One. At the moment of salvation, God plants the seed of this new lives in the believer. As John explains, "No one who is born of God [habitually] practices sin, because His seed abides in him; and he cannot sin [habitually], because he is born of God" (1 John 3:9).

John also writes about the strength we believers can derive from God's Word, which serves as a true and accurate mirror of reality and truth (John 17:17; 1 John 2:4, 21). God's truth as revealed in Scripture will increasingly transform our thoughts and actions. As Scripture progressively defines, modifies, and orders our world, we will become more honest, candid, and open to admitting those aspects of our lives where we do not yet resemble Jesus, where we are not walking as He walked, loving as He loves, or seeing as He sees.

The Holy Spirit, the body of Christ, the new nature within us, the Word of God—these determinants of spiritual growth impact our perceptions of and reactions to the events, the interpersonal encounters, and the decisive happenings in our lives and, by reminding us of God's sovereign work in our every moment, impact our faith story. Furthermore, the activity of the Holy Spirit in our hearts, our vital connections with members of Christ's body, the growth of our Christlike natures, and our commitment to knowing and following the Word of God keep discipleship from being formulaic and standardized: each of us believers is walking through life in an intimate, personal, and unique relationship with the Almighty God.

Issue: The Process That Guides Development

Conclusion 2: Spiritual growth is holistic.

Human beings are integrated wholes. Acknowledgment of the intertwining and relatedness of the different aspects of the human personality—of the mental, physical, psychological, emotional, and, yes, spiritual—is vital to understanding people and growth. Below, Habermas and Issler propose a view of personhood that integrates both structural and functional dimensions.[10]

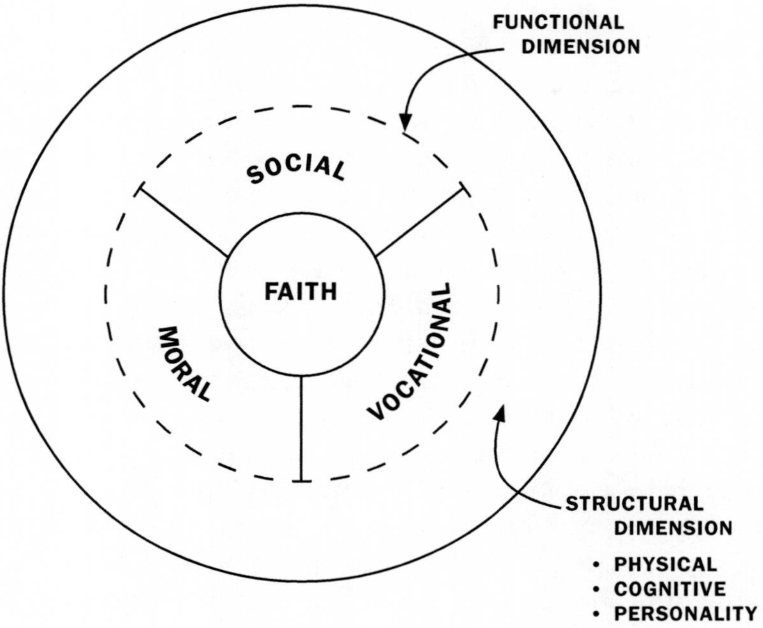

Note: The dotted lines indicate interactions within the four functional domains as well as between the functional and structural dimensions.

The structural dimension refers to inherited qualities, both material and immaterial, including physical attributes, cognitive abilities, and personalities. The functional domains of growth include faith/spiritual development, social development, moral development, and vocational development.

Jean Piaget provides an example of structural theory at work in his theory of cognitive development, which has been useful in understanding how individuals make sense out of experience or how thinking is done, not on what is being thought about. Lawrence Kohlberg's stage theory of moral reasoning and James Fowlers' stage theory of faith development are other examples of structural development. There are ages when certain stages are most likely, but an individual does not automatically pass through each of Piaget's stages. People can stall at any stage.

In the functional dimension, the focus is on how well a person progresses through the issues encountered in each stage of life, and these stages are cumulative. Erik Erikson's psychosocial theory is representative of functional theories. Erikson's stages are different from Piaget's, though, in that everyone goes through every stage, and these stages are related to chronological age. All of these structural and functional domains are integrated within each of us, and as we have acknowledged, each of us is enmeshed in a particular socio-cultural-historical-geographical environment. These two theories help us to understand two different aspects of human development; we should not merge the two into one or choose one over the other. Both of these developmental theories give us a vision of growth, wholeness, and maturity as people, and both can help us think about spiritual development.

Looking again at the Habermas and Issler model, notice that the domain of faith is at the core of the believer. Realize, however, that the growth of the self does not necessarily yield growth in faith, but the process of one's growth in faith will increasingly impact every other domain that comprises the whole person. Why is that observation significant? The substance and process of human development are basically universal, and most marks of maturity hold true for the believer and not-yet believer alike. Yet—and this is crucial—optimal human development is available only to the Christian. From a human development perspective, born-again people alone have the power to realize the full potential of human life.[11]

Professor and Christian educator Ted Ward effectively uses the human hand to illustrate the human fulfillment that is available to believers. Explaining that each finger represents one aspect of the human personality, Ward says that the spiritual essence of the person resides in the palm of the hand. Clearly, that spiritual essence influences every aspect of a person—the physical, cognitive, affective, social, and moral. Who God is to us is thus central to who we are, and the spiritual is not reduced to merely a single aspect of our humanity.[12]

Not surprisingly, Scripture gives us Jesus as an example of development. In his gospel, Luke reported that "Jesus kept increasing in wisdom and stature, and in favor with God and men" (2:52). As a twelve-year-old, Jesus was growing in all areas of His life—that is, cognitive, moral, spiritual, social, emotional, and physical—as well as in His relationships with God and human beings. Comprised as we are of these different domains, we risk toxic side effects if we neglect any one of the six. Each of these aspects of development is vital to a person's becoming whole; not one aspect can be neglected. Transformation is necessary in each and every area. Sin or brokenness in the mind must be overcome, but so must sin and brokenness in the emotions, sin and brokenness in the will, sin and brokenness in the body, sin and brokenness in relationships, and sin and brokenness in the spirit.

Again, the goal of spiritual formation is spiritual maturity. The biblical word meaning "mature, perfect, complete" is the Greek word *teleios*. In Matthew 5:48, Jesus exhorted believers, "Be perfect [*teleios*], as your heavenly Father is perfect." James 1:4 directs readers to "let endurance have its perfect [*teleios*] result, so that you may be perfect [*teleios*] and complete, lacking in nothing." Commentator William Barclay states that "the basic meaning of *teleios* in the New Testament is always that the thing or person so described fully carries out the purpose for which it was designed."[12] It is God's desire that we believers become whole, complete, and able to fully carry out the purpose He has designed us to fulfill.

The fog of the "riddle of sanctification" lifts and the "dilemma of the call to personal holiness" is resolved as we believers recognize the holistic and restorative nature of God's work in our lives. Seasoned Parents in the faith, who have traveled deep and far on their journeys toward Christlikeness and godly wholeness, are qualified to guide others in the body of Christ on a similar path.

Issue: The Process That Guides Development

3. Spiritual growth is normative.

The 1 John 2 paradigm of growing spiritually through stages is common to all men and women through the centuries and across various cultures and ethnicities. That is no surprise in light of the fact that God's eternal Word teaches these stages of spiritual growth and they, therefore, are normative for the universal experience of believers. These stages identify benchmarks along the path of a believer's lifelong journey of faith. First John 2:12–14 contains the timeless truth that every Christian is to grow deeper and go farther in faith throughout life. Recall that John Stott clearly differentiates three "stages of spiritual development" or "pilgrimage," where each stage represents a more fully developed and deeper believer. At each stage, believers are qualitatively different from the way they were in earlier stages. This radical metamorphosis (literally, change of form) is to be the experience of every follower of Christ.

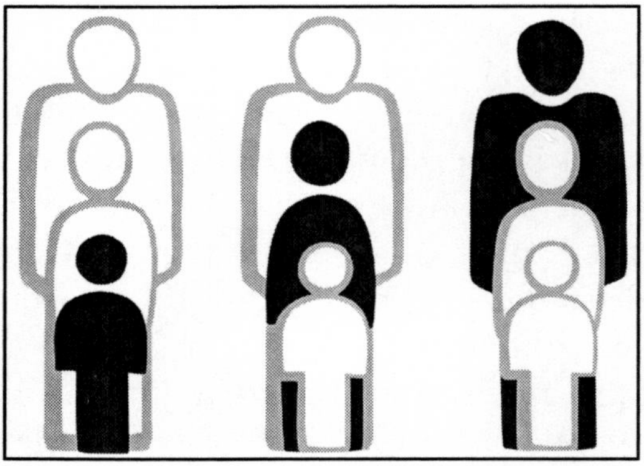

The stages of faith model describes the process of faith and a route to full-grown spiritual maturity. The model is clear about both the goal (a deep, transformative relationship with God) and the process involved in reaching that goal. Salvation marks the beginning of one's journey of faith; sanctification is the lifelong process of becoming increasingly "like Christ" (1 John 3:2). The Christian is to be metamorphosed from sinner to saint, from the point of new birth and spiritual immaturity to full-blown spiritual maturity and Christlikeness. This process occurs in three predictable stages of spiritual development, and certain milestones in each stage offer clear benchmarks by which we can reliably assess our growth as well as chart our course—or a fellow believer's course—for further progress.

Again, not strictly a Western model or a trendy, flash-in-the-pan approach to discipleship but a path based on God's eternal Word, these stages of spiritual growth will never become obsolete. First John 2:12–14 reflects the timeless truth that Christians are to continuously grow in faith throughout their lives. In fact, John's three stages of faith may be considered a path, featuring eight milestones along the way, signaling to believers how far they have traveled, the distance remaining to their destination, and suggesting possible routes to take to get there. As a path, these stages offer direction and the journey's end, but not a predetermined or standardized, "one-size-fits-all" route that will work for every believer. The milestones in John's model offer benchmarks by which believers can evaluate their growth and reliably chart a course. The milestones represent underlying, essential, core issues of spiritual growth; they are not remedial suggestions, simplistic solutions, or waste-of-time hoops to jump through.

John's stages of faith model can help guide our journeys of faith just as a trail map helps us journey through the mountains. When we are backpacking, we depend on a trail map to determine how far we've traveled. That map also helps us not to get lost along the way. John's model does the same things for us as we journey and grow in our faith. A trail map, however, does not consider our age, how healthy we are, what kind of shape we are in, or how experienced or motivated we are as we tackle the mountain hike. A map also does not report weather conditions that may affect the journey, nor does it indicate how much time it may take to get to a given destination. Likewise, John's model is not able to do any of these things for us as we travel our spiritual journeys. We who are hiking must, however, take note of these variables and how they will affect our journeys. Thankfully, we can turn to this biblical model for reliable direction; we do not need to look elsewhere for paths of spiritual growth.

But without the clarity of a biblical map to rely on for direction, believers continue to impatiently look elsewhere for new and improved approaches to spiritual growth. We live in an instant gratification culture—and we want instant sanctification now!

> Just sit near a vending machine and watch what happens when people do not get the product they have paid for. They will begin to complain to anyone handy or even begin to abuse the machine... If we do not receive the desired results almost instantly, we become impatient and frustrated... We adopt some new spiritual technique. We find a new coin and a new slot to put it in. We put it in and push a new button, but nothing seems to happen. We start kicking and beating on God: "Why don't You do something?" Or we discard that technique and go to find another machine and another coin.[13]

Knowing the path of stages and what the journey ahead looks like can save one missteps, aimlessness, worry, and wasted time. Like a driver's GPS or a hiker's map, the stages of faith path, with its eight milestones, can provide direction, purpose, and confidence for believers as they move ahead on their journeys toward spiritual maturity and Christlikeness.

Issue: The Process That Guides Development

Conclusion 4: Stages of faith are descriptive of both content and process.

An effective paradigm must be general enough to describe the Christian journey in a way that will not be situationally dependent; yet it will clearly explain how spiritual growth works. The paradigm must also be useful and valid for all believers at all times. John's model meets these criteria.

As we've seen in 1 John, the stages of faith model offers no traces of simplistic formulas or canned prescriptions. Faith that advances to maturity is best seen as:

Dynamic	Irregular	Elastic	Fluid	Flexible
Never static, fixed, or unchangeable				

In fact, the image that best represents the movement through stages of faith may be three distinct spirals. The growth is not hierarchical, nor does it involve a lockstep ascension of a ladder or stairs, where moving to the next rung or step suggests growth. This spiritual progression is not to be viewed as a hard and smooth, straight line, but neither is it random or haphazard.

Indeed, John's three-stage model contains vital clues to God's prescribed path for our lifelong journeys of faith. Although John's model is not exhaustive, it clearly suggests a Master Story as a guide, a Master Story that is sophisticated, sufficiently detailed, and user-friendly. John's model also allows for the reality that spiritual growth is uneven; it slows down, speeds up, and sometimes plateaus. His paradigm is not too simplistic or bare bones, but it is descriptive enough of the journey that we are able to locate our current position and track our progress. Nor is John's paradigm too complex and therefore inaccessible. Actually, believers will find John's model validated by their own experience and useful in helping them recognize their own progress on their spiritual journeys.

Faith as a Noun; Faith as a Verb

It is imperative that every believer recognizes that there are two dimensions to knowing (think back to Milestone #5). Neither dimension can be neglected or overemphasized without toxic side effects. The two dimensions must be kept in balance as we develop a deep and truly authentic Christian faith. First, genuine Christian faith is a biblically informed faith—focusing on the *what* or *content* of faith. Faith as a noun is the dimension of faith that we often focus on in ministry, in the church, and in the Sunday school classroom. John's model is comprised of rich content in each of the three milestones of the Childhood stage, three milestones of the Young Adulthood stage, and the two milestones of the Parenthood stage.

But genuine faith is more than a noun; it's more than just information about the eight milestones. Transformative faith is also a verb—focusing on the *why* and *how* of faith. This dimension of knowledge comes with the lived-out experience of the core truth of each milestone. Faith as a verb can be described as the process, action, movement, and transformation resulting from personalizing a milestone's truth. While believers today are more accustomed to thinking about their faith in terms of *what* people should believe, healthy spiritual growth needs to look farther than the *content* of faith. Perry Downs describes this common flaw:

> Historically evangelicals have attended to content but have ignored structure. We have been so concerned with guarding what people believe that we have failed to listen to *how* people believe. We have ignored the possibility of stages of faith, striving only to make faith stronger without being concerned with making faith more mature. We have tended to police its content and tried to strengthen its power, but we have neglected its maturity.[14]

Downs goes on to discuss the advantages enjoyed by the Christian educator or caregiver who employs a model of spiritual growth that attends to the *process* of faith, not just the content of faith:

> As Christian educators become sensitive to the stages of faith they will be able to hear the structure as well as content, and maturity as well as strength. They will understand people more deeply and have a more realistic perspective on the health of their congregations. Moreover, they will have better possibilities for designing educational approaches fit to the level of maturity of their people.[15]

In *Foundations of Spiritual Formation*, Paul Pettit also emphasizes that authentic growth is not static but is instead an ongoing process:

> Make no mistake: maturing as a Christian is a process. It is not a second step, a higher plane, a sacred blessing, or a lightning bolt moment when God invades and brings the Christian to a perfected place. A lifelong transformation is set into motion when one places his or her faith in Jesus Christ and seeks to follow Him.[16]

Mel Lawrenz shares the following observations about growth and form in *The Dynamics of Spiritual Formation*:

> Spiritual formation is the progressive patterning of a person's inner and outer life according to the image of Christ through intentional means of spiritual growth. It is neither a novel concept nor one limited to any particular tradition. Its biblical foundation is in the idea that God creates with form, and in a broken world, his work of salvation is best called trans*form*ation. The mission of the church in making disciples is to provide the means whereby fractured and misshapen lives can be re-*form*ed according to the pattern of the perfect man, Jesus Christ. We are to be con-*form*ed to him, not the world. Disciples of Jesus are those who are continually being reshaped in thought, word, and deed. Spiritual growth, as is the case with any kind of healthy growth, follows a certain form. It is not random, accidental, or arbitrary.[17]

He continues:

> Growth without form or structure is what happens with cancer—millions of cells that have escaped the normal forces regulating cell growth expand and divide, producing more tissue, but more corruption. Eventually a *growth* is discovered. But because it has not been formed according to the body's design, it represents sickness rather than health.[18]

Finally, as John's stages of faith model reflects—and as these other Christian writers agree—healthy spiritual growth comes when one's Christian faith is both a noun (solid in biblical content and truth about God and basic doctrine) and a verb (a lived-out experience of trusting in God).

Issue: The Importance of Age

Conclusion 5: Stages are loosely linked to chronological age.

Salkind requires that developmental theories answer the question, "What role does age play as a general marker of changes in development?" Those who study human development tend to take the view that no age period is any more important than any other period of development. The changes that occur during the adult years, for instance, are as significant as those that occur during childhood or adolescence.

But what part does age play in the *process* of change? Can age even be considered a cause of development? There has been a good deal of debate over whether or not age is a reliable measure for evaluating if development is appropriate or healthy. Complicating that issue is the fact that the term *age* has come to include the dimensions of chronological age, biological age, psychological age, functional age, and social age. Together these different aspects of one's age may provide clues to the extent of one's progress, but they do not automatically cause growth.

Addressing this matter of age, F. F. Bruce observed that "the threefold grouping [children, young men, fathers] relates to spiritual maturity, not years reckoned by the calendar... It is spiritual experience that is emphasized."[19] While his statement is true, I maintain that age is a clue as to the distance and depth of a believer's spiritual progress, but age, by itself, does not result in spiritual maturity.

Other social scientists whose Christian perspectives have informed their developmental theory—i.e., Levinson, Gillespie, Powers, and Steele—agree that age is a factor in tracking the spiritual progress of a believer. Consider how their insights (below) shed light on the 1 John model of spiritual development with respect to the element of age. The thoughts of these theorists may be useful, especially to a Parent in the faith, in describing and explaining one's story of faith, including its patterns, seasons, and rhythms.

- D. J. Levinson's developmental model has age factors built into it: He describes the seasons of one's adult years. He offers descriptive clues about issues the aging adult will need to attend to, and he addresses the patterns and mechanics of growing and changing. Levinson reports that the framework and sequence of periods and transitions apply to both women and men; although, women experience the path differently. His description of human life offers a map of adulthood that mentoring Parents in the faith can draw on as they guide fellow believers toward spiritual maturity.[20]
- Bernie Gillespie suggests that seven "experiences of faith" occur over one's life span: 1) Early Childhood: Borrowed Faith; 2) Middle Childhood: Reflected Faith; 3) Early Adolescence: Personalized Faith; 4) Later Youth: Established Faith; 5) Young Adults: Reordered Faith; 6) Middle Adults: Reflective Faith; and 7) Older Adults: Resolute Faith. The latter three are descriptive of an adult's process of coming to maturity in the Christian faith. Parents in the faith will look for evidence that younger believers are attending to a Reordered Faith, Reflective Faith, and Resolute Faith, depending on their ages.[21]
- Bruce Powers describes "five phases of faith development." The focus here is on the three adult phases, the first of which (ages nineteen to twenty-seven) involves reality testing. During this phase, individuals try out their faith in the arena of life to see if it will stand up. Also during this phase, some of the idealism of their youth is tempered and changed by the realities of life. The second phase (ages twenty-eight to thirty-five) involves making choices. In this phase of faith development, people truly own their faith, and their life is now, to some degree, shaped by what they believe. The third phase (age thirty-six+) is characterized

by active devotion. Significant to Powers' perspective is the idea that adolescents cannot yet truly own their faith. It is not yet incorporated into them because they have not had sufficient time or experience to test what they believe. Powers' model is especially helpful in understanding the apostle John's Young Adulthood stage of faith. "Young men" will be testing reality and making choices throughout their twenties and thirties. The Parent in the faith will guide these Young Adults (and Children in the faith as well), helping these believers apply God's Word to their life experiences, not merely absorb biblical content.[22]

- Relying on Erik Erikson's theory, Les Steele outlines seven "cycles of Christian formation," four of which occur in adulthood, that believers will need to work through as they age if they are to experience a steadily maturing and deepening faith. According to Steele, age is a factor that cannot be neglected in the Christian's approach to spiritual formation. At each stage of his trajectory of optimal human development and the characteristics of Christian formation common to them, Steele includes a polarity. Specifically, in later adolescence (ages eighteen to twenty-five), there is a tension between searching versus entrenching. This is followed in young adulthood by consolidation versus fragmentation, in middle adulthood by reappraising versus re-entrenchment, and in later adulthood by anticipating versus dreading.[23]

Steele's four cycles of Christian formation during adulthood provide an age framework that helps one understand the dynamic process of maturing faith. Adulthood can be like a second adolescence, a challenging time of reassessing and reordering the assumptions of one's life. Middle-aged adults will reappraise their lives to this point and renew their directions and faith. If adults don't face this challenge, they will re-entrench in old ways of living and being as Christians, and their spiritual growth will stall. The Parent in the faith benefits from the awareness of the dangers of entrenching, fragmentation, re-entrenchment, and dreading, all of which interfere with growth as a believer ages. These Parents will be better able to help adult Christians grow toward a firsthand, owned faith.

- Finally, the stages in John's model are loosely linked to chronological age. The children, young men, and fathers mentioned in 1 John 2:12–14 are metaphorical stages of spiritual growth, but chronological age does provide clues about the extent of one's spiritual progress. The Greek words for children, young men, and fathers actually tie those stages of life to certain ages.

Additionally, the readiness of the adult Christian to deal with each of the eight milestones demonstrates the connection and impact of age on spiritual progress. Furthermore, all four major developmental theorists—Jean Piaget, who addressed cognitive development; Lawrence Kohlberg, who addressed moral development; James Fowler who addressed faith development; and Erik Erikson who addressed psychosocial development—describe the ways age contributes to how people mature.

Likewise, I see a similar and definite connection between age and spiritual maturity. First, believers will not move beyond the Childhood stage of faith until they develop a solid sense of self, God, and others. The initial work involved in these three milestones will challenge and stretch the capabilities of chronological adolescents. Second, the stages of faith model suggests that the Young Adulthood stage of faith can begin for some as early as age seventeen or eighteen. Too, at twenty-five, a person may have attended to the milestones of Childhood and may be in the midst of owning one's faith in the stage of Young Adulthood. But it is not likely that any believer will have the *consistent* and *coherent* faith of the Young Adulthood stage until after the mid-twenties or even until the early thirties. Too many adults fail to adequately traverse this Young Adulthood stage of faith and plateau here—some permanently. Powers would point to the tasks of "reality testing" and "making choices" as age-appropriate for the mid-twenties, and Steele would say that the consolidation versus fragmentation polarity is an appropriate focus for twenty-five-year-olds.

One's chronological age, however, does not guarantee that he or she is a Parent in the faith. Advancing in years does not automatically bring spiritual maturity. In fact, John's stages of faith model helps us to better understand how believers can be churched for many years and yet be stuck in their Childhood stage ... or how they can participate in Bible study groups and be actively serving in the church and yet be stuck in the conforming faith of the Young Adulthood stage. Believers are not likely to begin to enter the stage of Parenthood until at least their mid-thirties—and then only if they have attended to the milestones of Childhood and Young Adulthood. Years of time and experience are required to fashion a believer into a veteran Parent in the faith. And it is critical to mention that individuals who become Christians at age fifty still need to attend to the formative milestones of Childhood (renewing one's concept of self, God, and others) as well as to the individual milestones of the Young Adulthood stage.

Lastly, realize that even if a person has been a Christian for fifty years, it is possible that he or she is stuck in the stage of Childhood or has plateaued in Young Adulthood. Age alone does not make a person a Parent in the faith. Advancing years do not automatically bring spiritual maturity.

So what part does age play in the process of change, specifically in the process of spiritual growth? To answer that question, I defer to Richard Lovelace, author of *Dynamics of Spiritual Life*, who wrote this about renewal: "It takes time, and the penetration of the truth, to make a mature saint."[24] Age is definitely a factor that, to one degree or another, impacts one's spiritual maturity.

Questions for Reflection and Action

1. Before reading this book, what had you read, heard, or learned about how to grow spiritually? What was helpful? What did you find helpful in this chapter?
2. Think back over the path you have traveled to get where you are today in your walk of faith. Earlier, you practiced telling

that story, so this week, schedule a time to get together with someone who knows you well to practice, and/or meet with a nonbeliever friend of yours and see if the Lord gives you an opportunity to share this life-giving truth.

3. Consider how far you have come in your relationship with God, His Son, His Spirit, and His Word since you began to follow Christ personally. What non-quantitative indications of growth can you cite? (Why aren't quantities like your number of quiet times per week or how many times a month you cross the threshold of your church indications of spiritual growth?)
4. Chapter 8 addressed five of the Twelve Conclusions. Choose two or three to comment on: Why is it key to understanding spiritual growth? What pressure might this insight take off a believer? What encouragement for growth might it spark?

    Conclusion 1: Nature and nurture interact.
    Conclusion 2: Spiritual growth is holistic.
    Conclusion 3: Spiritual growth is normative.
    Conclusion 4: Stages of faith are descriptive of both content and process.
    Conclusion 5: Stages are loosely linked to chronological age.

5. From your perspective, what value do the developmental insights add to the discussion of spiritual growth?

CHAPTER 9

THE *HOW* OF SPIRITUAL GROWTH, PART 2

- Describe when and how your journey of following Christ began. In other words, What unique circumstances led up to your decision to follow Christ?
- How far have you come in your spiritual growth since your journey of faith began?
- What do you need to understand and do in order to go farther in your spiritual progress and enjoy a deeper relationship with your heavenly Father?

WE FIRST ASKED these questions in the previous chapter. Now, in this chapter, we will address the remaining Twelve Conclusions that help describe the dynamic process of spiritual growth and, thereby, help you better understand the story of your own pilgrimage in the faith.

Before we do, consider what Richard Lovelace, in *Dynamics of Spiritual Life: An Evangelical Theology of Renewal,* calls a "sanctification gap"[1]: some believers are not sure what the journey forward, between salvation and ultimate glorification, looks like. It is the intention of *The Path* to clear up some of the uncertainty and to bridge "the gap."

Issue 4: The Rate of Development and Critical Periods

Conclusion 6: Change is triggered by scheduled and unscheduled events.

Having addressed the nature of human development, the process that guides development, and the impact of age on human development, N. J. Salkind now asks the question, "Are there certain sensitive or critical periods during development, and, if so, how are they related to the rate of development?"

Believers need to remember that the journey of faith is not characterized by a constantly increasing amount of growth that occurs in a steady, continuous fashion. Growth may happen for a season, but spiritual growth is best viewed as discontinuous and irregular. Growth is not an unbroken, seamless process. Growth will occur more rapidly during certain periods and less rapidly during others. Growth is complex and idiosyncratic, shaped by each individual's unique encounters with life and his/her attempts to make sense of it all. Be assured that there are substantial differences among believers as to both *when* and *how* such stages are experienced.

We should not expect to see measurable daily growth. Stepping back and seeing the big picture, though, can assure us that a spiritual metamorphosis is actually happening. But progress is often unimpressive, incremental, unremarkable, and imperceptible. But God *is* reshaping us into Christ's likeness (2 Corinthians 3:18).

Sometimes change is rapid and startling, as when we are surprised by a fresh glimpse of God's grace, when we gain freedom from an undesirable situation or personal habit, or when we make a fresh commitment to God's control and care. The norm, however, is that "steadily, progressively, constructively we are being transformed."[2]

Baltes suggests that three kinds of factors interact to produce human growth and change.[3] First, development occurs due to "normative age-graded influences" (likened to nature), and traditional developmental theory emphasizes these influences. Biologically determined developmental changes, for instance, normally happen at predictable ages. In addition, certain types of transitions are normative and expected according to the cultural and social norms at particular times of life. These transitions include graduation from high school or college, marriage, parenthood, grandparenthood, and retirement. These normative transitions, resulting from an internalized biological and social clock, partially regulate the timing of events in one's life.

The second kind of factors are "normative, history-graded influences" (likened to nurture), and this category includes historical factors, eras, and events that have dramatic effects on the individuals who experience them, effects that may persist for a lifetime. Human development is contextual: it can vary substantially depending on the historical and socio-cultural conditions in which it takes place. Therefore every age cohort (meaning the group of individuals born at a particular time) is unique because it is exposed to a unique segment of history. Members of a specific cohort experience certain decisive economic, social, political, and military events at similar junctures in life. Since society changes, each new generation exists in an environment different from what earlier generations knew, so the members of different cohorts develop in different ways. As a result of the unique events of the era in which they live, each generation tends to arrive at a somewhat unique style of thought and life. And, significantly, social influences are reciprocal: we both affect and are affected by the people around us.

Third, "non-normative influences" impact development. Such transitions are idiosyncratic. Because they are unusual, unexpected, or non-shared, these influences usually have a greater, more-disturbing, and longer-lasting impact than normative transitions. Non-normative influences are unique, unscheduled life events that decisively shape an individual. Divorce, the death of a spouse or a child, major health problems, job changes, business failures, moves, and many lesser events are examples of idiosyncratic or non-normative transitions.

But neither the events of life nor age alone can fully explain an individual's responses to the challenges that come and the human development that results. The meaning of any event depends on the person experiencing the event and the timing of that event. More specifically, the individual's perceptions of an event, determined by the personal context in which it is experienced, are key.

Non-normative influences especially involve unique turning points, where people change direction in their lives. Psychologist Bernice Neugarten explores the meaning of age and argues that even these non-normative events are "on time" if they follow a "normal expectable life cycle," and those "on time" events are less disruptive and less difficult to deal with than those that are "off time" or out of sync. Yet those unique, "off time," and unscheduled life changes are the ones most likely to trigger change, growth, and significant reassessment of one's self and one's life.[4]

It's a statement of the obvious to say that all of us can expect to encounter various types of upheaval, turmoil, and challenges that promote or foster both sudden growth spurts as well as gradual, ongoing growth. We cannot underplay or overemphasize either type of human development. In fact, we can come to appreciate a crisis not as a tragedy or a reason for extreme anxiety, but instead as a turning point that opens us to change. We can choose to embrace the way a crisis challenges our life structures, old assumptions, identities, and connections and requires new, adaptive resources.

In *Necessary Losses*, Judith Viorst shows how we grow and change through the multiple losses that are an inevitable and necessary part of life. Her words apply to the changes we can expect with all three kinds of triggers mentioned above. She argues that the unavoidable losses we all face include our "romantic dreams, impossible expectations, illusions of freedom and power, illusions of safety—and the loss of our younger self, the self that it thought would always be unwrinkled and immortal."[5] As we deal with our losses, she contends, we will grow and gain deeper perspective, true maturity, and greater wisdom about life.

William Bridges, in his *Making Sense of Life's Transitions*, describes three stages of transition or endings and makes it clear that new beginnings in our lives will emerge from experiences of disenchantment—whether scheduled or unscheduled. He writes, "The lifetime contains a long chain of disenchantments, many small and a few large: lovers who proved unfaithful, leaders who were corrupt, idols who turned out to be petty and dull, organizations that betrayed your trust." In such times—whether it is a minor disappointment or a major shock—you discover that your old view was sufficient in its time, but it is insufficient now. Old assumptions need to be discarded. Bridges adds, "For the whole idea of disenchantment is that reality has many layers, each appropriate to a phase of intellectual and spiritual development. The disenchantment experience is the signal that the time has come to look below the surface of what has been thought to be so."[6]

Within each stage of faith and between the three stages come periods of transition in which the believer's life structure begins to deteriorate and the creation of a revitalized life structure becomes necessary. These times of change are a major factor in the stimulation of faith development. At such points, a believer must ask, *What will I do with this hurt, this dark night of the soul? How will I fill the void caused by this loss?* In these periods of transition, our faith may change, and corrections and advancements are more likely to occur. Indeed, *crisis* can be defined as a change forced by dramatic, life-altering influences or events, and that change suggests that a point of decision is at hand: *How will I respond to this opportunity, this challenge? What is God inviting me to do?* Crises, too, shape us by reducing us, "tearing down things that they thought were strong and important, and exposing the position of one's personality and faith."[7]

Revisit now what Jesus and Paul said about tribulation and suffering:

> These things I have spoken to you, so that in Me you may have peace. In the world you have tribulation, but take courage; I have overcome the world.
>
> —Jesus (in John 16:33)

> But we have this treasure in earthen vessels, so that the surpassing greatness of the power will be of God and not from ourselves; we are afflicted in every way, but not crushed; perplexed, but not despairing; persecuted, but not forsaken; struck down, but not destroyed; always carrying about in the body the dying of Jesus, so that the life of Jesus also may be manifested in our body.
>
> —Paul (in 2 Corinthians 4:7–10)

Again, faith needs to be seen not as static and monolithic but as dynamic, changing, deepening, and maturing as we deal with the tribulations and afflictions the Bible promises that we'll encounter. Yet we believers tend to condemn the stressful times ... and sanction the calm periods.

As followers of the Way (Acts 9:2; 19:9, 23; 22:4; 24:14, 22), believers are travelers on a quest, a voyage, an odyssey, a journey, and we can expect the unexpected along the way:

> To follow Christ is to move into territory that is unknown to us and to count on his purposeful guidance, his grace when we go off the path, and his presence when we feel alone. It is to learn to respond to God's providential care in deepening ways and to accept the pilgrim character of earthly existence with its uncertainties, setbacks, disappointments, surprises, and joys. [8]

Depending on the tribulations we encounter along our particular life journeys, we will need to face and resolve as best we can those forced changes and significant hurts that could block spiritual as well as emotional and psychological growth. As our lives unfold, there will be critical seasons for reworking some of the underlying patterns of our emotional or relational life, a reworking that can bring healing. As research psychologist Daniel Levinson reports, in times of transition, "much from the past must be given up—separated from, cut out of one's life, rejected in anger, renounced in sadness or grief. And there is much that can be used as a basis for the future."[9] Inevitably, everyone's journeys through life mean growing into adulthood with emotions that, to some degree, are wounded or distorted. Involuntarily, we learned to hide these wounds from ourselves with what the psychoanalytical tradition calls "defenses." Our defenses keep us and, to some degree, keep others from seeing our wounds, but we must face these defenses and the wounds they cover if we are to grow.

In the apostle John's model of stages of faith, the seasoned Parent in the faith will look for and inquire about these triggers of change (normative age-graded influences, normative history-graded influences, and non-normative influences) and the believer's experiences with them. A Parent in the faith can be a powerful resource for a believer who is in the midst of change or darkness and who likely requires new skills and perspectives in order to process and grow from those experiences. The Parent in the faith can come alongside the believer in these times of darkness or pain because the Parent has personally been through such life transitions. The maturity that resulted enables a Parent to assist others on their journeys.

In *Seasons of the Soul*, Bruce Demarest shares this observation:

> The unsettling seasons we encounter on the journey are necessary both for our transformation in Christ and for gaining the wisdom to guide others on their homeward journeys. Our greatest need, therefore, is not to avoid distress and suffering, but to live into the process and patiently permit our hardships to do their transforming work.[10]

Issue: The Shape of Development

N. J. Salkind next asks, "Is development smooth and continuous, or do changes occur in abrupt stages?" The issues here concern whether or not developmental changes are characterized by clear-cut, abrupt shifts or come as the result of a slow, smooth, gradual, stable, uninterrupted, and incremental but steady progression. On this point, stage and non-stage developmental theories are mutually exclusive. Stage theories imply an abruptness or developmental discontinuity *between* stages but continuity *within* the stages. Do people grow (quantitative change) in an orderly sequence of stages, or does development (qualitative change) occur in a more continuous manner, without definite boundaries?

Conclusion 7: Change is discontinuous, but some continuity is evident.

John's model does not suggest steady, continuous, or seamless transitions from one milestone to the next or from one stage to the next. We believers can expect periods of stagnation as well as seasons of equilibrium. Also, some changes may occur more rapidly during certain periods of life and less rapidly during others. Sometimes progress is startlingly great after a crisis or a fresh commitment to obedience to Christ. But spiritual growth is not an ongoing phenomenon that always occurs in a steady, continuous fashion. Spiritual growth *may* happen like that, but development is basically discontinuous and irregular. Furthermore, we may be unaware of our incremental and imperceptible growth. In the midst of this uncertain journey, we must choose to believe that we are being transformed (2 Corinthians 3:18).

Author of *Conformed to His Image*, Dr. Ken Boa reminds us that spiritual growth is an uneven developmental process:

> Our task is to place ourselves under the conditions favorable to growth and look to God for our spiritual formation. He uses different paces and methods with each person. Since the inner life matures and becomes fruitful by the principles of growth (1 Peter 2:2; 2 Peter 3:18), time is a significant part of the process. As nature teaches us, growth is not uniform—like a vine or a tree, there may be more growth in a single month than in all the rest of the year. If we fail to accept this uneven developmental process, we will be impatient with God and ourselves as we wait for the next growth spurt or special infusion of grace.[11]

Author and seminary professor Bruce Demarest describes this discontinuous journey: "Hardly ever does spiritual growth and fruit-bearing advance in linear fashion consisting of static starts. Rather the journey is fluid and dynamic, involving starts, stopping places, digressions, reversions."[12] Like John Bunyan's pilgrim, disciples of Jesus face many uncertainties and bear many burdens as they travel the pathway to the Celestial City. Mel Lawrenz, author of *The Dynamics of Spiritual Formation*, observes that "spiritual growth is painfully slow—with a few leaps and bounds, but also long interludes and sometimes even regression."[13] Similarly, Demarest notes, "Just as recovery from major surgery often occurs slowly, so spiritual progress is gradual."[14] The process of becoming a deep and seasoned Parent in the faith happens only with both the intensity and extensity of the years. Along the way, believers will, ideally, learn to rely less on circumstantial evidence of growth, personal experiences, or emotions and instead learn to walk faithfully and obediently in God's love, trusting that He is doing His transforming work in them.

Seasons of stagnation, the deterioration of old ways, and periods of fresh beginnings can all be expected in life. Saint John of the Cross used the phrase "the dark night of the soul" to capture the emotional desolation that some times of transition can bring. Likewise, centuries later, Ken Boa notes that experiences of weakness and dryness can be expected as part of one's life journey. Those experiences bring us to our knees in deeper trust and greater closeness to God. He adds this:

> [Those experiences reveal to us] our desperate condition and our need to renounce our exaggerated estimates, our deluded images, and our attachment to reputation and accomplishment. Outward trials and inward dryness become means to grace when they drive us to a more profound realization of our helplessness and emptiness before God. They cause us to see that the false self is far worse than we ever imagined and that Christ is far greater than we ever dreamed. In this condition in which God exposes our absurd hiding places, we become more spiritually supple and willing to surrender to his loving purposes.[15]

Furthermore, this maturing process—outlined by John's three stages of faith—will not end until a believer's death or Christ's return (1 John 3:2–3). In other words, the full fruit of our initial salvation will not be manifest until we are present with Him. In the meantime, Christ's followers come to experience a real tension. First, we yearn for holiness in Jesus' absence, in the "now," so that we will better represent Him to those around us. Yet, at the same time, we long to be Home with Him; aware of the very real differences between Jesus and us, we experience the frustration of "not yet," of not yet being like Christ and not yet being with Him. We fall so far short of His likeness; none of us can say this side of heaven that we are ever fully transformed. No wonder the wise, old apostle John exclaimed in his nineties, "What marvelous love the Father has extended to us! Just look at it—we're called children of God! That's who we really are" (1 John 3:1 MSG). Having been a follower of Christ for over sixty years, John was amazed by his ever-present need to connect with the renewing love and grace of God.

Professor of Systematic Theology Ray Anderson illustrates for his seminary students how God works to train us to become like a master pianist and how we may not approve of the painful process:

> A woman, in her later years of life, decided to begin playing the piano. She searched for the best piano teacher she could possibly find and asked him how she could become a master pianist such as himself. He looked hesitatingly at her, asking her if she was sure she wanted to do this. He explained to her that at her age, the women's bones had naturally calcified and were configured in a certain way. To play the piano, she would need to engage in finger exercises that would break this calcium down, thereby giving her supple, flexible fingers that would allow her fingers to extend to various keys. He warned her that the finger exercises and the calcium breakdown would be excruciatingly painful, as if her fingers were being smashed.[16]

As we are being transformed to the likeness of Jesus, as we aspire to possess the skills of the Master Pianist, our own spiritual calcification must be broken down. We not only need to *learn* about God and grow deeper in our relationship with Him, but also we need to *unlearn* what we falsely believe about God, ourselves, and our walk with Him. Unfortunately, what we erroneously believe is often solidified and unyielding, so it is painful to break down. Such is a reality everyone experiences on the long journey of spiritual development.

Issue: The Shape of Development

Conclusion 8: Stages of faith are sequential.

The stages of faith outlined in 1 John 2:12–14 are a sequence of qualitative changes encountered by every believer in the exact same order. Spiritual growth unfolds incrementally and through definable stages, and these stages never vary. The three stages have a logical, sensible order to them. The formative Childhood stage precedes the individuative Young Adulthood stage, which, in turn, precedes the generative Parenthood stage, but this progression is no lockstep, smooth model of growth. Each successive stage consists of an integration and extension of the previous stage. Remember, progress through John's stages of faith is probably best seen as discontinuous, irregular, and "soft."

Each Christian will pass through the stages in the same sequence or order but not in the same way or at the same pace. The personal tempos and the intensity of growth will differ, but the path of growth follows a consistent pattern. Believers can trust that the Holy Spirit is directing an ongoing, concurrent, collaborative interaction between the milestones within each stage and between the stages. Progress is therefore best illustrated by an upward, spiral movement rather than a straight line or hierarchical staircase. View each of the three stages of faith in John's model as a spiral, "each turn on the spiral representing another visit to the stages—and an ever-changing relationship with God."[17] Easy or seamless transitions from one stage to the next are not likely, and failing to work adequately through any milestone will interfere with, delay, and undermine spiritual growth. Neither are there child prodigies or any spiritual elite (even among seminary graduates and pastors!) on the journey of faith.

Every believer must attend to each milestone and every stage. None can be skipped or hurried. There are no shortcuts to your growth in wholeness and Christlikeness.

According to stage theory, we can understand all the stages through which we have been, and we can grasp intellectually the ones immediately ahead of us. But we cannot fully comprehend the actual day-to-day existence of people who are more than one stage ahead of us. "It is like teenagers trying to understand what it means to be living in adulthood or middle-agers trying to understand the inner life of senior citizens. We have difficulty until we've been there ourselves."[18] Although 1 John 2:12–14 lays out a precise path through the three stages of spiritual development and although hikers may be informed ahead of time about each of the stages, the trekkers only grow as they follow the path and tend to the milestones along the way, thus experiencing the stages firsthand. Consequently, it is only the Parent in the faith who has traveled through all three stages and is therefore fit to guide others.

Issue: The Shape of Development

Conclusion 9: The stages are cumulative.

Each stage of growth lays a foundation for the next, and each stage incorporates the preceding. The result is a cohesive, synergistic relationship between the milestones within the stages. This relationship may also be described as collaborative and concurrent: there seems to be a natural affinity or confluence among the milestones within each stage. Each milestone seems to empower and fuel the next. Likewise, failure to attend to the milestones gives them the power to hold back or even diminish spiritual progress and growth. A strong beginning in the Childhood stage is therefore critical to future development.

Erik Erikson

An important quality of Erikson's psycho-social model is that the stages are cumulative. Each of the eight issues in his model is most evident at a particular stage in the life cycle, but every one of the eight appears to some degree throughout life. (For example, the first issue of trust is part of the resolution of the last stage.) Transformation is ongoing. Only a successful resolution of the crisis associated with each stage—a turning point or point of decision—allows the person to move into the next developmental stage with an increased sense of inner unity and a greater capacity to do well according to his or her personal standards as well as the standards of those whose opinion the person values most. It is almost as if a new person arises in the crisis of each stage. A positive resolution of one stage contributes to the positive resolution of the following stages. Conversely, if a crisis is not handled satisfactorily, the person continues to fight his or her early battles later in life so that the unresolved conflicts are carried forward. The resolution (or non-resolution) of each crisis becomes incorporated into the human personality.

And, Erikson notes, the issues of a particular stage do not "suddenly appear and then suddenly disappear; they are present in the infant as they are present in the elderly."[19] Each stage exists in some form prior to its point of ascendancy. "Each stage adds something specific to all later ones, and makes a new ensemble out of all the earlier ones"[20] Each stage is related to all other stages. Erikson's stages are "building blocks."[21] The earlier stages provide either strengths or weaknesses for people to negotiate later stages. In Erikson's view, all the stages build on and affect one another. The unsuccessful resolution of any one stage leaves the individual with unfinished business and unresolved conflicts that are carried forward to the next stage, making it then more difficult to resolve that stage successfully. Thus, Erikson is proposing eight stages that are inevitable, in a fixed sequence, and cumulative.

James Fowler

Fowler's six faith stages are broad categories and descriptions of growth. Because structural, developmental stages are not controlled exclusively by chronological growth, not all people progress to the later stages. "Persons may reach chronological and biological adulthood while remaining best defined by structural stages of faith that would most commonly be associated with early or middle childhood or adolescence."[22]

Yet Fowler maintains that the stages of faith development are invariant, sequential, and hierarchical and that no stage can be skipped. Each new stage builds on and incorporates into a more elaborate pattern the operations of the previous stage. Development from one stage to the next is always in the direction of greater complexity and flexibility. Fowler asserts that there is a qualitative increase in adequacy at each stage of faith development and that the more developed stages make possible a more genuine knowing than that which is experienced at less-developed stages: "The varying stages of faith can be differentiated in relation to the degrees of complexity, of comprehensiveness, of internal differentiation, and of flexibility that their operations of knowing and valuing manifest."[23] Put differently, each stage is characterized by a wider and more encompassing knowledge than the one that precedes it. This greater breadth fosters both a greater capacity for a sense of sureness and serenity and a greater capacity for personal wholeness, as well as for relationships with others.

The stages are not to be thought of as rigid, fixed, and totally discrete. In fact, a person is likely to live in more than one stage simultaneously, but he or she will be predominantly in one stage. As you chart your Spiritual Growth Profile results (see Chapter 10), you may notice varying degrees of progress in all three stages. That is quite likely, but it is vital to understand that you will operate out of one stage predominantly. "This is the place where we spend most of our time and energy."[24] This stage best characterizes where you are on your journey of faith, and this stage influences and, in part, determines the shape of your response of faith. Janet Hagberg and Robert Guelich support the idea that believers will find themselves predominantly in one stage (which they call a "Home stage") but will be dealing with issues from another stage at the same time.

Of interest at this point of the discussion are the effects of what Piaget, in his stage theory of cognitive development, calls "horizontal decalage." This phenomenon refers to our failure to extend our level of formal thinking into various other areas of our experience. Put differently, if we demonstrate the highest stage of thinking in one area, we may not do so in other areas of thinking. For example, someone may be on the cutting edge of complex computer or scientific knowledge, competent in issues of the law, or successful in the financial world but remain very simplistic or shallow in his or her understanding of the Christian faith. Such individuals will employ that high level of thinking primarily in areas of special interest or ability. They may know quite well the content of the Bible but not be able to think deeply about its application to their life experiences. Or certain people may demonstrate a high level of thinking in an aspect of their faith but be not as insightful or analytical in other areas of their faith.

Next, it may surprise you to learn that believers will often need to return to the dynamic milestones of the stages of Childhood Young Adulthood, and Parenthood throughout their lives if they are to mature in their relationships to God, their understanding of self, and their insights and care for others. Thus, in God's refining process, none of us will ever completely outgrow the Childhood, Young Adulthood, or Parenthood stages.

Echoing this truth about the spiritual life, sixteenth-century mystic Theresa of Avila observed, "... no one becomes so advanced that they don't have to return to the beginning."[25] I compare such returns to my trips to Kauai. The first time I vacationed on Kauai, I was awed by the island's beauty. The second time, I returned for a longer visit, and the third time, I traveled to different parts of the island I had not seen. Each time I return, I am impacted differently, and I develop a deeper wonderment about the island. So it is in the believer's spiritual life. Your relationship with God will be enriched as you revisit various milestones of the stages of faith over time.

On those return visits, you will more fully attend to areas of yourself, your heart, and your relationship with your heavenly Father that were previously unrecognized, denied, or unresolved. This concept of repeatedly recycling, revisiting, and revitalizing each milestone, and thereby furthering the work already done there, calls for a spiritual growth model that addresses one's entire life. This concept of revisiting milestones also negates the idea that believers must complete all the issues within one stage before moving on to the next stage. On their circuitous, spiritual journeys believers will continue to circle back to issues they have addressed before, but this time they will tackle the issues at a higher level. A believer's areas of unfinished business become the focus of God's agenda for continued growth. This continual process of returning to previously addressed milestones to attend to and nurture various aspects of the three stages of faith is not to be mistaken as regression, as may be the reaction of some Christians. It is important that believers do not see this time as one in which faith is weakening or diminishing.

Consider for a moment that this concept of revisiting complements the apostle John's idea of "walking in the light." That choice to walk in God's light enables believers to progressively come to grips with their personal darkness as well as with the obstacles that are holding them back from fuller obedience (the test of obedience, of whether or not we are walking as Jesus walked, indicates the strength of the vertical dimension of our faith), from deeper love (the test of love, of whether or not we are loving people as Jesus loved, indicates the strength of the horizontal dimension of faith), and from keener discernment (the test of belief, of whether or not we are recognizing and abiding in God's truth, seeing as He sees).

Believers may have carefully attended to a particular milestone as best as their awareness at the time permitted. But new life circumstances and events may call for a deeper or a fresh way of addressing that milestone. Christopher Bryant writes this:

> Spiritual development is no steady, regular advance, but is punctuated by crises in which growth appears to have come to a stop for a time, *old battles have to be refought and old experiences relived at a deeper level.* [26]

So don't be surprised that old issues prompt you to recall old battles and old experiences and that, with these recollections, issues resurface and need to be addressed again. Becoming deep and whole depends on realizing anew—again and again—that God is adequate.

Bruce Demarest writes this: "Subsequent seasons of darkness and distress … should prove less disorienting since priceless wisdom has been gained from past experiences."[27] This is definitely the process of growth that leads to the formation of character in the deep and seasoned Parent in the faith.

Now consider Bruce Demarest's observation from his *Seasons of the Soul*:

> The unsettling seasons we encounter on the journey are necessary both for our transformation in Christ and for gaining the wisdom to guide others on their homeward journeys. Our greatest need, therefore, is not to avoid distress and suffering, but to live into the process and patiently permit our hardships to do their transforming work.[28]

The Parent in the faith is a vital resource in the development of fellow believers as he or she moves progressively deeper and farther in the faith. As a matter of fact, moving from milestone to milestone, and from stage to stage, generally requires the help of another—a friend, someone in a small group, a pastor, a spiritual director, or a counselor. Without the guidance of a seasoned Parent in the faith, believers will find their spiritual growth slowed down.

Issue: The Shape of Development

Conclusion 10: Stages move the believer toward spiritual maturity and, ultimately, Christlikeness.

Developmental theorists ask, "Are changes qualitative or quantitative?" *Qualitative* changes involve change in structure or organization, change in kind or type. An example from nature is the qualitative change from egg to caterpillar to cocoon to butterfly. In contrast, *quantitative* changes are changes in amount, frequency, or degree. An example from nature is the quantitative change from kitten to cat. This change is gradual; it occurs in small increments. Likewise, quantitative change in the realm of human development comes as bits and pieces of knowledge are acquired, healthier habits are developed, and new skills are acquired. Most developmental theorists agree that both qualitative and quantitative types of change occur in human beings.

And such change—such growth—is to occur throughout our lives. The Word of God itself challenges believers to continue to grow deeper and go farther in spiritual maturity: "Therefore, let us leave the elementary teachings about Christ and go on to *maturity*" (Hebrews 6:1). In 1 Corinthians 13:11, Paul described his own growth by saying that when he was a child, he thought like a child and that becoming an *adult* meant he had to put away the childish thinking he had grown accustomed to.

Sometimes along the path to spiritual maturity, though, we have certain issues to "put away." Echoing this book's metaphor of growth being a journey, Robert Mulholland considers spiritual growth not only as a journey to wholeness but also as liberation from bondages:

> When spirituality is viewed as a journey, the way to spiritual wholeness is seen to lie in an increasingly faithful response to the One whose purpose shapes our path, whose grace redeems our detours, whose power liberates us from crippling bondages of the prior journey and whose transforming presence meets us at each turn in the road.[29]

Complementing Mulholland's point, Christian psychologist H. N. Malony uses the phrase "holy wholeness and whole holiness" to describe the ultimate goal of the interaction between one's faith and one's psychological well-being.[30] Traveling the journey toward authentic faith, believers will face and resolve as best they can the significant hurts, unhealthy habits, and unfulfilled hungerings in life, all of which block growth. The process of each believer's growth in faith will impact and restore all aspects of the whole person. Salvation is the starting point for what theologian Francis Schaeffer called "the substantial healing of the total person." Schaeffer referred to it, however, as the *substantial*, not the *complete*, healing of the individual. What we can experience is real and significant healing, but it will never be *complete* or total on this side of eternity.[31]

The stages model is clear about both the *teleos* (goal) and the process of spiritual growth. The trajectory and course of development John described emphasizes progressive movement toward an ultimate direction of wholeness, maturity, and Christlikeness. In sharp contrast, modern theories of development that focus on the ultimate goal of justice (Kohlberg), universalizing faith (Fowler), integrity (Erikson), or commitment in relativism (Perry) fall far short of this biblical goal of conformity to Christ's likeness.

Furthermore, the real issue in a Christian's spiritual development is not more faith (quantitative) but rather a *different* faith (qualitative), a different, more mature, and more godly perspective at each stage. In John's model of growth, the desired changes are not just more of the same: "Growth in the spiritual life is more like the growth of caterpillar to butterfly than kitten to cat."[32] More specifically, at each advancing stage, believers will reframe in a radical new way the meaning of the world as they once understood it. Profound transformation means a fundamental shift in the way one sees, and a new structure and stance come with that new perspective.

Growth can therefore be understood, in part, as a series of transformations in the way we make meaning. Believers will form new, more adequate ways of mentally organizing the world and making sense out of it. Development is an internal reorganization and construction of how people process their experiences. As individuals mature, they reorganize these inner categories of personal experiences and construct new categories. Consequently, spiritual development is evidenced when one relates to experiences and people in structurally different ways than before. Those differences result from a more adequate faith; a more accurate perception of reality; and a more fitting composition of self, God, and the world.

Consider this statement by James Wilhoit and John Dettoni:

> Development is a basic change in the internal categories of making meaning for oneself or one's experiences. Development is evidenced when learners relate to data, experiences, and people in structurally different ways. Developmental learning is a basic inner changes in how people process their responses

> to ideas, other persons, and events. As development occurs, the limitations of less mature perspectives are replaced by more and more mature ones. By doing so, one continually reduces the errors of understanding that come from immature internal structures of meaning. Instead, one has increasingly more adequate internal categories or internal structures of meaning with which to handle complex stimuli. [33]

Believers who are in the Young Adulthood stage of faith and Parenthood stage of faith will see, experience, and respond to life more fully, adequately, appropriately, and maturely than believers who are in the Childhood stage of faith. Perhaps a congregation memorizes a particular verse of Scripture or hears the pastor address a specific passage. Believers in the three stages of faith will understand and experience the verse or message very differently: they will experience the verse and message as a Child, a Young Adult, or a Parent in the faith. Likewise, believers can discover their spiritual gifts to employ in God's service, but such service will be exercised as a Child, a Young Adult, or a Parent in the faith. A Parent in the faith has climbed higher and can see farther and more broadly than the Child or Young Adult in the faith, but every believer—wherever he or she is in the journey—benefits from the memorization and preaching; and the body of Christ benefits from the service that Christians in all three stages of development offer.

Tragically, though, it seems that as the journey of faith continues and becomes something of a climb, more and more people get sidetracked along the way; they choose a favored peak for its unique view and stay or plateau at that level of spiritual maturity. Christians should value each stage for its unique richness—but we definitely need to keep moving! Also, while guiding others on the journey, we must be careful not to speak of an experience at one stage as if it is in any way better or inferior to another. Believers who have advanced to the Parent stage of faith are not better or superior Christians. They are, however, fundamentally and qualitatively different from the Child or Young Adult in the faith. The seasoned Parent in the faith has a greater experiential knowledge of the faith, a more intimate relationship with God, and a deeper, firsthand faith.

Parents in the faith have suffered more in battle and used more of their gifts to serve others. That's why Parents in the faith are able to challenge fellow believers and point them to the peaks ahead, where new blessings await.

In addition to experiencing greater richness in one's faith and one's relationship with Christ, growing also involves losing limitations. In the course of one's development, the limitations of less mature perspectives disappear as more mature perspectives are acquired. Believers can also expect a diminishing of distortion and the falling away of harmful or inadequate patterns of living as they move from stage to stage. Dr. Mark Young says that development is the "the process of overcoming, through the power of the Spirit working through the matrix of human development, the limitations (which are incurred because of the Fall) upon each person's capacity to bear the image of Christ."[34] As mentioned above, not all believers arrive at a full-grown, mature faith.

Let me close this discussion of the shape of development with these generalizations:

- It has already been demonstrated that all believers will cycle back and revisit unfinished areas, but some believers have done little or no work on the milestones of the Childhood stage, even though they may have been following Jesus for a long time. These believers, regardless of how long they have been Christians, will need to revisit the Childhood stage and grow in those areas that have been neglected.
- Too many Christians plateau or stall, some permanently, in the Young Adulthood stage. These believers get stuck in a borrowed, secondhand faith, a faith that is largely a set of correct but untested beliefs, a set of beliefs governed by a reliance on the approval of significant others.
- The church today is experiencing a shortage of seasoned, experienced Parents in the faith who are worthy models of maturity and Christlikeness and who assume the responsibility of skillfully guiding fellow believers along the path of spiritual growth.

Issue: Individual Differences

Finally, N.J. Salkind asks, "How does the theory explain differences in development between individuals of the same chronological age?" In response—and as stated above—spiritual growth is neither inevitable nor guaranteed. Spiritual growth does not happen automatically with the passing of time. Neither is it irreversible. Not every believer will continue to develop into the "likeness" (1 John 3:2) of Christ as he or she was created to.

Conclusion 11: Spiritual growth is idiosyncratic.

The social sciences have noted some descriptions, explanations, contours, mechanisms, and patterns at work in growing people and, consequently, suggest what Christians might experience through life. However, substantial differences as to when and how the process of growth will occur and be experienced exist among individual believers.

As demonstrated earlier, growth is complex and idiosyncratic for each believer: "These tectonic shifts happen in various ways, along a range of different fault lines in the same person."[35] Development is not an ever-increasing amount of growth that occurs in a steady, continuous fashion. It may do so, but development is also discontinuous and irregular. Some changes will occur more rapidly during certain periods and less rapidly during others. We can be comforted in knowing that God is patient in waiting and inviting each believer to grow at a pace that is just right.

The stages of faith model is broad enough to speak to all Christians, but we must acknowledge that the stages of development will be experienced differently, according to people's ages, cultures, genders, and personality types. Yet, whatever the specifics of who we are and when and where we live, Christian transformation is an ongoing process from the beginning to the end of our lives, and it impacts every area of our being—our thinking, feeling, choosing, behaving, and relating. Though everyone will pass common milestones, the experience and the timing will vary from person-to-person.

In other words, each of us will pass through the same stages in the same order, but not in the same way. There are substantial differences among believers as to the particulars of *when* and *how* the stages are experienced. Recall the three kinds of factors that interact and result in growth: normative, age-graded influences; normative, history-graded influences; and non-normative influences (see Conclusion 6). How are Christians to view these? First, we can appreciate the way both God's design and His personalized handiwork are exhibited in and through each of these three types of influences. We can also choose to cooperate with the unique purposes and work of God in our lives. Certainly there is mystery, but we as Christians can trust our God, who can and does creatively, sometimes unexpectedly, direct and develop His people's growth. As Paul Tournier observed, "Man, unlike nature, can have springtime in autumn."[36] (In circumstances like that, a Parent in the faith can help a fellow believer see God at work.)

A key aspect of the truth that God has a personal design for every believer's life is that no two believers travel identical paths. As Benedict Groeschel observes, "We all take the same journey and must pass through similar stages and ways. But like travelers across a continent, we have different experiences of the same reality."[37] Spiritual growth may be triggered by unique life experiences, significant events, and turning points that do not occur at any predictable or scheduled time. In such seasons of challenge, if not pain, people are most open to change. Whatever the emotions of those seasons of life—apprehension, disenchantment, fear, deliverance, relief, excitement, or something else—the result may be deeper faith.

An individual's experience of spiritual growth is also mediated by personality or temperament. The chart below describes four approaches to the Christian experience—approaches reflective of different personality types—and their respective emphases. You will likely see yourself in one or more of these emphases. All of us, for instance, know intellectual Christians who tend to be critical of those who emphasize spiritual intuition, and vice versa. We also know that activists get frustrated with the contemplatives, and the contemplatives wonder whether or not the activists will ever stop to appreciate God for who He is. Some believers invest great energy in categorizing intelligible theological propositions, and others understand theology in terms of a love relationship with God.[38] Our personalities definitely impact our relationships with the Lord and our approaches to Christian growth.

Emphases of Types of Christian Spirituality

The Activist Approach action engagement visibility pursuing God as holy	The Contemplative Approach quietism withdrawal hiddenness pursuing God as love
The Intellectual Approach intelligibility analysis activity pursuing God as truth	The Mystical Approach ineffability intuition passivity pursuing God as one

Regardless of our temperaments and our approaches to faith, every one of us believers must grow through the three stages of faith—Childhood, Young Adulthood, and Parenthood—en route to authentic spiritual maturity. During this process, believers will come to appreciate the limitations of their temperaments well as the value of other people's approaches.

In his book *Sacred Pathways*, however, Gary Thomas observes that many Christians have lapsed into a generic, prescribed routine, perhaps following the path of growth that someone else has followed. But "giving the same spiritual prescription to every struggling Christian is no less irresponsible than a doctor prescribing penicillin to every patient." The author then describes nine spiritual temperaments or ways "we relate to God, how we draw near to him."[39] He based these pathways on biblical figures, historic church movements, and various personality temperaments. Most of us have a certain predisposition for relating to God, and that mode is our predominant spiritual temperament. Thomas explores the strengths and pitfalls of each of these temperaments:

- Naturalists: loving God out of doors
- Sensates: loving God with the senses
- Traditionalists: loving God through ritual and symbol
- Ascetics: loving God in solitude and simplicity
- Activists: loving God through confrontation
- Caregivers: loving God by loving others
- Enthusiasts: loving God with mystery and celebration
- Contemplatives: loving God through adoration
- Intellectuals: loving God with the mind

A maturing Christian, Thomas suggests, will learn from all these temperaments and appreciate fellow believers who walk with the Lord differently than he or she does. God is bigger than we can possibly know via our limited temperaments and from our finite experiences. God wants each one of us to increasingly know Him and love Him so that we will confidently and expectantly walk with Him on a personalized route He specifically designed for us to travel on. Though our temperaments differ, we all will grow through the predictable stages of Childhood, Young Adulthood, and Parenthood in the faith.

I was recently reminded at the gym, of all places, that spiritual growth is one of a kind. I was ready to mount an elliptical bike for some cardio when I noticed a sign conspicuously posted on it: "Under Repair. We apologize for any inconvenience. Repairs will be made as quickly as possible. Parts are on order." Something on the bike was faulty, and management was taking care of the problem, so I moved on to another machine. Similarly, God knows where each of us has faulty parts that desperately need to be repaired so we can function as He designed us to function. The damage is not irreparable, the repairs are in process, and our Creator and Designer will restore us.

Issue: Individual Differences

Conclusion 12: Spiritual growth is not inevitable.

Spiritual growth is not inevitable, automatic, or irreversible. Growth can be interrupted, crippled, stalled, stalemated, and even reversed. In fact, neglecting or inadequately dealing with any developmental, spiritual milestone can endanger, delay, and distort spiritual growth. Unfinished business at one stage prevents the believer from fully engaging in the next stage.

As we saw in Chapter 3, an individual's spiritual development can be slowed and even stopped, and passages like 1 Corinthians 3:1–4; Hebrews 5:11–14; Ephesians 4:12–16; and 2 Peter 1:5–9 show that Christians can find themselves stuck and not growing. Some people, for whatever reason, refuse to change. It is, for instance, quite possible for a deeply committed Christian to be psychologically impaired at some significant level. Clearly, not all believers attain full maturity in every part of their lives. In *Nurture That Is Christian*, John Dettoni and James Wilhoit note that personal comfort and lack of nurture can arrest progress:

> Development can be thwarted or stalemated. Not everyone will continue to develop to what he or she was created to be. People often do not want to move from their state of equilibrium because it causes too much discomfort. Likewise, environment can play a thwarting role by not providing sufficient nurture and support to encourage growth.[40]

Benedict J. Groeschel, author of *Spiritual Passages*, observes that growing faith can stall if it becomes perfunctory or routinized:

> When the choices of life are not faced or made deliberately, the familiar picture of a lukewarm believer begins to emerge in midlife. Faith, while not destroyed, becomes perfunctory in its expression. Perceptible spiritual growth slows down or disappears.[41]

Perry Downs suggests that James Fowler's stages can help us understand the maturity of believers in our congregations and small groups. As Christian educators and faith shapers, we will need to listen to the structure of faith, not just the content of faith, and we will pay attention to the maturity of faith, not just the strength of faith.

> Lower stages of faith are not inappropriate for young persons. A young adolescent in stage-two faith can have a *strong* faith (a deep commitment to God), which is perfectly appropriate to his or her age. But if the same person continues in a stage-two structure well into adolescence or adulthood, the faith can be said to be strong, but immature. That is, it is not developmentally appropriate for the person's age and place in life.
>
> The young child who believes God will protect her from all harm has a strong belief in the sovereignty of God and the specific childlike perceptions of what God's love for her entails. Such a belief may be appropriate for a child. But when she becomes an adult, if she still believes that nothing "bad" can happen to her because of her faith, she is both misguided and immature.[42]

As life unfolds, every believer will encounter critical times for healing or reworking some underlying patterns of one's emotional or relational life. At these points, the mature adult must relinquish old patterns, habits, and assumptions. The deepest convictions and most profound hurts may require reexamination and reworking. But when we cease to grow or we stop being involved in the dynamic process of becoming more the Christlike individuals God wants us to be, we are in a negative process of becoming; we are in decline.

Janet Hagberg and Robert Guelich, authors of *The Critical Journey: Stages in the Life of Faith,* point out that we can get stuck, trapped, and "caged" as we journey, and then we are no longer making progress in the faith.

> We may rest on the way. We may even stop for periods of time to visit friends or sightsee. But we are still traveling. However … we can get stuck along the way; not just visiting people, sightseeing, or pausing to learn but stopping at a stage and getting bogged down in an unhealthy way … When stuck long enough, we get

> trapped. Frequently this happens unconsciously. When stuck, we generally do not think we are stuck. To others, however, it is very apparent. The stage has become for us a cage.[43]

Finally, John's stages of faith model offers its own predictions of individual differences in spiritual progress. It suggests, for instance, that many Christian believers, regardless of how many years have passed since salvation, will probably need to attend to the milestones in the formative Childhood stage of faith. Also, John's model may help explain why many believers fall short of the firsthand faith of the Young Adulthood stage and plateau in a secondhand, conforming faith. Finally, John's model, when informed by developmental theory, hints at why many believers do not progress to the full-grown Parenthood stage of faith, the goal of spiritual maturity.

The fact that growing in one's faith is not inevitable and can stall should prompt believers to be humbly open and vulnerable with God, as Saint Augustine was in his work *Confessions* (354–430 A.D.). Transformation is really God's business, and our responsibility is to rely on Him to reshape us. May we cry out as Augustine did:

> My soul is like a house, small for You to enter, but I pray You to enlarge it. It is in ruins, but I ask You to remake it. It contains much that You will not be pleased to see: this I know and do not hide.[44]

Conclusion

These two chapters on "The *How* of Spiritual Growth" outline some dynamic possibilities for change and growth that believers can expect to encounter on their lifelong journeys of faith. Having read these chapters, you may now more fully understand and therefore be better able to communicate your own history of spiritual growth. Besides offering insights into one's journey, the twelve Conclusions offer vital clues for those individuals who provide care, direction, and discipleship to others. In fact, maybe now we can better heed

Perry Downs's caution and listen to how people believe, pay attention to what they believe, and be concerned about helping their faith become more mature, not just stronger.

Again, Richard Foster's plea that believers become "deep" is a timely one, and the situation—in Donald Alexander's words—where divergent paths of sanctification cause confusion must be remedied. Believers in Christ need to become familiar with a way forward and upward that is biblical, sensible, and compelling.

Recall that Christian educators Ronald Habermas and Klaus Issler consider further study of biblical stages a promising way to describe the spiritual maturation process. Chapters 8 and 9 have sought to lift some of the fog by outlining a path of biblical stages by which believers can locate where they are on their journeys toward becoming increasingly transformed followers of Christ. Also, those who care for the spiritual development of other people can look to this stages of faith path as a tool for skillfully guiding others toward Christlikeness. The *how* of spiritual growth truly is an empowering and encouraging study.

Questions for Reflection and Action

1. Chapter 9 addressed seven of the Twelve Conclusions. Choose two or three to comment on: Why is it key to understanding spiritual growth? What pressure might this insight take off a believer? What encouragement for growth might it spark?

   Conclusion #6: Change is triggered by scheduled and unscheduled events.
   Conclusion #7: Change is discontinuous, but some continuity is evident.
   Conclusion #8: Stages of faith are sequential.
   Conclusion #9: The stages are cumulative.
   Conclusion #10: Stages move the believer toward spiritual maturity and, ultimately, Christlikeness.
   Conclusion #11: Spiritual growth is idiosyncratic.
   Conclusion #12: Spiritual growth is not inevitable.

2. Change—or spiritual growth—can result from scheduled as well as unscheduled, unanticipated events in life. Give an example of each.
3. In Conclusion 7, this observation was shared: "As we are being transformed to the likeness of Jesus ... our own spiritual calcification must be broken down." What calcification has been broken down in your life? Describe that process. What areas of calcification need to be addressed? If you're not sure, ask the Holy Spirit to show you not only the *what* but also the *how*.
4. Review the discussion of qualitative and quantitative growth (pages 197–201). What evidences do you see that you are following the growth path of caterpillar to butterfly rather than kitten to cat? Share, for instance, a new understanding of the world you have gained during your months or years as a believer.
5. Look again at the chart that shows different types of Christian spirituality (page 204). Do you see yourself more as an Activist, Comtemplative, Intellectual, or Mystical? Explain your choice with specific evidence from your life, personality, likes/dislikes, etc. What means of worship and therefore spiritual growth do the descriptions of the other three types suggest to you? Which one or two will you try this week?

CHAPTER 10

THE SPIRITUAL GROWTH PROFILE

WHAT KIND OF SHAPE ARE YOU IN?

WHEN R. L. Bassett took an empirical look at what it means to be a mature Christian, he examined the instruments commonly used to measure different dimensions of spirituality and maturity. He concluded that an instrument that measures discrete stages of spiritual maturity is much needed:

> A developmental perspective on Christian maturity would seem informative. Implicit in all of the instruments used in this study seems to be the assumption that Christian growth is a continuous process. Christians can be more or less mature, but there doesn't seem to be any recognition of the possibility that there may be *discrete stages of maturity*. Looking toward the future, it would seem that instruments specifically designed to measure Christian maturity could borrow important ideas from theories/instruments designed to measure religious maturity.[1]

Instruments that purport to measure some aspects of spiritual maturity do exist; although, none are widely used. I considered five of the most promising instruments that have been used more widely by Christians than others:

1. Allport's Intrinsic and Extrinsic Religiosity (Allport, 1959)
2. Spiritual Well-Being Scale (Paloutzian and Ellison, 1982)
3. Spiritual Maturity Index (Ellison, 1983)
4. Religious Status Interview (Malony, 1985)
5. Religious Status Inventory (Malony, 1988)

Do these tools truly measure Christian growth? After looking at their stated purposes, the underlying conceptual basis of each, and their empirical effectiveness and deficiencies, I developed the 1 John 2:12–14 stages of faith paradigm, a unique model by which an individual can measure spiritual progress.

Tools other than those listed above are more popular in certain corners of the Christian community. One resource is the *Spiritual Health Assessment and Spiritual Health Planner.*[2] Based on Rick Warren's *Purpose Driven Life*, this tool looks at "five vital signs" of a healthy Christian life: Worship, Fellowship, Discipleship, Ministry, and Evangelism. A second resource is *The Christian Life Profile: A Discipleship Tool to Access Christian Beliefs, Practices, and Virtues.*[3] Randy Frezee is the principal author of this tool and senior pastor of Pantego Bible Church in Fort Worth, Texas. Frezee notes thirty core competencies to help churches know when they are effectively guiding their members toward Christlikeness. Both of these tools, however, measure narrow aspects of the Christian life, focusing on external behaviors rather than describing a holistic, comprehensive picture or map of the believer's transformation.

I developed the Spiritual Growth Profile to operationalize the 1 John 2:12–14 stages model and to then measure a believer's progress in the three specific stages of faith. The eight milestones in John's model are not only describable but also measurable, even if only in relative or subjective terms. This instrument was developed in an attempt to reliably determine the distance a believer has already traveled along the journey of faith and to identify that Christian's strengths and weaknesses in the stages of Childhood, Young Adulthood, and Parenthood. These three stages offer followers of Christ a map to locate how far they have traveled, a means of determining the distance remaining to the destination of being more like Christ, and suggestions for possible routes to that God-ordained goal.

Within the Christian community, the Spiritual Growth Profile (SGP) will be useful for:

- Self-Discovery. How far along am I in my journey to Christian maturity? What are the strengths and weaknesses of my walk with Jesus? What can I do to experience spiritual health?
- Mentoring. The Christian who wants to disciple another Christian can use this tool to prompt the respondents to tell their stories and then to provide guidance for their further growth.
- Leading a *Stages of Faith* small group. Group members will discover their overall spiritual maturity and progress.
- Leading a Small Group Bible Study. A small group committed to study and support one another on their journeys of faith will find guidance in the SGP.
- Christian Counselors, Stephen Ministers, etc. Because stages of faith is a heuristic model, thoroughly grounded in the Scriptures and integrating research in human development and psychology, caregivers can rely on the SGP to give direction and understanding to those they minister to.
- Parents. The SGP will help moms and dads who want to skillfully guide and shape the spiritual progress of their family members. What will you emphasize? What are your goals for your child? What is spiritual wholeness for a child, a teenager, a young adult, and an older adult? At what stage of the journey are you? How will your level of spiritual development affect your children's growth?
- Teachers and Professors. Anyone who is nurturing Christian students in a college or seminary classroom will find the SGP a helpful tool.
- Preaching Pastors. The SGP can help pastors prepare messages for church members at diverse levels of spiritual development; counsel individuals, couples, and families;

provide spiritual direction to individuals; and understand their own spiritual journeys and growth.

- Leadership Training. Pastoral staff, elders, deacons, teachers, parents, youth workers, and children's workers can use the SGP as a tool in developing and training leaders.
- Leader Evaluations. This biblical paradigm of spiritual development can help leaders evaluate and guide the overall strategy of their ministry. How are we nurturing the congregation as they journey through these stages and milestones? What are our strengths as a church? In what areas are we weak? What are we doing to intentionally produce healthy Children, Young Adults, and Parents in the faith? At what point in the Childhood or Young Adulthood stages are people in our congregation likely to become stuck? What changes in strategy do we need to make to help people avoid getting stuck?
- Administrative Pastors and Staff. The SGP can prompt ideas and direction for those church leaders responsible for envisioning and planning spiritual growth strategies.
- Missions. Since the three stages and eight milestones are universal and timeless, they provide a cross-cultural map of spiritual growth. The SGP helps identify a culture's unique values and how those values are either allies or adversaries to the gospel and ongoing growth. These eight themes can help anticipate and avoid unnecessary tensions between culture and the gospel.

The Childhood, Young Adulthood, and Parenthood model offers a compelling description of the growth of a person's Christian faith as well as helpful insights into how the journey proceeds. Instead of looking at simplistic formulas or canned prescriptions, believers explore the rich metaphor of three stages of spiritual growth and the milestones that define each stage.

For a more thorough understanding of this metaphor, review in Chapters 8 and 9 the following characteristics of deep change:

1. Nature and nurture interact.
2. Growth is holistic.
3. Stages of faith are normative.
4. Stages of faith are descriptive.
5. Stages of faith are flexibly age-linked.
6. Change is triggered by scheduled and unscheduled events.
7. Change is discontinuous with elements of continuity.
8. Stages of faith are sequential.
9. Stages of faith are cumulative.
10. Stages move the believer toward spiritual maturity and Christlikeness.
11. Spiritual growth is idiosyncratic.
12. Spiritual growth is not inevitable.

It is my desire that, together, The Spiritual Growth Profile, the *Stages of Faith* book, and *The Path* serve as a map that both guides and interprets a person's spiritual growth. I hope you will also be encouraged, assured that God will use every believer's unique, personal story of spiritual progress to make an impact on others.

Stages of Spiritual Growth Can Be Measured

At this point, please go to www.stagesoffaith.com. At this website, you can complete the Spiritual Growth Profile free of charge and immediately see the results. Or, if you are using the profile found in the front of the *Stages of Faith* workbook, complete the profile, and then follow the instructions for scoring your "Journey of Faith" chart.

In the Spiritual Growth Profile, five statements attempt to fully define each of the eight milestones. For each of the profile's forty statements, you will indicate how true each statement is about you by using a Likert Scale of 1 ("Very unlike me") to 7 ("Very like me"). This range allows you to note the degree to which you have worked through each item. You will be instructed to respond to each of the forty items based on your own experiences, not on your beliefs, your sense of other people's expectations, or your own ideals for yourself. You will then see your progress on a graph—and, as is often the case, you may be surprised to see that you have made more progress than you thought in some areas and less progress than you expected in other areas.

This exercise will provide you with a window into your private, inner world. But, as with the results of any evaluation, you may intellectualize, deny, or rationalize away whatever is revealed. It remains up to you to look through that window with honesty and a willingness to learn from it. Transformation begins with awareness.

The Spiritual Growth Profile does not address or claim to address every aspect of spiritual growth. No single means of evaluation could. The profile does not, for instance, attempt to evaluate the orthodoxy of beliefs, the practice of spiritual disciplines, the performance of certain rituals—aspects of one's faith journey that do not necessarily serve as accurate benchmarks of Christian spiritual growth anyway. Also, the instrument does not attempt to measure spiritual well-being, religiosity, or intrinsic/extrinsic motivation, as other instruments commonly do. Gary Moon and David Benner, authors of *Spiritual Direction and the Care of Souls*, wisely issue this caution:

> When the character of mature spirituality has been reduced to specific behaviors or spiritual practices, serious souls have turned the indicators into goals and have approached maturity as a cause-and-effect achievement. [4]

What the Spiritual Growth Profile does do is affirm the areas in each of the stages of Childhood, Young Adulthood, and Parenthood where you are healthy and strong, as well as identify for you those specific areas that detain, interrupt, or thwart your spiritual growth, areas that you may have been blind to or may not yet have adequately addressed.

"My Journey of Faith" Chart

The Spiritual Growth Profile addresses who you are at the deepest levels of your being. The Journey of Faith chart provides you with a snapshot of where you are in regards to each of the eight milestones. The scoring intentionally avoids the use of scales and norms and thereby any suggestion of comparison, competition, success, or failure. Instead, your score for each Milestone suggests the extent of your progress, while the light portion suggests areas that may need your exploration and attention. Your scores for each item (based on your responses on the Spiritual Growth Profile) are also seen on the My Journey of Faith chart. These scores are clues to the distance and depth of the journey of faith you have traveled so far.

Now, before looking closely at the SPG results, review the Growth Chart on page 7 of *Stages of Faith* for an overview of the three stages and the eight milestones. Note that a core issue identifies the main focus of each milestone. This core issue consists of an all-important theme inherent in your life's story. Also, at each of the milestones, spiritual transformation can either occur or be halted.

As you note areas that may be detaining growth, realize that no stage is ever entirely free of areas that need our further attention. Also, although we human beings tend to too easily focus on our weaknesses, let yourself feel affirmed by those areas where you see health and growth.

Also, know that the lessons in the *Stages of Faith* book provide a sense of the content and the powerful influence of each of the milestones. As you complete each lesson in the *Stages of Faith* text, you will further understand where you are in your faith journey and what to do to move on. The *Stages of Faith* book can be read alone, but it is most effective in a small-group setting, where people can discuss answers to each question and hear one another's stories.

To learn from your profile, look at each of the five items of the three Childhood milestones. Each item is a clue to the depth of your spiritual progress. Note the items with the highest scores. Then observe those items with the lowest scores. Keep in mind that, even though we are adults chronologically, these Childhood milestones are not kid stuff, and we may have some significant work to do here. After all, these Childhood milestones form the foundation, the building blocks, for a life of deep spiritual growth. Repeat these steps for the Young Adulthood stage and the Parenthood stage.

What follows are the five key aspects that define each of the eight milestones identified in the Spiritual Growth Profile. Scattered throughout the profile are ten statements in the negative (1, 2, 6, 10, 12, 27, 28, 31, 35, and 39). That is done intentionally to keep respondents alert and thoughtful: they cannot assume that for each question, 1 is low and 7 is high. The computer reverses the score of those ten items so that, for example, if you scored a 3 on Item #1, it becomes a 5—and you will do the same on your hard copy of the profile. A score of 4 stays the same.

The Childhood Stage

#1. Grounded in God's Grace and Forgiveness

1. There are things about myself that I don't share with God. I often pretend and hide the "real" me from Him.

10. I have doubts and lingering reservations about whether God fully accepts me just as I am.

20. In the deepest places of my secret life, I feel God's love and approval.

27. I feel that I must do more to gain God's approval and acceptance. I seem to never quite do enough or be good enough for Him.

38. I have experienced God's love and healing in every hurt and disappointment of my childhood, adolescence, and adulthood.

#2. Embracing God as Father

6. I often experience God as punishing, unpredictable, or angry with me.

15. I experience God as safe, and I fully trust Him, without resistance, reluctance, or reservation.

18. I examine my faith for any inadequate and inaccurate ideas about God.

29. On a personal, emotional level, I experience God as close and caring.

35. I do not fully trust God or rest in His care.

#3. Growing Up Together

4. I have Christian friends who reach out to know me and touch my needs.

11. I have relationships where I openly and honestly express my needs and hurts. I can totally be myself—faults and all.

21. I have friends with whom there is a common commitment to know, support, and challenge one another toward personal growth and spiritual maturity.

31. I do not presently have friends who provide the kind of support and challenge that I need to grow stronger in my faith.

39. I don't share myself deeply with others. I don't let others fully know me.

The Young Adulthood Stage

#4. Owning a Firsthand Faith

2. I tend to believe and behave like other Christians expect me to.

12. My actions are determined by "What will other people think? Will I disappoint others or hurt their feelings?"

24. I have moved far away from conforming to other people's opinions, expectations, oughts, and ought nots.

32. I examine and am deliberate about the personal convictions, values, and beliefs that are guiding my journey.

40. I examine and modify the *what* and *why* of each of my beliefs, my values, and my lifestyle.

#5. Linking Truth and Life

5. I consistently and thoughtfully apply biblical principles to the problems, choices, and events of my daily life.

14. Every book of the Bible reshapes the way I think and the way I live my life.

19. God's Word challenges, modifies, and orients every area of my life.

26. I am practiced at examining and revising all my thoughts, emotions, and actions according to God's Word.

37. I daily study and apply God's Word to my day-to-day circumstances.

#6. Defeating the Enemies of Spiritual Growth

7. I see through the deceptions, lies, and illusions in the world around me.

16. I recognize and shore up my vulnerability to each of my arch-enemies—the world, the flesh, and the devil.

23. I am free of any hurt, habit, or hungering that would keep me from becoming whole and Christlike.

28. Certain habits or patterns of thought or behavior have a hold on me.

36. I discard the values of my culture that conflict with my loyalty to Christ.

The Parenthood Stage

#7. Empowering Others

8. I frequently help others discover their potential for spiritual growth and realize untapped possibilities for going farther on the journey.

13. People often look to me for insight, support, and challenge in their spiritual progress.

17. I frequently enable others to more fully follow God.

25. In my relationships, I am skilled at listening carefully and understanding accurately.

34. I offer a biblical perspective whenever I help others work through the struggles and questions they face in life.

#8. Seasoned by Time and Experience

3. My spiritual maturity is seasoned, proven, and full-grown.

9. I strongly resemble Christ in my character, conduct, and life purposes.

22. My character has been deeply refined by facing and overcoming painful struggles and adversities.

30. I have long experienced a deep faith in Christ and a spiritual maturity that nourishes and sustains me.

33. Life experiences have taught me to fully trust God no matter what the uncertainty, disappointment, or tragedy.

What Stage of Faith Am I In?

How far have I come in my spiritual journey? Am I in the Childhood, Young Adulthood, or Parenthood stage of faith? Looking at your Journey of Faith chart, you may note progress in the milestones of each of the three stages, but remember that we never completely outgrow a stage. Also, your Journey of Faith chart will show that you are living in more than one stage, but you will find yourself more at home in one of those stages. You will operate primarily out of that one stage, and that stage will affect your work in the other stages. This stage best characterizes where you are on your journey of faith, and this stage influences and, in part, determines your responses at each milestone. (This idea is developed more fully in Chapter 8, Conclusion 9: The stages are cumulative.)

A spiritual director or good companion in the faith will remind us that the journey is not a race to complete in record time. Nor is it a quest to acquire more information or champion certain spiritual practices. Authentic transformation takes time; it will not be hurried, nor will it be reduced to formulas or activities. These comments are meant to encourage you to be honest as you look at your Journey of Faith chart and the dominant stage of faith you are in, knowing that God is at work in you and seeing in the Journey of Faith chart where He is working.

In *Invitation to a Journey*, Robert Mulholland prompts us to look below the surface, just as the SGP enables us to:

> I do not know what your perception of Christian discipleship might be, but much contemporary spirituality tends to view the spiritual life as a static possession rather than a dynamic and ever-deepening growth toward wholeness in the image of Christ. When spirituality is viewed as a static possession, the way to wholeness is seen as the acquisition of information and techniques that enables us to gain possession of the desired state of spirituality . . .
>
> When spirituality is viewed as a journey, however, the way to spiritual wholeness is seen to lie in an increasingly faithful response to the One whose purpose shapes our path, whose grace redeems our detours, whose power liberates us from our crippling bondages of the prior journey, and whose transforming presence meets us at each turn in the road. In other words, spirituality is a pilgrimage of deepening responsiveness to God's control of our life and being.[5]

Realize, too, that you may have carefully attended to a particular milestone to the best of your ability at the time. But new life circumstances and events will call for a deeper or a fresh way of addressing that milestone. Christopher Bryant wrote this:

> Spiritual development is no steady, regular advance, but is punctuated by crises in which growth appears to have come to a stop for a time, old battles have to be refought, and old experiences relived at a deeper level.[6]

Again, God is at work in you, moving you toward deep, spiritual transformation and authentic Christlikeness with each milestone. So be alert to what you see in your Journey of Faith chart, and team up with someone who can provide skilled listening, interpretation, and direction.

The Skilled Guide

The Spiritual Growth Profile invites you to talk about your perceptions, feelings, attitudes, and experiences with someone who is farther along the journey of Christian faith. What you share will give clues to help you evaluate your spiritual progress, so this self-disclosing and history-giving should not be neglected. These actions enable you to take the vital step of acknowledging those experiences that have significantly shaped your life.

The Spiritual Growth Profile can reveal much about the significance of your life experiences and your progress on your spiritual journey, but often we ourselves are blind to the full meaning of our life experiences. That is where a skilled Parent in the faith (i.e., a pastor, counselor, Christian friend, or small-group leader) can play an important role in our spiritual growth. A mature Parent—who has already attended to the milestones in the three stages of faith—knows what threatens spiritual development and what can enrich your journey of faith. A seasoned Parent can help you develop a strategy uniquely tailored for you, one that addresses the needs identified in the Spiritual Growth Profile. With a mentoring Parent, you can develop a revitalizing strategy that addresses the present needs as revealed in the Spiritual Growth Profile. The plan will be individually tailored rather than a conveyor-belt, clone, or carbon-copy plan that is prescribed for all. This Parent can also provide you with the support, accountability, and prayer you'll need along the way.

Spiritual growth is best guided by one who has already traveled before us. The apostle John calls this seasoned, mentoring Parent a "father" (1 John 2:13, 14). These parents have deeply personalized the eight milestones, know the journey well, can share from their own stories, and are committed to being there with the necessary support and challenges for fellow believers who are in the Childhood, Young Adulthood, and Parenthood stages. Without the empowering presence and caregiving of a mature Parent, one's spiritual development is deficient, and the journey toward Christlikeness is more treacherous and less enjoyable.

This mentoring Parent is alert and sensitive to the catalytic core issue at each of the eight milestones. He or she is looking with you for evidence or symptoms of health and progress, as well as for clues as to what unfinished business remains in these vital, core areas. The mentoring Parent will use the SGP as a map to guide discussion, to assess and interpret strengths and weaknesses in the progress of faith, and to plan a course of action. Together, a believer and a Christian mentor can tailor a revitalizing strategy that fits the unique journey of that individual.

Therefore, discuss with a veteran Parent what your Journey of Faith chart and your scores on each milestone suggest about the distance and depth of your spiritual growth. Be prepared to share life stories that illustrate and give evidence of your scores. Together consider and begin charting the next steps you will take.

Once you have completed the Journey of Faith chart, you can attend to the issues that delay your spiritual growth. If you are a faith-shaper, the spiritual profiles of those people in your care will enable you to implement strategies of spiritual direction that are tailor-made for them. The Journey chart offers small-group leaders, counselors, parents, youth workers, teachers, Christian educators, church leaders, and pastors insight into how we grow spiritually, why we plateau or stagnate, and what they can do to nurture us toward spiritual maturity, wholeness, and Christlikeness.

The Spiritual Growth Profile identifies the primary issues that will either catalyze or slow your spiritual growth. The SGP also yields a Journey chart of your progress in the stages of Childhood, Young Adulthood, and Parenthood. These three stages are a convenient map for you. But remember: although a map shows you how far you have traveled, the distance remaining to your destination, and possible routes to take, it won't do the traveling for you.

Explore Your Possibilities

Consider the road you've been traveling and all that you've accomplished along your journey of faith. You may have:

- Completed the Spiritual Growth Profile.
- Created your Journey of Faith chart.
- Identified areas of spiritual strength and weakness.
- Done each of the lessons in the *Stages of Faith* book.
- Discussed in a small group the lessons and their significance to you.
- Gained a solid understanding of the apostle John's model of stages of faith as outlined in 1 John 2:12–14.
- Begun to understand what John's model says about your unique journey of faith.

Now it's time to explore your possibilities by answering the following questions. You and a skilled guide or mentor can decide which questions will be most rewarding and profitable for you to explore. Then meet together a few times to talk about your journey of faith and to discuss possibilities for your further growth.

1. Recall from "The *How* of Spiritual Growth" that stages of spiritual growth are flexibly linked to your chronological age (pages 174–178). What does your age suggest about the distance and the depth of your journey of faith?
2. What recent event(s), if any, may have influenced how you completed the Spiritual Growth Profile? Consider factors like depression, illness, stress, and loss as well as the exhilarating joy of success, accomplishment, and recognition.
3. What people, events, circumstances, factors, and forces have most slowed or interfered with your journey toward Christlikeness thus far? Be specific, and share your ideas about why they have had a detrimental effect on your spiritual growth.
4. Which of your Spiritual Growth Profile scores, if any, surprised you? Explain why you were surprised.
5. Take a minute to think about the Childhood stage of your faith. List the area(s) where you scored the highest. Then list the area(s) where you scored the lowest.

Now think about Young Adulthood stage of your faith journey. List the area(s) where you scored the highest. Next, list the area(s) where you scored the lowest.

Finally, consider the Parenthood stage of faith. List the area(s) where you scored the highest, as well as the area(s) where you scored the lowest.

6. Which of your scores, if any, reflect recent growth? Which, if any, suggest a step backward? Explain what prompted your movement in either direction.
7. In which specific stage—Childhood, Young Adulthood, or Parenthood—do you see God working most in you? Cite specific evidence as well as your ideas as to why this growth is happening.
8. Are you pleased with where you are in your spiritual growth? Why or why not? Would you be happy if you were at this same spot in a year? Why or why not?
9. At what point(s), if any, do you feel stuck? Be specific.
10. To move forward in your journey of faith and to grow spiritually, what might you need to do? List some possible steps you could take.
11. Think about a time when you intentionally tried to move forward. What did you do to foster spiritual growth? Describe your experience. What encouraged and/or interfered with the growth you'd hoped for? Did the growth that resulted last? Why or why not?
12. What risks does moving forward in your journey of faith involve? What or who might undermine your attempts to grow? Also, in what ways do you personally resist change? What might you do to overcome those tendencies and/or fears?
13. What are some of the possible consequences of choosing to remain right where you are on your journey of faith?
14. Do you know other people who may be wrestling with the same spiritual growth issue(s) you are? What steps are they taking? What do you think they (and you) could be doing to grow in faith?

15. Why would the support and challenge of a friend or a skilled spiritual guide help you to move forward? In what specific ways could a spiritually mature Christian help you along your journey? Who could fill this role in your life, or where will you go to find such a person?

As you explore possibilities for spiritual growth, know that the Lord Himself desires for you to grow even more than you do, and He will bless your efforts.

Questions for Reflection and Application

1. Complete the Spiritual Growth Profile if you haven't already. You can do so at www.stagesoffaith.com.
2. Now complete the My Journey of Faith chart if you haven't done so before now. What did you learn about yourself from this exercise? What surprised you most? What encouraged you most? What inspired you most?
3. Do you have in your life a spiritual mentor or Parent in the faith? If so and if you have met with that person to discuss your SGP and Journey of Faith chart, what insights were most helpful? If you don't have such a person in your life, make it a topic of prayer. You might also talk to a church leader who may know of someone interested in mentoring others in spiritual growth.
4. Fifteen questions are listed in this chapter's "Explore Your Possibilities" section (pages 225–227). What did you learn about yourself from your answers to the three parts of question 5?

   Also, as question 10 states, what might you need to do to move forward in your journey of faith and to grow spiritually? List some specific steps you could take and circle the one you will work on this week.

CHAPTER 11

THE CHILDHOOD STAGE OF FAITH

THE BIRTH OF FAITH THAT IS BIBLICALLY BASED AND DEVELOPMENTALLY INFORMED

AS CHAPTERS 5–7 show, the stages of faith model is deeply rooted in Scripture. However, the content, meaning, and importance of each milestone; the potential for spiritual growth at each milestone; and the effects if that milestone are neglected. Remember, every aspect of the metaphorical stages of Childhood, Young Adulthood, and Parenthood is always carefully and exclusively grounded in God's Word.

Now Chapters 11–13 will reveal how insights from the field of human development support each of the eight milestones of spiritual growth. Further shedding light on this powerful correspondence between spiritual and developmental growth, Table 6 describes each milestone more specifically than the table in Chapter 2 does. Table 6 includes the following information as well:

1. The core issue of the milestone's content
2. A summary statement that encapsulates the primary meaning of the core issue in each milestone
3. The developmental insights that support this aspect of spiritual growth

This synthesis of developmental research with the biblical model of stages of faith yields a description and explanation of the core issue of each milestone. These eight milestones, which powerfully shape or misshape a believer's development, need to be understood and nurtured throughout one's life. In addition, personal stories from believers illustrate not only the kind of deep spiritual transformation that can occur at each milestone but also the roadblocks we believers can expect the world, the flesh, and the devil to throw into our paths and slow our growth. Parents in the faith will hear such stories and gain skill in providing guidance.

Consider now an illustration of this stage of spiritual growth. Childhood is a time of intense learning. Think about all that you learned during those early years—everything from walking to reading, tying your shoes, and playing baseball. You were exposed to many new ideas and skills, many of them fundamental to life. Similarly, during the Childhood stage of faith, we need to learn many lessons that are fundamental to a lifetime of spiritual growth. The three milestones of Childhood review key truths that serve as the foundation for your lifelong walk of faith. Working through these milestones and deeply personalizing the truths they teach are essential steps in the Childhood stage of faith.

Table 6: The Childhood Stage of Faith and Developmental Growth

Milestone	Core Issue/ Content	Summary	Growth Process
#1 Experiencing God's Grace and Forgiveness	Concept of Self: A New Way of Relating to Self	God loves believers unconditionally. Every believer is secure and significant as a child of God. Confident of God's saving grace and full acceptance, believers can progressively receive God's restorative grace and increasingly see themselves as God sees them.	This is about learning to trust, progressively accepting God's grace and releasing the need to earn acceptance, and discarding pretense and performance.

Continued

Milestone	Core Issue/ Content	Summary	Growth Process
#2 Embracing God as Father	Concept of God: A New Way of Relating to God	Believers are trusting children of God who are bonded to their heavenly Father by faith in His unconditional love and care. To grow spiritually, Christians need to know God as Father, as the One in whom they can trust and to whom they can fully surrender. Believers will replace any distorted ideas of God with the truth about Him and then let their heavenly Father re-parent them.	This is about learning to be intimate with God and discarding false concepts of God.
#3 Growing Up Together	Concept of Others: A New Way of Relating to Others	Believers will grow spiritually as they progressively experience the mutually supportive and challenging relationships found in the family of God. God's children grow whole in community, not in isolation.	This is about growing as a result of supportive and challenging relationships with fellow believers.

These three milestones of Childhood give shape to critical aspects of faith as well as to a believer's inner and outer worlds. During the Childhood stage of faith, believers will increasingly come to see and experience self, God, and others in a more mature and biblical way.

- At Milestone #1, believers focus on God's full forgiveness, being significant in God's view, establishing an identity based on God's gracious acceptance and unconditional love, and coming to see themselves as God does.
- At Milestone #2, believers address not only their perceptions and feelings about God but also how God truly feels about them, resulting in greater trust and more complete surrender to Him. Together, Milestones #1 and #2 define the vertical or "Jesus and me" dimension of faith, a dimension of the believer's inner world.
- Milestone #3 of Childhood encourages the formation of distinctively Christian and genuinely intimate relationships, defining the horizontal or "Jesus and we" dimension of faith, a dimension of the believer's outer world of faith.

The three milestones work in concert, synergizing and reinforcing one another throughout a believer's life. All three need to progressively crystallize and coalesce in the believer's experience.

Why are these three milestones of the Childhood stage of faith important to spiritual growth? First of all, these milestones comprise God's agenda for personal renewal. Reflecting the divine curriculum for spiritual birth and new life in Christ, these Childhood milestones serve as the foundation for the Young Adulthood and Parenthood stages; therefore, they are determining the quality of future spiritual growth. Second, these Childhood milestones are important because God uses them to heal us, free us, and move us toward wholeness and Christlikeness. Growth in faith will be delayed if these three milestones are neglected or any of the work is left unfinished.

Note how the diagram below illustrates the interdependence of the milestones. The ribbon wrapping around the stages in the diagram suggests ongoing movement, because—as discussed in Chapters 8 and 9—spiritual growth is dynamic, elastic, fluid, flexible, and irregular; it is never static, fixed, or unchangeable. Notice that the new message in each milestone of John's stages is

Milestone #1

Experiencing God's Grace and Forgiveness

To grow spiritually, I need to believe that I am loved unconditionally. Once I am certain of God's forgiveness and confident that He accepts me in Christ, I will be able to discard pretense and my masks and receive His healing.

Milestone #2

Embracing God as Father

To grow spiritually, I need to know God as my Father, as the One in whom I can trust and to whom I can surrender my life. In order to know God as Father, I will replace my distorted ideas of God with biblical truth about Him and then let my heavenly Father re-parent me.

Milestone #3

Growing Up Together

To grow spiritually, I need to experience the mutually supportive and challenging relationships that can be found in the family of God. After all, we who are God's children grow whole when we're in community, not in isolation. We really do need one another.

derived from Scripture and enlivened by insights about human development.

Childhood Is Forever

Throughout your life, you will return again and again to each of the three milestones of Childhood for enrichment and reworking. Life events will trigger the need for renewal and for grounding yourself once again in God's truth about who you are as His child. Healthy Christians will strengthen their biblical concepts of self, God, and relationships with others throughout their lives. It will become apparent that the three milestones are not remedial or childish.

Christian adults will progressively work on these Childhood milestones throughout their lives, strengthening and revising their concept of self, God, and relationships with others. You and I will never outgrow these basic truths, and any progress we make along our journeys toward spiritual maturity depends on having this three-part guardrail in place. Furthermore, each of the three milestones serves as a powerful agent of change and growth. We cannot rush through or skip any of these milestones of Childhood. If any of these three formative milestones is neglected or if our efforts to resolve them are inadequate or incomplete, ongoing spiritual growth and wholeness will elude us—no matter how many years we have named Jesus as our Savior and Lord.

As mentioned above and as indicated in the diagram below, insights from the study of human development support and help explain these milestones of the Childhood stage of faith. The names in parentheses credit those social scientists whose ideas offer the basis for the discussions that follow.

Table 7: Social Science's Perspectives on the Childhood Stage of Faith

Milestone	Descriptive Title	Theorist
Milestone #1	Experiencing God's Grace and Forgiveness	Trust vs. Mistrust (Erikson)
Milestone #2	Embracing God as Father	God Concept (Rizzuto)
Milestone #3	Growing Up Together	Intimacy vs. Isolation (Erikson) Observational Learning (Bandura) The Affiliative Style of Faith (Westerhoff)

Milestone #1

Experiencing God's Grace and Forgiveness: A New Way of Relating to Self

Milestone #1 is about personalizing the reality of God's grace in thorough, deep, and restorative ways. As Christians progressively awaken to God's wholehearted and unshakable acceptance of them, they will be more able to grow stronger and travel farther in their faith.

In Milestone #1, there is to be the formation of the believer's identity or self-concept. Change and growth toward spiritual maturity take place when believers know that they are fully accepted and forgiven. God's grace restores brokenness and replaces shame. If believers neglect this milestone, self-condemnation, legalism, or perfectionism will misshape their faith as well as their identity. Believers will not likely be able to face their sin and brokenness honestly.

Based on 1 John 2:12 ("I am writing to you, little children, because your sins have been forgiven you for His name's sake"), Milestone #1 addresses the core issue of self-concept and identity. The truth to be progressively nurtured here is, "I am significant as God's child. I am unconditionally loved by Him. I am absolutely secure in His love." Certain of God's saving grace and confident that you are fully accepted, you can progressively receive God's restorative grace. The life you live will become grace-based, and you will increasingly see yourself as God sees you. You should be:

- *Moving away*... from dys-grace and toxic faith—from your sense that you are ineligible for God's love and forgiveness; from self-condemnation and self-justification; from being motivated by reward and punishment; from performing to please and an addiction to approval; from the legalism and tyranny of *ought*; from pretense; and from shame-based living that will sabotage your adult life.
- *Moving toward*... grace-based living—toward reprogramming your thinking about yourself based on God's grace and truth; toward finding security and significance as a child of God; toward confidence in God's certain, unconditional, and nonrepayable love; and toward experiencing divine healing of any crippling hurts, habits, or hungerings.

Every believer needs to personally discover that God's love is relentless, reliable, and restorative. You will again and again return to these Childhood milestones in order to deepen your experience of your heavenly Father's causeless, ceaseless, and measureless love for you.

Your ongoing spiritual growth will be sustained by your assurance that you are fully loved and fully forgiven by God. Your self-worth, your sense of security, and your awareness of your significance as a person must become grounded in God's certain, unconditional, and non-repayable grace. God's grace is the basis for spiritual renewal and all progress toward wholeness. The healthy formation of personality is related to the acceptance of one's intrinsic worth. The knowledge that God cares about you, the feeling of being accepted by Him, provides an incentive to commitment and change as it hints at the possibility of a progressively deeper, richer experience of Him.

If a believer does not attend to this milestone, an attitude of self-condemnation will lead to attempts to earn acceptance based on performance, and an inadequate self-esteem can take hold. Failure to embrace God's grace often results in an inadequate view of God (Milestone #2) and will prevent meaningful relationships or community with fellow believers (Milestone #3).

At the point of salvation, the believer accepts God's unconditional love and forgiveness, receiving Jesus as Savior and Lord. Then believers are to progressively "grow in … grace" (2 Peter 3:18) and be increasingly "strengthened by grace" (Hebrews 13:9). Sanctifying grace is the continuous renewal toward maturity by means of a grace-based system rather than a shame-based system. Paul prayed, "May grace and peace be yours in fullest measure" (1 Peter 1:2), suggesting that the Christian's experience of grace can enlarge. Peter went on to say, "Grace and peace be multiplied to you in the knowledge of God and of Jesus our Lord" (2 Peter 1:2).

But it is all too easy to forget who we are in Christ, to not see ourselves as God sees us. Some believers seem to limit God's salvation to the forensic act of His serving as judge in the courtroom, pardoning us, declaring us innocent, and dismissing the case. We are free to leave the cells that imprisoned us and to stand in the warm sunlight and breathe the fresh air outside. But now, as ex-convicts, we must learn to establish a new life outside the prison walls and to do so in dependence on the fact that He loves us as His children.

However, Pastor John Ortberg observes, "Too often people see the gospel as merely the front door to Christianity, or worse, 'heaven's minimum entrance requirement.'"[1] Many people's idea of the gospel is that some day we'll get to the bridge to paradise and be asked, "Why should you be allowed to cross?" As long as we answer correctly, we make it across. Answer wrongly, and we're cast into the abyss. The gospel is redefined as the announcement of the minimal entrance requirements for getting into heaven. In some churches, the question, "Why should you be allowed to cross?" is all that is asked of those who attend. So some know the words, thinking they know what their standing before God is based on.

Hear these other wise words of caution: "Ever since the Fall, we have shown a striking tendency to forget who we really are... We have suffered a profound memory loss regarding how life is to be lived in friendship with God."[2]

Writer Brennan Manning expressed his regret this way:

> My last twenty-five years of pastoral experience indicate that the stunning disclosure that God is love has had negligible impact on the majority of Christians and minimal transforming power. The problem seems to be that either we don't know it, or know it but cannot accept it; or we accept it, but are not in touch with it; or we are in touch with it, but do not surrender to it.[3]

God intends for us to rest in His love and be transformed by it. He also intends His grace to free us from the people-pleasing efforts and performances by which we too often try to earn or preserve His acceptance. Grace excludes self-condemnation, self-justification, and reliance on performance because we worry that God's acceptance of us is conditional. God's grace greets us at the moment of salvation, when our spiritual journeys begin, and then He walks with us on the lifelong journey.

Sanctifying or restorative grace focuses on the lifelong process of sanctification that follows salvation. During the Childhood stage of faith, we believers will need to become increasingly familiar with God's grace, by which He—among other things—builds up and reconstructs our inner lives. This is God's reprogramming, repairing, or reconstructive grace. This divine grace also releases believers from the control and patterns of sin as well as provides a way to deal with our sin. We believers learn that we need not hide, ignore, deny, resist, defend, project, or rationalize our sin (1 John 1:9; 2:1). We learn to come out from behind the walls we have built for protection. God's grace is also the power behind our personal transformation. His grace can free each Christian to live openly in His love and to receive His healing for wounds, both hidden and otherwise. God's grace will free us from the crippling wounds and bondages of the past. Whether a believer has been abused, shamed, neglected, driven to perfectionism, or, for whatever other reason, is ashamed of his or her past, that believer can—by God's grace—choose to receive God's love.

Although children and young people can and do personally experience God's love and grace, achieving a stable identity rooted in that love and grace is beyond the ability of even high school students. The ability to identify one's self clearly and solidly as a child of God and to live free of all the defenses and false ideas learned while growing up is central to a healthy adult faith, and that ability comes as one works on this milestone. Adolescents are very much in flux as they begin to shed their fixation on self and start to deal with the questions of identity that become increasingly pressing as high school years pass. Also, not all adolescents demonstrate the abstract thinking ability that facilitates identity formation. Nor are adolescents governed by the kind of internal, self-chosen principles that would enable them to move beyond the need to conform to significant others and win their peers' approval.

Whenever believers open themselves to it, though, God's restorative grace is completely accessible to them. His grace challenges Christians to let His love heal painful memories and free them from fermenting resentments. Grace also allows believers to accept God's love and the truth that, in Christ, they are totally worthy of that love. No better illustration of this Milestone #1 truth can be found than in Victor Hugo's *Les Miserables*. Jean Valjean has spent nineteen years in a labor camp, the sentence he received after being caught stealing food for his sister's family. Upon being released, he is required to carry a yellow passport that marks him as a convict. After being rejected by innkeepers who do not want to take in a convict, Valjean sleeps on the street. Then, growing more bitter as he searches futilely for a roof over his head, Valjean is finally encouraged to go to a bishop's house, and there he encounters unexpected grace. In the middle of the night, though, Valjean steals the bishop's silverware and leaves the house. When he is caught by the police, the bishop claims that the silverware was a gift, and at that point, he gives Valjean his two silver candlesticks as well, chastising him before the startled police for leaving in such a rush that he forgot these most valuable pieces. And what impact does the bishop's grace have on Valjean? The bishop's act of generosity breaks the man's cycle of anger and sin. Jean Valjean becomes a radically new man.[4]

Just as the bishop's interaction with Valjean reshaped his life, our early childhood experiences shape our personalities, motivations, and lives. We grow into adulthood with emotional wounds and distorted ideas about self, God, and relationships that can have a deep and lasting effect on us. In fact, these injuries and untruths can usher in a "false self," an identity that makes existence bearable for us despite emotional deprivation or abusive relationships. Later, at critical times of transition and change, we must find healing for these injuries and reconstruct our false thinking. And God's grace—that we come to know and accept in Milestone #1—plays a transforming role at this point, as do the support of the grace-based community (Milestone #3) and the influence of a mature Parent in the faith (Milestone #7).

Erik Erikson

As you may remember from Intro to Psych, Erik Erikson identified eight qualitatively different psychosocial stages extending over the entire life span, each stage centering around "a salient and distinct emotional concern." Transformation is ongoing but not smooth and discontinuous. To Erikson, a crisis is any experience of significant change or new challenges in one's life. Believers can profit by looking at their life journeys and taking note of the "turning points" or "crucial periods."

An important quality of Erikson's model is that the stages are cumulative. During your life span, you must periodically return to previous stages in order to reach higher resolutions of them. "Each stage adds something specific to all later ones, and makes a new ensemble out of all the earlier ones."[5] How a person deals with the earlier stages will make negotiating subsequent stages either easier or harder. The unsuccessful resolution of any one stage leaves an individual with unresolved conflicts that are carried forward to the next stage, making it then more difficult to successfully resolve that stage.

Erikson's first stage—addressing the issue of "Trust vs. Mistrust"—corresponds nicely with Milestone #1 of the spiritual journey. Erikson and others have pointed out that the nurturing one's parents give lays the groundwork, good or bad, for a child's understanding of God. A person's understanding of self, God, and others is unconsciously shaped and misshaped in the early years as that person learns or does not learn to trust. When a child is entirely dependent on parents or other adults for food, sustenance, and comfort and when responsible caretakers meet those needs with warmth, regularity, and affection, the infant will develop a sense of basic trust of the world and of oneself. Erikson identified hope as the strength that allows infants to trust, and for a trusting person, life becomes hopeful and hope-filled.

Alternatively, the sense of mistrust or fearful uncertainty can develop if caretakers fail to provide for a child's basic needs. By extension, if you experience your parents as trustworthy, then you can begin to understand God as trustworthy. When caretakers are untrustworthy and neglectful, children develop an unhealthy level of mistrust that will affect every future relationship that calls for trust, including, if not especially, their relationship with God and their ability to trust Him. (Conversely, if a child develops an overdependence on caretakers and places too much trust in the parent, that child may develop an inability to recognize the limits of that relationship.)

Despite the impact of our parents on our ability to trust God and other people, we believers cannot blame our parents, our culture, or our early life experiences for who we are today. Every believer is responsible for who he or she is and what he or she does in the present. No believer is a helpless victim, yet we believers dare not ignore the past. Rather, we take our pain and dysfunction before

God and the healing truths of the Childhood stage of faith. Parents in the faith will make rich use of the relationships and events from a believer's past as they encourage a Child's growth.

Experiencing God's Grace and Love

In Milestone #1, believers will become increasingly able to stand strong against five opponents of grace that can delay or stall the process of spiritual growth: the rival within the believer (human nature), the rival in the church (legalism), the home's influences, the culture's impact, and dark "high places" (1 John 2:15–17). These forces can diminish a Christian's experience of grace throughout the lifelong journey of faith.

In summary, Milestone #1, Experiencing God's Grace and Forgiveness, is about personalizing God's grace in more thorough and deeply restorative ways. As Christians progressively awaken to God's acceptance, they will be able to travel deeper and farther in their faith. These Christians will also be moving from pretense to personal authenticity. As Christians attend to Milestone #1, they will find themselves becoming increasingly genuine, whole, and free from the hold of the opponents of grace. Also, during the Childhood stage of faith, believers will have a healthy focus on *being* rather than *doing*.

What follows are several personal testimonies that reveal some of the challenges that may surface when a believer is working on this first milestone. If you are providing spiritual direction to believers, look and listen carefully for evidence of both progress and any obstacles that may hinder that progress. And draw on the five items for Milestone #1 in the Spiritual Growth Profile as a rich source of dialogue. You may discover that we adults have work to do on our ways toward becoming "deep" believers.

> This first milestone taught me that all of the bad traits I see in myself—like being overweight, pouring an insane amount of effort into trying to perfect my work, allowing myself to be easily irritated and frustrated—are forgiven by God. I have placed a set of standards on myself that are so high they are unreachable;

yet I internally chastise myself and think of myself negatively when I do not measure up to the standards that I have set. In this milestone, I learned and, more importantly, I am beginning to really internalize that the only standards that matter are God's, and if He can forgive me, I can forgive myself.

Growing up in the Asian shame-based culture, I learned that I was valued only if I succeeded. Therefore I developed a tremendous fear of failure. I've seen a counselor about this, and I still struggle at times in this area. The lessons of Milestone #1 showed me that I still try to please God and win His approval in the area of my performance at work. I am very wary of trying anything new that I am not good at, worrying that I may let God or other people down because I didn't do what I feel I should be capable of doing.

I was born with an incredible drive for perfection. My dad, who rarely found my efforts acceptable, compounded this tendency. My journey toward really understanding Milestone #1 began about three years ago, when God invited me to lay down this drive for perfection. The first step toward accepting that invitation was the scariest thing I think I've ever done, and the work that I've had to do since then has been difficult. As I have worked on these milestone lessons and as I reflect on what God has been doing the past three years, it's like everything came together and I really "got" God's love and grace. I can't even describe it, but I'm like a new person.

Growing up as one of three siblings who were very close in age, I found I was competing for the attention of Mom and Dad. I thought I could "win" by being the good kid. I studied hard to get good grades, attended church, and stayed out of trouble. Was that such a bad thing? Absolutely not, but it distorted my view of authority figures and caused me to believe I must exceed the expectations of others in order to gain recognition. I felt I needed to earn love. I continued with this behavior in each of the jobs I held over the years. I worked harder than everyone else, put in longer hours, and volunteered to travel, even though I would miss out on family events. What was important to me was getting praise from my boss and his affirmation that I was valuable to the company. I thought I was being myself, but I have come to realize that I was trying to be someone I was not. I'm so thankful

> that God sees me for who I really am and that His grace is given freely as a gift that I don't deserve.
>
> As I worked through this lesson, I often found myself in tears. I did not want to face painful areas that I had kept submerged throughout my life. I never felt I was loved for myself when I was a child. My parents didn't have time for me, teachers saw me as stupid, and peers rejected me as a friend, so why should God love me? I can say that I accept God's love for me, but I have a difficult time feeling it.
>
> As a result of many hurtful, shameful things in my past, I have struggled to truly accept or believe in God's unconditional love for me. During this study of Milestone #1, I have learned and really internalized the fact that He loves me. I can now accept that nothing I do can make Him love me more and that nothing I do can make Him love me less. This is a huge relief to me, as it removes the pressure of trying to earn brownie points with God.

Milestone #2

Embracing God as Father: A New Way of Relating to God

Milestone #2 addresses the core issue of a believer's concept of God. This milestone is based on the apostle John's statement in 1 John 2:13: "I am writing to you, children, because you know the Father." The truth to be learned here is that God is a believer's completely trustworthy Parent, the heavenly Father who consistently offers His unconditional love and care. To grow spiritually, Christians need to know God as their Father, whom they can trust and to whom they can fully surrender themselves and their lives.

It is impossible to have a healthy relationship with God without having a biblically correct understanding of who He is. An incorrect, confused, or distorted concept of God will result in an unhealthy and unhelpful response to Him. Believers respond to the God they know—or think they know. Pastor and writer A. W. Tozer observed, "What we believe about God is the most important thing about us." He added, "If [believers] could see beyond their little inadequate god, and glimpse the reality of God, they might even laugh a little and perhaps weep a little."[6]

Personal, spiritual renewal and optimal growth in the Childhood stage of faith are based on a person's relationship with God as Father. As one theologian put it, "There is one attribute of God through which we are able to see all the other facets of Him. It serves as a viewpoint from which we are able to view all the other facets of His personality. God is first and foremost, above and beyond everything else, a Father." What more can we ask for than a heavenly Father who cares deeply, understands us thoroughly, is completely trustworthy, and always acts on our behalf! Believers therefore need to replace any defective ideas about God with scriptural truth about Him and then let the heavenly Father re-parent them.

A. W. Tozer wrote this:

> Our real idea of God may lie buried under the rubbish of conventional religious notions and may require an intelligent and vigorous search before it is finally unearthed and exposed for what it is. Only after an ordeal of painful self-probing are we likely to discover what we actually believe about God.[7]

The dynamic growth process at this milestone includes our:

- *Moving away*... from any faulty and distorted but persistent impressions about God that interfere with our relationships with Him. You will let go of a God you have made in your image and work to resolve any contradictions between the God of your head and the God of your heart and the God of the Bible.
- *Moving toward*... a greater trust in God and the ultimate intimacy reflected by the title *Abba* ("Daddy"), which you as a believer are privileged to call Him. You will let your heavenly Father re-parent you and, as a result, be able to more fully surrender your life to your heavenly Father.

Every believer will need to learn to trust God without resistance, reluctance, or reservation. Our heavenly Father is absolutely trustworthy, completely safe, and utterly reliable—and this is as radical a thought in the twenty-first century as it was in the first.

In fact, "during the past few decades the concept of God has been investigated more than any other religious concept."[8] As Tozer pointed out earlier, the single most important thing in our minds is our idea or image of God. And, like one's concept of self, one's concept of God is shaped by relationships with parents and significant others as well as by experiences throughout childhood and young adulthood. It is our nature to project our own insecurities and fears onto God. So, in order to develop a healthy adult faith, we need to examine and revise any distorted images, misconceptions, or caricatures of God we have accepted as true. Such untruths need to be challenged and discarded, and at the point of adulthood, a person is uniquely prepared to do that. Since no parent flawlessly models the love, forgiveness, and care of the heavenly Father, every Christian will likely need to revise his or her concept of God.

If Christians do not attend to this milestone, inaccurate and distorted ideas about God—an inability to trust and surrender to Him, intellectual questions, theological doubts, neurotic perfectionism—may persist and even cripple their journeys of faith.[9]

Your Concept of God

Just what is a "God concept"? Christian psychotherapists William and Kristi Gaultiere write this:

> Your God Image is the collection of emotional images of God that you have deep inside your heart. It's your private experience of relating to God. You might think of your God Image as your perception of God's attitudes toward you or the way that you feel He relates with you. These perceptions form a certain set of expectations about how God will treat you. Your God Image is the picture of God you draw inside your heart with the different colored crayons of your emotions... This perceptual concept of God is different than your professed beliefs about God.[10]

Simply put, your God concept has to do with what you feel God feels about you. The Gaultieres continue:

> For many of us our image of God is like Dorothy and her friends' image of the Wizard of Oz. If you remember, Dorothy was lost in the land of Oz and was homesick for Kansas. The friends she met in the land of Oz also had some problems. The scarecrow needed a brain, the tinman needed a heart, and the lion wanted courage. They had been told that the Wizard of Oz was kind and wonderful and would give them their wishes. Filled with hope, they sang and skipped down the yellow brick road to Emerald City. When they had got there and met the wizard, they were shocked by a horrifying and ugly monster on a huge screen, blowing out smoke and thundering angry threats at them. The four of them trembled in fear before this image of a terrifying wizard.
>
> They had heard that the Wizard of Oz was so kind and wonderful and would help them, yet the wizard they saw on the screen was so mean he cruelly turned them away without offering any help. It wasn't until Toto pulled open the curtain that they saw the real Wizard of Oz wasn't the one up on the screen. He was a kind old man who was gentle and caring. In the same way you may be relating to a mistaken caricature of God on the screen of your heart. It's not enough for you to think that the One you turn to for help is supposed to be loving. You need to feel in your heart that God loves you. Many people cower in fear and back away from God until they're able to see that the real God isn't the mean figure on the screen but the gentle and kind One behind the curtain.[11]

Like Dorothy and her traveling companions facing the image of a frightening wizard, you may be relating to a mistaken caricature of God on the screen of your heart. Furthermore, research strongly indicates that inaccurate ideas about God can become part of one's way of experiencing Him.

The Source of Your God Concept

What is the source of the believer's concept of God? As mentioned above, like the concept of self (Milestone #1), one's concept of God is shaped by relationships with parents and significant others as well as by life experiences. We project on God attributes of our parents. As a result, each believer has a concept of God that is distorted or inadequate in some way (1 Corinthians 13:9, 12).

Missionary, pastor, and writer David Seamands noted the following five factors that can contribute to a false image of God:

1. *A series of negative interactions with significant people*—too often, we conclude that God will relate to us in the same negative way that we were treated by people who were supposed to love us.
2. *Mistaking the guilt-inducing condemnation of one's conscience for the voice of God*—if you experienced a legalistic brand of Christianity and are very works-oriented, you may perceive God as a demanding and perfectionistic drill sergeant, barking out orders. Consequently, you may constantly fight the inadequacy, guilt, and shame that have been programmed into your thinking. Your primary emotion toward God is fear. Afraid of triggering God's anger, you may be reluctant to venture too close to Him.
3. *Ineffective religious teaching and training*—often we learn not so much from what is said but from what is *not* said. For example, believers may grow up in a church that preaches primarily about sin, salvation, and separation from worldliness—and with parents who, consequently, do not let them go to the movies or dances. In the eyes of these believers, God is a killjoy, and life is to be endured rather than enjoyed. Likewise, these believers may never hear much about God's unconditional love, forgiveness, and grace. They also miss out on learning to be honest with God, themselves, and others.

4. *Traumatic circumstances for which we blame God*—the theology of some believers does not include pain and disappointment. So when a personal crisis strikes, these individuals find it difficult to see God as a supportive ally. They think that God must be punishing them for some sin. They also cannot admit to themselves or their heavenly Father their very real anger at Him. These believers find themselves wrestling with such questions and thoughts as "How could a good God allow this to happen?" and "This would not have happened if God really cared about me!"
5. *Misinterpreting Scripture*—we have preconceived ideas and beliefs that shape the way we read and interpret verses. Slow to discover and admit these preconceptions and, often, misconceptions, we read Scripture in such a way that reinforces our distorted image of God. (Consider Matthew 5:48, "You are to be perfect as your heavenly Father is perfect." This verse could fuel neurotic perfectionism for some.) We can find support for our own dysfunctions in the Bible, and such misreadings further keep us from knowing God as He really is.[12]

Only when believers truly know God as He is, according to the truth of the Bible rather than the experiences of childhood and youth, can they fully trust Him and surrender their lives to Him.

Ana-Maria Rizzuto

Based on her research, Ana-Maria Rizzuto described the childhood process of constructing an image of God. Rizzuto observed that the early creation of a God concept results from a child's experiences with a mother, a father, and other significant adults. Children construct an idea of God that has some of their parents' characteristics, and to whatever degree that idea contradicts biblical truth, the children's sense of self will be distorted. When defense mechanisms like splitting and dissociation take place due to abuse or neglect, the child will probably construct an image of the "bad" self who deserves to be punished by a demanding and justifiably angry God, who requires performance and perfection before He extends His acceptance. Failure causes shame and guilt and blocks out any experience of grace.

Children, Rizzuto also suggested, idealize their representations of God so as to correct and compensate for some of their parents' deficiencies. In fact, such concepts of God may replace, restore, and heal the wounds that resulted from absent or inadequate parents. A growing child's concept of God starts with parents, and Rizzuto's research "makes us [parents] more deeply mindful of how, in our weakness, neglect or abuse, we can deeply impair our children's emerging faith and cripple their spirits."[13]

David Johnson and Jeff Van Vonderen note some common distortions of God. Some see Him as:

1. A God who is never satisfied, who keeps setting higher and higher goals and is eager to let you find out how much you have missed the mark.
2. A mean, vindictive God, who is waiting for us to make a mistake. Then He is able to do what He would rather do anyway, which is to point out all of our failures or to punish and humiliate.
3. An apathetic God who watches when people are hurt and abused but does nothing to help because it would mean having to challenge an authority figure or structure.
4. A God who is asleep and does not notice even when people are hurt and abused.
5. A God who is awake, close, and who sees and cares but is powerless to help when people are hurt and abused.
6. A God who is a kind and fickle baby. His mood can be manipulated by our slightest mistake.
7. The "utterly holy God." He is like a spiritual burglar alarm, ready to go off any time you think about sin.[14]

Certainly, none of these seven is a biblical view of God; yet research strongly indicates that such ideas can become part of one's way of experiencing God. Such ideas—distorted images, misconceptions, myths, and caricatures of God—need to be examined and revised according to the truth of Scripture.

Even for the healthiest Christians, clarifying one's concept of God is a lifelong assignment and a central part of reaching maturity in Christ. Myths need to be discarded. Also, a person's perceptual image of God is not necessarily the same as his or her creedal, professed beliefs about God. Too many believers may be orthodox in faith but unable to connect with, trust, and surrender to God because they experience or perceive Him in some distorted way. Many of these misconceptions were framed in a person's early developmental experiences. But a believer can take courage and, by God's grace, face the pains and deficiencies of the past, see the effects of those pains and deficiencies on his or her way of relating to God, and then, as a remedy, choose the Bible's picture of God and of being in relationship with Him. Believers who are in the Childhood stage of faith need to be freed from inadequate, sterile, and unbiblical images of God in order for Him to re-parent them. Breaking free of preconceived images is a necessary step toward building a confident, genuine relationship with the God of the Bible.

In the following personal testimonies, believers talk about the challenges they faced as they worked on this second milestone:

> I spent a great deal of my life believing that my earthly father wasn't very proud of me and that, unless I did the things he wanted me to do, he didn't really like who I was. The lifestyle that evolved out of that was a lot of attempts to win his approval while I carried on another life in secret that I knew he would frown upon.
>
> I see God as an angry old man who is frowning and will yell at me the minute He looks in my direction. I realized from this Milestone #2 lesson that my perception of God was like my childhood experience with a priest from my parish who would pick on me in front of the whole congregation. I hated to go to church because he would embarrass and demean me so much

> that I wanted to crawl under a pew and hide. This is the way I still see God. No wonder I am so reluctant to go to Him and feel uncomfortable approaching Him! How could I have been so wrong!
>
> When my parents got divorced, there was no parent really picking me. They were picking new significant others and new career paths. My brother and I were just there. For him, it was juvenile court, and for me, it was whoever would accept me. Praise God for wanting to be around and loving those who were not deemed worthy and that His message is for people like me.

Milestone #3

Growing Up Together: A New Way of Relating to Others

The first two milestones of Childhood encourage Christians to develop the vertical dimension of their faith, their inner world. Milestone #1 invites you to stop trying to earn acceptance and love and to live a life based on God's gracious and unconditional acceptance of you. Milestone #2 challenges you to examine and revise any distorted ideas you may have about God. Now, at Milestone #3 (based on 1 John 2:7–11; 3:11–18; 4:7–21; 5:1–3), you move from the vertical dimension of your faith to the horizontal, from the deeply personal to the interpersonal. Believers who have adequately attended to Milestone #1 will be better able to experience intimacy with others in Milestone #3. The apostle John knew how important being in relationships with other believers is to one's journey toward Christlikeness and spiritual maturity. After all, the Christian's concepts of self (Milestone #1) and of God (Milestone #2) are relearned and reinforced and truly experienced in community.

The vertical and horizontal dimensions of a believer's faith are equally important to a healthy Childhood. None can be neglected, as their interconnectedness illustrates. First of all, identity precedes intimacy. Healthy relationships result when we have a renewed and genuine sense of being forgiven, significant, and worthy in Christ. When we Christians let God love us deeply, we can then love others deeply (1 John 4:10, 11, 19; 2 Corinthians 5:14). When we believers experience God's grace, we can extend His grace to others. Yet, at the same time that identity precedes intimacy, identity is also realized in intimacy. Deep, caring relationships serve as the context in which one's new identity in Christ can be recognized and affirmed. God's love and forgiveness come alive through people who love one another deeply. Without such intimacy, believers cannot experience a fully renewed identity. That is why "the pilgrimage of faith must be made in the company of others."[15]

So, at Milestone #3, believers focus on their relationships with other people, because we Christians are reshaped, refined, and strengthened in the grace-based family of God. I cannot follow Jesus alone—any more than I can get married alone. We are saved from our privacy. We Christians grow spiritually when we extend God's grace and unconditional love to one another. This relational, interactional context needs to be experienced if our faith is to grow strong. Christians are to come to know and experience grace together. In the transactional context of safe and healthy relationships, believers can learn to be honest about themselves and open with others, to perceive life and reality more accurately, and to receive support during the slow and sometimes painful process of growth toward Christlikeness.

Based on words of the apostle John, "I am writing to you, little children [*teknia*]" (1 John 2:12), "brethren" (3:14), "one another" (3:11), and "beloved" (4:7), Milestone #3 emphasizes the importance of relationships with fellow believers. After all, whether we are in the Childhood, Young Adulthood, or Parenthood stage of faith, we are all *teknia,* children of God. In Milestone #3, then, we focus on developing mutually supportive and challenging relationships: we are committed to one another's spiritual growth and wholeness. God's children grow whole in community, not in isolation. Believers really do need one another.

The dynamic growth process at this milestone includes the following aspects. We are:

- *Moving away*... from superficial, detached, impoverished, and unhealthy relationships. You will work on moving away from relationships of proximity, relationships that lack real community. (In Western cultures, such unhealthy relationships are often characterized by self-sufficiency and anonymity. People in Eastern cultures, however, are often overly dependent on family and friends, and that can also lead to unhealthy relationships.)
- *Moving toward*... relationships characterized by an empowering mix of support and challenge. You'll experience "group grace," a sense of truly belonging, collaborative care, interdependence, and efforts to ensure each person's wholeness in Christ. Believers are fighting for one another's wholeness. A special place for mentoring Parents exists in such a matrix of relationships.

Milestone #3 is similar to Milestone #1 and Milestone #2 in that, like having a clear identity grounded in God's grace and an accurate concept of God respectively, relational maturity is beyond the capabilities of young people. Adolescent interactions typically focus on gaining social acceptance and conforming to norms established by one's peers. Acutely aware of what kinds of behavior will earn them approval, adolescents imitate their peers. This awareness of what other people are doing and the importance of being accepted by them can manifest itself in loyalty and conformity. Also, adolescents tend to still be too concerned about establishing their own identity or sense of self to care about, much less work on, establishing truly intimate relationships with others.

Yet believers cannot fully know the reality of love, truthfulness, or trust apart from community. It is community that makes possible the experiencing of these in dynamic fashion. Dr. Henry Cloud and Dr. John Townsend, in *Christian Beliefs That Can Drive You Crazy*, remind us of the false assumption that "if I have God, I don't need other people."[16] God made us to need both Him and other people.

Deep and strong relationships are critical to our growth as disciples of Christ:

> We must have the community to support and correct our discipleship in the world. This seems so obvious, but our practice is so frequently individualistic. Christian discipleship is not for Lone Rangers (though in all fairness, even the masked man had Tonto as his sidekick). We must resist the individualism of our culture and cultivate deep and strong relationships with others. The challenges we face are formidable; without community they become impossible.[17]

But we may not be ready or able to enter genuine Christian community. In *True Faced: Trust God and Others With Who You Really Are*, the authors assert that it is not uncommon for adults to put on a mask and begin bluffing. We marshal our best appearance, smile a lot, and say that we're doing just fine. Sadly and cruelly, our masks not only leave us lonely, but also they deceive us into believing that we can hide our true selves. Not so. In time, people can usually see what we're trying to hide. No matter how beautifully they are formed, our masks eventually reveal us to be tragic figures … because masks always crack. Yet we're not just actors in this drama. We have become directors of a badly styled play, teaching those we love how to pose and masquerade around our false self; we memorize fake lines and rehearse empty expressions.[18] Milestone #3, in contrast, points toward transformational friendships that counter such pretense and superficiality.

If we believers do not complete this third milestone, we will remain tragically isolated from others. The absence of relationships with other Christians can impair spiritual growth. In positive terms, our intimate, godly relationships with fellow believers are powerfully linked to our spiritual progress. Yet recognition of the importance of this horizontal dimension of faith appears to be largely neglected in discussions of how faith develops. Even in churches that strongly encourage members to participate in a small-group Bible study, believers may not connect deeply with people because they are not open, honest, or vulnerable with one another. These individuals may gather faithfully for education, but they may not experience edification.

Hear this word of caution: it is more important to know about what is happening in the small groups than to determine what percentage of your congregation is involved in small groups! As Quaker scholar Elton Trueblood observed, Christian fellowship without "artificiality" can revive faith. He continued:

> What we need is not intellectual theorizing or even preaching, but a demonstration. One of the most powerful ways of turning people's loyalty to Christ is by loving others with the great love of God. We cannot revive faith by argument, but we might catch the imagination of puzzled men and women by an exhibition of a fellowship so intensely alive that every thoughtful person would be forced to respect it. If there should emerge in our day such a fellowship, wholly without artificiality and free from the dead hand of the past, it would be an exciting event of momentous importance. A society of genuine loving friends, set free from the self seeking struggle for personal prestige and from all unreality, would be something unutterably priceless and powerful. A wise person would travel any distance to join it.[19]

To enjoy an authentic and mature Christian faith, every believer needs to be sure to attend to Milestone #3.

Erik Erikson

As mentioned earlier, Erik Erikson identified eight stages of life. His sixth stage addresses the issue of "Intimacy vs. Isolation," and the ability to be intimate is impacted by the quality of work an adult has done in earlier stages of development. According to Erikson, only with a reasonably well-integrated identity will intimacy with other people be possible. For people with an unformed or incomplete identity, relationships will remain shallow, and these individuals will experience a sense of isolation or loneliness. Without any meaningful level of intimacy, a person becomes psychologically isolated, and relationships are mechanical, cold, and empty. Erikson said this:

> It is only after a reasonable sense of identity has been established that real intimacy with the other sex (or for that matter, with any other person or even with oneself) is possible... The youth who is not sure of his identity shies away from interpersonal intimacy; but the surer he becomes of himself, the more he seeks it in forms of friendship, combat, leadership, love, and inspiration.[20]

Also, Erikson describes the "radius of significant others" that affects the developing person. The radius increases as the individual develops and grows. In Milestone #3, the adult believer can choose to examine and revise the quality of the relationships that are within his or her radius in light of what God wants for His people.

Finally, interaction with other people can also serve as an impetus for change. Communities assist in shaping development. In fact, "the character of the community shapes the character of its people."[21] Educator, Lawrence Richards, emphasizing socialization and moral development, regards the relationships as absolutely essential. Richards contends, "It is Truth that is communicated in the context of a close and loving relationship that will be used by God to remold and renew the believers personally toward Christ."[22] Hauerwas clearly highlights the value of community for Christian character formation: "The most important social milestone of Christians is to be nothing less than a community capable of forming people with virtues sufficient to witness of God's truth in the world."[23]

Albert Bandura

Albert Bandura studied the process of social development and learning in a social context. Recognizing the importance of both acquiring new skills and information and altering old behaviors by watching others, he emphasized the role of imitation and observational learning as a means of acquiring new behavior.

Much social development results from the accumulation and integration of episodes of observational learning.[24] The church that acknowledges the value and effectiveness of this informal mode of education faces an enormous challenge, though, because church leaders wrongly assume that learning happens primarily in a formal classroom setting, with students detached from teachers. That error impacts ministry.

Bandura's research underscored the importance of both a believer's relationships (Milestone #3) and the role an exemplary Parent in the faith can play in his or her life (Milestone #7). A believer will grow in such informal relationships, so establishing opportunities for believers to develop relationships with fellow believers needs to be a priority for church leaders. The church is to function as a community, and its primary testimony to the unbelieving but watching world is to be the quality of relationships among its people (John 13:34–35). The world will know we are Christians by our real love for one another.

Once believers are involved in a community of faith, each person would be wise to seek out someone who could be a mentor and encourager. Scripture refers to the imitation of significant models as a means of change and growth. Paul, for instance, described himself to the Thessalonians "as a model for you, that you might follow our example" (2 Thessalonians 3:9). Paul also urged the Corinthians to "follow my example, as I follow the example of Christ" (1 Corinthians 11:1). Such role models, says Bandura, can serve as instructors, motivators, inhibitors, disinhibitors, social facilitators, and emotion arousers. Christians can pattern their thoughts, feelings, values, and actions after a model Parent in the faith.

John Westerhoff

Former minister and professor John Westerhoff placed a high value on a believer's relationships within the body of Christ, the "ecological community of faith," and regarded this interaction with others as an impetus and a context for spiritual formation and change. He also referred to four "styles of faith" when he talked about spiritual growth, pointing out that a group can actually keep one's faith from maturing.[25] His first style of faith is an experienced or inherited faith—that of the preschooler and young children. Many adults, Westerhoff contended, plateau in the second style of faith, the affiliative style that is characterized by the strong sense of belonging that comes when one's values and actions are determined largely by the church. Heritage and traditions shape faith. Typically, adults stall here, so care must be taken to develop relationships that do not merely conform the believer in an affiliative but stagnant faith.

The third style—searching faith—comes in late adolescence and early young adulthood as individuals examine and even challenge their own assumptions. At this point of spiritual development, every point of faith is up for scrutiny, some doubt arises, and critical judgment is necessary. It is not always an easy transition to move away from a faith that belongs to the community to a faith that is truly one's own. The last style is owned faith. At this point, one's faith is central to one's being and actions.

Returning to the discussion of Milestone #3, believers focus on the "Jesus and we" dimension of spiritual growth, where they will find in the community support and challenge, but they are not to become overly dependent on other members of the group to determine their beliefs or define their faith.

As the following testimonies reveal, the Christian community plays a key role in a believer's journey of faith:

> My plate is full of adversity, but I want all of you to know, my dear sisters [her small group of women], that because of God's love and your prayers and support, I AM NOT GIVING UP! A year ago, with the same pitfalls that lay before me now, I would have handled my situation in a totally different manner. I wouldn't have surrendered to God, and I would not have had all of you to guide me along my path. I do NOT have the Word of God (yet!) as my armor against the devil, but I DO have God's love. So, as I struggle to walk in grace, I can "armor" myself with God's love

while I endeavor to learn God's Word and dodge Satan's arrows. God and all of you are keeping this sinking ship afloat!

I can't begin to describe the experience I have had in this process. The brothers in my small group who have shared their experiences with me, as I have shared mine with them, have brought me an awareness of and a closeness to other men that I have never experienced before.

When I took the Spiritual Growth Profile, I discovered why I am afraid to reach out to others in a personal, meaningful way. While I enjoy serving others and I am not afraid to engage in conversations with others, I avoid getting in too deep. I believe this is because I am afraid that I will not measure up to other people's standards. Furthermore, I don't like the idea of showing my weaknesses. However, I have learned in this small group that everyone else is just as screwed up as I am. Sharing with the other men, I learned that we all experience similar obstacles.

Being a pastor, I feel that there are areas of my life that [members of my congregation] can't understand and won't understand. Therefore, I need to seek out a group of pastors whom I can relate to, knowing they understand what I'm going through and that they will allow me to be me, without fear of repercussions from my congregation.

In Milestone #3, I encountered an aspect of my journey where I have abundant room for growth. As I analyzed my scope of friends, I realized I didn't have any meaningful relationships outside of my family. Also, I discovered that the reason for this is my deliberate reluctance to allow others to get know the "real me." I don't open up easily, and the result is superficial relationships.

Prior to this Stages of Faith study, I made a conscious, albeit uncomfortable, decision to open up to the members of my small group and let God take away the anxiety. What an amazing decision! I was welcomed by the group of gals, and they provided such a safe environment for me to open up in. I definitely experienced the strength that is infused in me by having other people to bounce issues or ideas off and getting honest, safe, biblical feedback.

A Review of the Childhood Stage of Faith

Clearly, salvation—or accepting God's saving grace and acknowledging Jesus as Savior and Lord—is not crossing a finish line; it is instead the starting point of a new beginning. After all, God created us to grow.

In the Childhood stage, the three milestones of spiritual growth address fundamental and far-reaching core issues that are foundational to a Christian's spiritual maturity. None of the three milestones can be neglected without diminishing one's spiritual health and delaying, if not preventing, one's progress. Tending to these three milestones will both result in a strong foundation for ongoing spiritual growth and determine the quality of one's spiritual progress. These milestones are essential to choosing to experience the promised joy (1:4) that may often elude the Christian.

If we Christians do not attend to the three milestones of Childhood, we will likely have a difficult time fully attending to the milestones of Young Adulthood and Parenthood. Unfinished business from Childhood means struggles later. A skilled, seasoned Parent in the faith can be a significant guide to the Child in the faith, but on occasion, believers may need a competent professional counselor to help them work through any underlying issues that are paralyzing their attempts to establish a grace-based identity, a biblical concept of God, and intimate relationships with other people. Again, it cannot be overemphasized that a Christian's spiritual growth depends on the quality of work done at Milestones #1, #2, and #3. They are a precondition to transition into a healthy spiritual Young Adulthood.

It should be noted, however, that spiritual growth can be too fast or too slow; sometimes it even stops altogether. Too many adults remain dwarfed and stuck in the Childhood stage. (The apostle Paul termed this protracted spiritual infancy "carnality" in 1 Corinthians 3:1–4.) Spiritual growth can also be pushed too quickly. But healthy growth will not be hurried, pressured, or unduly accelerated. Hurrying a Child in the faith into the stage of

Young Adulthood violates that stage of Childhood. As a result, the development that is appropriate to that stage is neglected.

Assuming a healthy pace and solid spiritual growth in the Childhood stage, believers then move into the Young Adulthood stage with its own three milestones. There, believers will determine their own sense of ultimate purpose and meaning. They will decide what is really important to them. They will shape and internalize basic personal values, convictions, and commitments. The key concept at that stage will be *ownership*.

Questions for Reflection and Action

Milestone #1: *Experiencing God's Grace and Forgiveness*

1. **A New Way of Relating to Self**—review the statements about grace (pages 236–239). Which one or two do you especially wish you'd heard a long time ago? Think about your level of trust or mistrust. What experiences and/or relationships might be behind your ability or lack of ability to trust—and to trust God? Then comment on the following passage from the chapter. What about this point, if anything, is significant to you personally?

> Despite the impact of our parents on our ability to trust God and other people, we believers cannot blame our parents, our culture, or our early life experiences for who we are today. Every believer is responsible for who he or she is and what he or she does in the present. No believer is a helpless victim; yet we believers dare not ignore the past. Rather, we take our pain and dysfunction before God and the healing truths of the Childhood stage of faith.

Milestone #2: *Embracing God as Father*

1. **A New Way of Relating to God**—review the five factors that contribute to a false God concept. Which, if any, have

influenced you? What can you do—what *will* you do—to correct that inaccurate idea about God? Would you consider yourself orthodox in faith but unable to connect with, trust, and surrender to God for whatever reasons? What are your thoughts as to why that disconnect exists? What idea(s) of Ana-Maria Rizzuto and/or what statement(s) from the testimonials were especially significant to you? Share your thoughts as to why that is the case. What does work on Milestone #1 contribute to work on Milestone #2?

Milestone #3: *Growing Up Together*

1. **A New Way of Relating to Others**—be specific about the ways your concepts of self (Milestone #1) and of God (Milestone #2) have been relearned, reinforced, and/or truly experienced in community. For instance, what has your involvement in a Christian community taught you about God's love for you? What point(s) from Erik Erikson, Albert Bandura, and/or John Westerhoff helped you better understand Milestone #3? Explain why those points were significant. What does work on Milestones #1 and #2 contribute to work on Milestone #3?
2 In your own words, explain why these three milestones serve as a strong foundation for a believer's ongoing spiritual growth. Why do these three milestones also determine the quality of one's spiritual progress?

The Transition to the Young Adulthood Stage of Faith

At Milestone #3, we focused on community, the horizontal dimension of our Christian faith. We acknowledged our need to belong and the importance of supporting and challenging one another to grow in our walks of faith. Milestone #3 emphasized interdependence and strong connections with fellow believers. Now, in Milestone #4, a key task is separation, and these two—separation and connection—will remain in dynamic tension throughout our journeys toward Christlikeness. After all, the purpose of community is neither conformity (we believe and behave alike) nor obsessive reliance on others (we let others think for us). In healthy relationships, we are liberated to come into our own internalized, biblical faith.

There appears to be a strong connection between Milestones #3 and #4. The relationships formed in Milestone #3 are not intended to restrict and mold the values and beliefs of the Christian. On the contrary, these relationships are to offer the support and challenge necessary for a believer to come to a firsthand faith. Robert Kegan describes this tension that will continue for the believer as a story of "staying connected in the new way, of continuing to hold onto one's precious connections and loyalties while refashioning one's relationship to them so that one makes them up rather than gets them made up by them … 'deciding for myself' does not have to equal 'deciding by myself.'"[1]

So, in Milestone #3, there is a focus on "we," while in Milestone #4, there is a shift to "me." In Milestone #3, there is a sense of "I belong"; in Milestone #4, there is a transition to "I stand alone"—but not all alone. In Milestone #3, there is connection to and among believers; in Milestone #4, there is a separation from the group's hold and, to some degree, from the fear of disappointing others. The strong Christian is fully responsible and self-governing as authority shifts from external to internal. Faith has shifted from secondhand to firsthand, from borrowed to owned.

This transition from Milestone #3 to Milestone #4 may be accompanied by a tempestuous period of doubt and confusion, including feelings that range from exhilaration to mild apprehension to frozen fear. Some people describe their faith as "diminishing" or "weak"; they might even talk about "losing faith," despite the fact that they may actually be in the process of deepening a truly authentic faith. And this process involves revisiting, once again—and this won't be the last time—the three Childhood milestones.

During the transition from the Childhood stage to the Young Adulthood stage, the believer can expect several new issues to emerge. Believers will gain:

- **A New Role.** Each of the three Young Adulthood milestones is a powerful catalyst for change and growth. As you attend to the tasks of each new milestone, God will move you toward Christlikeness and spiritual maturity. During this stage, you will develop an additional repertoire of skills for use on the journey.

- **A New Perspective.** During the Young Adulthood stage of faith, you will come to see God, self, and others differently than you did when you were in the Childhood stage of faith. You will gain a deeper and increasingly mature Christian perspective on life, faith, and joy (1 John 1:4). You will experience greater freedom from conformity, gain a clearer sense of what is real and ultimate, and experience more fully the release from controlling forces and habits. An advantage of this risky advancing is that the higher you go, the farther you can see. To your surprise, you may also discover that a believer in the Childhood stage may be threatened by people like you who are farther along on the journey of Christian faith.

- **Some New Challenges.** One challenge of spiritual Young Adulthood comes as you attend to the tasks of Milestones #4, #5, and #6 and recognize the existence of unfinished business left over from the Childhood stage of faith. In addition, the Young Adulthood stage challenges you to learn to stand alone and be confident in your biblical convictions. The danger lies in not examining and revising your faith and instead simply believing what others believe and conforming to how they think and act. When we choose that option, our faith remains secondhand and borrowed.

- **A New Invitation.** Young Adults in the faith come to see more clearly their shortcomings and weaknesses, the lies they have believed, and the unhealthy patterns they have developed. Only when believers open their eyes to these things can they truly experience growth, grace, forgiveness, and divine healing. Young Adults in the faith are developing a faith that is owned and firsthand. The challenge is to base one's faith on personal convictions rather than merely going along with the accepted group-think. Sadly, too many Christians plateau at this point and stop growing. Choosing to go higher and farther than these believers is definitely worth the risks.

CHAPTER 12

THE YOUNG ADULTHOOD STAGE OF FAITH

THE OWNERSHIP OF FAITH THAT IS BIBLICALLY BASED AND DEVELOPMENTALLY INFORMED

DURING OUR SPIRITUAL Young Adulthood, we will determine our own sense of ultimate purpose and meaning and decide what in life is most important to us. Basic personal values, convictions, and commitments are shaped during this stage, and—as mentioned above—the key concept here is *ownership*. We must own our Christian faith rather than believe merely because someone else believes. So, during this Young Adulthood stage, you will do the hard work necessary to personalize and experience a faith that is truly your own.

There are three milestones in the Young Adulthood stage of faith (1 John 2:13, 14):

Milestone #4	Owning a Firsthand Faith "I am writing to you, young men because you are strong."
Milestone #5	Linking Truth and Life "I am writing to you, young men, because the Word of God abides in you."
Milestone #6	Defeating the Enemies of Spiritual Progress "I am writing to you, young men, because you have overcome the evil one."

These three milestones work in concert, synergizing and reinforcing one another throughout a believer's life. Note how the diagram below illustrates the interdependence of the milestones. The ribbon wrapping around the stages suggests ongoing movement, because—as discussed in Chapters 8 and 9—spiritual growth is dynamic, elastic, fluid, flexible, and irregular; it is never static, fixed, or unchanging. As always, the message in each milestone of John's stages is derived from Scripture and enlivened by insights about human development.

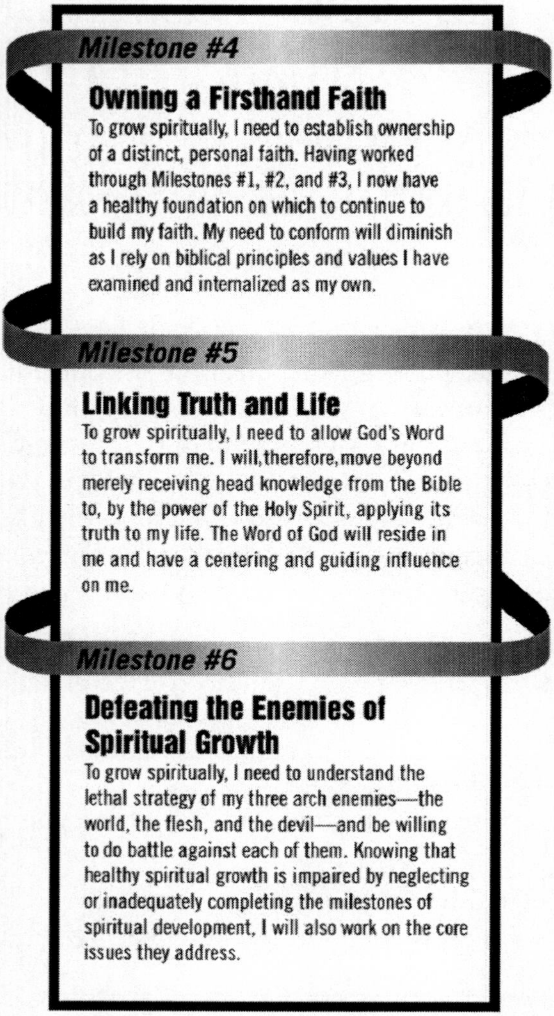
Milestone #4
Owning a Firsthand Faith
To grow spiritually, I need to establish ownership of a distinct, personal faith. Having worked through Milestones #1, #2, and #3, I now have a healthy foundation on which to continue to build my faith. My need to conform will diminish as I rely on biblical principles and values I have examined and internalized as my own.
Milestone #5
Linking Truth and Life
To grow spiritually, I need to allow God's Word to transform me. I will, therefore, move beyond merely receiving head knowledge from the Bible to, by the power of the Holy Spirit, applying its truth to my life. The Word of God will reside in me and have a centering and guiding influence on me.
Milestone #6
Defeating the Enemies of Spiritual Growth
To grow spiritually, I need to understand the lethal strategy of my three arch enemies—the world, the flesh, and the devil—and be willing to do battle against each of them. Knowing that healthy spiritual growth is impaired by neglecting or inadequately completing the milestones of spiritual development, I will also work on the core issues they address.

These stages of the believer's journey are sequential (we pass through them in the same order) and cumulative (they build on one another as we progress). All of us will address the same milestone issues along the way, but we won't travel at the same speed. Each of us has our own timetable. Just as no two people are alike, no two journeys towards wholeness and Christlikeness will be identical.

Readiness for the Young Adulthood Stage of Faith

What can we learn about John's young men by looking through the lens of developmental theory? What distinguishes the "young men" from believers in the Childhood stage of the faith? What advances have these young men made? What is taking place inside them? The goal in this chapter is to capture the content, meaning, and importance of each milestone; to adequately demonstrate the potential for spiritual growth that each milestone offers; and to show the effects if a specific milestone is neglected. Table 9 (below) integrates the three milestones and several human development theories.

First, though, think back to Chapter 8, "The *How* of Spiritual Growth," specifically to Conclusion 5: The Importance of Age and the discussion that stages of faith are only loosely linked to chronological age. Developmental theories help answer the question, "What role does age play as a general marker of changes in development?" So let's return to the 1 John 2:12–14 passage and think about age in relation to spiritual growth.

The Greek word for "young men" referred to someone in the age range of twenty-four to forty, so our usage of the phrase *young adult* in this study is not to be confused with the youthful adolescence of our western culture. (This study uses *young adult* instead of *young men* in order to include both genders.) It is important to note that the Young Adulthood stage of faith can *begin* as early as age seventeen or eighteen, the entry level being roughly concurrent with entering college. While chronological age offers a clue about one's growth in faith, age alone is no guarantee of the distance one has traveled because, as we've seen, spiritual growth is never automatic. Furthermore, we must remember that deep principled reasoning and true ownership of examined beliefs and values are beyond the capabilities of an adolescent.[2] A full expression of faith that is both consistent and coherent—repeated, practiced, tested, and thorough—is not likely before the age of thirty.

Now we will add the insights of several theorists who have studied the role of age in human and spiritual development. Chickering notes that the twenties are a period of "provisional adulthood."[3] Levinson calls this period of time "novice adulthood."[4] In Gillespie's model, the "established faith" of later youth, the "reordered faith" of young adults, and the "reflective faith" of middle adults are roughly parallel to the 1 John stage of Young Adulthood.[5] Then, in Bruce Powers's model—with the "reality testing" of ages 19 through 27, "making choices" between ages 28 and 35, and the phase of "active devotion" starting at age 36—can help describe and explain the way a believer is likely to mature during the Young Adulthood stage of faith.[6] Also, in Les Steele's model, later adolescence (ages 18 to 25) is characterized by a "searching versus entrenching" cycle, followed in young adulthood by "consolidation versus fragmentation," and then, in middle adulthood, "reappraising versus re-entrenchment."[7] Steele's paradigm also hints at applications to the Young Adulthood stage of faith. Specifically, the transitional struggle to Young Adulthood can be a protracted process that often takes place in the thirties and forties, but many adults plateau there permanently.[8] As you learn more about the three Young Adulthood milestones, you will begin to understand why.

To further shed light on this powerful correspondence between spiritual and developmental growth, Table 9 describes each milestone in greater detail than the table in Chapter 2 does. Table 8 includes the following information:

1. The core issue of the milestone's content
2. A summary statement that encapsulates the significance of the core issue in each milestone
3. The developmental insights that support this aspect of spiritual growth

Table 8: The Young Adulthood Stage of Faith Informed by Developmental Theory

Milestone	Core Issue/ Content	Summary	Growth Process
#4: Owning a Firsthand Faith	Convention or Conviction	To grow spiritually, believers will progressively establish ownership of a distinct, personal faith. Having attended to Milestones #1–3, believers now have in place the internal and external structures necessary for an owned faith. The need to conform and not disappoint diminishes as believers rely on principles and values that they have examined and internalized as their own.	Examined, Tested, Revised Faith
#5: Linking Truth and Life	Experiential Knowing	To grow spiritually, Christians will progressively allow God's Word to transform them. Individuals will move beyond head knowledge of the Bible and start applying its truths to their lives. The Word of God will reside in and have a centering influence on those believers who have begun the lifelong work of Milestones #1–#4.	Levels and Extent of Learning
#6: Defeating the Enemies of Spiritual Progress	Transcendent Spiritual Realities	To grow spiritually, believers must recognize and counter each of the three enemies that jeopardizes spiritual growth. Believers will progressively face the three rivals and successfully do battle where they are vulnerable. Knowing that healthy spiritual growth is impaired by neglecting or inadequately completing the preceding milestones of spiritual development, the Christian will continue to work on the core issues those milestones address.	Three-Dimensional Warfare

As mentioned above and as indicated in the diagram below, insights from the study of human development support and help explain these milestones of the Young Adulthood stage of faith. (The names in parentheses credit those social scientists whose ideas offer the basis for the discussions that follow.)

Table 9 Social Science's Perspectives on the Young Adulthood Stage of Faith

Milestone	Descriptive Title	Theorist
Milestone #4	Owning a Firsthand Faith	Searching and Owned Style of Faith (Westerhoff) Moral Development (Kohlberg) Stages 3-4 of Faith Development (Fowler)
Milestone #5	Linking Truth and Life	Stage 3 of Cognitive Development (Piaget) Extent and Degrees of Learning (Habermas and Issler)
Milestone #6	Defeating the Enemies of Spiritual Progress	Interactional Model of Nature-Nurture (Erikson)

Milestone #4

Owning a Firsthand Faith

Based on 1 John 2:14 ("I have written to you, young men, because you are strong"), Milestone #4 addresses the core issue of becoming a Christian who lives according to one's own choices rather than bowing unthinkingly to the pressure to conform to conventional Christian views. The truth to be lived out here is: "I am determining and owning the Christian values and biblical beliefs that, regardless of the cost, will guide my faith journey." To grow spiritually, a believer must gradually establish ownership of a distinct, personal faith, and if you have attended to Milestones #1–#3, you have in place the internal and external structures necessary for such an owned faith. The need to conform and not disappoint diminishes as you rely on godly principles and biblical values that you examine and internalize as your own. To become a strong Christian, you will need to shape and internalize personal values, convictions, and commitments. The process of growing strong includes:

- *Moving away...* from secondhand, borrowed faith and external conventions—from obsessive conformity and compliance; from the need to win approval; from being overly concerned about disappointing others; from "pew pressure" to live according to prescribed or stereotypical rules, standards, and expectations; from fictional sins; from unexamined faith and values; and from dependency and imitation.
- *Moving toward...* firsthand, owned faith and inner convictions; a consistent and coherent Christian faith; examined and revised but still biblical values; a faith governed by internalized and inviolable Christian principles; and tolerance of nonessential differences between you and fellow believers.

Believers who neglect Milestone #4 will remain weak Christians, motivated primarily by the need to conform and the desire to win the approval of people they deem significant. Critical thinking skills will remain undeveloped, and obedience to God will continue to be mechanical, obligatory, and burdensome.

The Strong Christian: A Profile

So what steps can we take to become strong Christians? What exactly makes a Christian strong? We'll begin to answer those questions by stating first that strong believers and weak believers are fundamentally different from one another. As we read in Romans 14 and 15, a weak Christian's beliefs and values are borrowed and often dependent upon the approval of significant others. A weak Christian's faith is largely unexamined and secondhand: it is a "default faith." (Think of the Jewish Christians clinging to hundreds of years of their inherited traditions.) It is not uncommon to hear statements like these or, perhaps more likely, to see those ideas implied in how people live:

- "The pastor said it, and that settles it!"
- "Others more qualified than I am have thought this through for me."
- "Everyone else seems to believe and behave this way."

Christians can also become dulled, cautious, stiff, and proper by letting the question, "What will others think?" guide their thoughts as well as their behavior. Such a secondhand faith is dangerous:

> [The danger is] a reliance on significant others to such an extent that personally held beliefs and values are never consciously adopted or reflected upon. What arises is a truncated value system in which one simply "buys into" the values of others in his or her life who are admired.[9]

Recall that, in Romans 14–15, Paul described the weak believers as those who focused on days and diets, on such nonessential issues that, although they don't matter, nevertheless become flashpoints of division and debate in the church. The weak will ascribe almost biblical authority to their private doctrines, and their *oughts* and *shoulds* become sacred. This kind of thinking—of being limited by strict boundaries—results only in pseudo-transformation. Just consider the "worship wars" fought in so many churches: Will the worship service be traditional or contemporary, contemplative or expressive? Do we use hymnals or sing praise choruses? Is the worship gathering focused on the evangelism of unbelievers or the edification of believers? Does the congregation dress up or dress down for church? What kind of separation from the world is expected of members? Can believers drink, dance, or attend movies? Must young people attend Christian schools or be homeschooled? (You can probably add more issues to this list.)

And this list, however incomplete it is, suggests—as promised above—why so many Christians get stuck and don't fully transition into the Young Adulthood stage of faith. Some of these people plateau because they don't move beyond the group's control and pressure to conform. The challenge is to dare to be different. Yes, there is risk in this time of renewed commitment, but strong Christians in the Young Adulthood stage have courageously developed a faith that is their own. They are living out a firsthand faith rather than a secondhand, conventional faith. They are rethinking and perhaps rejecting longstanding behaviors and even beliefs as they themselves explore the answer to the question, "What do I really want in my faith?"

By the time they have reached Milestone #4, these Young Adult believers have addressed the issues reflected in these basic questions: "*Why* do you believe and behave as you do?" and "To what degree are your beliefs and values largely determined by the approval of other people?" After all, your beliefs cannot be dictated by your parents, your pastor, your denominational statement of faith, your peer group, or a faith hero—and truly be *your* beliefs! To become a strong Christian, you need to clarify, be able to articulate, and truly own the biblical values and beliefs that will guide your journey of faith. Living for the approval of those people who matter to you will not serve you well for the long haul. Strong Christians understand that fact and have, therefore, learned to stand alone and confidently in their faith.

Let's now return to the various development theorists already mentioned. The chart below summarizes the studies of styles of faith (Westerhoff), moral commitment (Kohlberg), and faith development (Fowler)—three ways of looking at key aspects of the process of growing strong in one's faith. We will consider the contributions these social scientists made to understanding what distinguishes the strong believer from the weak in Milestone #4. To summarize, too often the spiritual growth of believers levels off at a borrowed, secondhand faith: these weaker Christians continue to look to others to determine their beliefs and behaviors, and these weak believers are fundamentally different from strong believers who own their faith.

Romans 14–15	Styles of Faith	Moral Commitment	Faith Development
Weak Believers	Experienced, Affiliative	Levels 1–2	Synthetic-Conventional
Strong Believers	Searching, Owned	Level 3	Individuative-Reflective

Perry Downs reminds us that evangelicals have paid attention to the *content* of their faith to the exclusion of the *process* of their faith. Understanding both this process of *how* people believe as well as *what* Christians believe is the purpose of *The Path*:

> Historically, evangelicals have attended to content but have ignored structure. We have been so concerned with guarding what people believe that we have failed to listen to how people believe. We have ignored the possibility of stages of faith, striving only to make faith stronger without being concerned with making faith more mature. We have tended to police its content and tried to strengthen its power, but we have neglected its maturity.[10]

Styles of Faith

The movement toward Christian maturity and the ownership of a strong faith is a dynamic and lifelong process; yet too often we believers neglect the process by which we can become strong Christians. If we make the decision to try to grow strong, we must consider not only our beliefs (are they biblical?) but also how we come to believe. Too often we believers neglect the process by which we can become strong Christians. Religious educator John Westerhoff offers one model with his styles of faith, a helpful way to look at this process, when he identifies four styles of faith and likens them to the rings of a tree. As a tree grows and matures, it adds rings, but the previously formed rings are still present in the central core of the tree's trunk. Keep that image in mind as you review the four styles of faith outlined next.[11]

Even if you became a Christian as an adult, you will experience each of the four styles.

John Westerhoff considers a believer's relationships in the body of Christ as an essential impetus for spiritual formation and change. When he identifies four styles of faith, Westerhoff shows that a group can play a role in keeping an individual's faith from maturing. The *experienced* style of faith of preschoolers and children is the inherited faith shaped by children's responses to their experiences with Christians they know. Children copy the faith of others as they observe and interact with members of the Christian community.

Next comes the adolescent *affiliative* style of faith, a style characterized by the strong sense of belonging that comes when one's values and actions are largely determined by the church's way of understanding faith ("My church believes …") as well as its heritage and traditions. Many adults, Westerhoff explains, stall at this stage of affiliative faith, which is largely a "borrowed faith," a secondhand faith.

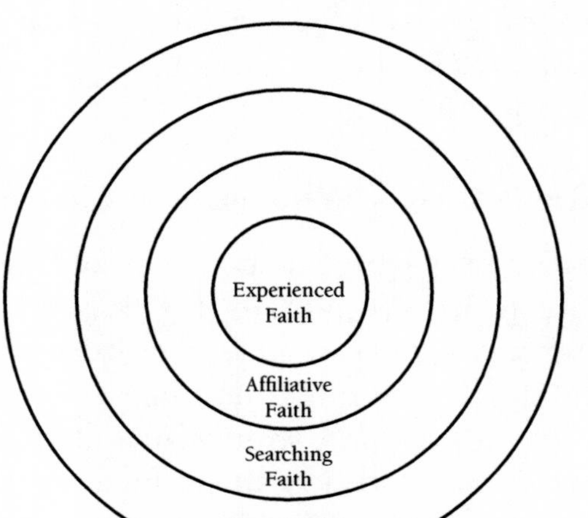

Next in this developmental sequence, *searching* faith comes in late adolescence and early young adulthood as believers examine and challenge their assumptions. Believers who move into this phase inevitably question the content and expressions of faith that were important to them during the affiliative period. Every point of their faith is now up for scrutiny, and some struggle, pain, and doubt are necessary and unavoidable at this point of spiritual development—and such struggle, pain, and doubt are not necessarily symptoms of sin, loss of faith, or carnality. Feelings associated with searching range from exhilaration to deep fear. For some, this phase is temporary; for others, it may last for years … or forever.

That said, keep in mind that it is almost never easy to move away from a faith that belongs to the community to a faith that is one's own. After all, we tend to shy away from stress and welcome calm, and transition can be stressful. Furthermore, times of searching never end completely, so a lack of courage and determination may also explain why many people do not transition to an owned faith. As Westerhoff warns, care must be taken to develop relationships that do not merely confine the believer to an affiliative faith.

Last—and ideally—searching faith brings a believer to a genuinely *owned* faith. Your faith is central to your being and actions. You have experienced a huge, inner reorientation in your movement from weak believer to strong. Your motivation to walk with the Lord is now internal.

Moral Development: The Development of Commitment

In our day-to-day lives, all of us may appear equally moral; yet we may choose to behave morally for very different reasons. Lawrence Kohlberg's studies of moral development identify three levels of moral development and outline the process of coming to personal commitment and strong faith. Both Kohlberg's and Catherine Stonehouse's studies of moral maturity also help us see when and why some believers get stuck. Study the following chart (it's not as complicated as it looks) to learn about the process of becoming morally mature.[12] Kohlberg makes the point that moral content is only one aspect of strong faith. *What* I believe to be right or wrong is the content of one's moral judgment. *Why* I believe something is right or wrong is what Kohlberg focused his studies on.

	LEVEL ONE		LEVEL TWO		LEVEL THREE
Source of Authority	Self-Interest	CRISIS POINT — OBEDIENCE — LIBERATING ELEMENT	External Standards and Models	CRISIS POINT — TRUST — LIBERATING ELEMENT	Internal Principles
What is Right?	Adult Command		Important People and Groups		Self-Chosen Values
Stimulus to Right Action	Reward or Punishment		Perform to Please		Commitment to Inviolable Principles
	COMPLIES		IDENTIFIES		INTERNALIZED

Level 1: The Preconventional Level (from ages 5–6)

The child's point of reference at this level is self. Choices are often determined by what the consequences of the actions will be, what explicit reward or punishment may result. Children are egocentric and oblivious to the needs of others (when this trait appears in adults, we call it *narcissism*), and they usually act with unquestioning deference to authorities at this point. Children rely on others to define what is right and wrong for them: bad is what parents forbid; good is what parents approve. (This may be likened to Westerhoff's "Experienced" or "Inherited" style of faith.)

Unfortunately, some adults use only Level 1 moral reasoning. (See 2 Corinthians 9:6–7 for what Paul says about financial stewardship based on Level 1, "under compulsion.") People at this level respond to God's gracious invitation of salvation in order to escape hell and to receive the benefits that God has promised believers. Indoctrinating children and youth with moral content will not necessarily produce or lead to moral living.

Level 2: The Conventional Level (teenagers and early adulthood)

At Level 2, the point of reference when it comes to making decisions is broader than the self. Now the individual internalizes and imitates standards and models, specifically the rules and expectations of family, peer groups, significant others, institutions, and society at large. Feeling the pressure to conform, accepting the judgment of others as final, and avoiding the stigma of standing out as different all encourage our obedience. Yet we should not be satisfied to know the right answer (content) without really engaging the reasons *why* the right is right. Consider the danger faced by the churched high-school graduates who have been equipped with all the right answers but go off to college unable to defend their faith and, as a result, see their faith crumble under the challenges of a secular campus. (In this sense, Level 2 may be likened to Westerhoff's "Affiliative" style of faith. The imitation, conformity, compliance, and dependency that result are largely subconscious.)

Individuals at Level 2 are preoccupied with rules and careful not to disappoint the people and groups they deem important. First Corinthians 3:3–4 ("I am of Paul, Cephas, Apollos, Christ …") offers an example of Level 2 reasoning: the believers were stalled in their faith because they were depending on these gifted leaders to do their thinking for them. "What will these leaders think?" was an important question. Consequently, Paul described them as "men of flesh" and "babes in Christ" (3:1). Similarly, when the apostle Peter acted in a Level 2 way, Paul called him on changing his behavior based on whom he was with (Galatians 2:11–14). This issue of conformity and convention suggests why too many Christians stall at Milestone #4 of the Young Adulthood stage of faith; it can be difficult to break away from community.

Level 3: A Postconventional Level

Teenagers and young adults have not had sufficient time to test their beliefs, but at Level 3—adulthood—this testing begins. Age, however, is no guarantee of arriving at this level where authority now shifts to you, to your "inner panel of experts" who reserve the right to choose and are prepared to take responsibility for their choices, and those choices function independently of peer groups and culture. Rather than relying on external sources of authority, authority is relocated within the self. After all, moral principles are now firsthand and owned, and those internalized principles have become the source of moral authority.

At Level 3, individuals search for the reasons behind the rules, and biblical principles become self-chosen, internal, inviolable, and owned. Signs of reaching this level may appear during late adolescence, but not until adulthood is this higher form of moral thought firmly established. At that point, the adult can draw on all three levels of moral reasoning, and Scripture itself makes moral appeals on all three levels.

Although a cognitive awareness of principles develops in adolescence, commitment to their ethical value for guiding behavior develops only in adulthood. During this Young Adulthood time of struggling for independence, people may describe their faith as diminishing because it involves the rethinking and perhaps even the rejection of traditional ideas that have been a part of their very being since childhood. In truth, these individuals may be growing or maturing in their faith. In this sense, Level 3 may be likened to Westerhoff's "Searching" and "Owned" styles of faith.

Important to consider, though, is whether or not Kohlberg's findings are in harmony with Scripture. Put differently, is his presentation of how people reason morally and the sequence of moral development consistent with God's Word? Although Kohlberg's research probed the patterns of moral reasoning, we are not presenting him as the authority of moral content. His findings simply offer insight and help us be more effective in guiding the growth of others. We see, for instance, that God's Word includes moral appeals to people at all three levels of moral development. Acts 5:29, for instance, captures the essence of Level 3: "We must obey God rather men." The convictions of Paul's strong believer are also apparent in Romans 14:5 ("Each person must be fully convinced in his own mind") and Romans 14:22 ("The faith which you have, have as your own conviction before God"). The weak believers Paul talked about in Romans 14:1–12 appear to be at Level 1 or 2 in their moral development. Furthermore, believers are likely to be strong in those areas where they have examined their faith and own it … and weak in those areas where their faith is yet unexamined and therefore still borrowed. Clearly, Scripture makes moral appeals to believers at all three levels of moral development.

Faith Development

Having looked at research from studies in moral development, we will now turn to James Fowler's model of faith development. Fowler traces the development of a person's faith through the entire span of life. His model may not be without error or theological bias, but it is helpful for describing and explaining how believers grow in faith. His research separates the content of faith (*what* people believe) from the structure of faith (*why* they believe it), and he then examines the deep structures of *how* people believe rather than *what* people believe. In his theory, the way people understand and experience their faith will emerge in predictable stages.

Professor Perry Downs does not think it is unreasonable that Christian faith will follow normal patterns of faith development. He sees compatibility rather than conflict between developmental patterns and the work of God. This kind of stage theory does not do injustice to the work of the Holy Spirit, nor does it remove the mystery and serendipitous experience of personal faith. The distinction between the Christian and the secularist is the *content* of faith, not the *fact* of faith.[13] A careful probing of someone's journey will reveal the core of ultimate beliefs and relationships that comprise that person's faith. Steele noted this:

> If it is true that God has created us to develop according to predictable patterns, could it not be true that faith also is subject to development? Because developmental stages allow for a great deal of flexibility within them, it is possible for God to work with each of us individually and yet to see predictable stages of faith designed by His hand.[14]

In Fowler's description of the construct of faith, Stages 1 and 2 are primarily childhood stages in which children believe what their parents and other primary caretakers teach them about God. Then comes Stage 3.

Stage 3: Synthetic-Conventional Faith

In Stage 3, children and many adults tend to be highly committed to a denomination, a particular theological seminary's teachings, or a particular doctrine, i.e., "I believe what the church believes." First Corinthians 1:11 and 3:4, for instance, show that one factor detaining the progress of many believers was their overdependence on the significant judgments and expectations of leaders or faith heroes such as Apollos, Paul, and Cephas to do their thinking for them. The way I see myself is rooted in how I think significant others see me. Consequently, Paul described them as "men of flesh" and "babes in Christ" (3:1).

In Stage 3, a deficiency or danger occurs when the expectations and evaluations of others are compellingly internalized—and sacralized—without reflection and examination. A person can be very articulate about what he or she believes and feel strongly about those beliefs but still be unable to think critically about them. Fowler notes that authority in this stage is located in traditional authority roles or in the consensus of a valued group. He concludes that much of the church life in this country can be accurately described as predominantly Synthetic-Conventional. Too many adults stall permanently in this stage.

> There can be great comfort in synthetic/conventional faith because there is a sense of community and belonging that is missing in much of contemporary society. Also categories tend to be sure, with clear delineations being made between truth and error and "the good guys" (us) and "the bad guys" (them). An ecclesiastical theology that stresses community and relationships and strong leaders can create and hold people in stage-three faith.[15]

Fowler's Stages 3 and 4 are particularly helpful when it comes to understanding the process of transitioning from weak to strong Christians.

> A limitation of Stage 3 is an over dependency on significant people within the community of faith. Pastors, youth leaders, or other significant persons are depended on for judgments regarding truth ("What do we believe about ...") and self-worth... In addition, in Stage 3 one is highly susceptible to the tyranny of "they," allowing external control to become all-important. (Perry Downs[16])

> While beliefs and values are deeply felt, they typically are tacitly held... There has not been occasion to step outside them to reflect on or examine them explicitly or systematically. (James Fowler[17])

> Many adults remained at this [Stage 3], which was conformist, accepting the judgments of significant others and lacking the security to construct their independent perspective. Strongly held beliefs and values were not viewed objectively. (Kenneth Hyde[18])

Believers may plateau at Stage 3 because the work of transitioning to Stage 4 causes too much discomfort, fear of rejection, and loss of the familiar.

> [Stage 3 Christians may] be highly committed to the church, and for them the church becomes an idealized extended family... God is perceived as an extension of interpersonal relationships and can be counted on as a close personal friend. In Stage 3 people have no problem believing that God has a perfect parking spot for them right in front of the store because He deeply loves them and is interested in their best interests... Those with synthetic/conventional faith are quite sure regarding who are the true people of God and who are not. (Perry Downs[19])

Also important to understand is that every group wants to define who is in the group and who is out, so they tend to establish boundary markers. According to sociologists, these markers are highly visible but relatively superficial practices. Conforming to these boundary markers too often substitutes for authentic transformation. Doctrine, behavioral standards, and even sanctified peculiarities may identify who's in the club, but they also may present the facade of pseudo-transformation, masking an unchanged life within. Authentic transformation happens differently.

Stage 4: Individuative-Reflective Faith

Over the years, there may be a shift from unexamined allegiance and what matters to others. Admittedly, people swing back and forth between Stages 3 and 4 while maturing from one stage to another. The shift from Stage 3 to Stage 4 can be precipitated by changes in relationships, the death of a parent, or leaving home. Or it can result from the challenges of moving, divorce, changing jobs, or discovering the inadequacies of one's Stage-3 faith. Maybe people visit another church or meet believers or a professor with different beliefs that challenge theirs. It is not until Stage 4 that older adolescents and adults begin to investigate their assumptions and values for themselves. At that point, believers begin the process of critically examining and owning their faith rather than simply accepting what they have been taught.

Note that the content of faith, or *what* a person believes, may not change in a person's growth from Stage 3 to Stage 4. It is *how* that person believes that changes. It is a point of inner reorientation and renewed commitment to God. Faith becomes "mine." A full expression of the Stage 4 individuative-reflective faith, however, does not become consistent and coherent until a person's late twenties or early thirties. For some adults, the transition can be a protracted process—if it comes at all—and may occur in their thirties or forties. Whenever it comes, believers then take responsibility for their commitments, lifestyles, and beliefs.

Not surprisingly, Stage 4 may not be a comfortable stage. For many people, this is a time of considerable upheaval and struggle, and they will describe their faith as diminishing, weakening, and lessening. They may experience considerable guilt as they experience "losing faith." At Stage 4, they may also become disillusioned with the established church and its "You mustn't question your faith" message. However, the fullness of maturity must include some dissonance of doubt and the facing of hard questions that often move against the current of popular belief. Spiritual maturity involves struggling with new concepts, rethinking, and sometimes even rejecting long-standing, traditional assumptions. No longer is faith characterized by the harmony and unity of Stage 3, where disagreements and disharmony are considered obstructions to faith.

Now think back to the discussion in Chapter 6 about the strong and the weak believers, based on Romans 14–15. Now, this Chapter suggests how weak believers and strong believers are fundamentally different from one another.

Note the following four distinctions between the strong and the weak:

- *The weak sabotage the Word of God.* As Romans 14 indicates, weak Jewish believers in the Roman church retained biases deeply rooted in their culture and experiences. They found it—as we do today—difficult to discard the shackles of an Experienced faith (Powers), an Affiliative faith (Westerhoff), and a Synthetic-Conventional faith (Fowler).

  For strong Christians, the Word of God is transformational as it speaks truth that they absorb and apply. Clearly, the powerful Word of God has not yet fully taken root in the hearts of weak believers who persist in their cultural values.
- *Weak believers allow their values and cherished beliefs to remain largely unexamined.* They have internalized and sacralized taboos about foods and Sabbaths. These weak believers are governed by the forces of conditioning, conformity, and convention.

  Strong believers, however, examine their values and cherished beliefs (Owned faith, Individuative-Reflective faith). Strong believers systematically reflect on and critically explore the issues, the presuppositions, and the "givens" of their faith. Again, this explains why the Word of God is a more effective agent of transformation in the life of a strong believer.

- *Weak believers continue to be governed by convention and external authorities.* The beliefs of the weak are still largely determined by both significant others and conditioning forces outside of themselves. The weak may have strong convictions, but these believers have not yet found freedom from the bondage of conforming to the beliefs of external authorities (Experienced faith, Affiliative faith, Synthetic-Conventional faith). The danger here is that weak believers can so completely internalize the expectations and evaluations of others that they find making decisions for themselves quite difficult.
- *The relationships of weak believers are impoverished.* The weak do not experience the support and challenge to their faith that is necessary for spiritual growth. Genuine moral development happens in an environment characterized by an exchange of ideas; perspective taking; exposure to the next level of reasoning; contact with situations that pose problems, raise questions, and challenge one's current moral structure (the resulting dissatisfaction helps move one to the next level); and freedom to openly discuss conflicting moral views. In this kind of environment, the weak believer—who has known only the tyranny of pressure from other weak believers and rejection and criticism from some of the strong—may come to understand the perspective of the strong and recognize the need to move on to higher levels of reasoning and maturity.

Likewise, in this kind of environment, the strong may gain some insights into the perspectives, feelings, and motivations of the weak. After all, the strong and the weak are "brethren" (Romans 14:10,13) who need one another; who are to work toward harmony rather than to judge, belittle, or criticize one another (14:1,3,10,13); and who are to admonish one another (15:14). Knowing this kind of support and challenge, strong believers reach a point of

> independence and personal ownership of their faith. At the same time, these strong believers are able to live out their faith in interdependent relationships with fellow believers.

The following personal testimonies reveal the kinds of challenges that a believer working on this milestone may encounter. If you are providing spiritual direction to believers, look and listen carefully for evidence of progress as well as any obstacles that may hinder that progress. Also, draw on the five items of Milestone #4 in the Spiritual Growth Profile as a rich source of dialogue. You may discover that we adults have work to do on our way toward becoming "deep" believers.

> Milestone #4 is the weakest area of my spiritual journey and needs special attention. I grew up in a Confucius culture, where conformity is considered a social norm, so my identity has been shaped by how other people perceive me. Their approval became more of a concern than honoring God as the primary authority in my life.
>
> I discovered that I am very tempted to conform to the beliefs, practices, and shoulds of others in the church. In order to feel good about myself, my faith, and my relationship with God, I often need those in leadership to think I'm a good, godly woman. This causes a lot of striving to please, guilt for setting boundaries, and high expectations of myself in ministry. Milestone #4 was actually comforting to me. Now I know that it's okay to have my own opinions that are different from others. This is a sign of growth and owning my own faith.
>
> I can think of two aspects of my faith that I have deferred to what our church believes without wrestling with the issues. These areas are: 1) women in ministry and 2) church and politics. These are two sensitive topics, and fear has kept me from owning them. I prefer to use the church's stance as a means of absolving myself from any criticism. I need to really take a look at what the Scriptures say about these matters and form my own beliefs.
>
> It is time for me to review everything, including the people who were significant in my life. God wants to know me as a personal believer, not as part of a group.

> Milestone #4 is actually a very scary place for me, as I have relied on others for over thirty years to formulate my faith. But I believe it is necessary for me to examine my beliefs, ask some tough questions, and move from the Affiliative to a Searching Faith.
>
> Milestone #4 has been a celebration of freedom for me, as I realized that I am embracing a relationship with God that is not dependent on what others think about me. I have spent many years very concerned with being acceptable to others... Now I consider God's opinion of me instead of other people's, and that switch has opened up a new, marvelous life to me.

Milestone #5

Linking Truth and Life

Milestone #5 addresses the core issue of internalization, of believers grounding their life in God's Word. This milestone is based on 1 John 2:14, "I am writing to you, young men, because the Word of God abides in you." The truth to be learned here is that the Word is ultimate, internal, and personal. To grow spiritually, Christians progressively allow God's Word to transform them. These individuals move beyond head knowledge of the Bible to applying its truth to their lives. The Word of God will reside in the believers and have a centering influence. The dynamic growth process at this milestone includes:

- *Moving away*... from abstract biblical information that doesn't result in transformation—from theology that has no impact on biography, from creedal and cerebral faith (the cognitive curse), from reflection without action, and from truth that is accepted but not life-changing.
- *Moving toward*... transformational knowing; having, by God's grace, more Christlike character; the integration of faith and practice; congruency of belief and behavior; a comprehensive Christian worldview; a master motive, a God-given goal that orients and orders your entire life and gives it meaning; and embodying or incarnating God's Word.

This is the second of John's three milestones in Young Adulthood, and it is not simply the explanation for the believer's strength in Milestone #4. Note that the sequential process of Milestones #1–#4 is clear:

- Milestone #1: the Christian obeys God's Word, certain of His love and forgiveness, having experienced a renewed identity and now free of legalism and oughts.
- Milestone #2: the believer obeys but not to earn acceptance or to avoid a perfectionistic God's punishment.
- Milestone #3: the Christian can experience "group grace" as well as the support and challenge of others.
- Milestone #4: the believer is moving away from obeying and believing because it is expected, as well as from simply conforming to the beliefs and behaviors of others who matter.

These four milestones are preparatory to God's Word abiding in the strong Christian. These milestones therefore shed light on how God's Word moves progressively from propositional "head" knowledge to visceral "heart" knowledge.

After all, factual knowledge of God is incomplete knowledge without experiential knowledge of Him. Heart knowledge of God enables believers to become increasingly competent at thinking and living according to a distinctive, Christian worldview. Scripture progressively defines, modifies, and orders their personal worlds. In undertaking the task of Milestone #5, Christians will findthemselves experiencing, not merely accepting, the Word of God.

Yet Donald Joy issues the following warning:

> Growth is only marginally related to "taking thought about growth" but is, instead, the direct product of the person's dealing with stress in distinctively personal transactions with people and events using the resources of previous experiences of reality... It is likely that "intellectualized growth" may tend to produce persons who learn the jargon of maturity and who delay entry into the experiences necessary to enter into the true maturity of higher levels.[20]

Certainly the Bible gives information about God not just so that we can pass an exam or win a debate but so that we can know God in intimate friendship and become like Him.

The Process of Spiritual Development

The apostle John offers three additional clues about the processes of abiding and of linking truth and life.

First of all, God reveals Himself to the obedient disciple. John records Jesus saying, "He who has My commandments and keeps them, he it is who loves Me; and he who loves Me shall be loved by the Father, and I will love him, and will disclose Myself to him" (John 14:21). Recall the discussion of "Faith as a Noun and Faith as a Verb" from Chapter 6. The objective dimension of knowing focuses on the content of a biblically informed faith. This is faith as a *noun*: the *what* of faith.

In addition to the objective dimension of knowing, there is the experiential or subjective and personal side of knowing; it focuses on owning one's faith and applying it to the particulars of life. This is faith as a *verb*: the *why* and *how* of faith. Authentic faith includes both propositional assent and personal allegiance. Milestone #5 is all about developing this intimate and obedient relationship so that, despite Jesus' physical absence from this earth, His people are in an exciting, dynamic relationship with Him. Obedient believers will experience fresh manifestations of the love of Jesus and the Father. We truly come to own our faith when we obey God's commands.

Second, the Holy Spirit is actively involved in the process of spiritual development. John says, "But you have an anointing from the Holy One… And as for you, the anointing which you received from Him abides in you, and you have no need for any one to teach you; but as His anointing teaches you about all things, and is true and is not a lie, and just as it has taught you, you abide in Him" (1 John 2:20, 27). John is not saying that believers do not need teachers. After all, John himself is teaching in this epistle. John is, however, emphasizing that the Christian does not need to rely solely on others to learn God's truth, understand His Word, and apply it in day-to-day life. The Holy Spirit enables each Christian to discover the meaning and application of the Scriptures without relying on the group or teachers as the primary authority. This step is indicative of the movement away from the secondhand faith and conformity that often stalls the believer at Milestone #4.

Third, abiding is not to be mistaken for accumulating abstract doctrine or gaining a merely cognitive understanding of the faith. Such efforts do not lead to either mature Young Adulthood in the faith or wholeness and Christlikeness. Heretical teachers ("anti-christs") intend to deceive Christians (1 John 2:26). So believers must learn to recognize and resist counterfeits that oppose faith (1 John 2:18–27), not merely identify errant doctrines.

Earlier, in Chapter 3, H. P. Owen showed that the author of Hebrews divides the Christian life into three successive stages, just as John does in 1 John 2:12–14. Owen sees the process of spiritual growth in Hebrews 5:11–6:3, beginning with the stage of the "babe" (verse 13). Apparently, the Hebrew believers had become "dull of hearing" and were quite stalled in this stage of infancy, failing to move on to Stage 2.

In Stage 2, Christians are to become skilled in distinguishing between good and evil and therefore able to make sound moral judgments about issues, beliefs, and behaviors. Owen writes that Stage 2 is an ethical and practical stage, much like the apostle John's Milestone #5 in the Young Adulthood stage of faith. Importantly, this moral reasoning is based on God's Word, not on what significant others think. Believers are practicing and in training (*gymnazō*), getting accustomed to a faith that is firsthand and owned. These believers' choices are now affecting their character. As John puts it, the Word of God is progressively abiding in these people.

Once the Christian "has acquired a reasoned pattern of behavior based on experience he can proceed to Stage 3 and receive the solid food"—to the stage of the "mature" believer (verse 14).[21] John's Milestone #5 in the Young Adulthood stage of faith concerns itself with gaining skill and experience in "practicing righteousness" (verse 14) and a "reasoned pattern of behavior" that is based on God's Word.

Cognitive Development

Jean Piaget is best known for exploring four stages of cognitive development from birth to adulthood. Piaget also helps us understand the Milestone #5 process of abiding. Times of growth come with our awareness that our existing ways of knowing and doing things are no longer sufficient for dealing with our present experiences. (Piaget calls this process *disequilibration.*) At such times, we must respond to the new challenges by constructing more adequate ways of knowing and valuing in order to deal with those challenges. The childhood explanations fail to satisfy the sophisticated mind of the adult, so the need to problem solve stimulates the mind to higher levels of reasoning, producing new capacities for dealing with life issues. Piaget helps us see that learning and change occur when adults face directly the most profound dilemmas and greatest tensions in life and then develop new ways of seeing, solving, and responding. The purpose of the Word of God is to shed light on the exact issues and problems the believer faces. Again, the abiding of Milestone #5 is not the mere transmission of biblical information. People are not merely empty sponges to be filled with knowledge but are active in the process of growth.

Piaget also believed that three factors stimulate cognitive development: maturation, experience, and social transmission. First, the mind matures just as the body matures, gradually developing new capacities for thinking and reasoning. The mind is strengthened at each level of development; yet the mind will not merely absorb biblical information as a sponge absorbs water. Learning is to be a transformative process. Second, experience prompts cognitive development by providing sensory input. Direct, active involvement, rather than mere passive, academic involvement, allows the learner to gain new and necessary information. The third factor that stimulates cognitive development is social transmission. A believer's development requires interactions with people who have different perspectives. The Christian needs more than solid, biblical lectures and good preaching for significant learning to occur. The Word of God comes to abide and transform as Parents in the faith or Christian teachers in the classroom take into account the roles of maturation, experience, and social transmission.

After all, children know and think about things differently than adults do. Children's capacities for understanding and processing biblical and moral concepts is limited, and they need to respond to biblical truths at their own level. We must, therefore, be careful not to expect or demand adult understanding from children. But with adolescence, thinking takes wing. The new stage of cognitive development—formal operations—means the ability to think about thinking, exercise deductive logic ("if … then"), form generalizations, and perform abstract thinking. The adolescent is now capable of going beyond immediate experience to examine various alternatives and solutions. This growth allows the adolescent to begin to consider the burgeoning questions of life and to construct a system of personal beliefs and meaning. Simple answers are no longer sufficient, so adolescents ask, "Why?" or, "What for?"

This more complex level of thinking is new for adolescents, and they will need to continue to develop these skills as they enter adulthood and then continue to sharpen these skills throughout their lives. Keep in mind, however, that not all adults regularly perform at this level. Also, theorists suggest that certain types of thinking are unique to adulthood. These may include accepting conflict, pragmatic problem solving, and understanding paradoxes. These changes in the ways we think come with time and experiences.

Yet not every adult thinks at the level of formal operations. Adults who fit into Piaget's concrete operations stage are limited in their thoughts to concrete problems and issues, to the empirically perceived world. These adults cannot mentally apply logic to verbal or hypothetical problems. Dettoni suggests that concrete-thinking Christian adults cannot fully appreciate theological formulae and will be unable to make sense out of abstract theological ideas:

> Abstract ideas, such as the Trinity and other theological formulae, cannot be fully appreciated by adults in the concrete stage. When the concept of God as a Trinity is taught in an abstract fashion to these adults, they either will not understand it, disregard it because it does not make sense to them (it is irrelevant);

> memorize it but will not be able to understand it nor explain it; or try to make sense out of it in a mistaken manner. Concrete thinking adults will seek to make sense out of abstract theological ideas and can unknowingly make up heresy.[22]

Piaget's Stage 4, formal operations, is the most mature level of mental maturity. At that point, adults can think about the possible, not just what they see and experience. Contemplating about the past, present, and future is possible for adults in the formal operations stage. However, just because adults can function at the level of formal operations, that does not mean that these adults always do so. Adults, like children and youth, function at the highest stage necessary to achieve what they need. Adults will function with abstract thinking if they find that they cannot adequately deal with an issue, concern, problem, or concept with just concrete thinking—and many mental operations for adults do not require formal thought. So adults use the skills of the cognitive development stage in order to achieve what they need, and they quite possibly miss too much of the Bible's meaning for their lives.

Dettoni states this:

> Because adults can function in the marketplace with abstract thinking, does not necessarily mean they will do so within the church ... It is not unusual to find a person who can think well on an abstract stage returning to a concrete way of thinking when it comes to spiritual matters. Such thinking is unfortunate since so much of Scripture is written on an abstract, not concrete, level ... Christians who cannot or will not think abstractly miss a significant amount of the Bible's meaning for their lives.[23]

Milestone #5 involves more than knowledge. In the journey toward maturity, believers will gradually understand the Word of God at a more sophisticated level.

Levels and Domains of Learning God's Word

In our discussion of the first five milestones on the journey of faith, we've seen the need to consider not only the content of our

Christian beliefs and values but also the processes by which we came to our beliefs and values. Looking at how we learn anything will help us to understand how we can come to a more mature faith in Jesus. To begin, learning takes place on the following levels:

1. Memorizing facts
2. Understanding principles
3. Realizing implications of facts and principles for life
4. Choosing to obey (now within the learner's reach)
5. Changing one's behaviors[24]

It should not surprise us that the Word of God abides in believers at differing levels. As believers gain a more thorough understanding of Scripture at each level, that increased knowledge results in greater transformation. We can learn the Bible on any level, but only at the "Realization" level, when the Word of God most fully abides in us, does it transform our lives. Learning God's Word less thoroughly (at a lower level) is unlikely to transform one's life.

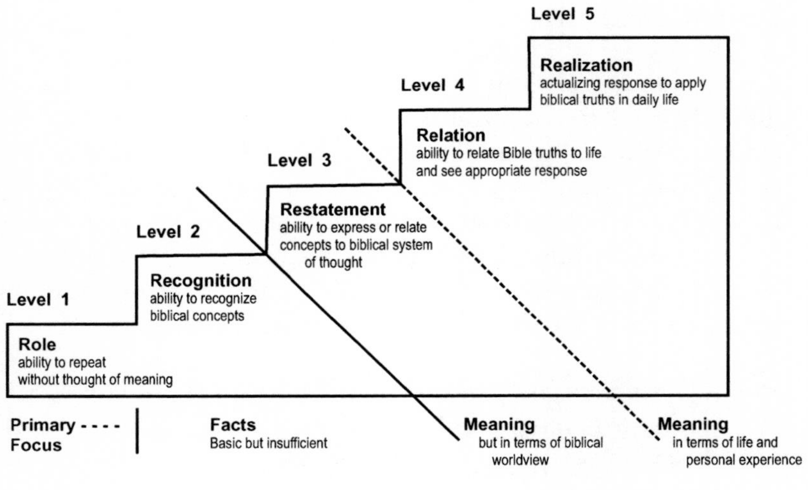

Then Habermas and Issler remind us that learning takes place in three domains and that one can grow and improve in each. Also, learning occurs in degrees (see Table 10 below). "The Word of God abides" in believers to different levels in each of the three domains (cognition, conviction, and competence), as well as in the three degrees of learning. Again, abiding is an ongoing process in a believer's life.[25]

Table 10: Domains and Degrees of Learning

Domain		Degree 1	Degree 2	Degree 3
Cognition:	Knowledge	Awareness	Understanding	Wisdom
Conviction:	Attitudes, values, and emotions	Sensitivity to others	Empathy	Compassion in action
Competence:	Physical skills and habits	Accom-plished with some difficulty	Accomplished with ease	Accomplished with improvisation

The significance of Milestone #5 lies in forging the link between biblical truth and everyday life. Yet that linking won't happen if the Word of God does not abide deeply in a Christian, and God's Word comes to dwell only in those believers who have adequately attended to the three milestones in the Childhood stage of faith and to the Young Adulthood Milestone #4.

In the following personal testimonies, believers talk about the challenges they faced as they worked on this second milestone of Young Adulthood:

> As a pastor, I've noticed that sometimes reading Scripture has become an assignment for me. Instead of asking, "What does it mean to me?" I find myself looking for teaching applications. How can I teach or preach this? What kind of illustration would best support this passage? Sometimes it feels that the Bible is a textbook and I'm just getting head knowledge from it. I need to carve out times for the purpose of reading the Bible devotionally, starting with one or two verses and really letting them take root in my life. I need to realize that the strongest teaching comes when I appropriate Scripture in my life.

> I grew up in the church, knew the Sunday school Bible stories, and had even read some of the Old Testament and all of the New… I had a lot of biblical information. However, when I interacted with more spiritually mature Christians, God showed me that I was lacking in the personal experience of the Bible's truths. I had been accustomed to simply reading rather than actually studying the Bible. As I opened myself to studying and personalizing God's Word, I began to find it easier to apply its truths to my daily life. He began to speak to me. The Word began to "abide" in me, as if it came alive in me. It is no longer restricted to head knowledge.
>
> My deeper yielding to God came by committing to spending time in His Word each day… As I did this … I began to have a strength within that I had never possessed before … to make a stand against the world, the flesh, and the devil.

Milestone #6

Defeating the Enemies of Spiritual Progress

Based on 1 John 2:13–14 ("I am writing to you, young men, because you have overcome the evil one"), Milestone #6 addresses the core issue of a lived-out faith in the God who has triumphed over the world, the flesh, and the devil. The truth to be learned here is: "I can recognize and counter each of the three enemies that threaten my spiritual growth." The dynamic growth process at this milestone includes:

- ***Moving away***… from the powerful influences of the world, the flesh, and the devil—from these three enemies that assault believers from within and without; and from bondage, compulsive drives, subtle and not-so-subtle deceptions, irrational beliefs, and points of vulnerability to these enemies, all of which jeopardize one's growth toward Christlikeness.
- ***Moving toward***… overcoming these enemies' efforts to undermine a Christian's personal holiness and wholeness—toward victory over the world, the flesh, and the

> devil; toward becoming a dynamic and authentic believer; and toward the freedom that comes from yielding oneself fully to God.

Knowing that healthy spiritual growth is impaired by neglecting or inadequately completing the preceding milestones of spiritual development, the Christian will continue to work on the core issues those milestones address. In the Childhood stage of faith, you will find that the three pernicious rivals will take aim at Milestone #1 and try to obstruct your experience of God's extravagant and amazing grace. These enemies also seek to distort your perception of how God, in His love and forgiveness, sees you and, therefore, prevent any deep renewal and repair. Then, at Milestone #2, these three enemies will try to distort your concept of God so that you won't let yourself trust Him or fully surrender to Him as your Father. At Milestone #3, these rivals conspire to keep you from deep relationships that provide the mix of Christian support and challenge you will need to grow strong and whole.

We have looked at two of the three milestones that characterize the Young Adulthood stage of faith. Milestone #4 has challenged the Christian to move past an Affiliative Style/Synthetic-Conventional stage of faith to a personally owned faith. Milestone #5 accents the centering and transforming influence of God's Word as it abides in the believer. At Milestone #6, the Christian is to become progressively aware that spiritual growth occurs on a battleground.

We are at war. We must be aware that there is a dark side of human nature—of both sin and suffering. The powerful forces of the world, the devil, and the flesh seek to conform and condition each believer, but you have to learn progressively to recognize and overcome each of these enemies. If Christians neglect this sixth milestone, they will be unprepared and unprotected in the inevitable spiritual battle that surrounds believers; they will find themselves vulnerable to the strategies of the enemies within and without. Overcoming or gaining victory over these rivals is a key aspect of the story of your spiritual journey that, as a Parent in the faith, you will share.

Eric Erikson

Let's look again to Erikson's psychosocial theory to explain child and adult development. He saw a changing child in a changing world and a system of culturally constructed contexts devoted to the socialization of children into the culture. According to Erikson, nature determines the sequence of the stages and sets the limits within which nurture operates, and the environment determines how those stages are resolved.[26]

Human development, including spiritual development, is shaped and determined by the mutually interactive and inextricably intertwined influences of nature and nurture. The influence of one is impossible to understand without considering the relative influence of the other. In other words, neither heredity nor environment exclusively causes development. Such changes occur as a result of the collaboration of inner and outer forces and factors. Also, the believer retains the option of choice, even in the face of strong and compelling forces. Finally, the external environment either enables or hinders a person's development, but it does not control it.

Recall the bottom line of the "The Enemies of Spiritual Progress" discussion in Chapter 4. Every believer, whether in the Child, Young Adulthood, or Parenthood stage of faith, encounters three deterrents to spiritual progress: the world, the flesh, and the devil. (These forces parallel the nature vs. nurture issue raised by the developmentalist.) The believer faces two external enemies (the world and the devil), as well as the internal enemy (the flesh). Spiritual progress can be impaired and delayed by any of these three rivals. In John's model of stages of faith, these enemies conspire to erode each of the eight milestones, which, if neglected or insufficiently attended to, will impair progress.

In John's model, the key forces of nurture or environment are the world and the devil. We believers, for instance, have not only absorbed unthinkingly the warped and twisted values, perspectives, and attitudes unique to our culture, but we have also been shaped and misshaped by those values. The world system socializes, secularizes, and conditions each person in ways counter to Christlikeness and spiritual maturity.

The second enemy, the Evil One, is the mastermind behind forces of the world and the flesh. Satan's lies and deceptions are designed to prevent believers from moving toward wholeness and full-grown Parenthood in the faith.

Nature or heredity is the third archenemy in John's model of spiritual growth. The Bible clearly teaches that human beings are not morally neutral; rather, each person is a sinner by nature (Romans 3:23). The "the lust of the flesh, the lust of the eyes, and the boastful pride of life" are strong, internal forces that believers must battle. *Lust* refers to the believer's instinct-driven desires, impulses, compulsions, habits, and motives that empower his or her efforts to be in control and the complete master of his or her life. As believers identify their vulnerabilities and appetites, they progressively yield to God's presence, power, and purposes.

A. W. Tozer wrote about the pain of parting from the "toys" that had a deep hold on him. He had discovered that only God could bring deep healing and renewal. We can expect the same experience as we experience victory over whatever holds us back from Christlikeness. Hear Tozer's prayer:

> Father, I want to know Thee, but my coward heart fears to give up its toys. I cannot part with them without inward bleeding, and I do not try to hide from Thee the terror of the parting. I come trembling, but I do come. Please root from my heart all those things which I have cherished so long and which have become a very part of my living self, so that Thou mayest enter and dwell there without a rival. Then shalt Thou make the place of Thy feet glorious. Then shall my heart have no need of the sun to shine in it, for Thyself will be the light of it, and there shall be no night. In Jesus' name, Amen.[27]

As the following testimonies reveal, the world, the flesh, and the devil play a key role in a believer's journey of faith:

> I discovered that my flesh is never satisfied and that sensual pleasures take up my time and keep me separated from the Lord's peace. I deal with this enemy daily in the areas of diet, exercise, and self-centeredness. I have been so hurt, being a single woman,

single mom, and fatherless daughter for so many years, that the enemy, the world, has so consumed much of my life with feelings of inadequacies, a sense of being unlovable, and the drive for self-sufficiency that much of my life is closed off to who God is and what He wants to do through me. Discovering this is helpful because it takes away a lot of the excuses that I make for being defeated off of the enemy, Satan, and makes my defeat my responsibility. I need to stop accusing Satan for my disobedience and start taking responsibility for my own sin. It is easy to say, "I'm defeated because my enemy is just too strong," but it takes responsibility to say, "I can overcome my enemy through Christ who will give me new strength over my flesh and the world He has already defeated."

I lived for many years in defeat ... having succumbed to the world around me. I was a prisoner to the desires within myself and a slave to the influences surrounding me. Milestone #6 helped me finally discover and recognize the areas where the enemy attacked. With a new understanding of what the enemy had done to me over the years, I was finally able to allow God into those areas of my life ... and now He has given me the victory, peace, and satisfaction I had been longing for. The deeper yielding came by committing to spending time in His Word each day... As I did this... I began to have a strength within that I had never possessed before ... to make a stand against the world, the flesh, and the devil. I had come to believe that there was no other way to have victory in these areas of life except through Jesus.

Young Adulthood in Review

The stage of Young Adulthood comprises three milestones. In the stage of Young Adulthood, believers will determine their own sense of ultimate purpose and meaning and decide what is really important to them. Basic personal values, convictions, and commitments are shaped and internalized here. Clearly, the key concept at this stage is *ownership*. Christians in the stage of Young Adulthood will own their faith rather than believe merely because someone else believes. During this Young Adulthood stage, believers will work to give shape and substance to a faith that can be truly their own.

The three milestones of the Young Adulthood stage of faith development must crystallize and merge if a believer is to move toward both ownership of an adult faith and a lifestyle grounded in and guided by God's truth. Like the three Childhood milestones, the milestones of Young Adulthood cannot be neglected without diminishing one's spiritual health and slowing growth toward Christlikeness and maturity. Working on the three milestones of Young Adulthood will lead to a consistent, coherent, and owned faith. Furthermore, attending to the milestones at this stage will determine the quality and health of the believer's spiritual progress in the Parenthood stage.

Work on the three milestones of Young Adulthood is certain to bring discomfort as believers experience the disequilibrium that comes with looking at why they believe what they believe. Such an appraisal of faith may mean discarding certain aspects of what they have, without examination, assumed true (and that may be painful), but this review can also mean a renewal of faith and a consolidation with faith at the center. This sort of stretching process is essential to genuine ownership of a Christian faith that is deeply penetrating, liberating, and healing. This kind of faith leads to knowing true joy in the Lord (1 John 1:4).

Many adults, however, plateau at the Young Adulthood stage of their journeys of faith and never move on and into the Parenthood stage. Why does this happen? A list of six contributing factors from Milestones #4–#6 follows.

1. *Expectations for growth may be too high.* A believer may be pushed, hurried on, or accelerated to bigger and better things at a pace that does not fit with his/her unique, personal timetable.
2. *Expectations for growth can be too low.* Sometimes believers receive insufficient support and/or challenge from the Christian community, and often they do not have the blessing of a Parent in the faith to serve as mentor and guide.
3. *Sterile religious teaching* may also contribute to an adult's stalling in the Young Adulthood stage. Well-intentioned

but poorly executed Sunday school lessons and even the influence of one's parents can fail to develop the believer's critical thinking skills. Such learning environments can arrest Christian development at Level 2 of moral reasoning.

4. *Churches that emphasize external performance, conditional acceptance, and creedal professions* can impede spiritual growth. In a setting like that, individuals may not have the opportunity to evaluate their beliefs, wrestle with the hard questions, and come to a point of truly owning their faith. The entire process that leads to owning one's faith may never even have a chance to begin.
5. *Believers may make sinful choices* that slow or even prevent their spiritual progress. One reason sin so effectively prevents spiritual growth is that it blinds believers to its paralyzing consequences. In fact, Christians can never know the full and far-reaching consequences of their sin. The Christians must also remember that they can stall at any stage of spiritual development.
6. *The comfort of an affiliative faith* can also hold back the believer in the Young Adulthood stage. Some believers have a strong desire to belong, to be accepted, and to not disappoint others, and that desire may contribute to their staying at the level of Westerhoff's affiliative faith. When believers begin to evaluate their faith and search out answers to hard questions, they can find the journey lonely, uncomfortable, even fearful, and those feelings may keep certain Christians in a conforming faith.

Each believer has his or her own timetable for spiritual growth; yet God promises that He is at work in each Christian (Philippians 1:6). And it's good to remember that He has a limitless number of creative ways to get a Christian—to get *you*—moving forward again.

Review the goals of the Young Adulthood milestones:

- Milestone #4: Owning a Firsthand Faith—strong believers are self-governing and skilled at determining their own values and beliefs apart from the input and influences of others. These believers will always need the support and challenge of fellow Christians, but they will no longer be dependent on that support.
- Milestone #5: Linking Truth to Life—God's Word has become internalized and is the centering, orienting influence for all that a believer does.
- Milestone #6: Defeating the Enemies of Spiritual Progress—the powerful forces of the world, the devil, and the flesh seek to form and condition the believer, but the Young Adult has learned to recognize and overcome each of these enemies.

Throughout your journey as a Christian, you will refine and more fully flesh out the three milestones of Young Adulthood. Time spent working on these milestones will keep your relationship with God alive and prevent mere rituals from setting in. As new life situations and spiritual challenges arise, you will address those issues as well, in order to become mature and seasoned in the faith.

Questions for Reflection and Action

Milestone #4: Owning a Firsthand Faith

1. What can prompt someone to wrestle with the questions "*Why* do I believe and behave as I do?" and "To what degree are my beliefs and values largely determined by the approval of other people?" What tools, experiences, and study can help a believer clarify and articulate biblical values and beliefs? Review what Lawrence Kohlberg wrote about moral development and James Fowler said about faith development. Identify two or three points that help you better understand the journey of faith.

Milestone #5: Linking Truth and Life

1. What can Christians do to allow God's Word to transform them? What evidence do you see in your life that God's Word has had a transformational impact on you? Be specific. The apostle John calls us to obey, rely on the Holy Spirit to teach us, and learn to abide in Christ. Why will each of these steps enable us to better link truth to everyday life? In what ways do Piaget's ideas about cognitive development and the discussion of the domains and degrees of learning support Milestone #5? Give two or three examples.

Milestone #6: Defeating the Enemies of Spiritual Progress

1. Erik Erikson wrote about the influence of both nature and nurture on human development. Explain how that parallels the biblical discussion of how the world, the devil, and the flesh are impacting spiritual development. Identify the ways each of these enemies attack—or have attacked—you. What enables you to recognize when these enemies are at work in your thoughts and your circumstances? Share any ideas about how to overcome these pernicious enemies.
2. Why is genuine ownership of one's Christian faith deeply liberating and healing?
3. Review the six factors that can contribute to stalling at the Young Adulthood stage. Which of these are you most at risk of succumbing to? Why? Now turn to Ephesians 6:10–18. What does God give His people so they can stand strong against the enemies of spiritual progress? Which piece of armor is most important at this point of your journey? Explain why.

The Transition to the Parenthood Stage of Faith

What does spiritual maturity look like? Where does a lifelong journey of Christian faith take a believer? What will the Christian's faith be like when he or she gets where he or she should be? What is the ultimate goal of spiritual development? What fruit will these stages of faith and their respective milestones bear? The apostle John's model of stages of faith offers a robust answer to these probing questions and a compelling vision of spiritual maturity. Around 95 A.D., John wrote to a first-century church in which some individuals had known Christ for as long as sixty-five years. Some of these seasoned veterans in the faith had become fathers or Parents in the Christian faith and in some very real ways, these fathers had become like *the* Father.

Just as the apostle John did, John Stott clearly differentiates three "stages of spiritual development," each one representing a more mature and stable believer. The veteran Parent in the faith is qualitatively and constitutionally different from the Child or Young Adult in the faith: "the fathers possess the *depth* and stability of ripe Christian experience."[1]

W. E. Vine similarly observed that "*father*s refers to those who have been Christians the longest and have the *deepest*, ripest, and most mature development. They are the older men in the heavenly family; those who by reason of experience are looked up to for sympathy, guidance and assistance."[2]

Recall the urgent need for *deep* believers expressed by Richard Foster: "Superficiality is the curse of our age. The doctrine of instant satisfaction is a primary spiritual problem. The desperate need today is not for more intelligent people nor gifted people, but for *deep* people."[3] The apostle John considered believers in the Parenthood stage to be those deep people, and it is the supreme goal of the church to produce this kind of mature disciple.

Yet as believers move toward Parenthood, even deeply committed Christians can still be impaired at some level. The doctrine of sin teaches the utter impossibility of perfection (Romans 3:23), but Parents in the faith will continue to become more like Jesus.

Christian psychologist R. E. Butman states this:

> While we can reasonably expect that a deeply internalized faith commitment will enhance an individual's psycho-spiritual

> wholeness, we cannot expect that Christians will ever become fully self-actualized or sanctified.[4]

Thus, the Parent will return to earlier milestones to address whatever issue has been neglected, avoided, or left unfinished. Parents will have become accustomed to this process, and this vulnerable willingness to acknowledge and address spiritual weakness is key to their effective parenting of other believers in the faith.

In the transition from Young Adulthood to Parenthood, believers can expect to find several new advances in their faith journeys. These advances include:

- **A New Role.** At Milestone #7, in order to be a catalyst of spiritual transformation, a Parent works to become a skilled guide, an example worthy of imitation, and a bold advocate for other believers traveling the journey toward wholeness and Christlikeness. Parents have moved from hurting to being healed and able to help others along on their healing journeys. Each Parent has a powerful and personal story of spiritual growth to share. Later, in Milestone #8, holiness and wholeness most fully merge.
- **A New Perspective.** Profound changes and growth can continue throughout one's life, and the Parenthood stage marks the culmination of some of these changes. Milestone #7, for instance, climaxes the movement from self-absorption to sacrificial love. Milestone #8 encourages Parents to share the wisdom of their seasoned, rich, and full faith—wisdom that is free of pretense and imbalances, wisdom that only comes with age and the real-life experiences of an owned, firsthand faith.
- **New Dangers.** Remember that any unfinished business left over from Childhood and Young Adulthood will interfere with the milestones of Parenthood. Also, the following four warnings are specific to the Parent stage:

1. Don't grow comfortable and let yourself stagnate or retire.
2. Don't neglect the next generation of Christians.
3. Avoid formulas of discipleship that can too easily result in the superficial production of spiritual clones.
4. Continue to grow in your faith by staying centered on the Lord Jesus Christ.

- **A New Invitation.** Children and Young Adults in the faith can benefit greatly from a Parent's spiritual caregiving, and that fact is a challenging invitation to the mature Christian to assume responsibility for the next generation of believers (Milestone #7). In addition, as the lifelong journey of faith continues for the Parents, they find themselves challenged by unfamiliar issues that come with aging (Milestone #8). And, of course, the Parent continues to work on Milestones #1–#6, because any unfinished business from Childhood and Young Adulthood will interfere with the two milestones of Parenthood.

CHAPTER 13

THE PARENTHOOD STAGE OF FAITH

MODELING FAITH THAT IS BIBLICALLY BASED AND DEVELOPMENTALLY INFORMED

JOHN ADDRESSED THE fathers in the faith (1 John 2:13–14), those individuals who had come to recognize that no undertaking in this life is more important than empowering others along their faith journeys and knowing Christ intimately or, said in another way, skillfully influencing others for Christ and knowing Him deeply. With these two eternal values governing the lives of those who are Parents in the faith, these believers pass on to others the spiritual realities they have come to know deeply and, always looking to the stages of faith map, guide these fellow believers on their own spiritual journeys. Key to the Parents' influence is their own personal testimony about God's love, care, and healing.

Two surpassing values guide the Parents in the faith (1 John 2:13–14):

Milestone #7	Empowering Others "I am writing to you, fathers ..."
Milestone #8	Seasoned by Time and Experience "I am writing to you, fathers, because you know Him who has been from the beginning."

Notice in the diagram below that the new message in each milestone of John's stages is derived from Scripture and enriched by insights from developmental theory. Also, recall that the ribbon wrapping around the column suggests ongoing movement, because—as discussed in Chapters 8 and 9—spiritual growth is dynamic, elastic, fluid, flexible, and irregular; it is never static, fixed, or unchangeable.

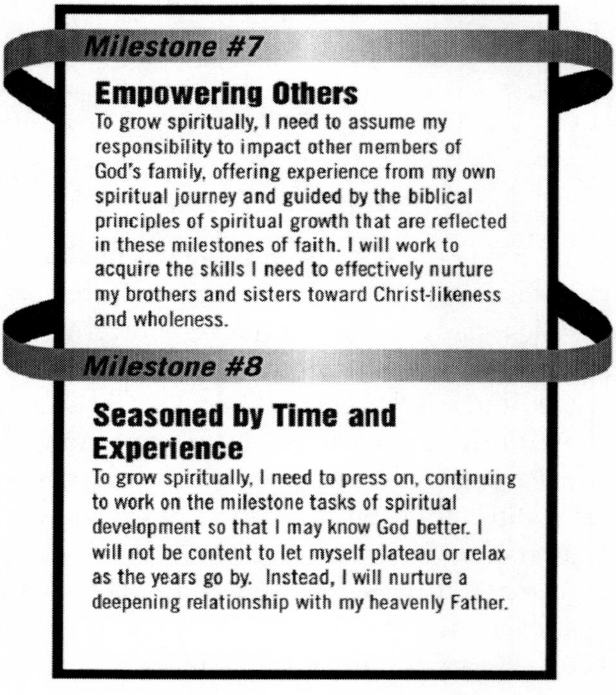
Milestone #7
Empowering Others
To grow spiritually, I need to assume my responsibility to impact other members of God's family, offering experience from my own spiritual journey and guided by the biblical principles of spiritual growth that are reflected in these milestones of faith. I will work to acquire the skills I need to effectively nurture my brothers and sisters toward Christ-likeness and wholeness.
Milestone #8
Seasoned by Time and Experience
To grow spiritually, I need to press on, continuing to work on the milestone tasks of spiritual development so that I may know God better. I will not be content to let myself plateau or relax as the years go by. Instead, I will nurture a deepening relationship with my heavenly Father.

Readiness for the Parenthood Stage of Faith

The growth of a Parent's faith results not from the number of years he has walked with the Lord but with the intensity with which he has pursued that relationship. Since both a substantial length of time spent walking with the Lord and a variety of life experiences are prerequisite for spiritual maturity, Parents in the faith are likely to be at least forty years old. Spiritual maturity is simply not possible without years of development. We saw, for instance, that the Young Adulthood stage is beyond the capabilities of the teenager and early adult; the Young Adulthood stage is not likely to be consistent and coherent until after age thirty.

Even when a person has attended to the milestones of Childhood and Young Adulthood, middle-age adulthood is generally the *entry* point to Parenthood in the faith. More likely, the believer will *begin* the stage of Parenthood sometime after age thirty-five. Of course, none of us believers should wait until middle-aged adulthood to guide and encourage others to grow in their faith, but as we mature, we will grow in the ability to influence others. And remember that if a Child, Young Adult, and Parent are each involved in serving others in the same ministry, the Parent's service flows from the heart of one who is entirely different from a Child and Young Adult. Because Parents in the faith have worked on Milestones #1–#6 through the years, they are uniquely qualified to walk with and guide Children and Young Adults on their spiritual journeys.

This chapter will highlight the contents, meanings, and gravity of the two milestones of Parenthood, demonstrating the potential for spiritual growth and identifying the effects if those tasks are neglected. As Table 12 integrates input from human development theories into the two milestones, the dynamic process and the possibilities for change and growth at each of the milestones of Parenthood will become clearer. To further shed light on this powerful connection between spiritual and developmental growth, Table 11 describes each milestone more specifically than the table in Chapter 2 does by including the following information:

1. The core issue of the milestone's content
2. A summary statement that encapsulates the primary meaning of that core issue
3. Developmental insights that support this aspect of spiritual growth

Table 11: The Parenthood Stage of Faith—Informed Developmental Theory

Milestone	Core Issue/Content	Summary	Growth Process
#7: Empowering Others	Procreative and Generative	To continue to grow spiritually, Christians will parent other believers, offering experience from and an account of their own spiritual journeys based on the milestones of each stage. Believers will gain skills needed to effectively nurture others toward Christlikeness and wholeness.	Journey guide, caregiver
#8: Seasoned by Time and Experience	Wholeness and Holiness Merge	To continue to grow spiritually, believers will come to know God even more deeply, still working to enrich their spiritual development at each milestone so that they may finish the journey well. Believers will not be content to plateau and relax as the years go by. Instead, these Parents will nurture deep and stable relationships with their heavenly Father.	Seasoned, proven

As mentioned above and as indicated in the table below, insights from the study of human development support and help explain these milestones of the Parenthood stage of faith. The names in parentheses credit the social scientists whose ideas serve as the basis for the discussions that follow. Table 12 lists the developmental researchers and their contributions to understanding the milestones of the Parenthood stage of faith.

Table 12: Social Science's Perspectives on the Parenthood Stage of Faith

Milestone #7	Empowering Others	Generativity vs. Stagnation (Erikson) Mentoring (Daloz)
Milestone #8	Seasoned by Time and Experience	The Dream (Levinson) Interiority (Neugarten) Four Challenges (Peck) Integrity vs. Despair (Erikson)

As has been shown, no stage of spiritual development can be skipped or hurried. The stages are also cumulative; each milestone builds on preceding milestones. More specifically, the formative milestones of Childhood and the individuative milestones of Young Adulthood are preparatory to generative Parenthood in the faith. While there are no shortcuts to spiritual maturity, there is an important source of help within the body of Christ. That source is a Parent in the faith.

Parents in the faith have progressed beyond Children and Young Adults in the faith and become even more "like Christ" (1 John 3:2). Recall the apostle John's three tests of genuine faith (described in Chapter 4 and set forth in 1 John 2:3–11). First, the test of obedience (2:3–6) reveals that Parents in the faith walk more as Jesus walked and more deeply and fully than a Child or Young Adult can. Parents resemble Jesus more closely, and their obeying God as Jesus did offers others a worthy example of spiritual maturity.

Second is the test of love (2:7–11). Mature believers are now able to love others more deeply and fully than the Child or Young Adult can, and a Parent's love for others is a worthy model of relational skills.

The third test is the test of discernment (2:18–27): seasoned Christians now see the world more biblically and clearly than the Child or Young Adult does. These veteran believers, however, are not flawless (1 John 1:6–2:2).

As believers age, the reality dawns on them that the values they have internalized from the secular culture (the world) and the addictions to which they may be vulnerable (the flesh) do not lead to the meaning and purpose for which these believers long. Actually, this reality may motivate Parents to offer less-experienced believers accounts of their life stories in order to help them. As D. J. Maitland points out, older adults may be better able to recognize the illusory nature of much that society values today and, as a result, set aside some of the social conventions that block many from seeing the truth clearly.[5] In Bernie Gillespie's model, the "Resolute Faith" of older adults parallels the stage of Parenthood in the faith.[6]

In another paradigm, Bruce Powers describes a period of "active devotion" after age thirty-six.[7] Les Steele offers another model that can guide the Parent in the faith: "Reappraising vs. Re-Entrenchment" in middle adulthood and "Anticipating vs. Dreading" in later adulthood.[8]

Christian maturity will always reflect the dynamic interplay between a believer's psychological and spiritual dimensions. The cultivation of a more Christlike character is, from a believer's perspective, perhaps the ultimate in spiritual and psychological well-being. Although certainly related and often interdependent, psychological and spiritual maturity will have points of divergence as well as convergence. Malony uses the phrase "holy wholeness and whole holiness" to describe some of the ways that psychodynamics and religious faith interact.[9] Any significant movement toward greater psychological health restores, at some level, a part of the image of God within a Christian.

Milestone #7

Empowering Others

Based on 1 John 2:13–14 ("I am writing to you, fathers ..."), Milestone #7 addresses the core issue of influencing others to grow toward mature faith. The dynamic growth process at this milestone challenges Parents in the faith to guide and nurture others toward wholeness and Christlikeness. This involves:

- *Moving away*... from self-absorption—from avoiding giving care to younger believers and neglecting their needs, from failing to bear fruit as a believer, from formulas and methods of discipleship that turn out clones rather than believers whose faith reflects their uniqueness and their own personal relationship with Jesus Christ, from using power to control others, from doing for others what they can do for themselves, and from fixing others.
- *Moving toward*... self-donation—toward catalyzing others with the kind of support, challenges, and vision that will spur their growth; toward mediating grace and providing skilled guidance to a Child or Young Adult's journey; toward being a faith-shaper and wounded healer, a real-life example of a believer who has been healed and transformed by God's power; toward empowering others on their faith journeys; and toward being an example of someone who continues to work on the milestones of spiritual growth.

For the Sake of Others

The Path charts a believer's journey through three biblical stages of faith, highlighting the interactive nature of community and the mutual support and challenge such a community offers (Milestone #3). But each one of us needs not only a map to follow but also personal, skilled, and experienced guidance from a Parent. The Christian faith is best communicated person-to-person. Spiritual growth is best guided by one who has traveled the road ahead of us. Because a

Parent in the faith has diligently worked on the eight milestones of spiritual growth through the years, he or she is uniquely qualified to skillfully guide the Child and the Young Adult along their own journeys of faith. Parents have traveled far and grown mature in the Christian faith; they can personally testify to God's love and healing and share that story with others.

So Milestone #8 focuses on the special contribution of Parents in a community of believers. Christian educator Terry Mulholland stated that "spiritual formation is the process of being conformed to the image of Christ *for the sake of others.*"[10] A mentoring Parent can be that kind of guide, and a believer's relationship with a Parent will be among the believer's most prized relationships. Spiritual growth requires a relationship with sure-footed guides.

Remember that spiritual progress is not some sort of private self-actualization. Instead, spiritual progress takes us increasingly in the direction of Christlikeness, and Christlikeness will, in turn, take us to the place of assuming and sustaining responsibility for the spiritual growth of fellow believers. Over the years, the process of spiritual growth moves believers from hurting to healing to helping. At that point, we are to pass on the lessons we have learned on our own faith journeys. If Parents do not sufficiently develop the essential skills of nurturing others and mediating grace to believers who are wrestling with each milestone, their own spiritual growth may be impoverished.

Having let go of pretense (1 John 1:6–2:2), Parents in the faith are credible and authentic people who have nothing to prove, no image to maintain, and no facades to preserve. Paul described himself as "the least of all the apostles" (1 Corinthians 15:9) and, in his later years, "the foremost of all sinners" (1 Timothy 1:15). It would appear, then, that Parents in the faith have grown to fully acknowledge their sin and failures; yet they truly experience and rest in God's grace.

> The unsettling seasons we encounter on the journey are necessary both for our transformation in Christ and for gaining the wisdom to guide others on their homeward journeys. Our greatest

> need, therefore, is not to avoid distress and suffering, but to live into the process and patiently permit our hardships to do their transforming work.[11]

Such experiences would uniquely prepare a Parent in the faith to be approached by others who also know sin and brokenness firsthand.

Furthermore, Parents in the faith do not exercise mechanized, routine, or stereotypical disciple-making efforts in an attempt to make Christian clones. Instead, mature and godly Parents have acquired the skills that will help free others to move toward Christlikeness and the wholeness that God designed people to know in Him. Parents will tailor their parenting to the unique needs of a specific individual.

As the authors of *Adult Development and Aging* put it, "Perhaps adulthood is the time during the life span to develop an understanding or perspective on the information one has gained and to pass this information on to others."[12] In light of that possibility, Dallas Willard highlights a serious omission in the church's work:

> Have we done what is necessary to bring the earnest convert into his or her possession as a child of God, as a brother or sister of Jesus Christ in the new life? Unfortunately, the answer to this question must be a clear no. It is not an exaggeration to say that this dimension of practical theology is not even taken as a matter of great seriousness by most of our teachers and leaders, probably because it doesn't seem imperative to succeed in doing so immediately. So we can only describe the phrase, "teaching them to do all things whatsoever I have commanded you," as the Great Omission from the Great Commission of Matthew 28:19–20.[13]

We believers need to—and developmental psychology supports this idea—come alongside brothers and sisters in the faith to offer support, encouragement, a role model, and prayer. In other words, we need to disciple them.

Eric Erikson

In his studies of human development, Erikson theorized that individuals in midlife must confront the issue of "Generativity vs. Stagnation." *Generativity* refers to establishing, guiding, and passing the torch to the next generation, leaving a legacy and investing in something that outlives the self.[14] Generativity includes rearing children, training students, serving as a mentor to a younger worker, and generating new ideas. Generativity refers to all that a person produces and leaves behind, and spiritual formation definitely falls into this category. A parent, teacher, pastor, small-group leader, mentor, discipler, or friend can guide that spiritual formation. If a person does not choose opportunities to reach out to younger individuals, stagnation occurs, bringing with it a feeling of boredom, a life of impoverishment, and an excessive preoccupation with oneself.

Indeed, a major problem in our culture is self-absorption. Too many people remain more concerned about themselves than about others—to the peril of future generations. This situation has huge implications for the Christ-follower as well as for the church's education and formation ministry. To be specific, the Parent stage of one's faith journey is a critical time for caregiving and guiding others along the way. The Parent in the faith assumes responsibility for attending to the spiritual growth of others. A Parent has, through the years, shifted from journeying *with* others to journeying *for* others. This mature, veteran believer will note the strengths and weaknesses of Children and Young Adults in the faith and come alongside to help shore up those weaknesses.

Knowledgeable about the markers that indicate forward movement on this path, Parents are also familiar with the pitfalls, detours, trials, and temptations along the way. Having experienced the process of becoming deep, whole, and more like Christ, a Parent in the faith offers no banal formulas for spiritual growth. Instead, Parents offer the Child and Young Adult the relational and incarnational dimension of spiritual nurturing: they invite people to be with them (Mark 3:14) in a variety of settings, which is a greater commitment of time and effort than the formal learning a classroom requires.

> *The Path* has carefully described the overarching biblical pattern and dynamics of the three stages of faith and the eight milestones to be attended to. But we believers need to know what the model looks like experientially or practically as well. So this text blends the descriptive with the challenge of a prescriptive approach. The Parent in the faith is to help believers experience and cultivate a lived-out relationship with God. The church needs generation after generation of such authentic and deep believers.

Laurent Daloz

After investigating the skills needed to help people grow, Laurent Daloz developed the following strategy from an adult development perspective. He found that teachers/mentors guide development by providing support and engendering trust, issuing a challenge, and formulating a compelling vision. Daloz further explains:

> People grow best [developmentally] where they continuously experience an ingenious blend of support and challenge… Environments that are weighted too heavily in the direction of challenge without adequate support are toxic; they promote defensiveness and constriction. Those weighted too heavily toward support without adequate challenge are ultimately boring; they promote devitalization. Both kinds of imbalance lead to withdrawal or dissociation from the context. In contrast, the balance of support and challenge leads to vital engagement.[15]

The Christian community is to be a place of unconditional love, and that makes it an ideal place for both support and challenge. Within this community, mature, seasoned Parents in the faith can guide others. Their modeling and the personal relationships they establish provide impetus for change and growth. "Indeed, the presence of this gifted enabler has often changed a 'happening' into a 'formative experience.'"[16] Put differently, a Parent in the faith can help attach valuable meaning to another believer's experiences.

As the diagram below illustrates, though, the support and challenge that a Parent offers need to be in balance if a Child or Young Adult is to grow:

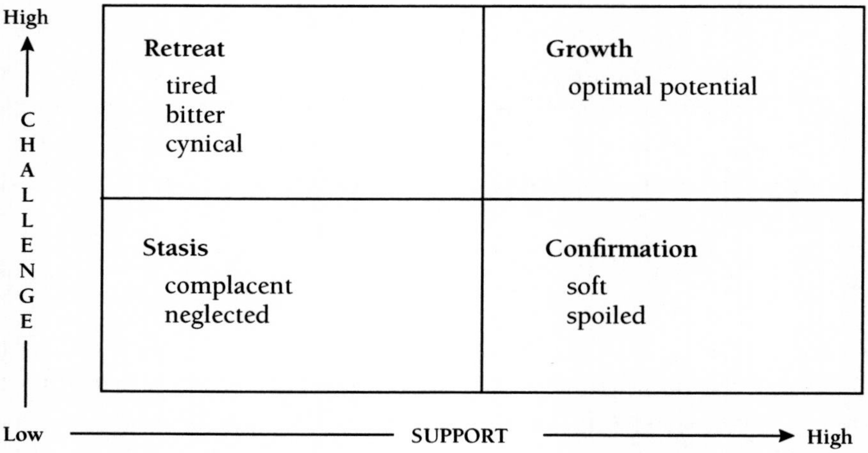

- First, if support is high but challenge to their faith is non-existent or weak, believers will merely receive *confirmation* for where they are on the journey. Such high support and low challenge do nothing more than preserve the status quo. Again, the high support will make younger believers feel good about themselves, but they are not likely to go anywhere.
- Second, when both support and challenge are low, the result is *stasis*. Low support means that no mentoring Parent is available to offer the much-needed support and challenge required for spiritual growth to happen. As a result, the believer will feel alone and disappointed—and will be going nowhere.
- Third, too much challenge from the Parent without appropriate support can result in *retreat*: a Child or Young Adult can lose interest in the spiritual journey and/or rebel. Too much challenge may also cause some Christians to

dig in deeper and become tirelessly perfectionistic. They may become "churchaholics" who try to measure up to the expectations of others and the probably too-strict expectations they imagine God has for them.

- Fourth, an appropriate mix of support and challenge results in optimal *growth*. A balanced blend of support and challenge encourages Christians to risk entering new territory in their faith, prods them to keep moving when they get bogged down, and gives them a vision to move toward. Parents will empower fellow believers to envision the changes they want to make and to bravely face the risks those changes involve.

Just as no two people are alike, no two spiritual journeys are alike. Therefore, all believers need a seasoned Parent in the faith who can help them navigate their unique journeys. A skillful and loving Parent tailors expectations to the particular strengths and weaknesses of each pilgrim. Furthermore, Parents in the faith are able to encourage a Child or Young Adult toward further spiritual growth because they themselves (the Parents) have been working on the milestones of spiritual development. Parents offer a deeper meaning, speak to the younger believer's vulnerabilities, and ask profound questions. Children and Young Adults in the faith need the prayerful and wise support of a nurturing Parent as they face the complexities of life and the questions that come with living out one's Christian convictions.

Furthermore, the story of the Parent's personal journey of faith, of the transformative work the Spirit has done at each of the milestones, will be a means of empowering fellow believers. The seasoned Parent in the faith has a personal message of growth and healing to share, and it is important that these older Christians tell their stories. Linda Vogel says this:

> I believe that older adults should be the story bearers, as they are given encouragement and opportunity to share their faith stories. If we do not grasp the opportunity, these stories—and those of

> that generation's parents and grandparents—will be lost from the community memory.[17]

Note, however, that a believer's need for support, challenge, and vision does not diminish, even though he or she has become a Parent in the faith. The absence of adequate support, challenge, and vision may cause stagnation, resignation, plateauing, or regression in a Parent, just as it can in a Child or Young Adult. Wise Parents, therefore, seek the support of fellow Parents and even find encouragement, support, challenge, and vision in their relationships with Children and Young Adults in the faith.

Two other aspects of Milestone #7 need to be clarified. First, the message here is not at all that prior to middle-age adulthood and the Parent stage of faith development Christians cannot serve, teach, or disciple fellow believers. Actually, Milestone #7 emphasizes that ministry (doing) grows out of who you are (being) and that truth applies to believers at all stages of growth. Second, Christian leaders, pastors, seminary graduates, and missionaries are not automatically in the Parenthood stage of faith. They may be educated, trained, and salaried to do what Parents do, but they may not be Parents in the faith experientially.

Consider the following examples:

> I now see that some of my performance baggage is affecting the way I shepherd others. Being bent on performance, I am not as patient as I should be with their spiritual development because I feel that their lack of development is a reflection on me. In one sense, it is because I am trying to rush them. I need to sit down with each of them, listen to where they would like to grow, and help them. I need to realize that, even though I am their shepherd, God is the One causing them to grow, not me. Most of them are in the Childhood stage of their faith and need a nurturing parent. I am using Stages of Faith to help me develop a vision for their spiritual growth.
>
> As a result of several short-term mission trips that were rebuilding and construction efforts after large-scale natural

disasters [Asian tsunami, Katrina, etc.], I had the increasing desire to minister to the soul of the local people versus simply rebuilding their homes or villages. The rebuilding was the easy part; the empowering of others (Milestone #7) was where I needed help and preparation. The challenge I faced was where to find the skills to be an effective "faith coach" without attending seminary. The answer for me was Stages of Faith, where I discovered rich, organic, deeply nourishing principles of faith empowerment and encouragement. My takeaways from Milestone #7 became the tools I was searching for to become a faith coach. I have become a skillful listener, a more effective rebuilder of hope, and more unselfish.

I used to think that the "parenting phase" of Christianity referred to raising one's own children, but the Stages of Faith study brought home the point that I could be an example to other men in the church. Milestone #7 points out that "nothing in this life surpasses knowing Christ intimately and empowering others to do the same." What a challenge! At my tender age of sixty-three, it would be easy to rationalize that I have done a lot of mentoring throughout my years of walking with the Lord and that it is time to let younger men step up and stand in the gap. Milestone #7 provided the impetus I needed to keep on being involved in ministry to men.

Milestone #8

Seasoned by Time and Experience

Based on 1 John 2:13–14 ("I am writing to you, fathers, because you know Him who has been from the beginning"), Milestone #8 addresses the core issue of developing and enjoying a mature, vintage faith in which wholeness and holiness come together. To grow spiritually, believers will progressively come to know God better, continuing to enrich and enhance the milestones of spiritual development so that they may finish the journey well. These believers will not be content to plateau and relax as the years go by. Instead, these Parents will nurture a deep and stable relationship with their heavenly Father.

The dynamic growth process of Milestone #8 includes:

- ***Moving away***... from stagnation—from the tendency to withdraw or retire, from plateauing and resting comfortably on one's laurels and the results of earlier spiritual growth, from being mentally rigid and closed to new ideas, and from fear and anxiety about aging and physical decline.
- ***Moving toward***... a rich and full-grown faith—toward a deep, proven, stable friendship with God; toward ongoing appraisal and renewal of one's spiritual direction and life-giving faith; toward the point where personal holiness and God-given wholeness merge; toward a lifestyle characterized by godly wisdom; toward continuing the long obedience to God; toward consistent attention to the milestones of spiritual growth; and toward finishing the journey of faith well.

Recall John Stott's observation: "The fathers have progressed into a *deep* communion with God" (emphasis added).[18] In a similar fashion, James Montgomery Boice noted this: "It is the fathers who, as a result of a lifetime of spiritual experience, have known the Eternal One and have come to fully trust Him. The fathers have acquired the gift of spiritual wisdom, having lived longer in the faith and thus have come to know Him who is from the beginning in a *deeper* way."[19]

So how does a Christian become a *deep* believer? We find some answers at Milestone #8. Consider, for instance, the truth that since growth is such a long journey, requiring sufficient time and experience, we need to expect to come face-to-face with pain, discomfort, and unexpected and unwanted events, all of which play an important role in our development. As a result of those hard times, we will learn or be reminded firsthand that God is reliable, that He can be trusted no matter what, and that He is present and active in every moment of our lives, shaping and forming us into the image and likeness of Christ.

Seasoned by Inevitable Challenges

When John's brother James became the first of the original disciples to be martyred, John bore the loss in a more personal way than the other disciples did. Then, as each of those other disciples was martyred, one by one, John suffered additional grief and pain. John's friends and companions were gone, and he alone was left. In some ways, that solitude may have been the most painful suffering of all. Additionally, in his later years, John was exiled on the island of Patmos, where he lived in a cave, a harsh environment for an aged man.[20] Yet, during John's more than ninety years on this planet, God used every experience and every ounce of pain to transform John from Son of Thunder to the Apostle of Love.

In light of John's experience, we can be confident that our trials, distress, and disorienting seasons have a definite purpose in God's plans for our lives and for our spiritual growth. God uses our hard times to make us seasoned Parents in the faith, and these hard times will become key chapters in the personal testimony that we, as Parents in the faith, will share with others.

A widely read modern-day allegory is Hannah Hurnard's *Hind's Feet on High Places*. In this parable, God calls Much-Afraid to journey to the high country with two companions, Suffering and Sorrow, who will help her along the way. Stunned that God would call her to travel with such unattractive friends, she pleads with the Shepherd:

> "I can't go with them," she gasped. "I can't. I can't. O my Shepherd, why do you do this to me? How can I travel in their company? It is more than I can bear. You tell me that the mountain way itself is so steep and difficult that I cannot climb it alone. Then why, oh why, must you make Sorrow and Suffering my companions? Couldn't you have given Joy and Peace to go with me, to strengthen me, and encourage me and help me on this difficult way? I never thought you would do this to me!"[21]

Parents in the faith are not unaccustomed to facing trials and choosing to trust God's purposes during these disorienting seasons. Illustrating this truth, Much-Afraid becomes less afraid and more trusting of her traveling companions. Similarly, Parents in the faith draw on the ultimate and glorious goal of their heavenly destination. They are assured of meeting Jesus at the journey's end, regardless of the challenges, the suffering, and the sorrows that they face along the way.

Developmental theorists identify different goals in life. The goal of Kohlberg's moral development theory is justice, and he points to Mahatma Gandhi, Martin Luther King, Jr., and Mother Teresa as examples of Stage 6 moral reasoning. The goal of Fowler's faith development is a universalizing faith, and he mentions Mahatma Gandhi, Thomas Merton, Martin Luther King, Jr., and Dietrich Bonhoeffer as examples of universalizing faith. Fowler's actual research has identified only one current interview functioning at Stage 6.

Scholar and religious educator Gabriel Moran noted that there is a flaw in a system based on the highest stages that very few people reach.[22] Also, we are not called to identification with the Ground of Being (Fowler). Rather than this kind of universalizing faith, the goal of the 1 John 2:12–14 paradigm is likeness—a striking resemblance—to the character of Christ. This end is to be the pursuit of all believers, and such Christlikeness is to be especially characteristic of the seasoned Parent in the faith.

Knowing God *in* Midlife

Upon entering adulthood chronologically, individuals confront issues they did not face when they were younger. In middle adulthood, these issues can trigger new spiritual growth, and believers can come to know God on a deeper level. Research in human development by Robert Peck, Bernice Neugarten, Daniel Levinson, and Eric Erikson offers clues to understanding issues that arise with the progress and the decline that characterize adulthood.

Robert Peck

Peck researched Erikson's concept of the tension between generativity and stagnation in midlife and noted four challenges that middle-aged adults face:[23]

- With the decline of their physical powers, adults must value wisdom rather than physical strength.
- Adults must redefine relationships with both sexes. This involves learning to socialize relationships instead of sexualizing them. The challenge here is to stress companionship rather than sexual intimacy or competitiveness.
- Adults must either develop "cathectic" flexibility or face "cathectic" impoverishment. By this, Peck means that adults need emotional support from soul friends as they face the death of their parents, the drifting away of friends, and the moving away of their children. Midlife can be, then, a time to establish new and deep friendships for the journey ahead.
- Adults must develop mental flexibility rather than becoming rigid in their thinking. Often middle-aged adults are stereotyped as dogmatic, set in their ways, and closed to new ideas. Middle-aged adults must be open to fresh ideas and willing to change if they are to continue to grow.

Consequently, as midlife believers face these four challenges, they can experience a fresh and deeper maturity based on the strength that comes from wisdom, richer marriages and friendships, and a shift to new ideas to guide their lives.

Bernice Neugarten

According to Bernice Neugarten, one positive change that comes at midlife is "interiority," which she defines as the tendency to be more philosophical and reflective.[24] A middle-aged adult and Parents in the faith beyond age forty tend to reflect on where they have been in life and where they are going. Middle-aged adults also experience a shift in their perspective on time, thinking now in terms of the time they have left rather than the time since they were born. They are aware that they have more yesterdays behind them than tomorrows ahead of them. This, therefore, is a key time for Parents in the faith to challenge men and women in midlife to take their faith more seriously.

Daniel Levinson

Supporting Neugarten's conclusions, Daniel Levinson advises that midlife adults, including Parents in the faith, take stock of their lives up to that point.[25] Questions like "Who am I?" and "Where am I going?" again become important at this point that is something of a second adolescence. Evaluating their personal achievements in light of their lifelong goals and dreams, these middle-aged adults begin to recast their dreams and set new goals as they answer the questions "Who am I?" and "Where am I going?"; as they personally hear God's call to follow Him; and as they choose to influence others deeply. Midlife adults can experience an enormous shift from centering the world around themselves and their successes to winning others to Christ and influencing and guiding believers' spiritual growth.

Knowing God *Beyond* Midlife

Even after midlife, other events trigger spiritual growth and maturity. After all, Christians are not immune to the challenges, losses, and struggles that life brings after age forty-five or fifty. Even in life's final chapters, growth need never stop. Challenges can continue to bring believers into a deeper relationship with God. Struggles can further ground the Parent in the Lord's truth, His power, and His hope. Even in their spiritual Parenthood stage, believers need not decay, plateau, or stagnate. Knowing God deeply makes the difference.

Eric Erikson

Erikson identifies the conflict "Integrity vs. Despair" as the primary issue of older adulthood.[26] In this last stage of development, *integrity* refers to the emotional integration and sense of coherence and wholeness that enable one to be at peace with oneself in the face of decline and death. In contrast, despair is emotional disintegration, a lack of coherence and wholeness, and the inability to accept one's inevitable death. Despair results in fear, anxiety, and the feeling that one's life has not been worth living. The following factors can influence growth (integrity) or stagnation (despair) in midlife and beyond:

1. Changing cultural values and patterns regarding aging
2. A sense that one's productive life is past and the end is near
3. Reaching one's life goals
4. Evaluating one's failures and disappointments
5. Decreasing physical strength and failing health
6. Reduced income
7. Forced retirement
8. Leisure time
9. Ingratitude of those one loves
10. Tragedies and disappointments
11. An empty nest
12. Widowhood
13. Dependency
14. The reality and inevitability of death

Followers of Christ must honestly ask themselves, "Has my life had real value? Did my life count for God? Has my life impacted other people positively? Have I lived with purpose and found fulfillment? At my funeral, will it be said that I lived life well? And am I ready today to be with the Lord tomorrow?"

Parents in the faith have been and continue to be seasoned by the fourteen kinds of experiences listed above. Their relationships with God make a difference in how they face these tough issues that come in adulthood. Success in meeting these challenges depends, to a great extent, on how well they have worked through the milestones of Childhood and Young Adulthood. Finally, in their older adulthood, Parents in the faith need to exercise the body, mind, and spirit as never before, and the church cannot miss the opportunity to encourage older adults to keep growing.

Consider these examples:

> Imagine serving almost fifteen years as a leader in church and parachurch ministry when everything suddenly changes. Well, that has been my experience ... at sixty years old! My comfortable, scripted, Christian lifestyle was no longer working, and, like Humpty Dumpty, I couldn't put it back together again. As a result, I crash landed in the wilderness with my companions anger, denial, and disillusionment. The Stages of Faith Milestone #8 not only provides the framework but also the connectedness for my stay in the wilderness as God and my companions help equip me for my transition into being a seasoned believer. I am committed to continue working through this experience because I know that God's purpose is to prepare me for finishing well as His servant and His friend.

> I love Milestone #8! I was reminded lately that each of the stages of growth emphasizes one's "readiness" to deal with the spiritual tasks at hand. I am seventy-three years old and have walked with and served the Lord since my conversion forty-three years ago. Two years ago, I began to believe that it was time to cut back on ministry, not remembering that cutting back on ministry really means cutting back on my own spiritual growth! So at that time, the Lord in His mercy called me to a new ministry that is more complex and challenging and time-consuming than I have experienced in some time! The purpose, I believe, is to increase my capacity to rest in the Lord, to encourage me to embrace new challenges and new experiences, and to help me be completely open to whatever the Lord is doing next!... I haven't thought about age for the last two years!

Review of Parenthood

"What does spiritual maturity look like?" "Where is this lifelong journey of faith taking the Christian?" Human development has suggested the following responses to these Milestone #7 and #8 questions.

At Milestone #7, Empowering Others, Parents in the faith intentionally enter into caregiving relationships with younger believers in order to influence and empower them on their spiritual journeys. A Parent will resist simplistic formulas and prescriptions when guiding others toward wholeness and Christlikeness. When Parents neglect this milestone, however, they slow the progress and healing of other believers, whose growth requires a relationship with experienced guides. When Parents do not sufficiently develop the skills essential to nurturing others and mediating grace to believers wrestling with each of the milestone issues, the spiritual health and growth of those younger believers may be impoverished.

At Milestone #8, Seasoned by Time and Experience, Parents in the faith have come to know Christ and His ways intimately and experientially. They also continue to have a passion for the Lord and a desire to finish their journeys of faith well. When Parents in the faith neglect this milestone, they plateau, stall, and fall short of attaining the depth of character and degree of spiritual transformation God desires for them.

Some believers are in the Childhood stage, others are in the Young Adulthood stage, and still others are in the Parenthood stage of this lifelong, transformational process. Over the years, Parents in the faith have become more like the Father; for them, holiness and wholeness merge. God's desire is for His Spirit to so transform Christians that they progressively reflect the character of God and live according to His purposes. Parents in the faith have a seasoned and mature faith, and therefore, they offer a compelling, real-life illustration of a deep, spiritual reality.

Summary

Chapters 11–13 have focused on the integration and synthesis of John's model (described in Chapters 5–7) with the developmental theory set forth in Chapters 8-9. Chapters 11–13 described and explained the process, content, and course of the three stages of faith outlined in 1 John 2:12–14. It is hoped that, first, the dynamic process and possibilities of change and growth at each stage have become clearer and more comprehensible and that, second, the "riddle of sanctification" and the "dilemma of the call to personal holiness" are less confusing.

Questions for Reflection and Action

Milestone #7: *Empowering Others*

1. Why is learning from someone who has walked the road before you more effective than learning from books?
2. Why do you think such coming alongside others has become—according to Dallas Willard—"the Great Omission from the Great Commission"?
3. What keeps believers from mentoring and encouraging fellow believers?
4. In what aspect of life and learning have you experienced a helpful balance of challenge and support? What resulted?
5. What has resulted when all you knew was an imbalance between challenge and support?
6. What would a good balance of challenge and support look like for spiritual growth to result? Be specific.
7. Wherever you are on your journey, to what fellow believer can you offer challenge and support? Describe what that will look like.

Milestone #8: *Seasoned by Time and Experience*

1. What hard times in your life have helped you learn or relearn that God is reliable, that He can be trusted no matter what, and that He is present and active in every moment of your life? Describe that experience.
2. Review what Robert Peck, Bernice Neugarten, and Daniel Levinson say about believers in midlife. What unexpected challenges or surprising benefits do you find mentioned there? Be specific.
3. Look again at the list of fourteen experiences that Eric Erikson says come post-midlife. What advantages do believers have when they encounter these circumstances? What about their faith enables them to experience integrity rather than despair?
4. Explain the meaning the italicized phrase in this statement has for you personally: "*holy wholeness and whole holiness* ... describe some of the ways that psychodynamics and religious faith interact." You might begin by defining *holy wholeness* and *whole holiness*.
5. Why are those appropriate goals for Christians?
6. If someone were watching your life for any length of time, what evidence would he or she see that you are trying to be God's light and reflect His image in the world?
7. Who in your life serves as a compelling, real-life illustration of a deep, spiritual reality? Go out for coffee with that person so you can get to know him or her better. Learn what has been key in that person's journey of faith, the journey toward Christlikeness.

CHAPTER 14

DISCIPLES IN SEARCH OF DIRECTION

THE PATH HAS presented a comprehensive, biblically based, and developmentally informed overview of how disciples grow and become more like Christ. We have seen that a Christian's growth takes place not at a steady, predictable, or scheduled pace, but slowly and over a lifetime. Since believers never fully arrive at Christlikeness this side of heaven, our spiritual growth continues every day of our lives. Some believers will travel farther than others, and others have not traveled as far as they think they have.

In this chapter, we will explore some ways to ensure that the lessons learned and the maturity resulting from a believer's growth and gradual transformation are available for God to use in that believer's local church or in a disciple-making ministry. In fact, professor and author Dallas Willard strongly advocates the central role of the church in the spiritual transformation of its members:

> Local congregations, the places where Christians gather on a regular basis, *must resume the practice of making the spiritual formation of their members into Christ-likeness their primary goal, the aim which every one of its activities serves*... Unless this course of action is adopted in the local or neighborhood congregations, the now widespread talk about "spiritual formation," and the renewed interest in practices of the spiritual life in Christ, will

> soon pass, like other superficial fads that offer momentary diversion to a bored and ineffectual church primarily interested only in its own success or survival.[1]

Many churchgoers as well as church leaders today complain that their churches lack a coherent plan for adult discipleship and spiritual growth. This observation prompted the development of a plan to help believers become deep and whole, transformed rather than merely informed. Later in this chapter, I propose five vital, if not comprehensive, steps that can guide the spiritual growth of people in different stages of spiritual development. This chapter is also immediately relevant to Christian higher education, discipleship ministries, or mission organizations.

Understand People More Deeply

As stated in Chapter 1, "Uncovering a Neglected Path," we leaders in the church too often ignore the *process* of coming to mature faith because we are focused on whether or not the *content* is acceptable, biblical, and orthodox. But we need to consider more than the content of faith if we are to experience genuine transformation into Christlikeness. Recall the words of Christian educator Perry Downs:

> Historically evangelicals have attended to content but have ignored structure. We have been so concerned with guarding *what* people believe that we have failed to listen to *how* people believe. We have ignored the possibility of stages of faith, striving only to make faith stronger without being concerned with making faith more mature. We have tended to police its content and tried to strengthen its power, but we have neglected its maturity.

Downs then describes the advantages of attending to both the process of faith as well as the content of faith:

> As Christian educators become sensitive to the stages of faith, they will be able to hear the structure as well as content, and maturity as well as strength. They will understand people more deeply and have a more realistic perspective on the health of

> their congregations. Moreover, they will have better possibilities for designing educational approaches fit to the level of maturity of their people.[2]

Ideally, we as the church will develop ministries that recognize biblical principles of learning and genuine transformation while avoiding simplistic formulas and prepackaged programs. Of course, there is a place for curriculum and pragmatic approaches to discipleship, but we cannot neglect ministry that nurtures the whole person.

Casting a Vision for the Church

Pastors and church leaders are responsible for creating and sustaining a vision for the church, including how to foster the spiritual maturing of the flock. Church leaders should take seriously this biblical commitment to disciple men and women and support their growth toward Christlikeness. Enabling such genuine spiritual growth is a core element of a Bible-based church's mission. More important than anything else is the development of a church that values becoming a disciple, and *Stages of Faith* could play a vital role in that.

- Ideally, all pastoral staff and key leadership teams will complete *Stages of Faith*. Each pastor and leader will discover the strengths and weaknesses of his or her own spiritual growth. They will become conversant about the model and competent in the application of its ideas. Consider being a small group for all of the thirteen lessons. If pastors are too busy to consider this kind of commitment, their unspoken message might be that *Stages of Faith* is just another program for the congregation—as if the members of their congregation aren't busy!

  By the way, trying to do a two-hour lesson in just one hour will reduce the course to a sterile academic exercise, with minimal transformative value. Completing *Stages of Faith* together does require a sacrifice for a season.

Another way for leaders to complete *Stages of Faith* is to have each member of the pastoral staff lead a *Stages of Faith* small group within his or her particular area of ministry. For instance, the pastor of youth/student ministries could guide his or her leadership team through the study.

- The profound truths discussed in each lesson and the rich level of group sharing that *Stages of Faith* encourages make it unique among discipleship materials. Imagine the deepening of relationships as fellow pastors and church leaders learn to care for and trust one another as they share some of the highlights and hurts that shape their personal stories. This shared "Jesus and we" experience will spill over into the way members of the small-group study relate to one another in the future, as well as the ways these participants model and lead.
- Once they have journeyed through *Stages of Faith*, pastoral staff could then explore how to adapt *Stages of Faith* for their particular areas of ministry. Staff involved with children could consider how to integrate into their ministry the three milestones of the Childhood stage. Staff involved with junior and senior highers could see immediate applications of principles from the Childhood and Young Adulthood stages of faith. (*Stages of Faith* would need to be translated into the language and experience of youth who are ready to explore faith at a new and deeper level.) College-age and young adults in their twenties can more directly apply *Stages of Faith* since it is naturally more relevant to their life experiences. *Stages of Faith*, however, will be most fully and easily used by adults; it also proves more significant for them. Adults are more able and ready to see their need for both being transformed into Christlikeness and becoming deep in their faith. Put simply, the more life experiences, the greater the impact of *Stages of Faith*.
- Your church may already have a well-defined path of discipleship. In that case, *Stages of Faith* will need to earn its way into the starting lineup. Perhaps a pastor or leader overseeing adult education, spiritual formation, or ministry to men and women or small groups could be the advocate for *Stages of Faith* and

integrate it into existing groups and programs. A good starting point for the thirteen-week material is a trial run in a solid small group for men and a strong small group for women. This pastor could communicate his findings to the senior pastor and board as he expands his use of *Stages of Faith*. Over time, *Stages of Faith* will gain the reputation of being well received and essential to the toolbox of every small-group leader and faith-shaper.

Wanted: Skilled Guides for the Journey

Do you remember *Lord of the Flies*? That story clearly illustrates that an island inhabited by just children—with no adult presence at all—is disorderly and deadly. Likewise, the church needs an adult presence. Parents in the faith are crucial to the church. Sadly, there is a shortage of veteran Parents in the faith. Therefore, the identification and ongoing training of seasoned guides is paramount to having one's church be a center of spiritual formation.

Said another way, the success and longevity of any discipleship plan will depend on the quality of the men and women who are the shepherds and guides. The pastor involved with adult ministries and discipleship, together with select Parents in the faith, will, therefore, make it a priority to develop leaders, both men and women, who will provide for other's support, challenges, and the vision for spiritual maturity and Christlikeness.

These men and women will, looking to the *Stages of Faith* map, lead or participate in small groups, teach classes, provide one-on-one guidance to fellow believers, and assume various roles of ministry. These skilled guides could be available to provide spiritual direction, to debrief with a person the results of his or her Spiritual Growth Profile, and to discuss the "Explore Your Possibilities" exercise. Every believer would benefit from occasional time with a coach who can help guide the journey of spiritual growth from Childhood to Young Adulthood to Parenthood. The seasoned guides could be called on to assist believers as they find they need help progressing through the "Five Steps of Spiritual Direction" (see page 342 and following).

What Kind of Shape Are They In?

The Spiritual Growth Profile (SGP) can help you—and others who are skilled guides—discern how far people in your congregation have traveled, where they are strong, what obstacles may be delaying their progress, and some possible steps to take to jumpstart their growth. The SGP is key in each *Stages of Faith* small group, and the group leaders will, as they gain hands-on experience, come to appreciate its value. Pastors and counselors could also become skilled in coaching men and women as to what steps to take toward spiritual growth based on the results of their Profiles.

Encourage participants to take the Profile online for free at www.spiritualgrowthprofile.com and then print their results. The SGP is also located in the *Stages of Faith* book, along with valuable information that will help individuals better understand their SGP. Questions in "Explore Your Possibilities" (at the end of Chapter 10) will be useful in helping people develop a plan for getting into spiritual shape. Encourage them to also become familiar with Chapter 10, "The Spiritual Growth Profile: What Kind of Shape Are You In?"

Five Steps of Spiritual Direction

The following five steps offer direction for guiding the growth of the believers in your care. As you will discover, each step focuses on an essential part in moving a believer along. Also, be innovative in the implementation of these essential steps in your plan for adult discipleship. Change the names of the steps or add your own unique distinctives and emphases if you want to.

Realize that these steps are *not* to be mistaken for a prescription for an orderly, lockstep, linear, rigid, sequential path. Often leaders want to translate the steps into a succession of courses that can be quickly completed with the guaranteed outcome being a mature believer. These five steps provide much-needed direction, but they can be individually tailored to each believer's unique journey. Also, the hiker can get on the path anywhere along the way.

Keep in mind that not everyone attending your church wants or is ready to engage in personal spiritual development. These people may need to hear regularly that church leaders expect men and women to get into groups that encourage and support spiritual transformation and hear personal testimonies of the transformation that individuals have experienced in a small group. These can help convince the reluctant of the value of the experience. Also, people on the fringes of church involvement may begin to actively travel the path of spiritual growth when they meet someone who invites them into a small group.

Your church may want to establish a small group for seekers, for those individuals who have yet to become followers of Christ, but who are willing to consider the message of the Bible and its answers to their questions. From the seeker's group, the new believer could transition to a New Direction group.

New Direction

Purpose: The journey begins with surrender to Christ, and that journey takes you in a new direction. If you have recently accepted Christ as your personal Savior or if you are rededicating your life to Him, join a New Direction group.

The early stage of a believer's journey of faith is critical to the process of spiritual growth. Starting the journey well is vital; a good beginning enables believers to travel far and safely on the journey.

New Direction groups are designed for new and young believers who are taking initial steps in a new direction. All believers, however, can benefit from completing this series, because too often believers start the Christian life without this critical foundation in place. Surprisingly, too many believers have failed to develop these basic skills.

Leadership may assign someone to follow up with those who decide either to receive Christ or to make a fresh commitment to follow Him. Be aware that new believers may be guarded and cautious about entering a group: "Will I be accepted? I haven't been in a church for a long time! Is it safe here? What did I get myself into?" Inviting, assimilating, and gaining trust are vital to reaching and winning such adults to a New Direction group.

Church leaders need to find and equip teams of men and women to facilitate this six-week series. The best teachers will be those who clearly remember what it is like to be a new believer entering a new group and taking those first steps in a new direction. The teachers will need to be gifted at genuinely connecting with people and modeling to them the love of God, while at the same time, creating a rich environment for learning and growing. These teachers will not be surprised by anything they hear when group participants share their stories of brokenness and emptiness. The teachers are privileged to be the first ones to connect with these people and to provide guidance as they get to know better the One who can transform their hearts and guide their paths of spiritual growth. Such teachers can often be found from within the Go the Distance small groups.

New Direction members will learn about the three milestones of the Childhood stage of spiritual growth from *Stages of Faith*. (You can order the New Direction workbooks at www.stagesoffaith.com.)

Milestone #1	I am irreversibly loved and certain of God's forgiveness.
Milestone #2	I can trust and surrender to the Father.
Milestone #3	I need friends who support and challenge me on the journey.

Significantly, students also experience being part of a caring small group. And, hopefully, they will continue to do so even after they complete the New Direction course.

In the six weeks of a New Direction class, participants may hear many ideas that are new to them, ideas about the Bible; God's restorative love; people who accept one another; healing from physical, emotional, and spiritual brokenness; and more. These individuals cannot be hurried. Upon completing New Direction, group members may want to stay together. Allow this time for the intentional building of relationships as they learn to journey together. Over time, this care and feeding of the new and young believers will have a huge and positive impact on your church. Be sure to find materials that prepare these young believers for ongoing spiritual growth. (For example, a six-week study of John 1–3 can focus on the joyful discovery of basic Bible truths that inform their new or refreshed relationship with Christ.)

When New Direction participants are ready, their next step is likely to be joining a Go the Distance group. This transition should be made carefully, intentionally, and prayerfully. During the last week of the New Direction group, let members know what groups are available, and then let Go the Distance leaders know who will be joining their groups. These new members should be welcomed and celebrated as they take this next risky step forward.

Go the Distance

Purpose: Ongoing support, challenge, and spiritual direction are essential for the long-haul journey of discipleship.

Recover ***Koinonia***: Believers benefit from participating in a large-group setting for preaching, teaching, and corporate worship. Large-group and small-group gatherings are best viewed as complementary to one another, each serving a unique and important role in a believer's life. In fact, believers suffer if they neglect either large- or small-group involvement. In general today, the transformative,

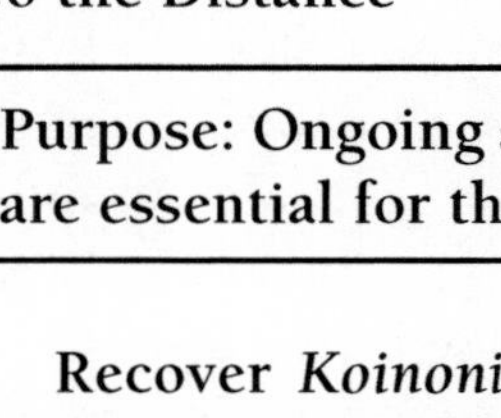

face-to-face gathering of the small group is usually the neglected involvement, and those small-group connections need to be recovered. We need to be *big* on *small*.

Small groups are one way the church can fulfill the clear mandate of Jesus' Great Commission (Matthew 28:19–20): make disciples. Once again, quoting Mulholland's definition, we want disciples who are "being transformed to the likeness of Christ for the sake of others"[3] and who will go the distance on the lifelong journey of spiritual growth. Sadly, not all believers have the time, energy, or level of commitment necessary for this kind of personal growth. A church must nonetheless offer groups that foster such spiritual growth.

Be Governed by God's Word: Believers are not to rely on creeds, church traditions, human reasoning, or their personal experiences as the primary authority for leading a Christian life. Rather, the believer's authority is to be the Bible. One result of personally applying God's Word is a believer's transformation into a greater likeness of Christ. Small groups for men and women, therefore, prioritize the study of God's Word and the personal application of its truth.

Grow Spiritually in Relationship: On the journey, we need one another. Optimal spiritual growth can't happen in isolation. Men need to know and be known by other men; women need to know and be known by other women. Spiritual growth happens as men and women meet intentionally in relationships that offer support, challenge, and accountability.

We understand that busy men and women will give themselves only to causes that pay dividends. Believers, therefore, need to be assured that small groups are a worthwhile investment in their spiritual growth. Again, the purposes of a small group need to be clearly defined: to study God's Word, to support one another during the ups and downs of life, and to challenge one another to go higher and farther on our unique spiritual journeys. So, in addition to asking, "What percentage of our church is in small groups?" church leaders need to ask, "What is happening in those groups? Is authentic, deep transformation occurring?" Authentic transformation happens when there is both learning and caring. Each small group, therefore, needs to be led by people who excel in caring and guiding others.

Establish Separate Ministries for Men and for Women: Having men and women meet in separate small groups is a very important aspect of Go the Distance and recovering *koinonia*. Men and women benefit by being in an environment that is safe, a place where they can learn to let go of pretenses, practice being completely honest, and risk being real. Of course, those things don't happen automatically, simply by being in same-gender groups, but being with the same gender definitely helps those things happen—and happen faster.

Biblical Supersedes Cultural: Strong social and psychological factors contribute to the reluctance of men to gather regularly in small groups. It is my observation that many men have a distorted or inadequate view of discipleship, fellowship, and group Bible study. Plus, men have likely learned firsthand not to let others get too close. Then, of course, the demands of family and profession make it difficult for us men to commit to a small group.

Ministry to men must counter these negative forces as well as provide an opportunity for new experiences in groups that are healthy and strong. Social and psychological explanations cannot keep us from developing transformative small groups, and we must select and train the best among the men to become leaders of these small groups. The mindset needs to be that the most coveted position of church leadership is for men to shepherd the spiritual progress of a small group of other men.

As I mentioned earlier, though, many believers have jumped through commonly prescribed hoops or adopted certain spiritual disciplines in hopes of growing spiritually. The methods and formulas included more Bible study, more prayer, more witnessing, more memorizing, more giving, more attending, and more surrendering, more serving, and more praising. Many sincere believers subscribed to these demands, expecting to grow spiritually, but their efforts resulted in only a weary admission of disillusionment and disappointment. Participating in a good, healthy small group, however, can enliven and transform believers.

Let Small Groups Be a Training Ground for Leaders: In the rich context of small groups, certain men and women will be identified as having the character, skills, and giftedness to be teachers and leaders. Their ability to relate to and communicate with group members will be noted. These people will need to be groomed as leaders for New Direction groups as well as Foundations of Faith and Go the Distance discipleship groups. Other men and women will be prepared to serve in ministry to children or in the discipleship of youth. Elders and deacons may also be found in these small groups. Identifying and preparing men and women for significant leadership roles is both critical to the health and strength of the church and vital to the family, the community, and the world of business.

Core Courses for Men and Women

What can these Go the Distance groups study together? The curriculum must both build community and encourage personal application of transformational biblical truth. Also, the core courses should offer a good blend and balance of both *preparation* at home and *participation* in small groups. There is real power in this combination of learning to study and listen to God's Word independently and then in meeting with others to share findings and personal applications. Group members learn to be real and open as they interact alone with God's Word … and real and open as they interact with one another.

Yet too many books and studies either have no questions or have questions limited to lower levels of learning (see Milestone #5: Five Levels of Learning) and, therefore, little or no transformational value. Similarly, books are too often unconcerned about the development of relationships, the dynamics of becoming a transforming community, and helping one another go the distance. Also, some books that belong on a personal reading list are not effective for study by a small group.

For five field-tested Go the Distance titles for small-group study, please see Appendix 1. Each book listed there—all written by this author—shows readers how to personally study God's Word and how to respond to searching questions that encourage *knowing, doing, being,* and *relating.* Small-group members can expect to invest about two hours in preparation each week and two hours of participation at their weekly meeting. This time commitment may be more than members are accustomed to, but the experience will definitely prove worth it. These books can be ordered at www.stagesoffaith.com.

A few more comments: These five core Go the Distance courses comprise two-and-a-half years worth of study. If that seems like a long time, remember that authentic relationships and personal renewal don't happen overnight. Also, many groups intersperse the book studies listed in the Appendix with topical studies, adding to the time spent as a Go the Distance group. The best choices for topical studies are those that contribute to the goals of building community and deepening the spiritual transformation and growth of the small-group members. Experienced small-group leaders understand the importance of selecting curriculum that leads to heart and life transformation.

In your church, other Bible studies and fellowship groups for men, women, or couples may be meeting at different times during the week, and some groups may meet in homes as well. Each of these groups has its own place in—and makes a unique contribution to—the life of the church and the growth of the individual believer. Church leadership will want to come alongside these small-group leaders to inform and invite them to be a part of the Five Steps of Spiritual Direction.

Foundations of Faith

Purpose: On the journey of life, God's Word is our map.

Another step toward spiritual formation is the Foundations of Faith small-group experience. Remember, though, that these steps are not necessarily to be tackled sequentially, one after the other.

Foundations of Faith works well as a core course for a Go the Distance group. Foundations of Faith could also be offered to anyone who wants to become a church member or anyone interested in exploring eight bottom-line, essential truths that distinguish the Christian faith—the biblical doctrines of the Bible, God, Jesus Christ, the Holy Spirit, man and sin, salvation, the church, and things to come. Knowing what you believe enables you to make your faith your own. In this nine-week series, believers will consider the mission, values, and beliefs of the church. Each participant will gain confidence in his or her faith and even learn to defend it.

Every believer can profit from this series and the crucial opportunity it provides to identify and examine one's personal beliefs. Too often a believer's knowledge of God and His Word remains largely secondhand, and any unbiblical ideas need to be corrected. Not only do many believers need to sharpen their "Christian thinking" skills, but also they need to learn to more effectively apply vital doctrines to their personal, day-to-day lives. Group leaders are not indoctrinating students; they are guiding the acquisition of information that the Holy Spirit will use to transform character.

Select a book or study guide that reflects your church or denominational distinctives and that is accessible to group members. Some books may be too lofty or unwieldy for a small group. Also, student workbooks for *Foundations of Faith* are available at www.stagesoffaith.com. These workbooks emphasize the discussion and personal application of each of the eight basic Christian doctrines.

Stages of Faith

Purpose: Believers need a map for their journeys toward personal spiritual growth.

Many believers have never seen a biblically based map for a lifelong journey of Christian faith. The apostle John, however, described three metaphorical stages of spiritual growth—Childhood, Young Adulthood, and Parenthood—and noted the distinguishing characteristics of each stage. *Stages of Faith* is a small-group study of the apostle John's map of the journey of spiritual growth found in 1 John 2:12–14.

It is strongly recommended that every adult believer completes this thirteen week study, which has been well received by many churches and small groups as a unique and biblical approach to discipleship. In the *Stages of Faith* series, believers will be introduced to a biblical map for the lifelong journey of spiritual growth, locate how far they have traveled in each stage, identify the obstacles that delay spiritual progress, chart steps to take on their journeys, and learn how they can skillfully guide others toward maturity and Christlikeness. Group members will complete the Spiritual Growth Profile, which is found in the *Stages of Faith* workbook and can also be taken free of charge online at www.spiritualgrowthprofile.com.

But *Stages of Faith* is not just another study to complete and put on the bookshelf. Nor is it a race to hurry through and then move on to something else. After all, no one will become a mature Parent in the faith in the span of four months. Rather, *Stages of Faith* is best seen as a map for believers to become skilled at using over their adult life span. An alert and prayerful leader will be able to know their group members' hearts and hurts. These leaders will not just police *what* their group members believe, but they will also listen to *how* they believe. After small groups complete the *Stages of Faith* series, they will select another course.

One of the Go the Distance small-group studies, *Stages of Faith* appears as a separate and significant step on the path, and it is. A biblically based curriculum that allows for great discussion, *Stages of Faith* should be in every small-group leader's toolbox. Church leaders should expect all small groups to go through *Stages of Faith* at some time in their life together.

You can order *Stages of Faith* books and find a useful Leader's Guide PDF at www.stagesoffaith.com.

Base Camp

Purpose: Believers need to be revitalized and prepared for the journey of faith.

Periodic workshops, seminars, retreats, and special events provide both challenges and refreshment for believers as they climb higher and travel farther on their spiritual journeys. Base Camps offer hikers occasional opportunities for respite and reflection, recovery from past spiritual and emotional injuries, the development of new goals, and preparation for the demands of the journey ahead.

This step appears as the last one on the path, but it will actually be taken at any time. Base Camps are designed to be an open door, enabling us to meet and even lead men and women who are seeking to start traveling their own paths of spiritual growth. Base Camps are short, focused, and always immediately practical. The goal is to be informative and transformative. Examples of Base Camps are a Saturday morning men's breakfast, a semiannual Friday night special speaker for men and or women, retreats, and an overnight camping trip.

New Direction, Go the Distance, Foundations of Faith, Stages of Faith, Base Camp—these five steps contribute to a believer's growth as an authentic follower of Jesus. These five steps can enrich a church's efforts to disciple men and women.

And every church absolutely needs a disciple-making strategy, but such strategies are too often talked about and measured in terms of *more*—more study, more commitment, more memorization, more service, more attendance, etc. But as stated earlier, in the words of Richard Foster, "… the desperate need today is not for *more* intelligent people nor gifted people, but for *deep* people."[4] In support of that truth, the intention of this book has been to present a new way of thinking about the Christian's journey … and to provide tools and ideas about *how* believers can grow deep as well as *how* they can guide others in spiritual growth.

Did we succeed? And have you accepted the challenge? Let's work together to grow deeper believers for their good and for God's glory!

Questions for Reflection and Action

1. Of course, it is crucial that the *content* of one's Christian faith is acceptable, biblical, and orthodox. As we come to the end of *The Path*, however, explain why understanding the *process* of coming to that mature faith is important as well.
2. The Five Steps of Spiritual Direction are listed here:

    New Direction
    Go the Distance
    Foundations of Faith
    Stages of Faith
    Base Camp

    a. What does each step contribute to a believer's spiritual journey?
    b. Which of these needs for spiritual direction is your church currently meeting?

c. What might be the next aspect of spiritual direction your church will address—and what will that entail?

3. Under "Go the Distance," believers are encouraged to:

   Recover koinonia.
   Be governed by God's Word.
   Grow spiritually in relationship.
   Let the biblical supersede the cultural.

   a. Take a few minutes to reflect on the importance of each category, and consider how well you're doing in each area.
   b. What do your answers suggest about an action step toward spiritual growth that you would be wise to take?

4. As you close this book, write down two things:

   What challenge are you taking away with you?
   What message of encouragement did you find here?

May, by God's grace, this balance of challenge and support foster spiritual growth and empower you on your journey toward Christlikeness.

APPENDIX 1

IN ADDITION TO *New Direction*, *Stages of Faith*, and *Foundations of Faith*, the following books can be ordered online at www.stagesoffaith.com.

Ecclesiastes: The Search for Meaning

In a small-group study of the Old Testament book of Ecclesiastes, we explore one man's search for meaning when God is not at the center of his life. King Solomon candidly reflects on his experiences of emptiness and futility. Sadly, he searched in all the wrong places to fill a void that only God can fill. We will learn from Solomon's experiences how to be fully alive and deeply satisfied by a life with God at the center. Inductive Bible study and workbook questions will invite rich sharing.

Colossians: Jesus, First Place in Everything

Paul's desire is that Christ be "first place in everything" (1:18), supreme, and without rivals in our lives. Paul's letter to the church at Colossae raises primary issues that we believers need to examine if Jesus is to truly be "first place." In contrast to the lessons in Ecclesiastes about where *not* to look for meaning and fulfillment,

Colossians helps us to see that all that we need is found in Christ. Inductive Bible study and workbook questions will prompt rich discussion and soul-searching.

The Marching Orders of Jesus: Studies in Jesus' Farewell Message, John 13–16

On the night before His crucifixion, Jesus met with His disciples in the Upper Room to prepare them for their mission to change the world. How are we—Jesus' disciples in the twenty-first century—to live in His absence? No believer can answer that question or go the distance on the journey of faith without knowing Jesus' farewell message in John 13–16 and letting those teachings govern his or her life. Applications and insights will come with the inductive Bible study and workbook questions provided.

ENDNOTES

Chapter 1: Uncovering a Neglected Path

1. Richard Foster, *Celebration of Discipline: The Path to Spiritual Growth* (New York: Harper and Row, 1978), 1.
2. Don Alexander, *Christian Spirituality: Five Views of Sanctification* (Downers Grove, IL: InterVarsity, 1988), 7, 10.
3. Perry Downs, *Teaching for Spiritual Growth* (Grand Rapids: Zondervan, 1994), 121.
4. Downs, 122.
5. Bruce Demarest, *Soulguide* (Colorado Springs, CO: NavPress), 185.

Chapter 2: The Case for Stages of Faith

1. Richard Foster, *Celebration of Discipline: The Path to Spiritual Growth* (New York: Harper and Row, 1978), 1.
2. Don Alexander, *Christian Spirituality: Five Views of Sanctification* (Downers Grove, IL: InterVarsity, 1988), 7, 10.
3. Howard Hendricks, *Exit Interviews* (Chicago: Moody Press, 1993), 276–277.
4. Hendricks, 276–277.

5. Ronald Habermas and Klaus Issler, *Teaching for Reconciliation: Foundations & Practices of Christian Educational Ministry* (Grand Rapids: Baker, 1992), 98.
6. Tom Ashbrook, *Mansions of the Heart: Exploring the Seven Stages of Spiritual Growth* (San Francisco, CA: Jossey-Bass, 2009), 12.
7. John Calvin, *Commentary on the First Epistle of John* (T.H.L. Parker, Trans.), in *Calvin's Commentaries Series* (Grand Rapids: Eerdmans, 1961), 251.
8. S. Smalley, *1,2,3 John*, in *Word Commentary*, vol. 51 (Waco, TX: Word, 1984), 69.
9. Raymond Brown, *The Epistle of 1 John*, The Anchor Bible (New York: Doubleday).
11. John Stott, *The Epistles of John* (Grand Rapids: Eerdmans, 1991), 101.
12. G. H. King, *The Fellowship* (London: Marshall, Morgan and Scott Ltd., 1954), 40.
13. Robert Law, *The Tests of Life*, 3rd ed. (Grand Rapids: Baker, 1914), 313.
14. Law, 313–314.
15. August Van Ryn, *The Epistles of John* (New York: Loizeaux Brothers, 1948), 61–62.
16. A. W. Pink, *Spiritual Growth* (Grand Rapids: Baker, 1971), 93.
17. F. F. Bruce, *The Epistles of John* (Old Tappan, NJ: Fleming Revell, 1970), 58.
18. W. E. Vine, *The Epistles of John: Light, Love, and Life* (Grand Rapids: Zondervan, 1970), 31.
19. James Montgomery Boice, *The Epistles of John* (Grand Rapids: Zondervan, 1979), 72.
20. Zane Hodges, "1 John," in *The Bible Knowledge Commentary*, J. F. Walvoord & R. Zuck, eds. (Wheaton: Scripture Press, 1983), 890.
21. C. H. Dodd, *The Johannine Epistles* (London: Hodder and Stoughton, 1946), 38–39.
22. H. Marshall, *The Epistle of John: New International Commentary on the New Testament* (Grand Rapids: Eerdmans, 1994), 137.

23. Raymond Brown, *The Epistle of 1 John*, The Anchor Bible (New York: Doubleday, 1983).
24. Stott, 102.
25. B. F. Westcott, *The Epistles of St. John* (Grand Rapids: Eerdmans, 1966); Alexander Ross, *The New International Commentary on the Epistles of James and John* (Eerdmans, 1972); A. Plummer, *The Epistles of St. John* (Cambridge University Press, 1894); A. E. Brooke, *A Critical and Exegetical Commentary of the New Testament* (Edinburgh: T. & T. Clark, 1912).
26. James Houlden, *A Commentary on the Johannine Epistles*, Black's New Testament Commentary, (London: A. & C. Black, 1973).
27. Brown, *The Epistle of 1 John*, 298–300.
28. R. C. H. Lenski, *The Interpretation of 1 and 2 Epistles of Peter, the Three Epistles of John and the Epistle of Jude* (1966); B. F. Westcott, *The Epistles of St. John* (1960); A. Plummer, *The Epistles of St. John* (1954).
29. Westcott, 57.
30. Westcott, 59.
31. Marshall, 137.
32. Stott, 96.
33. A. E. Brooke, *A Critical and Exegetical Commentary on the Johannine Epistles, The International Critical Commentary* (London: T. & T. Clark, 1912), 283; *Thayer's Greek-English Lexicon of the New Testament* (Peabody, MA: Hendrickson Publishers, 1996).
34. A. Plummer, *The Epistles of St. John*, in *The Cambridge Greek Testament for Schools and Colleges* (Cambridge: Cambridge University, 1894); B. F. Westcott, *The Epistles of St. John* (Grand Rapids: Eerdmans, 1966).
35. Brooke, 41.
36. James Montgomery Boice, *The Epistles of John* (Grand Rapids: Zondervan, 1979), 73.
37. Stott, 96.

Chapter 3: Evidence Beyond a Reasonable Doubt

1. Wayne Grudem, *Systematic Theology: An Introduction to Biblical Doctrine* (Grand Rapids: Zondervan, 1994), 746.
2. Gregg Allison, "Salvation and Christian Education," in James Estep, Michael Anthony, and Gregg Allison, *A Theology for Christian Education* (Nashville: B & H Academic, 2008), 217.
3. Paul Pettit, ed., *Foundations of Spiritual Formation: A Community Approach to Becoming Like Christ* (Grand Rapids: Kregel, 2008), 21.
4. H. P. Owen, *The Stages of Ascent in Hebrews 5:11–14*, in New Testament Studies (1956–1957), 3 243–253.
5. Owen, 244.
6. Ray Stedman, *Body Life* (Ventura, CA: Gospel Light, 1972).
7. Elton Trueblood, *Alternative to Futility* (New York: Harper & Brothers, 1948).
8. R. J. Bauckhman, *Word Biblical Commentary*, Vol. 50 (Waco, TX: Word, 1983), 190.
9. Stephen Paine, *The Wycliffe Bible Commentary*, 2 Peter (Chicago: Moody, 1962), 148.
10. Bauckhman, 189.
11. Paine, 148.
12. Perry Downs, *Teaching for Spiritual Growth: An Introduction to Christian Education* (Grand Rapids: Zondervan, 1994), 112.
13. B. Arndt and W. Gingrich, *A Greek-English Lexicon of the New Testament* (Chicago: University of Chicago, 1952), 714.

Chapter 4: An Aged Apostle's Ideas About Spiritual Progress

1. Robert Yarborough, *1, 2, 3 John*, Baker Exegetical Commentary of the New Testament (Grand Rapids: Baker Academic, 2008), 21.
2. Eusebius, *Ecclesiastical History* (Loeb Classical Library, 1926), 3.23.1–2.
3. S. Smalley, *1, 2, 3 John*, in Word Commentary, Vol 51 (Waco, TX: Word, 1984), 16.
4. Alexander Ross, *Commentary on the Epistles of James and John*, The New International Commentary on the New Testament, Ned B. Stonehouse, ed. (Grand Rapids: Eerdmans, 1954), 115.

5. Smalley, 18.
6. A. E. Brooke, *A Critical and Exegetical Commentary on the Johannine Epistles*, The International Critical Commentary (London: T. & T. Clark, 1912), 15.
7. B. Arndt and W. Gingrich, *A Greek-English Lexicon of the New Testament* (Chicago: University of Chicago, 1952), 35–36.
8. Robert Law, *The Tests of Life,* 3rd ed. (Grand Rapids: Baker, 1914), 141–145.
9. Augustine, *Confessions of St. Augustine* (New York: An Image Book, Published by Doubleday, 1960).
10. Smalley, 45.
11. C. H. Dodd, *The Johannine Epistles* (London: Hodder and Stoughton, 1946), 32.
12. John Stott, *The Epistles of John* (Grand Rapids: Eerdmans, 1991), 95.

Chapter 5: The Childhood Stage of Faith—The Birth of Faith

1. H. E. Dana and Julius Mantey, *A Manual Grammar of the Greek New Testament* (Toronto: The Macmillan Company, 1955), 179.
2. James Montgomery Boice, *The Epistles of John* (Grand Rapids: Zondervan, 1979), 74.
3. Francis Schaeffer, *True Spirituality* (Carol Stream, IL: Tyndale, 1971), 323.
4. Glen G. Scorgie O'Neill, in *A Little Guide to Christian Spirituality,* as quoted by Anne Lamott, *Traveling Mercies* (NY: Anchor, 2000), 112.
5. Lewis Smedes, *Shame and Grace: Healing the Shame We Don't Deserve* (San Francisco: Zondervan, 1993), 108.
6. Dallas Willard, "The Gospel of the Kingdom and Spiritual Formation," in *The Kingdom Life: A Practical Theology of Discipleship and Spiritual Formation*, Alan Andrews, ed. (Colorado Springs: NavPress, 2010), 51.
7. Smedes, 109.
8. J. I. Packer, *Knowing God* (Downers Grove, IL: InterVarsity, 1973), 41.

9. A. E. Brooke, *A Critical and Exegetical Commentary on the Johannine Epistles,* The International Critical Commentary (London: T. & T. Clark, 1912), 14.
10. Collin Brown, ed. *The New International Dictionary of New Testament Theology* (Grand Rapids: Zondervan, 1986), 393.
11. J. B. Phillips, *Your God Is Too Small* (New York: Macmillan, 1961), 32.
12. John Stott, *The Epistles of John* (Grand Rapids: Eerdmans, 1991).
13. A. W. Tozer, *Knowledge of the Holy* (New York: Harper and Row, 1961), 10.
14. Henri Nouwen, *The Return of the Prodigal Son* (New York: Doubleday, 1992), 12.
15. John Stott, *One People* (Downers Grove, IL: InterVarsity, 1968), 78.
16. Larry Crabb, *The Safest Place on Earth* (Nashville, TN: Word, 1999), 27, 32.

Chapter 6: The Young Adulthood Stage of Faith—The Ownership of Faith

1. R. C. H. Lenski, *The Interpretation of 1 and 2 Epistles of Peter, the Three Epistles of John and the Epistle of Jude* (Minneapolis: Augsburg, 1966); B. F. Westcott, *The Epistles of St. John* (Grand Rapids: Eerdmans, 1966); A. Plummer, *The Epistles of St. John,* The Cambridge Greek Testament for Schools and Colleges (Cambridge: Cambridge University, 1894).
2. D. W. Burdick, *The Letters of John the Apostle* (Chicago: Moody Press, 1985); B. F. Westcott, *The Epistles of St. John* (Grand Rapids: Eerdmans, 1966).
3. James Montgomery Boice, *The Epistles of John* (Grand Rapids: Zondervan, 1979), 76.
4. Alan Johnson, *Romans*, The Freedom Letter, vol. II (Chicago: Moody, 1985), 119.
5. James Dunn, *Romans 9–16*, in Word Biblical Commentary, vol. 38 (Dallas: Word, 1988), 795.

6. F. F. Bruce, *The Epistle of Paul to the Romans* (Grand Rapids: Eerdmans, 1971), 243.
7. James Stifler, *The Epistle to the Romans* (Chicago: Moody, 1960), 223.
8. Charles Shelton, *Adolescent Spirituality* (Chicago: Loyola University, 1983), 72.
9. C. E. Cranfield, *The Epistle to the Romans*, The International Critical Commentary, vol. 2 (Edinburgh: T. & T. Clark, 1979), 814.
10. Charles Swindoll, *Swindoll's New Testament Insights: Insights on Romans* (Grand Rapids: Zondervan, 2010), 292.
11. Anders Nygren, *Commentary on Romans* (Philadelphia: Fortress, 1949), 445.
12. Colin Brown, ed., *The New International Dictionary of New Testament Theology*, vol. 3 (Grand Rapids: Zondervan, 1983), 223–229.
13. B. Arndt and W. Gingrich, *A Greek-English Lexicon of the New Testament*, 504–505.
14. J. I. Packer, *Knowing God* (Downers Grove, IL: InterVarsity, 1973), 50.
15. Henry Alford, *The New Testament for English Readers: The Gospel of St. John and the Acts* (Nabu Press, 1865), 867.
16. John Stott, *The Epistles of John* (Grand Rapids: Eerdmans, 1991), 102.
17. Robert Law, *The Tests of Life,* 3rd ed. (Grand Rapids: Baker, 1914), 148.
18. C. S. Lewis, *Mere Christianity* (New York: Macmillan, 1943), 36.
19. C. H. Dodd, *The Johannine Epistles* (London: Hodder and Stoughton, 1946), cited in John Stott, *The Epistles of John,* 105.
20. Robert Law, *The Tests of Life,* 3rd ed. (Grand Rapids: Baker, 1914), 151.
21. A. W. Tozer, *The Pursuit of God* (Camp Hill, PA: Christian Publications, Inc., 1982), 31.

Chapter 7: The Parenthood Stage of Faith—Empowering Faith

1. Colin Brown, ed., *The New International Dictionary of New Testament Theology* (Grand Rapids: Zondervan, 1983), 300.
2. R. C. H. Lenski, *The Interpretation of 1 and 2 Epistles of Peter, the Three Epistles of John and the Epistle of Jude* (Minneapolis: Augsburg, 1966), 418–419; B. F. Westcott, *The Epistles of St. John* (Grand Rapids: Eerdmans, 1966), 59–60, 177; A. E. Brooke, *A Critical and Exegetical Commentary on the Johannine Epistles,* The International Critical Commentary (London: T. & T. Clark, 1912), 45.
3. E. H. Hiebert, *An Expositional Study of 1 John, Bibliotheca Sacra* (1988), 432.
4. John Stott, *The Epistles of John* (Grand Rapids: Eerdmans, 1991), 102.
5. P. R. Van Gorder, *In the Family: Lessons from First John* (Grand Rapids: Radio Bible Class, 1978), 74.
6. Larry Richards, *Expository Dictionary of Bible Words* (Grand Rapids: Zondervan, 1985), 266–267.
7. Heibert, 429.
8. W. E. Vine, *The Epistles of John: Light, Love, and Life* (Grand Rapids: Zondervan, 1970), 31.
9. J. M. Dettoni & J. C. Wilhoit, eds., *Nurture That Is Christian* (Wheaton, IL: Victor, 1995), 28.
10. Brother Lawrence, *The Practice of the Presence of God* (Grand Rapids: Fleming Revell, 1958), 112.
11. Bruce Demarest, *Soulguide* (Colorado Springs, NavPress, 2003), 185.
12. Stott, 102.
13. Stott, 102.
14. Westcott, 59.
15. Robert Law, *The Tests of Life,* 3rd ed. (Grand Rapids: Baker, 1914), 312.
16. Law, 313.
17. C. E. Cranfield, *The Epistle to the Romans*, vol. 2, in *The International Critical Commentary* (Edinburgh: T. & T. Clark, 1979), 261.

18. Bruce Demarest, *Seasons of the Soul* (Downers Grove, IL: InterVarsity, 2009), 153–154.
19. James Montgomery Boice, *The Epistles of John* (Grand Rapids: Zondervan, 1979), 74.
20. A. E. Brooke, *A Critical and Exegetical Commentary on the Johannine Epistles, The International Critical Commentary* (London: T. & T. Clark, 1912).
21. Colin Brown, ed., *The New International Dictionary of New Testament Theology* (Grand Rapids: Zondervan, 1983).
22. R. E. O. White, *Open Letter to Evangelicals, A Devotional and Homiletic Commentary on the First Epistle of John* (Grand Rapids: Eerdmans, 1964), 99.
23. E. H. Heibert, 430.
24. Stott, 97; C. H. Dodd, *The Johannine Epistles* (London: Hodder and Stoughton, 1946), 38; F. F. Bruce, *The Epistle of John* (Old Tappan, NJ: Fleming Revell, 1970).
25. C. S. Lewis, *Mere Christianity* (New York: Macmillan, 1943), 120.

Chapter 8: The *How* of Spiritual Growth, Part 1

1. John Stott, *Christianity Today, Evangelism Plus* (October 13, 2006).
2. Robert Mulholland, *Invitation to a Journey* (Downers Grove, IL: InterVarsity, 1993), 12.
3. Perry Downs, *Teaching for Spiritual Growth* (Grand Rapids: Zondervan, 1994), 73.
4. Greg Allison, *A Theology for Christian Education* (Nashville: B&H Academic, 2008), 195.
5. John Dettoni, "The Developing Person: Contemplating Theories of Major Sculptors," in Ronald Habermas, *An Introduction to Christian Education and Formation* (Grand Rapids: Zondervan, 2008), 74.
6. Dettoni, 74.
7. John Yeatts, "Helpful but Inadequate: A Critique of the Developmental Paradigm," *Christian Education Journal*, 13 (1): 49–60.

8. N. J. Salkind, *Theories of Human Development*, 2nd ed. (New York: John Wiley & Sons, 1985), 257.
9. John Cavanaugh, *Adult Development and Aging*, 3rd edition (Brooks/Cole Publishing Company, 1997), 8–9, in P. B. Baltes & O. G. Brim, eds., *Life-Span Developments and Behaviors* (New York: Academic Press, Vol. 2), 255–279.
10. Ronald Habermas and Klaus Issler, *Teaching for Reconciliation: Foundations & Practices of Christian Educational Ministry* (Grand Rapids: Baker, 1992), 77.
11. Habermas and Issler, 96.
12. William Barclay, *Hebrews* (Philadelphia: Westminster, 1976), 26.
13. Mulholland, 19–20, 22.
14. Downs, 121.
15. Downs, 122.
16. Paul Pettit, *Foundations of Spiritual Formation: A Community Approach to Becoming Like Christ* (Grand Rapids: Kregel, 2008), 21.
17. Mel Lawrenz, *The Dynamics of Spiritual Formation* (Grand Rapids: Baker, 2000), 15–16.
18. Lawrenz, 16.
19. F. F. Bruce, *The Epistles of John* (Old Tappan, NJ: Revell, 1970), 58.
20. D. J. Levinson, *Seasons of a Man's Life* (New York: Ballantine, 1978).
21. B. Gillespie, *The Experience of Faith* (Birmingham, AL: Religious Education, 1988), 176–225.
22. Bruce Powers, *Growing Faith* (Nashville: Broadman, 1982).
23. Les Steele, *On the Way: A Practical Theology of Christian Formation* (Grand Rapids: Baker, 1991).
24. Richard Lovelace, *Dynamics of Spiritual Life, An Evangelical Theology of Renewal* (Downers Grove, IL: InterVarsity Academic, 1979), 143.

The following resources will help you to explore human development from a Christian perspective:

- John Dettoni, "The Developing Person: Contemplating Theories of Major Sculptors," in Ronald Habermas, *An Introduction to Christian Education and Formation* (Grand Rapids: Zondervan, 2008), 74–82.
- Perry Downs, *Teaching for Spiritual Growth* (Grand Rapids: Zondervan, 1994), 69–123.
- Les Steele, *On the Way: A Practical Theology of Christian Formation* (Grand Rapids: Baker, 1991), 67–98.

Chapter 9: The *How* of Spiritual Growth, Part 2

1. Richard Lovelace, *Dynamics of Spiritual Life, An Evangelical Theology of Renewal* (Downers Grove, IL: InterVarsity Academic, 1979), 229.
2. Mel Lawrenz, *The Dynamics of Spiritual Formation* (Grand Rapids: Baker, 2000), 147.
3. John Cavanaugh, *Adult Development and Aging*, 3rd edition (Belmont, CA: Brooks/Cole Publishing Company, 1997), 8–9, in P. B. Baltes & O. G. Brim, eds., *Life-Span Developments and Behaviors,* vol. 2 (New York: Academic Press), 255–279.
4. Bernice Neugarten, ed., *Middle Age and Aging*, Bernice Neugarten, "The Awareness of Middle Age" (Chicago: University of Chicago, 1968), 93–98.
5. Judith Viorst, *Necessary Losses* (New York: Fawcett Columbine, 1986), 15–16.
6. William Bridges, *Making Sense of Life's Transitions* (Reading, MA: Addison-Wesley, 1980), 99, 101.
7. Lawrenz, 142.
8. Kenneth Boa, *Conformed to His Image: Biblical and Practical Approaches to Spiritual Formation* (Grand Rapids: Zondervan, 2001), 257.
9. Daniel Levinson, *Seasons of a Man's Life* (New York: Ballantine, 1978), 51.

10. Bruce Demarest, *Seasons of the Soul: Stages of Spiritual Development* (Downers Grove: InterVarsity), 153–154.
11. Boa, 258.
12. Bruce Demarest, "Reflections on Developmental Spirituality: Journey Paradigms and Stages," in *The Journal of Spiritual Formation and Soul Care* (Fall, 2008), Volume 1, Number 2, 164–165.
13. Lawrenz, 30.
14. Demarest, *Seasons of the Soul,* 156.
15. Boa, 171.
16. Kyle Strobel and Cassie Blair, "Calcified Faith," The Semi, Fuller Theological Seminary, April 25–29, 2005, www.fuller.edu/student_life/SEMI/semi.asp.
17. Janet O. Hagberg and Robert A. Guelich, *The Critical Journey: Stages in the Life of Faith* (Salem, WI: Sheffield, 1985), 252.
18. Hagberg, 9.
19. Les Steele, *On the Way: A Practical Theology of Christian Formation* (Grand Rapids: Baker, 1990), 95.
20. R. I. Evans, *Dialogue with Erik Erikson* (New York: E. P. Dutton, 1969), 41.
21. Steele, 96.
22. James Fowler, *Faithful Change: The Personal and Public Challenges of Postmodern Life* (Nashville: Abingdon, 1996), 57.
23. James Fowler, *Stages of Faith: The Psychology of Human Development and the Quest for Meaning* (San Francisco: Harper & Row, 1981), 101.
24. Hagberg and Guelich, *The Critical Journey*, 162.
25. Cited in Gerald May, *The Dark Night of the Soul* (New York: Harper San Francisco, 2004), 187.
26. Christopher Bryant, "The Nature of Spiritual Development," in C. Jones, G. Wainwright & E. Yarnold (eds.), *The Study of Spirituality* (New York: Oxford University), 566.
27. Demarest, "Reflections," 165.
28. Demarest, *Seasons of the Soul*, 153–154.
29. Robert Mulholland, *Invitation to a Journey: A Road Map to Spiritual Formation* (Downers Grove: InterVarsity, 1993), 12.

30. H. N. Malony, The Clinical Assessment of Optimal Religious Functioning, Review of Religious Research, 30 (1), 3–17.
31. The Complete Works of Francis A. Schaeffer: *A Christian Worldview, Christian View of Spirituality*, Volume 3 (Wheaton, IL: Crossway Books, 1982), 327.
32. B. J. Leonard, ed., *Becoming Christian: Dimensions of Spiritual Formation* (Lexington, KY: Westminster/Knoxville, 1990), 26.
33. James Wilhoit & John Dettoni, eds., *Nurture That Is Christian: Developmental Perspectives on Christian Education* (Grand Rapids: Baker, 1995), 36.
34. Mark S. Young, "Nurturing spirituality in the matrix of human development," in *Christian Education Journal*, 10(2), 87–88.
35. Laurent Daloz, *Mentor: Guiding the Journey of Adult Learners* (San Francisco: Jossey-Bass, 1987), 139.
36. Paul Tournier, *The Seasons of Life* (Louisville, KY: John Knox Press, 1972), 9.
37. Benedict J. Groeschel, *The Journey Toward God* (Ann Arbor, MI: Servant, 2000), 247.
38. Gary Thomas, *Sacred Pathways* (Grand Rapids: Zondervan, 2000), 22–31.
39. Thomas, 21.
40. Wilhoit and Dettoni, 36.
41. Benedict J. Groeschel, *Spiritual Passages: The Psychology of Spiritual Development* (New York: Crossword, 1983), 57.
42. Perry Downs, *Teaching for Spiritual Growth* (Grand Rapids: Zondervan, 1994), 122.
43. Hagberg and Guelich, 9.
44. James Houston, *The Desire: Satisfying the Heart* (Colorado Springs, CO: Cook Communications, 1990), 85.

Chapter 10: The Spiritual Growth Profile—What Kind of Shape Are You In?

1. Rodney Bassett, et al, "Measuring Christian Maturity: A Comparison of Several Scales," *Journal of Psychology and Theology* (Spring 1991, Volume 19, Number 1), 91.

2. Steve Gladden and Todd Olthoff, *Spiritual Health Assessment and Spiritual Health Planner*, *The Purpose Driven Life* (Saddleback Church Resources).
3. Randy Frezee, *The Christian Life Profile: A Discipleship Tool to Access Christian Beliefs, Practices, and Virtues* (Grand Rapids, MI: Zondervan, 2005).
4. Gary Moon and David Benner, *Spiritual Direction and the Care of Souls* (Downers Grove: IL, InterVarsity, 2004), 107.
5. Robert Mullholland, *Invitation to a Journey* (Downers Grove, IL: InterVarsity, 1993), 12.
6. Christopher Bryant, "The Nature of Spiritual Development," in C. Jones, G. Wainwright & E. Yarnold, eds., *The Study of Spirituality* (New York: Oxford University, 1986), 566.

Chapter 11: The Childhood Stage of Faith—Informed by Developmental Theory

1. John Ortberg, "True (and False) Transformation," in *Leadership Journal* 24, no. 3 (2002), 102.
2. Gary Moon and David Benner, eds., *Spiritual Direction and the Care of Souls: A Guide to Christian Approaches and Practices* (Downers Grove, IL: InterVarsity, 2004), 14.
3. Brennan Manning, *The Signature of Jesus* (Sisters, OR: Multnomah, 1996), 163.
4. Victor Hugo, *Les Miserables* (New York: Random House, 1961).
5. E. H. Erikson, *Identity and the Life Cycle* (New York: W. W. Norton & Company, 1959), 101.
6. A. W. Tozer, *Knowledge of the Holy* (New York: Harper and Row, 1961), 40.
7. Tozer, 10.
8. R. W. Hood, ed., *Handbook of Religious Experience* (Birmingham, AL: Religious Education Press, 1995), 279.
9. See Chapter 7, "Distorted Concepts of God," in David Seamands, *Healing of Memories* (Wheaton, IL: Victor, 1985), 107–120.

10. William and Kristi Gaultiere, *Mistaken Identity* (Old Tappan, NJ: Revell, 1989), 21.
11. Gaultiere, 23–24.
12. See chapter "Creating God in Your Parents' Image," in David Seamands, *Healing of Damaged Emotions* (Wheaton, IL: Victor, 1981), 55–72.
13. A. M. Rizzuto, *The Birth of the Living God* (Chicago: The University of Chicago, 1980), 53.
14. David Johnson and Jeff Van Vonderen, *The Subtle Power of Spiritual Abuse* (Minneapolis, MN: Bethany House, 1991), 42.
15. Sharon Parks, "Love Tenderly," in Sharon Parks, W. Brueggemann, and T. Groome, *To Act Justly, Love Tenderly, Walk Humbly* (Mahwah, NJ: Paulist, 1986), 33.
16. Henry Cloud and John Townsend, *Christian Beliefs That Can Drive You Crazy* (Grand Rapids: Zondervan, 1994), 111.
17. David Gill, *The Opening of the Christian Mind* (Downers Grove, IL: InterVarsity, 1989), 135–36.
18. Bill Thrall and Bruce McNicol, *TrueFaced: Trust God and Others with Who You Really Are* (Colorado Springs, CO: NavPress, 2003), 21.
19. Elton Trueblood, *The Company of the Committed*, as quoted in Bill Hull, *Choose the Life: Exploring a Faith That Embraces Discipleship* (Grand Rapids: Baker, 2004), 214–215.
20. E. H. Erikson, *Identity and the Life Cycle* (New York: W. W. Norton & Company, 1959), 101.
21. C. Dykstra, *Vision and Character: A Christian Educator's Alternative to Kohlberg* (Mahwah, NJ: Paulist, 1981), 55.
22. Lawrence Richards, *A Theology of Christian Education* (Grand Rapids: Zondervan, 1975), 43.
23. S. Hauerwas, *Character and the Christian Life: A Study in Theological Ethics* (San Antonio: Trinity University Press, 1975), 3.
24. Albert Bandura, *Social Learning Theory* (Englewood Cliffs, NJ: Prentice-Hall Rinehart and Winston, 1970).
25. John Westerhoff, *Will Our Children Have Faith?* (New York: Seabury, 1976), 87–91.

Chapter 12: The Young Adulthood Stage of Faith—Informed by Developmental Theory

1. Robert Kegan, *In Over Our Heads: The Mental Demands of Modern Life* (Cambridge, MA: Harvard University, 1994), 221–222.
2. Charles Shelton, *Adolescent Spirituality* (Chicago: Loyola University, 1983), 72.
3. A. W. Chickering, *The American College* (San Francisco: Jossey-Bass, 1981).
4. Daniel Levinson, *The Seasons of a Man's Life* (New York: Ballantine, 1978), 73.
5. Bruce Gillespie, *The Experience of Faith* (Birmingham, AL: Religious Education, 1988).
6. Bruce Powers, *Growing Faith* (Nashville: Broadman, 1982).
7. Les Steele, *On the Way: A Practical Theology of Christian Formation* (Grand Rapids: Baker, 1991), 146–149.
8. James Fowler, *Stages of Faith: The Psychology of Human Development and the Quest for Meaning* (San Francisco: Harper and Row, 1981), 172.
9. Charles Shelton, *Adolescent Spirituality* (Chicago: Loyola University, 1983), 7.
10. Perry Downs, *Teaching for Spiritual Growth* (Grand Rapids: Zondervan, 1994), 121.
11. John Westerhoff, *Will Our Children Have Faith?* (New York: The Seabury Press, 1976), 87–91.
12. C. Stonehouse, *Patterns in Moral Development* (Waco, TX: Word, 1980), 36.
13. Downs, 121.
14. Downs, 114.
15. Downs, 116–117.
16. Downs, 116.
17. Fowler, 173.
18. Kenneth Hyde, *Religion in Childhood and Adolescence* (Birmingham: Religious Education Press, 1990).
19. Downs, 116.

20. Donald Joy, ed., *Moral Development Foundations: Judeo-Christian Alternatives to Piaget/Kohlberg* (Nashville: Abingdon, 1983), 210.
21. H. P. Owen, The Stages of Ascent in Hebrews 5:11–14, New Testament Studies (1956–1957), 243–253.
22. J. M Dettoni & J. C. Wilhoit, eds., *Nurture That Is Christian* (Wheaton, IL: Victor Books, 1995), 79–80.
23. Dettoni & Wilhoit, 80.
24. Larry Richards, *Creative Bible Study* (Chicago: Moody Press, 1970), 75.
25. R. Habermas & K. Issler, *Teaching for Reconciliation* (Grand Rapids: Baker, 1992), 10.
26. P. H. Miller, *Theories of Developmental Psychology,* 3rd ed. (New York: W. H. Freeman, 1993), 169.
27. A. W. Tozer, *Knowledge of the Holy* (New York: Harper and Row, 1961), 31.

Chapter 13: The Parenthood Stage of Faith—Informed by Developmental Theory

1. John Stott, *The Epistles of John* (Grand Rapids: Eerdmans, 1991), 102.
2. W. E. Vine, *The Epistles of John: Light, Love, and Life* (Grand Rapids: Zondervan, 1970), 31.
3. Richard Foster, *Celebration of Discipline: The Path to Spiritual Growth* (New York: Harper and Row, 1978), 1.
4. R. E. Butman (1990), *The Assessment of Religious Development: Some Possible Options. Journal of Psychology and Theology*, 9, 15.
5. D. J. Maitland, *Aging as Counter-Culture: A Vocation for the Later Years* (New York: Pilgrims Press, 1991).
6. B. Gillespie, *The Experience of Faith* (Birmingham, AL: Religious Education Press, 1988), 208–225.
7. Bruce Powers, *Growing Faith* (Nashville: Broadman, 1982).
8. Les Steele, *On the Way: A Practical Theology of Christian Formation* (Grand Rapids: Baker, 1991), 162–173.
9. H. N. Malony, (1988), The Clinical Assessment of Optimal Religious Functioning, *Review of Religious Research*, 30 (1), 3–17.

10. Robert Mulholland, *Invitation to a Journey* (Downers Grove: InterVarsity, 1993), 15–44.
11. Bruce Demarest, *Seasons of the Soul* (Downers Grove: InterVarsity, 2009), 153–154.
12. J. Rybash, P. Roodin, & W. Hoyer, *Adult Development and Aging*, 3rd ed. (Chicago: Brown E Benchmark, 1995), 4.
13. Dallas Willard, *Spirit of the Disciplines* (San Fransisco: Harper & Row, 1988), 15.
14. Erik Erikson, *Childhood and Society*, 2nd ed. (New York: W. W. Norton & Company, 1964), 2.
15. Laurent Daloz, *Effective Teaching and Mentoring* (San Francisco: Jossey-Bass,1985), 215.
16. Julie Gorman, *Christian Formation*, *Christian Education Journal* (10, 65–73, 1990), 70.
17. Linda Vogel, *Teaching and Learning in Faith Community: Empowering Adults Through Religious Education* (San Francisco: Jossey-Bass, 1991), 60.
18. Stott, 97.
19. James Montgomery Boice, *The Epistles of John* (Grand Rapids: Zondervan, 1979), 74.
20. John MacArthur, *Twelve Ordinary Men* (Nashville: The W Publishing Group, 2002), 114.
21. Hannah Hurnard, *Hind's Feet on High Places* (Shippensburg, PA: Destiny Image Publishers, 1993), 86.
22. Gabriel Moran, *Religious Education Development* (Minneapolis: Winston, 1983), 118.
23. Robert Peck, "Psychological Developments in the Second Half of Life," in *Middle Age and Aging: A Reader in Social Psychology*, ed. Bernice Neugarten (Chicago: University of Chicago Press, 1968), 88–92.
24. Neugarten, 93–98.
25. Daniel Levinson, *Seasons of a Man's Life* (New York: Ballantine, 1978).
26. Erik Erikson, *Childhood and Society*, 2nd ed. (New York: W. W. Norton & Company, 1964), 267.

Resources for Further Study

- James Loder, *The Logic of the Spirit: Human Development in Theological Perspective* (San Francisco: Jossey-Bass, 1998).
- Patricia Miller, *Theories of Developmental Psychology,* 4th ed. (New York: Freeman and Company, 2002).

Chapter 14: Disciples in Search of Direction—Proposing a Disciple-Making Path

1. James Wilhoit, *Spiritual Formation As If the Church Mattered: Growing in Christ Through Community* (Grand Rapids: Baker Academic, 2008), 10.
2. Perry Downs, *Teaching for Spiritual Growth* (Grand Rapids: Zondervan, 1994), 121–122.
3. Robert Mulholland, *Invitation to a Journey* (Downers Grove, IL: InterVarsity, 1993), 19–20, 22.
4. Richard Foster, *Celebration of Discipline: The Path to Spiritual Growth* (New York: Harper and Row, 1978), 1.

STAGES *of* FAITH
Spiritual Guidance. Life-long Transformation.

We want to hear from you!

Please send your comments about this book

by visiting our website:

www.StagesofFaith.com

WinePressPublishing
Great Books, Defined.

To order additional copies of this book call:
1-877-421-READ (7323)
or please visit our website at
www.WinePressbooks.com

If you enjoyed this quality custom-published book,
drop by our website for more books and information.

www.winepresspublishing.com
"Your partner in custom publishing."

DISCOVER STAGES OF FAITH

Stages of Faith: 8 Milestones That Mark Your Journey is the companion workbook to *The Path*. This 13-week curriculum is a transforming resource for personal and small-group study, and should be in every small-group leader's toolbox of essential materials.

Based on 1 John 2:12-14, *Stages of Faith* provides a biblical "map" of the journey of faith and a compelling description of how spiritual growth takes place through three dynamic stages of transformation—Childhood, Young Adulthood, and Parenthood. *Stages of Faith* will help believers understand how far they have traveled, identify obstacles delaying their journey, and chart their way forward. Completing this study will change the way you think about your progress on the journey.

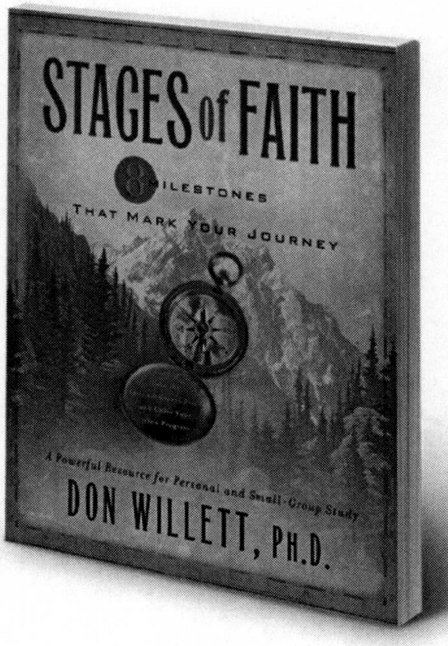

TAKE THE FREE SPIRITUAL GROWTH PROFILE

www.StagesofFaith.com

CPSIA information can be obtained at www.ICGtesting.com
Printed in the USA
LVOW080622200612
286840LV00002B/3/P

9 781414 121925